The Jurist and the Theologian

Islamic History and Thought

5

Islamic History and Thought provides a platform for scholarly research on any geographic area within the expansive Islamic world, stretching from the Mediterranean to China, and dated to any period from the eve of Islam until the early modern era. This series contains original monographs, translations (Arabic, Persian, Syriac, Greek, and Latin) and edited volumes.

The Jurist and the Theologian

Speculative Theology in Shāfiʿī Legal Theory

Mohamed Ahmed Abdelrahman Eissa

Gorgias Press

2017

Gorgias Press LLC, 954 River Road, Piscataway, NJ, 08854, USA

www.gorgiaspress.com

This dissertation was submitted to the Freie Universitaet Berlin (D 188)

2017

ISBN 978-1-4632-0618-5

Library of Congress Cataloging-in-Publication Data

A Cataloging-in-Publication record is available from the Library of Congress.

Printed in the United States of America

ربنا لا تؤاخذنا إن نسينا أو أخطأنا

To Magdy and Diana

TABLE OF CONTENTS

ACKNOWLEDGMENTS

First of all, I would like to thank my parents. Without their help and guidance, I could not have received any proper education. The support and encouragement I received from members of my immediate and extended family was overwhelming, especially from my late uncle Madgy Khalifa. This book is based on my doctoral dissertation that I wrote at the Berlin Graduate School Muslim Cultures and Societies, Freie Universität Berlin. My studies were financed by a doctoral fellowship from the German Research Foundation (DFG). I completed revising my dissertation during a fellowship financed by the Dahlem Research School and the German Research Foundation. I would also like to express my gratitude for my doctoral supervisors Prof. Dr. Birgit Krawietz and Prof. Dr. Christian Lange. The help and support I received from Prof. Dr. Lange, before and during my doctoral studies, was particularly very valuable. Prof. Anver Emon and Prof. Abdelsamad Belhaj very kindly read extended parts of this study; their comments helped me avoid many mistakes. Finally, no words of gratitude are enough to pay the debt I owe to many of the wonderful teachers I encountered during my school and university years.

INTRODUCTION

Numerous factors shape the creation of any given law. The process of creating a law is a sophisticated process; Islamic law (*fiqh*) is no exception. Muslims believe that their law has sacred origins. However, most Muslim jurists would agree that not all aspects of Islamic law are determined by the divine. Muslims, their societies and their social customs play a role in shaping and creating their religious laws. Furthermore, humans use their own 'imperfect' rational faculties to deduce laws from the available religious texts (Qurʾān and Prophetic Sunna). Jurists develop methods that allow them to interpret those texts with the purpose of creating new laws. Those methods are subsumed under the discipline of legal theory (*uṣūl al-fiqh*). The latter is the philosophical and theoretical framework that discovers and creates new laws and justifies existing ones. Numerous studies have been written on the factors that shaped pre-modern Islamic law. However, we still lack detailed studies on the factors that shaped legal theory. Medieval works of legal theory usually list three main sources from which jurists deduce their legal theory, namely the Arabic language, law and speculative theology (*ʿilm al-kalām*).[1] In this study, I explore the role speculative theology play in the formation of a jurist's legal theory.

The primary aim of this study is to examine the relationship between speculative theology and legal theory and evaluate how far the former informs and shapes the latter. To understand and analyse the relationship between both disciplines, my study will primarily focus on comparative legal theory (*uṣūl al-fiqh al-muqāran*). As

[1] See for instance, ʿAlī b. Muḥammad al-Āmidī (d. 631/1233), *al-Iḥkām fī uṣūl al-aḥkām*, 4 vols ed. ʿAbd al-Razzāq ʿAfīfī (Riyadh: Dār al-Ṣaymaʿī, 1424/2003), 3:294; Ghazālī, *Mustaṣfā*, 1:21.

a case study, I compare the legal theory of four jurists who belong to the same school of the law, the Shāfiʿī, but follow three different theological traditions, namely the Muʿtazilī ʿAbd al-Jabbār al-Hamadhānī (d. 415/1024), the Ashʿarīs Abū Isḥāq al-Shīrāzī (d. 476/1083) and Abū al-Maʿālī al-Juwaynī (d. 478/1085), in addition to the traditionalist Abū al-Muẓaffar al-Samʿānī (d. 489/1096).[2]

This comparison aims to investigate the impact of speculative theology on legal theory, exploring, in particular, the influence of a jurist's theological doctrines on determining his stands in legal theory. I examine in what way, if ever, speculative theology informs the legal theory choices of the four Shāfiʿīs at the heart of this study. Are there theological foundations for their stances in legal theory? To what extent are their legal theories different or similar? Do they favour legal theory positions as a result of their theological convictions? Does the adoption of particular theological doctrines require favouring specific stances in legal theory? Do theological disagreements necessarily lead to discrepancies in legal theory? Most importantly, many Sunnī schools of law include jurists from various theological backgrounds. In this case study, we have Muʿtazilī, Ashʿarī and traditionalist jurists who are all members of the Shāfiʿī legal school but who vehemently refuse each other's theological doctrines. Scholars often describe followers of other theological schools as deviants, if not infidels. However, legal disa-

---

[2] I use the term 'traditionalist' in the same manner that George Makdisi and Christopher Melchert use it. Both historians employ this term in reference to *ahl al-ḥadīth* or *aṣḥāb al-ḥadīth*; those are jurists critical of speculative theology and the rational non-textually based arguments and methods common among the specialists of this discipline. Traditionalists rather prefer to base their dogma on the Scriptures (Qurāʾn and Sunna) and support their doctrines primarily by textually based arguments. The term traditionalist is not to be confused with the term traditionist (*muḥaddith*). Makdisi and Melchert utilize the latter term as a reference to specialists in the transmission of Prophetic traditions (sg. *ḥadīth*). See George Makdisi, 'Ashʿarī and the Ashʿarites in Islamic Religious History I: The Ashʿarite Movement and Muslim Orthodoxy', *Studia Islamica* 17 (1962), 49; Christopher Melchert, *The Formation of the Sunni Schools of Law* (Leiden: Brill, 1997), 2.

greements rarely trigger accusations of deviancy and infidelity. In terms of legal theory and law (*fiqh*), jurists exist in harmony; they accept the legitimacy of each other's legal opinions, despite the presence of legal variances. But how do they manage to tolerate and legitimize the legal teachings of the same jurists when they refuse their theological teachings and accuse them of deviancy? How do jurists from different theological backgrounds exist harmoniously in the same school of law?

Many features of Muslim intellectual history reveal the intertwined and intricate relationship between speculative theology and legal theory. It is common, for instance, to find influential legal theoreticians who are also prominent theologians. Many scholars who wrote on legal theory have also authored books on speculative theology, including the four jurists under the spotlight here. Doctrinal discussions often appear in manuals of legal theory and theological writings are not free from legal references. To answer our questions, however, requires more than merely noticing these phenomena. They say nothing on the nature of the relationship between speculative theology and legal theory. They do not demonstrate in what way theology has managed to influence legal theory. They also shed no light on why, if theology had a great impact on legal theory, didn't each theological school create its own legal school based on its theological postulates? Why is it not uncommon to find jurists from diverse theological backgrounds members of the same legal school and adopting similar views in legal theory?

A comparative study, between jurists who belong to the same legal background, but follow three different theological traditions, might help answer some of these questions and shed further light on the relationship between both disciplines. Such a comparison is vital for understanding the process through which pre-modern legal theory was formed and developed. The current study focuses on jurists who mostly lived in the fifth/eleventh century. Wael Hallaq describes the legal theoreticians of this century as those who 'produced some of the most influential treatises for the course of theoretical developments in the centuries to come'.[3] Therefore,

---

[3] Wael Hallaq, *Sharīʿa: Theory, Practice, Transformations* (Cambridge: Cambridge University Press, 2009), 72.

analysing legal theory developments during this specific century is crucial for understanding the development of Muslim legal theory at later stages. Furthermore, this century offers a unique opportunity to compare the legal theory of four jurists who share the same legal school but belong to three different theological traditions. This mix of legal and theological beliefs allows a more nuanced understanding of inter-sectarian roles and interaction within a Sunnī school of law. It also offers a better opportunity to analyse the function of speculative theology in legal theory and understand how diverse theological traditions exist and interact within the same legal school and influence its legal theory.

RESEARCH METHODOLOGY

If legal theoreticians consider their theological doctrines as important factors shaping and informing their legal theory, we may assume the presence of legal theory disagreements among jurists following different theological traditions and legal theory similarities between jurists who share a common theology. If this assumption is incorrect, why should a common theology not lead to the adoption of a common legal theory? Why do different theological positions do not always lead to disagreements in legal theory? In this study, I have searched for consistent and significant differences and similarities in the legal theory of the four Shāfiʿī jurists. The existence of consistent and significant differences in their legal theories may entail that their theological disagreements are among the reasons causing discrepancies in their legal theory. If no significant differences are noticed in their legal theory, this may imply that their theological disagreements do not always lead to divergences in legal theory.

However, it is important to note that jurists may disagree in legal theory on grounds other than – or in addition to – theology. Furthermore, the legal theory of the Shāfiʿī School is not monolithic; there are legal theory variations among Shāfiʿīs. This is also true about other Sunnī schools of law. Therefore, the presence of legal theory disagreements is not, in themselves, a sufficient sign proving the impact of speculative theology on legal theory. In order to identify the differences in legal theory that are motivated by theological debates rather than other legal or hermeneutical disagreements, I have paid special attention to analysing the evidence and arguments each jurist presents to support his legal theory choices and rebut that of his opponents. This analysis should better uncover his motives for favouring or rejecting specific legal theory positions. If a jurist uses theological doctrines as evidence to justify his legal theory choice and refute that of his opponents, this may imply that his legal theory decision is informed (or perhaps determined) by his theological beliefs. If the arguments mentioned are largely legal or hermeneutical, and include no references to theology, this may entail that his theology does not play a major role in shaping this specific legal theory stand. Therefore, this research is not only concerned with comparing legal theory positions, but it is also, primarily, concerned with analysing arguments for and against those positions.

Although the current study focuses only on four Shāfiʿī jurists, it will be sometimes useful to take a step backward, when relevant, and briefly compare the arguments of those four jurists to that of other non-Shāfiʿī scholars. For example, to better understand the impact of Muʿtazilī theology on ʿAbd al-Jabbār's legal theory, I have at times compared his legal theory to that of other non-Shāfiʿī authors who also follow Muʿtazilī theology. The same also applies to the other three Shāfiʿīs. Juwaynī and Shīrāzī may be compared to other Ashʿarī jurists who belong to schools other than the Shāfiʿī school. Samʿānī may be compared to traditionalist scholars who follow the Mālikī or the Ḥanbalī legal school. These comparisons help to identify the differences or similarities between the legal theory of jurists who follow the same theological tradition but are members of different legal schools. In particular, they help to identify whether or not a common theology encourages jurists to favour similar positions in legal theory.

This study of the four Shāfiʿī scholars is mainly based on their own primary sources – the legal theory positions expressed in their legal theory literature. Each of the four Shāfiʿī scholars studied here left us at least one book on legal theory. ʿAbd al-Jabbār is the only exception; none of his books dedicated to legal theory have been, hitherto, discovered. However, his *magnum opus al-Mughnī fī-abwāb al-tawḥīd wa-l-ʿadl*, a multi-volume work on speculative theology, includes one volume (number 17) dedicated to legal theory.[4] This volume provides a good, though incomplete, survey of his legal theory. Furthermore, all four Shāfiʿīs left behind, in various quantities, works on speculative theology; those works provide the major source of information on their dogmas. In addition, works on legal theory and speculative theology by other fifth/eleventh century authors provide further information on the intellectual context in which the four Shāfiʿī scholars lived and expressed their ideas. Some of the legal theory literature written centuries after the fifth/eleventh century is also important and relevant. Writers such as Fakhr al-Dīn al-Rāzī (d. 606/1209), Sayf al-Dīn al-Āmidī (d. 631/1233), and Badr al-Dīn al-Zarkashī (d. 794/1392) have a wonderful bird's-eye view of earlier sources; they have access to writings by our four jurists that are hitherto undiscovered. Later texts, although written in different times and contexts, include valuable information on the legal theory debates of earlier centuries and they often analyse the ideas of preceding jurists. Nonetheless, such texts are secondary sources of information commenting, from their own perspectives, on ideas and writings expressed in former centuries.

The conclusions of this study are primarily deduced from comparing the position of four specific Shāfiʿī jurists, who lived mostly in the fifth/eleventh century, on three specific questions in legal theory. Space and time restraints have prevented me from adopting a wider scope for my study that would include a larger sample of legal theory questions. Would examining a different sample of jurists or a different sample of legal theory topics modify (or change) the conclusions I have reached? Perhaps. I believe, however, that the jurists examined here and the selected legal theory topics offer a good (but not comprehensive and decisive) indication of the impact of theology on legal theory in the Shāfiʿī School during the fifth/eleventh century. My frequent references to jurists from other legal traditions (and other periods of time) may also point to the impact of theology on the legal theory of other schools

[4] ʿAbd al-Jabbār b. Aḥmad al-Hamadhānī (d. 415/1024), *al-Mughnī fi abwāb al-tawḥīd wa-l-adl*, 20 vols, ed. Ṭahā Ḥusayn and others (Cairo: Wizārat al-Thaqāfa wa-l-Irshād al-Qawmī, 1960–9).

of law. The relationship between both disciplines is still under studied and I hope that my research will provoke further examination of the interactions between both religious disciplines.

It has become a custom in recent studies to use gender 'sensitive' language. Rather than only use male pronouns, authors are expected to shift between male and female pronouns or use both at the same time. The disciplines of legal theory and speculative theology, in the medieval period, are primarily male dominated. The language used in the examined literature is dominated by male pronouns. Furthermore, unfortunately, I am unaware of a published medieval work written by a female jurist or speculative theologian whose work is relevant to my study. Therefore, I do not use what some modern historians would consider a gender-neutral language. I use male pronouns in reference to the jurists and theologians of the pre-modern period, simply because it has been impossible to access works by female authors.

DEFINING SPECULATIVE THEOLOGY AND LEGAL THEORY

Before going further, we should briefly define the terms 'speculative theology' (*ʿilm al-kalām*) and 'legal theory' (*uṣūl al-fiqh*). The most common definition of speculative theology is a functional definition. Muslim scholars, in pre-modern times, often define it as the discipline concerned with defending and protecting the correct creed and rebutting deviant ones.[5] This functional definition fails to

---

[5] See for instance, Abū Ḥāmid al-Ghazālī (d. 505/1111), *al-Munqidh min al-ḍalāl*, ed. Saʿd Karīm al-Fiqī (Alexandria: Dār Ibn Khaldūn, n.d.), 13–4; Abū al-Yusr Muḥammad al-Bazdawī (d. 493/1099), *Uṣūl al-dīn*, ed. Hans Peter Linss (Cairo: al-Maktaba al-Azhariyya li-l-Turāth, 1424/2003), 15; Abū Naṣr Muḥammad al-Farābī (d. 339/950), *Iḥṣāʾ al-ʿulūm*, 2nd ed., ed. ʿUthmān Amīn (Egypt: Maṭbaʿat al-Iʿtimād, 1949), 107–8. For later scholars, see for example Saʿd al-Dīn Masʿūd b. ʿUmar al-Taftazānī (d. 793/1390), *Sharḥ al-maqāṣid min ʿilm al-kalām*, 2 vols (Pakistan: Dār al-Maʿārif al-Nuʿmāniyya, 1401/1981), 1:18; ʿAḍud Allāh wa-l-Dīn ʿAbd al-Raḥmān b. Aḥmad al-Ījī (d. 756/1355), *al-Mawāqif fī ʿilm al-kalām* (Beirut: ʿĀlam al-Kutub, n.d.), 7. For a survey of pre-modern definitions of the

reveal the topics and content (*mawḍūʿāt* or *masāʾil*) of speculative theology. The best method to uncover these topics is a brief survey of the indexes of pre-modern theological literature. This survey shows that the following are among the major topics that receive special attention in this genre: contingency of the universe, existence of God, divine attributes, ethics, metaphysics, soteriology, eschatology, political authority, in addition to epistemology. Speculative theology, then, is an overarching discipline under which various topics, disciplines, and sub-disciplines are discussed.[6] It is difficult to find an accurate translation for *ʿilm al-kalām*, but a common one is speculative theology.[7] The contents of the Muslim discipline of *ʿilm al-kalām* and those of speculative theology, in its Christian context, certainly overlap, however they are not identical.[8] Therefore, translating *ʿilm al-kalām* as speculative theology is only an approximation and I have used the Arabic term and its English translation interchangeably.[9]

---

term, see Ḥasan Maḥmūd al-Shāfiʿī, *al-Madkhal ilā dirāsat ʿilm al-kalām*, 2nd ed. (Karachi: Idārat al-Qurʾān wa-l-ʿUlūm al-Islāmiyya, 1422/2001), 9–19.

6 For a modern survey of the contents of speculative theology, see Muḥammad Ṣāliḥ Muḥammad al-Sayyid, *Aṣālat ʿilm al-kalām* (Cairo: Dār al-Tawfīq al-Namūdhajiyya, 1986), 61–70.

7 Other modern scholars prefer to translate it as philosophical theology, see for example W. M. Watt, *Islamic Theology and Philosophy*, 2nd ed. (Edinburgh: Edinburgh University Press, 2003), 37. Robert Wisnovsky translates *kalām* as 'Islamic doctrinal Theology' in his *Avicenna's Metaphysics in Context* (London: Duckworth, 2003), 301. Ahmed El Shamsy translates *kalām* as dialectic theology, see his 'The Social Construction of Orthodoxy', in *The Cambridge Companion to Classical Islamic Theology* ed. Tim Winter (Cambridge: Cambridge University Press, 2008), 98.

8 See Tim Winter, Introduction to *The Cambridge Companion to Classical Islamic Theology*, ed. Tim Winter (Cambridge: Cambridge University Press, 2008), 2–4. Winter argues that *ʿilm al-kalām* is a more inclusive term than theology; *kalām* incorporates aspects of mysticism and philosophy in addition to theology.

9 There are other Arabic terms used in reference to the discipline of *ʿilm al-kalām*, e.g. *uṣūl al-dīn, al-fiqh al-akbar, al-ʿaqliyyāt, al-ʿulūm al-ʿaqliyya, ʿilm al-tawḥīd*, and *al-ʿaqīda*. For a survey of the different terms used in

Legal theory or *uṣūl al-fiqh*, on the macro level, is the 'theoretical and philosophical foundation of Islamic law'.[10] On the micro level, legal theory is composed of the methods and theories jurists use to read and interpret the Qurʾān and the Prophetic Sunna to reach and justify their conclusions in law (*fiqh*). The latter is a group of moral guidelines, positive laws, legal procedures, rituals, imperatives and prohibitions that Muslims are expected to follow. Legal theory includes the tools through which laws are deduced or justified and through which the Qurʾān and the Prophetic Sunna produce positive laws that Muslims can apply in their daily lives. In this sense, legal theory is composed of abstract and theoretical methods whereas law or *fiqh* is the body of concrete rules and regulations deduced from the Qurʾān and the Prophetic Sunna via legal theory.[11]

---

reference to this discipline, see Shāfiʿī, *Madkhal ilā dirāsat ʿilm al-kalām*, 20–9.

[10] Wael Hallaq, *A History of Islamic Legal Theories* (Cambridge: Cambridge University Press, 1997), vii.

[11] For more details on the definition of legal theory, see Abū al-Ḥusayn Muḥammad b. ʿAlī b. al-Ṭayyib al-Baṣrī (d. 436/1044), *Kitāb al-Muʿtamad fī uṣūl al-fiqh*, ed. Muḥammad Ḥamīdullāh and others (Damascus: al-Maʿhad al-ʿIlmī al-Faransī li-l-Dirāsāt al-ʿArabiyya, 1965), 10–1; Abū Isḥāq Ibrāhīm b. ʿAlī b. Yūsuf al-Fīrūzābādī al-Shīrāzī (d. 476/1083), *Sharḥ al-Lumaʿ*, 2 vols, ed. ʿAbd al-Majīd Turkī (Beirut: Dār al-Gharb al-Islāmī, 1988), 1:157–63; Abū al-Maʿālī al-Juwaynī (d. 478/1085), *al-Burhān fī uṣūl al-fiqh*, 2 vols, ed. ʿAbd al-ʿAẓīm al-Dīb (Mansoura: al-Wafāʾ, 1418[/1979]), 1:78–9; Abū Ḥāmid Muḥammad b. Muḥammad al-Ghazālī (d. 505/1111), *al-Mustaṣfā min ʿilm al-uṣūl*, ed. Ḥamza b. Zuhayr Ḥāfiẓ (Medina(?): Sharikat al-Madīna al-Munawwara li-l-Ṭibāʿa (?), 1413/1992 (?)), 1:5. One must note that there is debate among scholars based in the West regarding the function (thus the definition) of legal theory. A number of scholars see that legal theory is used for constructing new jurisprudential laws in addition to justifying and rationalizing existing ones. See for example Wael Hallaq, 'Considerations on the Function and Character of Sunni Legal Theory', *Journal of the American Oriental Society* 104.4 (1984): 679–689; Hallaq, *Sharīʿa*, 73–9. Other scholars see legal theory not as a tool that creates new laws but one that only justifies, retrospectively, exist-

Textual interpretation is an important part of the process leading to deducing laws from the Qurʾān and the Prophetic Sunna. Pre-modern Muslim legal theoreticians are well aware of the complications entailed in the process of textual interpretation. Therefore, legal theory manuals often include detailed and sophisticated discussions of linguistics, grammar, rhetoric, hermeneutics, epistemology, logic, philosophy and theology – to mention only a few. Those disciplines constitute integral components of legal theory. Legal theoreticians use these disciplines to create an approach to – if not a philosophy of – language that enables a 'close reader' to interpret a text. This approach should help the jurist understand the messages of the Qurʾān and the Sunna and uncover the intent of their authors. Furthermore, legal theory is the discipline that provides jurists with the methods to deduce the deontic qualifications of actions on which revelation does not comment.[12] The two most prominent methods that are applied in this context are consensus (*ijmāʿ*) and *qiyās*, in addition to other non-textual tools such

ing ones, see for instance Sherman Jackson, 'Function and Formalism: Toward a Functional Analysis of Usul al-fiqh', in *Studies in Islamic Legal Theory*, ed. Bernard Weiss (Leiden: Brill, 2002): 177–201; Behnam Sadeghi, *The Logic of Law-making in Islam: Women and Prayer in the Legal Tradition* (Cambridge: Cambridge University Press, 2013).

[12] Referring to the Prophetic Sunna as revelation may be problematic. Muslims believe that the Qurʾān is the verbatim Word of God. On the other hand, although Muslim religious scholars often note that the content of each Prophetic tradition is inspired by God, the Prophet phrases this inspiration in his own words. Therefore, Prophetic traditions cannot strictly be considered revelation (*waḥy*). However, I often use the term revelation as a translation for the Arabic term *sharʿ* which include a reference to both to the Qurʾān and Sunna. I also use the term Scriptures in reference to the Qurʾān and Sunna. Since there is no one particular agreed upon text including all probative Prophetic traditions, it might also be also problematic to refer to the Sunna as a text or Scriptures. Nonetheless, to avoid repeating the words Qurʾān and Prophetic Sunna every time I need to refer to them, I use the terms revelation, religious texts, or Scriptures in reference to both.

as individual and communal best interest (*maṣlaḥa*) and social practice (*ʿurf*).

WHY THE SHĀFIʿĪ SCHOOL OF LAW?

To study the relationship between speculative theology and legal theory, I have compared the legal theories of jurists who belong to the same school of law but follow different theological traditions. This has allowed me to be in a better position to explore the impact of speculative theology on legal theory. One way to study this impact is to examine whether the adoption of different theological doctrines leads to divergences in legal theory. Comparing the legal theory of jurists belonging to the same school of law, while following various theological schools, has allowed me to recognize the legal theory differences that may be a product of theological disagreements rather than legal theory variances caused by disagreements among the various schools of law.

Why choose the Shāfiʿī School and take the fifth/eleventh century as the timeframe for this research? Most of the Sunnī legal theory literature available and accessible to us today is written by jurists who usually belong to one of four theological traditions: Ashʿarī, Māturīdī, Muʿtazilī and traditionalist. The available Ḥanafī legal theory literature is authored by jurists who are Māturīdī or Muʿtazilī; the Mālikī legal theory literature is written by Ashʿarī or traditionalist jurists, whereas most Ḥanbalī legal theory writings known to us are authored by traditionalist jurists. The available Shāfiʿī legal literature, on the other hand, is written by scholars who are Ashʿarī, Muʿtazilī, or traditionalist.[13] Therefore, the available and accessible Shāfiʿī legal theory writings seem more theologically diverse than that of other schools of law. Taking the Shāfiʿī School as our case study in this research allows us to compare jurists who

---

[13] The accepted wisdom is that most Muʿtazilīs joined the Ḥanafī School of law. This may have been correct. However, there are some Muʿtazilīs who joined the Shāfiʿī school, see Wilferd Madelung, *Der Imam al-Qasim b. Ibrahim* (Berlin: Walter de Gruyter, 1965), 15–6 quoted in David Vishanoff, *The Formation of Islamic Hermeneutics* (New Haven, Connecticut: American Oriental Society, 2011), 210 f.n. 117. See also Melchert, *Formation*, 83–6.

share the same legal background but belong to three different theological traditions rather than only two or even one.

To make use of this unique opportunity provided by the Shāfiʿī School, it is essential to include the Muʿtazilī scholar ʿAbd al-Jabbār al-Hamadhānī in this study. To the best of my knowledge, he is the only Muʿtazilī jurist who follows Shāfiʿī law and whose legal theory writings have been, albeit partially, discovered and published.[14] The choice of ʿAbd al-Jabbār enforces a specific time frame on this research. To analyse the relationship between speculative theology and legal theory I have examined the extent to which theological disagreements lead to discrepancies in legal theory. In the context of this research, comparing the legal theories of jurists belonging to distant historical settings disregards the changes and developments that occurred in legal theory during the passage of long centuries. I have therefore decided to adopt a synchronic approach to the history of legal theory and compare jurists who are – more or less – contemporaneous. This allows me to focus on legal theory differences that are caused by conceptual and/or theological disagreements rather than discrepancies in the legal theories of jurists belonging to different historical settings caused by the passage of time and changes in surrounding circumstances.

ʿAbd al-Jabbār spent most of his adult life in the second half of the fourth/tenth and the first two decades of the fifth/eleventh century. I then searched for other Shāfiʿī jurists who are, to the best possible extent, contemporaries of ʿAbd al-Jabbār and wose writings on legal theory and speculative theology are available in sufficient quantities. Among the few jurists who satisfy both criteria are Shīrāzī, Samʿānī and Juwaynī.[15] All were born in the

[14] For *only* an indicative list of the extant manuscripts by Muʿtazilī scholars, see Fūʾād Sazkīn, *Tārīkh al-turāth al-ʿarabī*, trans. Maḥmūd Fahmī Ḥijāzī, ʿArafa Muṣṭafā and Saʿīd ʿAbd al-Raḥīm (Riyadh: Jāmiʿat al-Imām Muḥammad b. Saʿūd al-Islāmiyya, 1411/1991), 1/4: 18–21, 59–88.

[15] For lists (certainly not *inclusive* ones) of the extant Shāfiʿī legal theory works authored before the sixth/twelfth century, see Carl Brockelmann *Geschichte der arabischen Litteratur* (Leiden: Brill, 1943), 1:188–92, 482–502; Carl Brockelmann, *Geschichte der arabischen Litteratur. Erster Supllement-*

fifth/eleventh century and passed away before the nineties of the same century. Although they are not strict contemporaries of ʿAbd al-Jabbār, their works on legal theory and speculative theology are extant and accessible. Moreover, all four scholars belong, to a great extent, to the same historical period.

TYPOLOGIES OF LEGAL THEORY

In an oft-quoted passage, ʿAbd al-Raḥmān b. Khaldūn (d. 808/1406) categorizes legal theoreticians into followers of two main methods, namely the method of the jurists (*ṭarīqat al-fuqahāʾ*, he also calls it the method of the Ḥanafīs) and the method of the theologians (*ṭarīqat al-mutakallimīn*, he also refers to it as the method of the Shāfiʿīs). Ibn Khaldūn describes the legal theory method of the jurists as more relevant to law. This method, he adds, is characterized by deducing legal theory principles from the already-existing body of laws. Works of legal theory based on this method frequently include references to and illustrations from *fiqh*. On the other hand, he notes that followers of the theologians' method isolate the process of constructing legal theory from law and often base their legal theory positions on rational deductions. In their legal theory writings, the theologians are influenced, according to Ibn Khaldūn, by the rational methods common in speculative theology.[16] Later at the end of his chapter on legal theory, Ibn Khal-

---

band (Leiden: Brill, 1937), 1:666–86; Sazkīn, *Tārīkh al-turāth al-ʿArabī*, 1/3:31–127, 179–213.

[16] ʿAbd al-Raḥmān b. Khaldūn (d. 808/1406), *al-Muqaddima*, 5 vols, ed. ʿAbd al-Salām al-Shaddādī (Casablanca: Khizānat Ibn Khaldūn Bayt al-Funūn wa-l-ʿUlūm wa-l-Ādāb, 2005), 3:18. Ibn Khaldūn writes that 'jurists' [legal theory] writings are more relevant and akin to law, since they deduce their legal theory from existing laws and include many legal examples and illustrations. Theologians free these issues [i.e. legal theory] from law, and tend, as far as possible, to utilize rational deductions (*wa-l-mutakallimūn yujarridūn ṣiwar tilaka al-masāʾil ʿan al-fiqh wa-yamīlūn ilā al-istidlāl al-ʿaqlī mā amkan*), for this is akin to and a product of the methods they often use [in speculative theology]. Ḥanafī jurists were the most skillful in delving deep into the fine details of law to deduce the rules of legal theory'.

dūn alludes to the existence of a third method established by the Ḥanafī Fakhr al-Dīn b. al-Sāʿātī (d. 694/1294) in which he mixed both methods of legal theory. However, he provides no description of this third trend nor does he name it.[17]

Ibn Khaldūn's description of both methods lacks detail, so it is not surprising to find modern scholars disagreeing on the typifying features Ibn Khaldūn attributes to each of his categories. For example, Bernard Weiss sees that Ibn Khaldūn is categorizing authors of legal theory manuals according to their field of speciality; authors specialized in speculative theology occupy one category; those specialized in law occupy the other.[18] George Makdisi is not explicit. Yet, it seems that he considers jurists who include theological discussions in their legal theory writings as followers of the theologians' method and those who avoid such discussions as followers of the jurists' method.[19] Robert Gleave and Gregor Schwarb mention, in passing, that Ibn Khaldūn categorized jurists according to the source material they use to create and form their legal theory. Followers of the theologians' method deduce their legal theory from their theology and allow their theological doctrines to inform their legal positions. Followers of the jurists' method deduce their legal theory, retrospectively, from the established laws within their legal school, without much regard to theology.[20]

---

[17] Ibn Khaldūn, *Muqaddima*, 3:19.

[18] Bernard Weiss, *The Search for God's Law*, rev. ed. (1992; repr., Herndon, VA: International Institute of Islamic Thought 2010), 18–20.

[19] George Makdisi, *Ibn ʿAqīl: Religion and Culture in Classical Islam* (Edinburgh: Edinburgh University Press, 1997), 76–85. See also George Makdisi, 'The Juridical Theology of Shâfi'î: Origins and Significance of *Uṣûl al-Fiqh*', *Studia Islamica* 59 (1984): 41–2.

[20] Robert Gleave, forward to *The Economy of Certainty*, by Aron Zysow (Atlanta, GA: Lockwood Press, 2013), xv; Gregor Schwarb, 'Capturing the Meanings of God's Speech: The Relevance of *uṣūl al-fiqh* to an Understanding of *uṣūl al-tafsīr* in Jewish and Muslim *kalām*', in *A Word Fitly Spoken: Studies in Medieval Exegesis of the Hebrew Bible and the Quran*, ed. Meir M. Bar-Asher (Jerusalem: The Ben-Zui Institute for the History of Jewish Communities in the East, 2007), 126–7, 148.

Ibn Khaldūn categorizes ʿAbd al-Jabbār and Juwaynī as followers of the theologians' method.[21] Modern authors often confirm this categorization.[22] Shīrāzī's and Samʿānī's categorizations are less straightforward. Goerge Makdisi writes that Shīrāzī does not include theological discussions in his works on legal theory. Therefore, he notes that Shīrāzī is a follower of the jurist's method.[23] Yet, it seems to me that Ibn Khaldūn's description of the theologians' method is applicable to Shīrāzī's legal theory works *al-Lumaʿ fī uṣūl al-fiqh* and *Sharḥ al-Lumaʿ*. In fact, most modern authors, writing in Arabic, consider Shīrāzī to be a follower of the theologians' method.[24]

Samʿānī, in the introduction to his *Qawāṭiʿ al-adilla fī uṣūl al-fiqh*, states that he is committed to the method of the jurists in legal

---

[21] Ibn Khaldūn, *Muqaddima*, 3:18. He even describes ʿAbd al-Jabbār's book *al-ʿUmad* (hitherto undiscovered) and Juwaynī's *al-Burhān fī uṣūl al-fiqh* as two of the four pillars of the legal theory methods of the theologians. The other two 'pillars' are Abū Ḥāmid al-Ghazālī's *al-Mustaṣfā min ʿilm al-uṣūl* and Abū al-Ḥusayn al-Baṣrī's *al-Muʿtamad fī uṣūl al-fiqh*. The latter is ʿAbd al-Jabbār's student, who followed Muʿtazilī theology and Ḥanafī law.

[22] On ʿAbd al-Jabbār, see for instance Muḥammad Zakariyyā al-Bardīsī, *Uṣūl al-fiqh* (Cairo: Dār al-Thaqāfa li-l-Nashr wa-l-Tawzīʿ, n.d.), 13; Muṣṭafā Saʿīd al-Khunn, *Dirāsa tārīkhiyya li-l-fiqh wa-uṣūluh* (Damascus: al-Sharika al-ʿArabiyya al-Mutaḥida li-l-Tawzīʿ, 1984/1404), 193. On Jūwaynī, see for example Muḥammad al-Khuḍarī, *Uṣūl al-fiqh*, 6th ed. (Cairo: al-Maktaba al-Tijāriyya al-Kubrā, 1389/1969), 9; Muḥammad al-Zuḥaylī. *Al-Imām al-Juwaynī*, 2nd ed. (Damascus: Dar al-Qalam, 1992), 165.

[23] George Makdisi, 'The Sunni Revival', in *Islamic Civilization, 950–1150*, ed. D. S. Richards (Oxford: Bruni Cassirer, 1973), 159; Makdisi, *Ibn ʿAqīl*, 81.

[24] See for example, Muḥammad Ḥasan Hītū, *al-Imām al-Shīrāzī* (Beirut: Dār al-Fikr, 1980), 16; Muḥyī al-Dīn Dīb Mistū and Yūsuf ʿAlī Bidīwī, introduction to Abū Isḥāq Ibrāhīm b. ʿAlī b. Yūsuf al-Firūzābādī al-Shīrāzī (d. 476/1083), *al-Lumaʿ fī uṣūl al-fiqh*, ed. Muḥyī al-Dīn Mistū and Yūsuf ʿAlī Bidīwī (Beirut: Dār al-Kalim al-Ṭayyib, 1416/1995), 5; Muṣṭafā Saʿīd al-Khunn, *Abḥāth ḥawl uṣūl al-fiqh* (Beirut: Dār al-Kalim al-Ṭayyib, 2000/1420), 288; ʿAbd al-Karīm b. ʿAlī b. Muḥammad al-Namla, *al-Jāmiʿli-masāʾil uṣūl al-fiqh al-Islāmī* (Riyadh: Maktabat al-Rushd, 2000/1420),16.

theory. He is also quite critical of scholars who follow the method of the theologians.[25] However, from my examination of Samʿānī's *Qawāṭiʿ al-adilla*, it appears to me that his book shows little signs of commitment to the features Ibn Khaldūn associates with the method of the jurists. Samʿānī, for instance, rarely refers to the laws espoused by early Shāfiʿī authorities as evidence for his positions in legal theory. This is probably why many modern scholars have categorized Samʿānī among the scholars following the method of the theologians.[26] This raises the question how the terms *ṭarīqat al-fuqahāʾ* and *ṭarīqat al-mutakallimīn* were understood during Shīrāzī's and Samʿānī's time, three centuries before Ibn Khaldūn. Ibn Khaldūn's typology is not the earliest attempt to categorize legal theory methods and literature. Others have made similar attempts and used similar categories.[27] Yet, all these pre-modern typologies are greatly under studied.[28] As it currently stands, we cannot claim sufficient knowledge of the categorizing criteria of pre-modern typol-

---

[25] Abū al-Muẓaffar Manṣūr b. Muḥammad b. ʿAbd al-Jabbār al-Samʿānī (d. 489/1096), *Qawāṭiʿ al-adilla fī uṣūl al-fiqh*, 5 vols, ed. Muḥammad Ḥasan Ismāʿīl al-Shāfiʿī (Beirut: Dār Iḥyāʾ al-Kutub al-ʿIlmiyya, 1997), 1/2:6–7.

[26] See for example, Jamāl al-Dīn ʿAṭiyya, *al-Tanẓīr al-fiqhī* (n.p.: n.p., 1987), 30; al-Khunn, *Abḥāth ḥawl uṣūl al-fiqh*, 289; al-Namla, *Jāmiʿ*, 17.

[27] For other attempts to typologize pre-modern legal theory literature, see ʿAlāʾ al-Dīn Abū Bakr Muḥammad b. Aḥmad al-Samarqandī (d. 539/1144?), *Mīzān al-uṣūl fī natāʾij al-ʿuqūl* in ʿAbd al-Malik b. ʿAbd al-Raḥmān Asʿd al-Saʿdī, '*Mīzān al-uṣūl fī natāʾij al-ʿuqūl*' (PhD., Umm al-Qurā University, 1404/1984), 1–3; Samʿānī, *Qawāṭiʿ*, 1/2:5–7.

[28] I am not aware of a work in a European language dedicated to an analysis and a study of the pre-modern typologies of legal theory. In Arabic there are few, however most of them focus on Ibn Khaldūn's typology. See for example, Quṭb Muṣṭafā Sānū, *Qirāʾa maʿrifiyya fi-l-fikr al-uṣūlī* (Kuwait: Wizārat al-Awqāf wa-l-Shu'ūn al-Islāmiyya, 1428/2007); Muḥammad Aḥmad al-Qaḥṭānī, *Manāhij al-uṣūliyyīn fi-l-taʾlīf* (n.p.: Dār al-Wafāʾ li-l-Ṭibāʿa wa-l-Nashr, n.d.); Yūsuf Aḥmad al-Badawī, 'al-Khaṣāʾiṣ al-uṣūliyya li-madrasat al-mutakallimīn', *al-Majalla al-Urduniyya fi-l-dirāsāt al-Islāmiyya* 5.4 (2009): no page numbers.

ogies of legal theory writings. Treating this lacuna requires an independent study and cannot be undertaken here.

What I can say, briefly, is that the so-called method of the theologians includes jurists with very different approaches to legal theory; so different that they cannot all be crammed into the same category. Furthermore, Bernard Weiss, Ahmad Ahmad and others have already noted that Ibn Khaldūn's typology appears too rigid; legal theoreticians, of all sorts, often utilize both rational reflection and juristic precedence to construct legal theory.[29] I believe that Ibn Khaldūn's typology is not sufficient to categorize the various trends in Muslim legal theory. In this study, I will neither take his typology for granted nor will I depend on it to categorize the jurists examined here. Most importantly, his categories, method of jurists and method of theologians, will not be used to understand the function of theology in a jurist's legal theory. I will not assume that a jurist who belongs to the method of the theologians allows his theology to shape his legal theory whereas those who belong to the method of the jurists do not.

Overview of Chapters

This book is divided into five chapters. The first chapter is a review of the modern literature that has examined or touched upon the relationship between speculative theology and legal theory. I discuss the major trends within this literature and explain how the current study is different. Chapter two describes the political and the intellectual context in which the four jurists, around whom this study revolves, lived and produced their ideas. This chapter has three main parts. The first presents a brief survey of some of the major political events in Iraq and Iran during the fourth/tenth-fifth/eleventh century, the time and place in which the four jurists

[29] Ahmad Atif Ahmad, *Structural Interrelations of Theory and Practice in Islamic Law* (Leiden: Brill, 2006), 15–8, 34–5, 191–2; Weiss, *Search for God's Law*, 18. For more critical remarks on Ibn Khaldūn's typology, see Vishanoff, *Formation of Islamic Hermeneutics*, 269–71; Aron Zysow, *The Economy of Certainty: An Introduction to the Typology of Islamic Legal Theory* (Atlanta, Georgia, Lockwood Press, 2013), 2; Rumee Ahmed, *Narratives of Islamic Legal Theory* (Oxford: Oxford University Press, 2012), 7.

lived. The second part discusses some of the important intellectual developments that might have influenced a jurist's perception of the relationship between speculative theology and legal theory. Among the intellectual developments that I discuss here is the ongoing dialogue between rationalist and traditionalist trends in Islam, the strong traditionalist presence in educational institutions, the traditionalization of legal theory, the speculative theologian's membership in Sunnī schools of law, in addition to what Wael Hallaq calls the rationalist-traditionalist synthesis in legal theory. The final part of this chapter presents brief biographies of each of the four Shāfiʿī jurists studied here.

In the second chapter, I argue that the ascendance of traditionalism and the strong presence of traditionalist scholars in educational institutions, at least in Iraq, probably placed some pressures on speculative theologians to distance some aspects of their speculative theology from their legal theory. This may have been motivated by the fact that many traditionalist scholars considered speculative theology to be a 'deviant' discipline. Furthermore, speculative theologians were keen to join Sunnī schools of law. This membership is an important mark of identity, crucial to facilitate employment opportunities and vital for gaining acceptance within the intellectual community. Most schools of law include jurists from various theological backgrounds. To maintain conformity within each school of law, jurists were keen to limit the legal theory discrepancies produced by their theological disagreements. This was done by keeping the most divisive theological controversies at some distance, as much as possible, from legal theory.

Chapter three compares the four jurists' use of *qiyās* as a tool in reaching and supporting legal conclusions. Due to space restraints, I mainly focus on one aspect of *qiyās*, namely the *ratio legis* (*ʿilla*), its deduction process and its function in law-making. The nature of *qiyās* and the *ratio legis* as legal tools makes them relevant to a number of important theological debates, such as the one around natural causality (*sababiyya*) and the controversy around the definitions of divine justice (*ʿadl*) and wisdom (*ḥikma*). The four Shāfiʿīs studied here often adopt different positions on these theological debates. Nonetheless, their conceptions of *qiyās* and the *ratio legis* are not significantly different. This indicates that their significant theological disagreements do not always lead to equally significant discrepancies in *qiyās*. These significant similarities, I argue, are a product of a deliberate effort by the jurists to limit the impact of their theological differences on their common legal theory.

Yet, this does not mean that the four jurists, who are studied here, adopt identical positions on the different aspects of *qiyās*. Disparities certainly exist; some of them are a product of theological disagreements. For example, ʿAbd al-Jabbār depends heavily on benefit or interest (*maṣlaḥa*) and unaided human reason (*ʿaql*) to deduce the *rationes legis* behind Qurʾānic and Prophetic deontic qualifications (sg. *ḥukm sharʿī*).[30] He uses the Muʿtazilī doctrines of optimism (*al-ṣalāḥ wa-l-aṣlaḥ*) and his rational moral theory (*al-taḥsīn wa-l-taqbīḥ al-ʿaqlī*) to justify his *ratio legis* deduction methods. On the other hand, Juwaynī and Samʿānī limit the use of interest and human reason to deduce *rationes legis*. They refer to their textualist moral theory (*al-taḥsīn wa-l-taqbīḥ al-sharʿī*) and their rejection of optimism as supporting evidence. This is certainly a legal theory discrepancy produced by a theological disagreement. Interestingly, ʿAbd al-Jabbār's Muʿtazilī student Abū al-Ḥusayn al-Baṣrī and the earlier Muʿtazilī authority Abū Bakr al-Jaṣṣāṣ both use optimism and rational moral theory to argue for a deduction method that is almost identical with Juwaynī's and Samʿānī's. Here we find Muʿtazilī jurists adopting the same theological positions as ʿAbd al-Jabbār, but disagreeing on the legal theory consequences of their common doctrines. We also find jurists adopting contradicting theological positions, yet all are using their different theologies to argue for the same legal theory methods.

These and similar incidents indicate that speculative theology certainly influenced the legal theory choices of individual jurists. However, at a group and school level, this influence is not entirely consistent. Jurists, from the same theological background often disagree on the legal theory consequences of their common dogmas. Therefore, sharing a theological dogma does not guarantee adopting a similar legal theory nor do theological disagreements always lead to variations in legal theory. Jurists who adopt the same legal theory position but use different (sometimes contradicting) theological justifications for their shared legal theory are in fact

[30] I borrow this translation from Zysow, *Economy of Certainty*.

disagreeing on the theological foundations of their common position in legal theory.

Chapter four studies what might appear to be a hypothetical legal theory question, namely the deontic qualification of human actions prior to the advent of divine revelation (*ḥukm al-ashyāʾ qabla wurūd al-sharʿ*). This legal theory debate asks the following question: before humans receive revelations from God (or in the absence of this revelation), are their actions permitted (*mubāḥa*) or proscribed (*maḥẓūra*), or should deontic qualifications rather be suspended until the advent of revelation (*waqf*). For example, are humans allowed to consume fruit and drink wine before they receive any divine messages informing them of the state of these actions? The theological debate that appears to have the greatest impact on this legal theory question is the one around moral epistemology (*al-taḥsīn wa-l-taqbīḥ*). ʿAbd al-Jabbār holds that all harmless actions are permitted even before the advent of revelation. He justifies his position mainly by demonstrating that human reason is capable of ascertaining moral and deontic knowledge without the assistance of divine revelation. On the other hand, Shīrāzī, Juwaynī and Samʿānī note that all judgments should be suspended until humans receive divine guidance. To support their position, they try to prove that human reason, without the assistance of revelation, is incapable of discerning moral and deontic knowledge.

Another relevant theological controversy is the debate around the definitions of divine justice and wisdom. Muʿtazilīs define divine wisdom and justice as a group of constraints that God placed on Himself. Their understanding of both divine attributes entails that God will always (or must) permit harmless actions and prohibit harmful ones. Therefore, ʿAbd al-Jabbār argues that divine legislations are predictable even before the advent of revelation. Humans can ascertain the deontic qualification of actions in the absence of revelation. Shīrāzī, Juwaynī and Samʿānī, as Ashʿarī and traditionalist scholars, vehemently refuse the Muʿtazilī understanding of divine wisdom and justice. They hold that nothing can place any obligations on God. Nothing guarantees that He will permit harmless actions and prohibit harmful ones. Their understanding of divine omnipotence renders divine laws and actions unpredictable. Therefore, for them, in the absence of revelation, humans cannot ascertain deontic qualifications and must suspend all judgments until they receive divine guidance. Those are only few examples of the theological arguments that appear in discussions of the 'before revelation' question. The presence of these arguments reveals the strong impact of speculative theology on this aspect of legal theory.

Having said this, one must note that the impact of theology on this part of legal theory does not seem consistent. As explained earlier, jurists often disagree on the legal theory implications of their common theological doctrines. This is again noticeable in the 'before revelation' debate. It is common to find followers of the same theological tradition using the same doctrine to justify different answers to the 'before revelation' question. It is also common to find jurists from different theological backgrounds using contradicting theological beliefs to argue for the same position. This shows that theological disagreements do not necessarily lead to discrepancies in legal theory. The use of theological arguments to justify legal theory conclusions demonstrates the impact of theology on legal theory. However, this impact is not uniform. Theology informs the legal theory choices of each individual jurist. Disagreements over the legal implications of theological beliefs hinder theology from leading to consistent results in legal theory. Therefore, sharing the same theology does not guarantee sharing the same choices in legal theory.

What appears to have a more consistent impact on forming a jurist's position on the 'before revelation' debate is his position on various hermeneutical questions. Among those questions is the interpretation of doubt: when in doubt about the legality of a particular action or thing, should a jurist favour permission or proscription? Another relevant hermeneutical debate is that around the legal significance of the silence of revelation. In other words, if revelation does not comment on a particular action, can this be taken as evidence for permitting or proscribing this action? It appears that a position on these hermeneutical questions consistently leads to adopting particular stands on the 'before revelation' debate. For example, jurists who refuse to consider the silence of revelation as evidence entailing any particular deontic qualification (*ḥukm sharʿī*), often adopt suspension. Scholars who regard the silence of revelation as of legal significance adopt either permission or proscription. Jurists who deem doubt to be an aspect of evilness favour proscription, whereas those who refuse to conceive doubt as an evil aspect favour permission. The impact of these hermeneutical positions on the jurists' answer to the 'before revelation' debate appears more consistent than speculative theology. Jurists who adopt permission, proscription, or suspension share a common position on the above hermeneutical questions, regardless of their theological discrepancies.

Chapter five examines another famous theoretical debate within Muslim legal theory, namely the controversy around the plurality of truth (*taʿaddud al-ḥaqq*) in law. Is truth single and universal, or are there various and multiple valid truths? Put differently, can there exist various, yet equally correct, deontic qualifications for the same human action? Or is only one juristic opinion correct and all opposing ones nothing but error? Insisting on the singularity of truth is a position often named *takhṭiʾa*; scholars who favour this perception are named *mukhaṭṭiʾa*. Those who acknowledge the multiplicity of legal truth adopt a position called *taṣwīb* and are often named *muṣawwiba*. I compare the position of the four jurists under study on this debate. My comparison is chiefly an analysis of their arguments supporting their own stand and their rebuttals of their opponents. As with previous chapters, the main aim of this analysis is to explore and evaluate the impact of a jurist's speculative theology on his stance regarding this legal theory question. It is important to mention here that this chapter depends on the distinction between the different aspects of (or divisions within) speculative theology.

It appears that jurists disagree on the aspects of speculative theology that are relevant to this legal theory debate. For example, Shīrāzī, Samʿānī and Juwaynī do not utilize any doctrinal or creedal aspects of theology in their arguments supporting their adoption of the singularity of truth. On the other hand, ʿAbd al-Jabbār's argument for the plurality of truth depends on his Muʿtazilī understanding of divine justice, especially on a derivative doctrine that excludes the possibility of God requiring an impossible obligation (*ʿadam taklīf mā lā yuṭāq*). This might indicate that, for ʿAbd al-Jabbār, an acceptance of both doctrines should lead to the adoption of *taṣwīb*.

Other Muʿtazilī and non-Muʿtazilī authors raise theological discussions in their sections on this debate in their legal theory writings. The two theological debates that often appear in discussions of this question are those around optimism and the possibility of God requiring an impossible obligation. A review of this literature reveals, again, that jurists are far from unanimous on the legal theory consequences of accepting or rejecting these doctrines. Optimism and the impossibility of God requiring an unachievable obligation are used, by different jurists, to argue for and against *taṣwīb* and *takhṭiʾa*. Those who reject both doctrines also use their theological positions to support contradicting positions on the plurality of truth debate. The fact that jurists often use both theological doctrines as evidence for and against adopting a particular position on the *taṣwīb-takhṭiʾa* debate indicates that these doctrines shape their position on this aspect of legal theory. However, they certainly disagree on the legal theory consequences of accepting or rejecting both theological doctrines. Theology certainly inspires each individual jurist to favour one or the other legal theory opinion. However, jurists interpret the legal implications of their common doctrines differently; doctrinal aspects of theology do not, therefore, always have a consistent impact on group level. A group of scholars sharing common theological doctrines do not always share similar legal theory preferences.

Rather than the doctrinal and creedal aspects, it appears that epistemology is the single aspect of speculative theology with the most consistent impact on a jurist's stance on this debate, both on an individual and group level. A jurist's position on a number of epistemological questions such as the goal of *ijtihād*, the role of probability (*ẓann*) in law-making and the epistemological value of inconclusive evidence (*amāra* or *dalīl ẓannī*) consistently determine whether he adopts *takhṭiʾa* or *taṣwīb*.[31] Jurists who elevate the epistemological value of inconclusive evidence often embrace *takhṭiʾa*. On the other hand, jurists who undermine the epistemological value of this type of evidence usually favour *taṣwīb*. *Muṣawwiba*, moreover, generally allow probability a greater role in law-making; probability in itself can be a goal for *ijtihād*. The *mukhaṭṭiʾa* refuse to consider probability as a goal for *ijtihād*. The latter, for them, aspires to uncover the divinely determined deontic qualification and

[31] Inconclusive evidence is a reference to any textual or non-textual evidence (i.e. an ambiguous Qurʾānic verse or a process of legal reasoning) that can only yield probable knowledge (*ẓann*). Conclusive evidence (*dalīl qaṭʿī*) is one that is capable of producing certain knowledge (*qaṭʿ* or *ʿilm*); this type of evidence is very rare in the field of law.

not only probable knowledge of it. Therefore, the *mukhaṭṭiʾa* do not share common theological beliefs; they rather share a similar epistemological outlook. This is also true of the *muṣawwiba.* I argue that the main difference between the *muṣawwiba* and the *mukhaṭṭiʾa* is a group of epistemological rather than doctrinal disagreements.

The final part of this study is the conclusion in which I argue that, for many jurists, the disciplines of speculative theology and legal theory are closely related. The legal theory writings of the four jurists examined here, and others, often include theological references and discussions. Legal theoreticians are also usually eager to harmonize their stands in legal theory with their theological beliefs. Each jurist adopts the legal theory positions he believes to be in harmony with (or the logical outcome of) his theology. Jurists often put forward theological arguments as evidence for the validity of their choices in legal theory. The aim behind these arguments is to demonstrate the harmony between the jurist's positions in legal theory and his theological doctrines. Therefore, I argue that a jurist's theology often influences which legal theory positions he adopts. However, jurists who belong to the same theological trend do not always agree on the legal theory requirements of their common theology. They disagree which legal theory positions are the logical outcome of their common theology. These disagreements entail that theology informs the legal theory of individual jurists; however, on theological school level this influence is not consistent.[32] Two jurists may share the same theological doctrine, yet each interprets the legal theory entailments of this doctrine differently. Therefore, sharing a common theology does not always lead to adopting common positions in legal theory. This prevents theological schools from creating their distinct legal theories that is based on a common understanding of the legal theory consequences of their shared dogma.

In this study, I also highlight the disagreements around the theological foundations for legal theory. Excluding the Ḥanbalī School of law, the other three Sunnī schools include jurists from diverse theological backgrounds. The Shāfiʿī legal school, for in-

---

[32] I am grateful to Prof. Dr. Christian Lange who helped me articulate this conclusion.

stance, include Ashʿarī, Muʿtazilī and traditionalist jurists; all believe that their legal theory positions within the Shāfiʿī School are in harmony with their theology. We often find jurists using different (sometimes contradicting) theological doctrines to support the same position in legal theory; each jurist believes that his theology is the one in harmony with his Shāfiʿī legal theory. The same can be noticed within the Ḥanafī and Mālikī schools of law; jurists, from various theological backgrounds, use different theological doctrines to support the legal theory of their choice, some of those choices are quite similar. This reveals a disagreement around the theological foundations of legal theory; jurists sharing the same position in legal theory use different theological doctrines as evidence vindicating their common position in legal theory. Each jurist considers his own theology as the proper foundation for their common legal theory stance.

These disagreements entail that the adoption of a particular legal theory does not always require the adoption of a specific theology. Doctrinal disagreements rarely prevent jurists from joining the same school of law and sharing similar opinions in legal theory. Therefore, we rarely find a legal theory position common within the Shāfiʿī, Ḥanafī, or Mālikī schools monopolized by any one particular theological trend. Membership in any of these schools does not necessitate embracing specific theological doctrines, other than accepting the Muslim message, the authority of the Qurʾān and the Prophetic Sunna. Jurists from various theological backgrounds coexist within the same legal school. Each of these jurists believes that his theology informs his legal theory. Different theological doctrines are often utilized as pillars supporting the validity of the legal theory stands common within the same legal school. Yet, none of the Sunnī schools of law (excluding the Ḥanbalī) is monopolized by any one particular theological trend. Theology did manage to inform the legal theory choices of individual jurists. However, theology did not significantly shape or inform the legal theory of a school of law. In the following chapter, I survey some of the modern studies that examined (or are relevant to) the impact of *ʿilm al-kalām* on *uṣūl al-fiqh*.

CHAPTER ONE: MODERN SCHOLARSHIP ON THE RELATIONSHIP BETWEEN THEOLOGY AND LEGAL THEORY

INTRODUCTION

The relationship between speculative theology and legal theory is the subject of many modern studies. In the coming pages I briefly survey the different views available on this relationship and explain the methods and arguments often used to justify these views. A full survey of all relevant studies cannot be done here; I only present a sample of such works. Even the works presented, full justice to their arguments and conclusions requires a more extensive examination. A succinct review is, however, sufficient for the purpose of this study.

The majority of modern historians, in both East and West, hold that speculative theology played a crucial role in the formation of legal theory. Two main arguments are often utilized to validate this view, the first is what I call the 'historical argument', and the second is the 'causal argument'. Other scholars, like David Vishanoff and Murteza Bedir, identify certain trends in legal theory that are more theologized than others. Only few authors argue that theology had no significant impact on legal theory, among those are Fazlur Rahman and Baber Johansen. Other studies, although not always focusing on the relationship between both disciplines, provide important insights on the nature of this relationship. Robert Gleave argues that there was some form of 'compartmentalization' among Muslim religious disciplines that makes tracing the interrelations among these disciplines difficult. Ahmed Elshamsy and Christian Lange draw attention to what they consider to be anomalies between particular legal theory positions and certain theological doctrines. Unpacking the arguments of the previous scholars will allow us to situate the current study in its wider context.

THE HISTORICAL ARGUMENT

To prove that theology influence the formation of legal theory, scholars adopting the historical argument depend mainly on a historical analysis tracing the development stages of legal theory. Theological doctrines and legal theory positions are not, in this argument, juxtaposed or analysed to clarify the interdependence of both disciplines. In addition to legal theory writings, scholars following this method also refer to historical chronicles and biographical dictionaries as sources of information on the relationship between both disciplines. Probably the best representative of the historical argument is George Makdisi. In his article 'The Juridical theology of Shāfiʿī', Makdisi mentions three main arguments uncovering the strong impact theology left on legal theory.[1] First, he compares the contents of *Risāla* by Muḥammad b. Idrīs al-Shāfiʿī (d. 204/820),[2] whom he considers the founder of legal theory, to the contents of later works on legal theory. Makdisi argues that Shāfiʿī founded a purely traditionalist legal theory that was not influenced by speculative theology. *Risāla* is, therefore, free from theological and philosophical discussions. By the fifth/eleventh century, theologians started authoring books on legal theory.[3] This development, argues Makdisi, transforms the contents of legal theory writings 'from [the] thoroughly traditionalist content of the *Risāla*, two centuries

---

[1] Makdisi, 'Juridical Theology', 5–47. Some aspects of his argument appeared before in George Makdisi *The Rise of Humanism in Classical Islam and the Christian West* (Edinburgh: Edinburgh University Press, 1990), 2–13, 39–43; Makdisi, 'Ashʿarī and the Ashʿarites', 37–80. However, I focus here on 'Juridical Theology' as it includes the most comprehensive presentation of Makdisi's views on the relationship between theology and legal theory.

[2] Muḥammad b. Idrīs al-Shāfiʿī (d. 204/820), 2nd ed., ed. Aḥmad Shākir (Beirut: Dār al-Kutub al-ʿIlmiyya, 199?).

[3] For the motivations behind the theologians' involvement in legal theory, see Makdisi, 'Juridical Theology', 26, 43; Makdisi, *Rise of Humanism*, 39–43.

previously, to one in which *kalām* and legal philosophy played a prominent part'.[4] The theologians' involvement allowed them to theologize legal theory and include theological discussions not previously considered part of this legal discipline. Makdisi adds that the theologians' efforts were so successful that many traditionalist jurists felt compelled to include theological questions in their legal theory literature.[5]

Makdisi's second argument proving the strong impact of theology on legal theory is based on a list of the most prominent men who died in the first years of the fifth/eleventh century compiled by Shams al-Dīn al-Dhahabī (d. 748/1347).[6] Makdisi argues that, in his compilation, Dhahabī does not always mention the legal affiliation of those individuals. Moreover, he excludes prominent traditionalist-Shāfiʿī jurists who should have appeared on this list. Instead, Dhahabī includes Shāfiʿī speculative theologians such as the Ashʿarī Abū Isḥāq al-Isfarāʾīnī (d. 418/1027) and the Muʿtazilī ʿAbd al-Jabbār al-Hamadhānī, without noting their legal affiliation but rather emphasizing their theological orientation. Makdisi argues that Dhahabī, himself a traditionalist Shāfiʿī, was deliberately attempting to uncover and scandalize those speculative theologians who entered 'unnoticed' the Shāfiʿī School. For Makdisi, this is a sign that theologians managed to penetrate Sunnī schools of law and that traditionalist scholars, like Dhahabī, were trying to resist their involvement in legal disciplines.[7]

Finally, Makdisi briefly surveys the pre-modern debate on the validity of including theological topics in legal theory literature.

---

[4] Makdisi, 'Juridical Theology', 42. For his complete argument, see Makdisi, 'Juridical Theology', 14–8; Makdisi, *Rise of Humanism*, 3–5. For a sample of the topics added, see Makdisi, 'Juridical Theology', 16; Makdisi, *Rise of Humanism*, 4.

[5] Makdisi, 'Juridical Theology', 44–5.

[6] Makdisi does not mention in which of Dhahabī's books this list is to be found. The original source may be lost as he notes that the list is preserved in Abū al-Faḍl ʿAbd al-Raḥmān b. Jalāl al-Dīn al-Suyūṭī (d. 911/1505), *Tarīkh al-khulafāʾ* (Cairo: al-Maṭbaʿa al-Munīriyya, 1351/1932), 276.

[7] Makdisi, 'Juridical Theology', 22–7.

Some jurists express their position on this debate in their introductions to their legal theory manuals; Makdisi studies a sample of those introductions. He quotes jurists and theologians on both sides of the debate, accepting or rejecting the inclusion of theological questions in legal theory writings.[8] For him this is evidence that at least some jurists (in fact he believes them to be a majority) consider speculative theology to be an integral part of legal theory and allow their theological doctrines to determine the shape of their *uṣūl al-fiqh*. Those are the three arguments Makdisi presents as evidence for the incorporation of theology in pre-modern Muslim legal theory. Makdisi sees the integration of theology in legal theory as a development that took place after theologians became involved in legal theory. He presents the history of legal theory in developmental stages revealing the stage which led to integrating theology in legal theory literature. However, his argument does not pay enough attention to the technical interrelations between both disciplines. He proves that theological topics were added to legal theory works, yet he does not explain how these new additions changed legal theory.

Quṭb Muṣṭafā Sānū is another scholar who adopts a historical argument, almost identical to Makdisi's, to prove the same conclusion.[9] Sānū argues that Shāfiʿī's *Risāla* is free from theological discussions. Starting from the middle of the fourth/tenth century, more theologians begin writing books on legal theory. Their writings offer them the opportunity to integrate their theology into the discipline of legal theory. They also attempt to create legal theories that are in harmony with their theological doctrines. To support his argument, Sānū compares the topics discussed in Shāfiʿī's *Risāla* to

---

[8] Makdisi, 'Juridical Theology', 13–18. See also Makdisi, *Rise of Humanism*, 33–40; Makdisi, *Ibn ʿAqīl*, 79–85.

[9] Quṭb Muṣṭafā Sānū, 'al-Mutakallimūn wa-uṣūl al-fiqh qirāʾa fī jadaliyyat al-ʿilāqa bayn ʿilmay al-uṣūl wa-l-kalām', *Islāmiyyat al-Maʿrifa* 9 (1997): 37–70. A modified version of this article appeared again in chapter two of the same author's monograph *Qirāʾa maʿrifiyya*, 83–120. Sānū was a professor of comparative law and Islamic finance at the Department of *fiqh* and *uṣūl al-fiqh*, International Islamic University in Malaysia. In 2011 he was appointed as the Guinean minister of International Cooperation.

topics included in later legal theory literature.[10] He notes that *Risāla* is mainly concerned with four issues, namely: *sharʿī* evidence, methods of deducting laws from those evidence, preponderance (*tarjīḥ*) between evidence,[11] and finally the different types of *ijtihād*.[12] Theologians, writes Sānū, add other topics that did not appear in the *Risāla*, such as their discussions of Greek logic and linguistics.[13] He adds that, in their legal theory writings, theologians include 'purely' theological and philosophical discussions such as the definition of reason, its function and its relationship to revelation.[14] Furthermore, continues Sānū, theologians introduce abstract debates that have little practical relevance to legal theory such as obligating the non-existent (*taklīf al-maʿdūm*), whether permission (*ibāḥa*) constitutes an obligation, and the responsibility of non-believers to follow the details of Muslim law. Sānū admits that theologians contributed to the sophistication of legal theory. They help maintain vigour within this discipline and created the tools used to renew and revitalize it. Yet, Sānū also notes that many of the theological and philosophical questions they added to legal theory are barely relevant to the process of law finding and its application.[15]

Both Sānū and Makdisi depend on a diachronic and developmental analysis to show the gradual integration of theology into legal theory. They trace the early history of legal theory by comparing what they consider to be the earliest legal theory book to later works in the same discipline noting changes and developments. Both authors hold that theology started as a traditionalist discipline that was later theologized by speculative theologians. Their main supporting evidence is the new theological and philosophical questions that appear in later works of legal theory. The theologians' involvement in legal theory is certainly one factor contributing to

[10] Sānū, 'al-Mutakallimūn wa-uṣūl al-fiqh', 55–63.

[11] The translation of *tarjīḥ* as preponderance is borrowed from Weiss, *Search for God's Law*, 721–30.

[12] Sānū, 'al-Mutakallimūn wa-uṣūl al-fiqh', 56–7.

[13] Sānū, 'al-Mutakallimūn wa-uṣūl al-fiqh', 59.

[14] Sānū, 'al-Mutakallimūn wa-uṣūl al-fiqh', 59.

[15] Sānū, 'al-Mutakallimūn wa-uṣūl al-fiqh', 61–2.

the appearance of such new questions in legal theory literature. However, this conclusion in itself does not clarify the impact those new additions left on legal theory. Neither Makdisi nor Sānū clarify how the introduction of speculative theology changed legal theory. They do not show which theological doctrines influenced which aspects of legal theory. They do not explain how is theologized legal theory different from the legal theory of jurists who refuse to mix both disciplines. None of them explain the internal dynamics that allows (or hinders) theology to inform a jurist's legal theory choice. Leaving those stones unturned obscures the nature of the relationship between theology and legal theory. My study attempts to examine some of these questions hoping to clarify the nature of the relationship between both disciplines and recognize the extent to which a jurist's theology informs his legal theory.

THE CAUSAL ARGUMENT

Other scholars try to establish the interdependence of theology and legal theory by showing causal relationships between particular theological doctrines and specific legal theory positions. They identify certain theological doctrines as the reason behind favouring specific positions in legal theory. The most famous study, in the West, to adopt this method is Aron Zysow's *The Economy of Certainty*.[16] Zysow notes that his study focused on the Central Asian tradition of the Ḥanafī School of law, especially on one particular member of this legal trend, namely ʿAlāʾ al-Dīn al-Samarqandī (d. 539/1144?).[17] At the very beginning of his book, and throughout, Zysow argues that 'developed theology, above all in the form of

[16] His book is almost an unmodified version of his famous doctoral dissertation 'The Economy of Certainty: An Introduction to the Typology of Islamic Legal Theory', (PhD diss., Harvard University, 1984). In his published version, Zysow only added a short preface and at the end of each chapter he includes a short commentary updating some of the sources and briefly commenting on some of his arguments.

[17] Zysow, *Economy of Certainty*, 2. However, he also makes extensive references to the legal theory literature of other schools of law.

Muʿtazilism, managed to penetrate to the very heart of legal theory'.[18]

Having said this, Zysow also identifies areas in legal theory that resisted and escaped the influence of speculative theology. This is clearer in his article 'Muʿtazilism and Māturīdism in Ḥanafī Legal Theory', in which he once again focuses on Central Asian Ḥanafīs, whom are mostly Māturīdī. Zysow notes that Central Asian Ḥanafīs borrowed many of the legal theory positions of the Iraqi Ḥanafīs, whom are predominantly Muʿtazilī. Zysow reminds his readers that Iraqi Ḥanafī legal theory is influenced by Muʿtazilī theology, yet this does not pose a problem for the Central Asian Ḥanafīs. However, Zysow writes that late in the fifth/eleventh and early sixth/twelfth century Māturīdī-Ḥanafī scholars, such as ʿAlāʾ al-Dīn al-Samarqandī and Abū al-Muʿīn al-Nasafī (d. 508/1114), tried to identify and remove Muʿtazilī influences from Ḥanafī legal thought. They also attempt to create a legal theory based on their Māturīdī doctrines. Zysow describes this effort as an attempt to theologize and de-Muʿtazilize Ḥanafī *uṣūl al-fiqh*. However, Zysow concludes that their endeavour to theologize Central Asian legal theory was of limited success. After the sixth/twelfth century, Central Asian Ḥanafīs continue holding almost the same legal theory positions they inherited from Iraqi Ḥanafīs. The links between those positions and Muʿtazilī theology gradually fade away. For Zysow, this indicates, that Māturīdī theology did not have a profound impact on the formation of Central Asian Ḥanafī legal theory.[19]

It is important here to demonstrate how Zysow identifies the cases in which theology informs legal theory and those in which it fails to practice significant influence. He singles out particular theological doctrines, identifies their logical consequences in legal theo-

---

[18] Zysow, *Economy of Certainty*, 4. Gregor Schwarb makes a similar remark. He says that 'it is a fact that the discipline of *uṣūl al-fiqh* underwent a fundamental change with the first Muʿtazilite treatise on the subject'. See his 'Capturing the Meanings of God's Speech', 127 f.n. 64.

[19] For his complete argument, see Aron Zysow, 'Muʿtazilism and Māturīdism in Ḥanafī Legal Theory', in *Studies in Islamic Legal Theories*, ed. Bernard Weiss (Leiden: Brill, 2002): 235–65.

ry and monitors the cases in which these consequences are adopted by jurists. When jurists accept the legal theory repercussions of a theological doctrine, this would be a case where their theology managed to inform their legal theory. When the opposite occurs, this would show that their theology failed to produce its expected outcome in legal theory. I mention here only one example. Zysow examines the legal theory debate around the default denotation of general expressions (*ʿumūm*): are general expressions (such as 'the Muslims' and 'the sinners') a default reference to generic categories that applies to all of its referents? Or are general expressions metaphorical references to many but not all of the referents? For example, when Qurʾān 82:14 says '*wa-inna al-fujjār la-fī jaḥīm*' (and the wicked will burn in the Fire),[20] is the general (*ʿāmm*) term *al-fujjār* (the wicked) a generic reference to all sinners or only a reference to most of them? Zysow suggests that early Ḥanafīs (fourth-fifth/tenth-eleventh centuries) are divided in their answer to this question along theological lines. Ḥanafī jurists who follow Muʿtazilī theology hold that general expressions apply, by default, to all its referents. In other words, the term *al-fujjār* mentioned above is a reference to all sinners. On the other hand, Ḥanfīs who adopt the theology of Irjāʾ (the Murjiʾa) often prefer a minimalist interpretation of general expressions. Unless there is evidence proving otherwise, general expressions should be interpreted as a reference to the majority of referents and not to all of them. Therefore, for those Ḥanafīs, the term *al-fujjār* in the previously-mentioned verse is an allusion to most, but not all, sinners.[21]

---

[20] For translations of Qurʾānic verses, I use The Qurʾān, trans. M. A. S. Abdel Haleem (2004; reprint, Oxford: Oxford University Press, 2005).

[21] The relationship between this hermeneutical debate and the fate of grave sinners in the afterlife has been examined by other scholars, see for instance Muḥammad b. ʿAlī al-Jīlānī al-Shtīwī, *ʿAlāqat ʿilm uṣūl al-fiqh bi-ʿilm al-kalām* (Beirut: Maktabat Ḥasan al-ʿAṣriyya,1431/2010), 460–473; Muḥammad al-ʿArūsī ʿAbd al-Qādir, *al-Masāʾil al-mushtaraka bayna uṣūl al-fiqh wa-uṣūl al-dīn*, 2nd ed. (Riyadh: Maktabat al-Rushd, 1430/2009), 201–5; Ignaz Goldziher, *The Ẓāhirīs: Their Doctrine and Their History*, trans. Wolfgang Behn (Leiden: Brill, 1971), 113–5.

Zysow notes that the above hermeneutical disagreement is a product of the theological debate around the fate of grave sinners in the afterlife. Muʿtazilīs believe that all grave sinners, who pass away without repenting, will face eternal punishment in the world to come. On the other hand, the Murjiʾa (as well as the Māturīdīs) accept the possibility that God may forgive at least some of those sinners. Zysow argues that a jurist's stand on this theological controversy determines his position on the hermeneutical debate mentioned in the previous paragraph. Each group of scholars adopts a certain hermeneutical position that would support its theological stance. In order to harmonize Qurʾān 82:14, and similar verses, with their theology, Muʿtazilīs must consider general terms such as *al-fujjār* to be an inclusive generic reference to all grave sinners. This will confirm their belief that no grave sinner will escape punishment. The Murjiʾa, on the other hand, adopt a minimalist interpretation of general terms like *al-fujjār*. This interpretation allows the Murjiʾa (and later the Māturīdīs) to argue that verses such as Qurʾān 82:14 do not preclude the possibility of forgiveness for at least some grave sinners in the next world. Zysow shows that since each theological group adopts the legal theory repercussions of their theological doctrine, therefore this would be a good example of demonstrating the impact of theology on legal theory. Theology in this instance is the cause behind favouring particular legal and hermeneutical positions and abandoning others.[22]

Zysow notes that within the Central Asian tradition of the Ḥanafī School, the influence of Māturīdī theology on their legal theory is not particularly strong, especially after the middle of the sixth/twelfth century. To prove this conclusion, in his article 'Muʿtazilism and Māturīdīsm in Ḥanafī Legal Theory', Zysow mentions three cases where Central Asian Ḥanafīs do not adopt what he considers to be the logical legal outcome of their Māturīdī theology. For example, despite being predominantly Māturīdī, most Central Asian Ḥanafīs hold that general expressions apply, by default, to all of its referents. The Māturīdī jurist Abū al-Muʿīn al-Nasafī tries to convince his fellow Ḥanafīs that this position entails adopting the Muʿtazilī position on the fate of grave sinners in the

[22] Zysow, *Economy of Certainty*, 78–82.

afterlife. Nonetheless, later Central Asians do not change their position.[23] Abū al-Muʿīn al-Nasafī and his younger Ḥanafī contemporary ʿAlāʾ al-Dīn al-Samarqandī argue that Māturīdī jurists should base their legal theories on their own theological doctrines. Yet, as mentioned before, Zysow notes that their efforts largely go in vain. Central Asian Ḥanafīs continue adopting legal theory positions that are associated with Muʿtazilī theology and do not conform to the 'requirements' of their Māturīdī doctrines. For Zysow, this is a sign that Māturīdī theology failed to significantly inform Ḥanafī legal theory. Therefore, he concludes that Central Asian Ḥanafīs were not entirely interested in theologizing their legal theory.[24]

Despite the resistance of some Central Asian Ḥanafīs, Zysow reaches the conclusion, at least in his book, that theology made a significant impression on Muslim legal theory. The impact of the debate around the fate of grave sinners in the afterlife on legal theory is only one of the many examples Zysow presents to support his conclusion. The majority of modern historians of Islam would agree with Zysow's general position. The causal analysis Zysow adopts is also utilized by many scholars to uncover the impact of speculative theology on legal theory. Haytham Khazna and Muḥammad al-Shtīwī are examples of scholars, writing in Arabic, who use a similar causal analysis to highlight the marks theology left on legal theory.[25] The method these scholars use to demon-

---

[23] Zysow, 'Muʿtazilism and Māturīdism', 252–7; Zysow, *Economy of Certainty*, 76–86.

[24] For his complete argument, see Zysow, 'Muʿtazilism and Māturīdism'.

[25] Haytham ʿAbd al-Ḥamīd ʿAlī Khazna, 'al-Ikhtilāfāt al-uṣūliyya bayna madrasaty al-ʿIrāq wa-Samarqand wa-atharuhā fī uṣūl al-fiqh al-Ḥanafī' (PhD., Jordanian University, 2004); al-Shtīwī, *ʿAlāqat ʿilm uṣūl al-fiqh bi-ʿilm al-kalām*. See also ʿAlī b. Saʿd b. Ṣāliḥ al-Ḍuwayḥī, *Ārāʾ al-muʿtazila al-uṣūliyya* (Riyadh: Maktabat al-Rashīd, 1995). For authors writing in English also adopting this causal argument, see Christian Lange, 'Sins, Expiation and Non-Rationality in Ḥanafī and Shāfiʿī *Fiqh*', in *Islamic Law in Theory*, ed. A. Kevin Reinhart and Robert Gleave (Leiden: Brill, 2014): 143–175; Vishanoff, *Formation of Islamic Hermeneutics*. Only few scholars have managed to mix both the historical and the causal argu-

strate the interrelations between speculative theology and legal theory are different from Makdisi's and Sānū's method. It goes deep into analysing highly technical legal theory debates and links them to theological questions. It mainly presents the relationship between both disciplines as a cause and effect relationship where the adoption of particular theological doctrines functions as the cause for favouring specific legal theory positions.

This causal analysis may have a major shortcoming; it imagines the influence of theology on legal theory to be one mainly of implication, where one theological doctrine produces a particular outcome in legal theory.[26] It does not pay enough attention to other forms of impact. Theology, for instance, frequently shapes and influences the arguments each jurist uses to support his choices in legal theory. A jurist's theological doctrines may also inform the language and terms he uses to express his legal theory positions. These different forms of interactions are largely lost in an analysis that only focuses on causal influences. Moreover, this causal analy-

---

ments, see for instance A. Kevin Reinhart, *Before Revelation: The Boundaries of Muslim Moral Thought* (Albany, N.Y.: State University of New York Press, 1995); A. Kevin Reinhart, "Like the Difference Between Heaven and Earth:' Ḥanafī and Shāfiʿī Discussions of *farḍ* and *wājib* in Theology and *Uṣūl*', in *Studies in Islamic Legal Theory* ed. Bernard Weiss (Leiden: Brill, 2002): 205–234.

[26] Zysow is critical of perceiving the relationship between both disciplines as one based on implication; he writes that '[i]t is appropriate to speak of associations because the relation between theology and legal theory is not in most cases one of implication in the strict sense; that is to say, theology generally undermines legal theory, and legal theory is far from an infallible guide to theology'. See his 'Muʿtazilism and Māturīdism', 235. Zysow does not clarify what he means by a relationship of implication. It appears to me that he is referring to implication as in logic which is a 'relationship between two propositions in which the second is a logical consequence of the first', see *Encylopædia Britanica* s.v. 'Implication'. Despite his previous statement, Zysow presents the relationship between theology and legal theory as one dominated by implication and causality. He does not sufficiently examine other forms of interactions between both disciplines.

sis implicitly assumes that jurists agree on the legal outcomes of their common theological doctrines. This study shows that jurists from the same theological background disagree on the legal theory consequences of their common theological doctrines. Furthermore, jurists, from the same legal school, debate the 'proper' theological foundations of their common positions in legal theory. These debates and the presence of different forms of influence from speculative theology to legal theory do not receive enough attention in the studies that depend on a causal analysis to examine the impact of *ʿilm al-kalām* on *uṣūl al-fiqh*.

DENYING THE RELATIONSHIP

Now we turn to the minority position that undermines the influence of speculative theology on legal theory. Among those who adopt this position are Fazlur Rahman and Baber Johansen. In the introduction to his *Contingency in a Sacred Law*, Johansen argues that speculative theology had almost no influence on *fiqh*.[27] He very briefly discusses the relationship between speculative theology and legal theory. Johansen notes that theology left no great impact on legal theory. He writes that speculative theology is largely a rational discipline that rejects the reliance on texts. Theologians often refuse the jurists' use of *qiyās* and relegate textual evidence (Qurʾān and Sunna) to a secondary position. On the other hand, jurists elevate texts above all other types of evidence. Furthermore, jurists are not enthusiastic about the theologians' involvement in legal subjects and they often do not take account of their opinions when forming a consensus (*ijmāʿ*) on a legal question. Johansen seems to be arguing that, excluding a brief period during the fourth/tenth century, epistemological and methodological differences created a rift between speculative theology and legal theory that hindered mutual influence between both disciplines.[28]

---

[27] Baber Johansen, *Contingency in a Sacred Law: Legal and Ethical Norms in the Muslim Fiqh* (Leiden: Brill, 1999), 1–76.

[28] For his comments on the relationship between speculative theology and legal theory, see Johansen, *Contingency in a Sacred Law*, 28–33.

Fazlur Rahman presents a different explanation for the limited impression theology left on legal theory. He argues that a lack of a Muslim moral philosophy created a gap between both disciplines. For him, this moral philosophy is the 'necessary link between theology and law'.[29] Fazlur Rahman mentions three main factors behind the absence of a Muslim moral philosophy. First, theology confined itself to a 'purely theological circle of considerations' and remained aloof from legal and moral issues. It focused on the nature of the divine and did not pay enough attention to human nature and actions.[30] This preoccupation with the divine nature, argues Fazlur Rahman, did not encourage Muslim intellectuals to create a moral philosophy that would focus on humans.[31] Second, he notes that Muslim scholars' approach to the Qurʾān is largely atomistic rather than holistic. Scholars of the Qurʾān are mainly occupied with interpreting individual verses. They fail to deduce overarching moral principles from the aggregate of laws, rules and regulations mentioned in the Qurʾān. Constructing a Muslim moral philosophy, argues Fazlur Rahman, is possible only after a holistic reading of the Qurʾān. Finally, Fazlur Rahman argues that *fiqh*, as a religious discipline, developed before theology and ethics. After the development of Muslim theology, scholars could not integrate theology and ethics into *fiqh*, as this may upset the already established legal principles.[32]

Fazlur Rahman states that the absence of a moral philosophy led to contradictions between a jurist's legal theory and the theology he embraces. For example, he argues that Ashʿarī theology undermines the assumptions required to uphold any divine law. Their belief in divine predetermination entails removing punishment and blame from sinners. Their denial of good and evil as inherent quali-

---

[29] Fazlur Rahman, *Islam and Modernity* (Chicago: The University of Chicago Press, 1982), 154. See also Fazlur Rahman, 'Functional Interdependence of Law and Theology', in *Theology and Law in Islam*, ed. G. E. von Grunebaum (Wiesbaden: Otto Harrassowitz, 1971), 94.

[30] Fazlur Rahman. 'Functional Interdependence', 89.

[31] Fazlur Rahman, 'Functional Interdependence', 90–2.

[32] Fazlur Rahman 'Law and Ethics in Islam', in *Ethics in Islam*, ed. R. G. Hovannisian (Malibu, California: Undena publications, 1985): 3–15.

ties in human actions and their insistence on adopting theistic subjectivism weakens any justification to obey divine law.[33] Yet, their involvement in law entails accepting human freedom of action and implicitly acknowledges that each human action has an inherent moral value. Therefore, notes Fazlur Rahman, Ashʿarīs' legal and theological writings appear to be in contradiction. The Muʿtazilīs, for Fazlur Rahman, are not in a better position. He argues that their law and legal theory are similar to that of Ashʿarīs because they failed to recognize the legal implications of their Muʿtazilī theology.[34] Elsewhere he argues that major Muslim scholars, such as Abū al-Ḥasan al-Ashʿarī (d. 324/935–6) and Abū Ḥāmid al-Ghazālī (d. 505/1111), were not even interested in integrating theology into law. On the contrary, they made efforts to create some distance between both disciplines.[35]

Fazlur Rahman is considered to be a reformist Islamic thinker. His comments above are part of the plan he suggests to reform Muslim law. One way to reform Muslim legal thought, argues Fazlur Rahman, is by theologizing law and legal theory.[36] For him

---

[33] Theistic subjectivism is the term George Hourani uses to describe the Ashʿarī belief that particular actions are good because they are condoned by God in revelation whereas other actions are evil because they are condemned in revelation. Hourani uses the term Theistic objectivism to describe the Muʿtazilī position. For them, God condones an action because it is inherently good whereas He condemns an action because it is inherently evil. See George Hourani, *Islamic Rationalism: The Ethics of ʿAbd al-Jabbār* (Oxford: Clarendon Press, 1971).

[34] Fazlur Rahman, *Islamic Methodology in History* (Karachi: Central Institute of Islamic Research, 1965), 137, 152–7; Fazlur Rahman, *Revival and Reform in Islam* (Oxford: One World, 2000), 67–8, 148–56.

[35] Fazlur Rahman, 'Functional Interdependence', 90–2.

[36] For other scholars who made similar suggestions, see Khaled Abou El Fadl, *The Great Theft: Wrestling Islam from the Extremists* (New York: Harper One, 2007); Tariq Ramadan, *Radical Reform: Islamic Ethics and Liberation* (Oxford: Oxford University Press, 2009), 126–155; Mohamed Fadel, 'The True, the Good, and the Reasonable: The Theological and Ethical Roots of Public Reason in Islamic Law', *Canadian Journal of Law and Jurisprudence* 21.1 (2008): 1–65.

pre-modern Muslim jurists failed to integrate theology into the legal disciplines. They failed to recognize the legal consequences of Muslim theology. He notes that creating a moral philosophy for Islam would be the first step to integrate theology into law.[37] Interestingly, other Muslim authors see legal theory as too theologized. They suggest that, to reform legal theory and make it more relevant to modern needs, 'irrelevant' theological debates should be removed.[38] Few Wahhābī writers would even prefer removing all elements of speculative theology from legal theory.[39]

I believe that Fazlur Rahman and Johansen have undermined the interconnections between theology and legal theory. This study does not claim that theology left no marks on legal theory. Theology certainly influences how jurists phrase their legal theory opin-

---

[37] Fazlur Rahman did attempt to create such a moral philosophy based on his 'holistic' reading of the Qur'ān, see his *Major Themes of the Qur'an*, 2nd ed. (Chicago: University of Chicago Press, 2009).

[38] See for example Muḥammad Mahdī Shams al-Dīn, *al-Tajdīd fi-l-fikr al-Islāmī* (Beirut: Dār al-Manhal al-Lubnānī, 1417/1997), 22–3; Quṭb Muṣṭafā Sānū, *Adāwāt al-naẓar al-ijtihādī al-manshūd fī ḍū' al-wāqiʿ al-muʿāṣir* (Beirut: Dār al-Fikr, 2000), 111–2; Khālid ʿAbd al-Laṭīf Muḥammad Nūr ʿAbd Allāh, *Masā'il uṣūl al-dīn al-mabḥūtha fi-uṣūl al-fiqh* (Medina: Islamic University, 1426/[2005]); Abū al-Faḍl ʿAbd al-Salām b. Muḥammad b. ʿAbd al-Karīm, *al-Tajdīd wa-l-mujaddidūn fī uṣūl al-fiqh*, 3rd ed. (1424/2003; reprint, Cairo: al-Maktaba al-Islāmiyya, 1427/2007), 401–3, 539, 561–2. For a brief survey examining the positions of modern Muslim scholars on the role theology should or should not play in modern legal theory, see al-Shtīwī, *ʿAlāqat ʿilm uṣūl al-fiqh bi-ʿilm al-kalām*, 34–43.

[39] See for instance Abū Muḥammad Ṣalāḥ b. Fattīnī Kantūsh al-ʿAdnī, *Akhṭā' al-uṣūliyyīn fi-l-ʿaqīda* (Sanaa: Dār al-Āthār, 1427/2006). Other Wahhābī authors wrote legal theory works to identify the legal theory positions that are based on 'erroneous' theological beliefs (those are usually the doctrines of speculative theologians) and create a legal theory based on the 'correct Salafī' (or more accurately Wahhābī) doctrines. See for example Muḥammad b. Ḥusayn b. Ḥasan al-Jīzānī, *Maʿālim uṣūl al-fiqh* (Dammam: Dār Ibn al-Jawzī, 1416/1996); Zakariyyā b. Ghulām Qādir al-Bākistānī, *Tawḍīḥ uṣūl al-fiqh ʿalā manhaj ahl al-ḥadīth* (Damman: Dār Ibn al-Jawzī, 1428[/2007]); ʿAbd Allāh, *Masā'il uṣūl al-dīn*; ʿAbd al-Qādir, *al-Masā'il al-mushtaraka*.

ions. It also occasionally informs the evidence a jurist uses to justify his legal theory choices. Theology is also an important factor shaping the legal theory positions of individual jurists. However, disagreements on the legal implications of theology impede it from having a consistent impact on group and school level. Furthermore, Fazlur Rahman does not recognize the debates among pre-modern jurists on the 'correct' legal theory consequences of theology. He imposes, on pre-modern jurists, his own understanding of the legal implications of Muʿtazilī and Ashʿarī theology. He blames Muʿtazilīs and Ashʿarīs for adopting legal theory positions that contradicts their theology, according to his interpretation of this theology and its ramifications in legal theory. This study pays close attention to the theological arguments jurists use to justify their positions in legal theory. These arguments aim to demonstrate the harmony between a jurist's theology and his legal theory. I compare the arguments that appear in the legal theory texts authored by jurists from various theological and legal backgrounds. I try to recognize, and analyse, the differences in the jurists' perceptions of the legal theory requirements of their theology. I make an effort, as much as possible, to avoid accusations of contradiction and understand that different jurists interpret the impact of their theology on their legal theory differently.

THEOLOGIZED AND UNTHEOLOGIZED LEGAL THEORY

Some scholars try to identify particular trends in Muslim legal theory that are more 'theologized' than others. David Vishanoff is one such example. His book *The Formation of Islamic Hermeneutics* is a study of the emergence and formation of Muslim legal hermeneutics from the second/eighth until the fifth/eleventh century.[40] Vishanoff identifies two main trends in Muslim hermeneutics, a

---

[40] The whole discipline of *uṣul al-fiqh* is sometimes referred to as legal hermeneutics. However, Vishanoff uses the term hermeneutics in reference to a particular aspect of legal theory, namely the linguistic methods and tools jurists use to interpret the Qurʾān and the Prophetic Sunna in order to deduce laws from them. See Vishanoff, *Formations of Islamic Hermeneutics*, xiii.

law-oriented and a theology-oriented trend. The goal of the latter is to 'integrate revelation into their theological discourse, so they tended to opt for hermeneutical principles that they could reconcile with their theological premises…'.[41] Within theology-oriented hermeneutics there are two sub-theories. The first is adopted mainly by the Basran Muʿtazilīs and the Ẓāhirīs. Vishanoff argues that this theory is shaped in response to the Muʿtazilī understanding of divine justice. He argues that the Basran Muʿtazilīs' notion of divine justice entails that revelation must be perfectly clear and comprehensible to any human who possess sound reason. This clarity encourages humans to understand revelation as literally as the text allows. The result is the creation of a literalist approach to revelation. The best representative of this theory is the Muʿtazilī theologian and Shāfiʿī jurist ʿAbd al-Jabbār al-Hamadhānī. Vishanoff states that ʿAbd al-Jabbār subdued his hermeneutics to the dictates of his Muʿtazilī theology. He, therefore, describes ʿAbd al-Jabbār's hermeneutics as more of a 'theological than a legal enterprise'.[42]

The second sub-theory within theology-oriented hermeneutics is adopted mainly by Ashʿarī jurists including the famous Mālikī Abū Bakr al-Bāqillānī (d. 403/1013). Vishanoff writes that for Bāqillānī revelation is ambiguous. Bāqillānī depends on his Ashʿarī concept of divine speech to justify his perception of revelation. Like many Ashʿarīs, he believes that God's internal speech (*kalām nafsī*) is eternal whereas physical copies of the Qurʾān are temporal representations of the eternal divine Word. These temporal representations can never be an accurate expression of God's eternal Speech. Therefore revelation will always remain an ambiguous representation of the divine message. This hermeneutical theory, notes Vishanoff, is squarely based on Ashʿarī theology.[43]

The law-oriented theory occupies a middle position between the two sub-theories of theology-oriented hermeneutics. It admits that the language of revelation is ambiguous, yet this language is clear enough for the deduction of laws from revelation. What is

---

[41] Vishanoff, *Formation of Islamic Hermeneutics*, 270–1. See also p. 252.

[42] Vishanoff, *Formation of Islamic Hermeneutics*, 150. For his full explanation of this trend, see 109–151.

[43] Vishanoff, *Formation of Islamic Hermeneutics*, 152–89.

important to note here is that Vishanoff argues that the law oriented theory undermines the links between speculative theology and legal hermeneutics. Followers of this theory (such as the Ḥanafī and Muʿtazilī Abū al-Ḥusayn al-Baṣrī (d. 436/1044) and the Ḥanbalī Abū Yaʿlā b. al-Farrāʾ (d. 458/1065)) see hermeneutics as a legal and a linguistic discipline more than a theological and a philosophical one. They are not interested in developing a hermeneutic that is in harmony with any specific theology. Vishanoff points that Abū al-Ḥusayn al-Baṣrī, unlike his teacher ʿAbd al-Jabbār, curtails the impact of his Muʿtazilī doctrines on his hermeneutics. He even subdues his theology to the dictates of his Ḥanafī legal hermeneutics, and not the opposite. The result, writes Vishanoff, is the production of a paradoxical and 'theologically rootless' hermeneutic.[44]

Vishanoff concludes that all three theories of legal hermeneutics co-existed until the turn of the fifth/eleventh century. Afterwards, law oriented hermeneutics dominated Sunnī legal theory and virtually eliminated the more theologized trends. Even speculative theologians, notes Vishanoff, adopted the legal-oriented model and started to keep their theology at a distance from their hermeneutics.[45] My study argues that this attitude is, occasionally, noticeable in other aspects of legal theory, such as *qiyās*. Legal theoreticians, including speculative theologians, sometimes try to limit the legal theory discrepancies caused by theological disagreements. These attempts include distancing some of the most divisive debates in speculative theology from legal theory.

In his doctoral dissertation 'The Early Development of Ḥanafī *Uṣūl al-Fiqh*', Murteza Bedir also makes a distinction between the-

---

[44] Vishanoff, *Formation of Islamic Hermeneutics*, 275. For his full argument see, pp. 190–253.

[45] Vishanoff, *Formation of Islamic Hermeneutics*, 252–3. He notes that the reasons behind the dominance of the law-oriented theory is primarily not conceptual or theoretical but rather what he describes as 'mundane factors', such as the resurgence of traditionalist Sunnī Islam in the fifth/eleventh century, marginalization of speculative theology from the *madrassa*s (i.e. educational institutions), in addition to his argument that the law-oriented theory 'buttressed the social authority of the juristic class'. See Vishanoff, *Formation of Islamic Hermeneutics*, 252.

ologized and untheologized trends in legal theory, though his study mainly focuses on the latter.[46] Bedir accepts the traditional division of legal theory into two major methods, the method of the theologians (*ṭarīqat al-mutakallimīn*) and the method of the jurists (*ṭarīqat al-fuqahāʾ*). Bedir notes that the method of the jurists dominated the Ḥanafī School of law. He argues that followers of this method are characterized by largely isolating their legal theory from their theology. They confine legal theory discussions to legal concerns and avoid theologizing their legal theory.[47] His dissertation focuses on comparing the legal theory of five Māturīdī-Ḥanafī jurists. He argues that all five scholars show little interest in creating a legal theory informed by their Māturīdī theology. Therefore, they often adopt legal theory positions that were previously common among Muʿtazilī-Ḥanafīs or ones entailing the acceptance of Muʿtazilī doctrines. Only briefly, in the sixth/twelfth century, some Ḥanafī jurists try to 'purify' Ḥanafī legal theory from Muʿtazilī elements. Like Zysow, Bedir notes that their efforts are unsuccessful and later Ḥanafī scholars continue adopting the old positions undisturbed by their theological implications.[48] In my study, I argue that keeping some aspects of speculative theology at a distance from legal theory is not only a character of the Ḥanafī School of law and the so-called method of the jurists; a similar attitude can occasionally be noticed among the four Shāfiʿī scholars studied here. All of them are classified as members of the theologians' method in legal theory.

THE COMPARTMENTALISATION OF RELIGIOUS DISCIPLINES

In an interesting article, Robert Gleave examines the attitude of Shīʿī Akhbārī jurists towards Sufism between the eleventh/seventeenth and fourteenth/nineteenth centuries in Safavid

---

[46] Murteza Bedir, 'The Early Development of Ḥanafī Uṣūl al-Fiqh', (PhD. diss. University of Manchester, 1999).

[47] Bedir, 'Early Development', 12–7.

[48] Bedir, 'Early Development', 16.

Iran.[49] Akhbārī legal theory is characterized by a scripturalism that relies primarily on textual evidence as a source for religious knowledge. It often undermines the validity of reason and non-textual sources as means for reaching legal conclusions.[50] On the other hand, Ṣūfism emphasizes the use of speculative and non-textual methods as tools for acquiring knowledge. Gleave shows that despite their common scripturalist legal theory, Akhbārīs are strongly divided on the validity and legitimacy of mystical and philosophical theology. Two trends co-exist within the Akhbārī School: pro-Ṣūfī and anti-Ṣūfī. This diversity of attitudes towards Ṣūfism, argues Gleave, indicates that Akhbārīs do not agree on the theological and philosophical consequences of their common scripturalist legal theory. Some Akhbārīs believe that their legal theory requires adopting a position against Ṣūfism, others hold the opposite. Others probably believe that their legal theory has no impact on their position on mystical knowledge and philosophy altogether. Most importantly, their contradicting positions on mystical philosophy do not ruin the common legal theory foundations of the Akhbārī School. Gleave concludes that the Akhbārī School 'was defined by a set of legal doctrines, and as such could either be conjoined with theological, philosophical and mystical doctrines, or (alternatively) used to denigrate these academic disciplines'.[51] In other words, the common framework that unites Akhbārī jurists is their common legal theory, regardless of theological and philosophical discrepancies. Therefore, theological and philosophical disagreements do not ruin the common legal theory of the Akhbārī School.

The question that begs itself here, is how can jurists with contradicting theological and philosophical views fit comfortably in the

---

[49] Robert Gleave, 'Scriptural Sufism and Scriptural Anti-Sufism: Theology and Mysticism amongst the Shīʿī Akhbāriyya', in *Sufism and Theology*, ed. Ayman Shihadeh (Edinburgh: Edinburgh University Press, 2007): 158–176.

[50] For more information on the Akhbārī School, see *EI*², s.v. 'Akhbāriyya' (W. Madelung); *EI*³, s.v. 'Akhbāriyya and Uṣūliyya' (Robert M. Gleave); Robert Gleave, *Inevitable Doubt: Two Theories of Shīʿī Jurisprudence* (Leiden: Brill, 2000).

[51] Gleave, 'Scriptural Sufism', 172–3.

same legal trend? Why the theological and philosophical disagreements among Akhbārīs do not cause divergences in their legal theory? In the introduction of his article, Gleave writes that '[p]re-modern Islamic literature generally, and classical Shīʿī literature in particular, is characterized by well-defined generic boundaries'. He adds that between the fifth/eleventh and thirteenth/late eighteenth century '[w]orks of jurisprudence, law, theology, and Qurʾānic exegesis displayed remarkable stable structural features'. After the eighth/fourteenth century, the structure of the texts addressing these disciplines is largely stable and the appearance of innovative views becomes, for the most part, rare and incremental. He concludes that this

> structural rigidity of the various genres inevitably encouraged a compartmentalisation of scholarly activity. At times the interrelationship between the intellectual structure of *taṣawwuf*... and the genres of *fiqh* (law), or *kalām* (theology) and *uṣūl al-fiqh* (jurisprudence) within a scholar's works is difficult to detect, since his writings on such topics confirm to generic standards which do not always permit 'interdisciplinarity'.[52]

Interrelationships between the different Muslim religious sciences, argues Gleave, are difficult to detect because of 'compartmentalisation'. Boundaries between disciplines hinder interdisciplinarity and may also obstruct cross-disciplinary influence. This phenomenon, according to Gleave, is not a late development. It is rather a feature of Muslim religious sciences during the classical and post-classical periods. Gleave, here, appears to be arguing that interdisciplinary boundaries created barriers among the different religious disciplines. They undermine interdisciplinarity and hinder scholars from, for instance, deducing legal conclusions from their theological doctrines and deriving theological conclusions from their legal positions. Scholars, to a degree, keep the doctrines and findings of each discipline at some distance from other fields of knowledge. Therefore, it becomes common to see jurists belonging to the same legal trend, despite their very different theological and philosophical orientations.

---

[52] Gleave, 'Scriptural Sufism', 158.

It is difficult to describe pre-modern Muslim scholars as lacking interdisciplinarity. Moreover, Gleave seems to be exaggerating the boundaries between religious disciplines. Pre-modern Muslim scholars are often involved in multiple disciplines. It is common, for example, to find a legal theoretician who was also a theologian, grammarian, Ṣūfī, or and/or a philosopher. Works in one discipline often includes numerous references to other disciplines. Legal theory literature, for instance, usually includes many allusions to theology, law, linguistics and philosophy. This study argues that jurists are aware that theology is relevant to legal theory. They know that their theology should somehow inform their legal theory. Yet, in some occasions, they try to keep legal theory at a distance from the most divisive doctrinal debates of speculative theology. This distance is necessary to prevent theological controversies from ruining the common legal framework of each legal school. Jurists, moreover, feared importing the factionalism common among theologians to the field of law. The distance between theology and legal theory is not due to a lack of interdisciplinarity, but rather the product of a deliberate effort to maintain some degree of conformity within the legal schools and limit the impact of controversial aspects of theology on legal theory.

THE COUNTERINTUITIVE EFFECT

A number of recent studies highlight what appear to be contradictions between the theological doctrines adopted by jurists and the legal theory positions they espouse. Among those is Ahmed El Shamsy's article 'The Wisdom of God's Law'. In this article, the author examines the influence of Muʿtazilī doctrines on Shāfiʿī legal theory especially on ascertaining the *ratio legis* (*ʿilla*) in *qiyās*.[53] He notes that, in the late tenth century (late third and early fourth Hijrī century), a group within the Shāfiʿī School adopted some aspects of Muʿtazilī theology including their moral theory. Among those scholars are Abū Bakr al-Khaffāf (fl. middle of the fourth/tenth century) and al-Qaffāl al-Shāshī (d. 365/976). Both adopt a rational moral theory and consider human benefit (*maṣlaḥa*) as the ultimate

[53] For a definition of *qiyās*, see pp. 94–7.

goal of Sharīʿa.[54] However, El Shamsy adds that fourth/tenth century jurists use reason and the concept of human benefit mainly to justify religious law, defend its existence and argue in support of the practice of *qiyās*. Nevertheless, *maṣlaḥa*, notes El Shamsy, 'played no role in the actual process of legal reasoning [i.e. *qiyās*]' or in law-making in general.[55] For example, *maṣlaḥa* was not used to deduce the *ratio legis* behind deontic qualifications mentioned in revelation, a step necessary for any operation of legal theory. Instead Qaffāl and Khaffāf depend mainly on methods borrowed from dialectics (*jadal*) such as *al-ṭard wa-l-ʿaks* (consistency and convertibility, to borrow El Shamsy's translations), but do not utilize *maṣlaḥa* for this purpose. Therefore, El Shamsy concludes that *maṣlaḥa* in the fourth/tenth century was largely an apologetic tool rather than one of law-making.[56]

El Shamsy juxtaposes Qaffāl's and Khaffāf's use of *maṣlaḥa* in *qiyās* to that of the Ashʿarī theologian and Shāfiʿī jurist Abū Ḥāmid al-Ghazālī (d. 505/1111). He explains that Ghazālī adopts theistic subjectivism; a moral theory that undermines the ability of unaided reason to distinguish between good, evil, harms and benefits. Moreover, Ghazālī, like many Ashʿarīs, denies any connection between the beneficial nature of the law and divine nature. In other words, nothing in God's nature compels Him to make human wellbeing the main goal of His laws. God, rather, voluntarily chooses to impose on humans laws that would enhance their lives. He could do otherwise if He wishes.[57] Nonetheless, unlike the early Shāfiʿīs, Ghazālī does not depend on dialectic methods to uncover the *ratio legis* behind deontic qualifications mentioned in revelation. Instead, he makes extensive use of *maṣlaḥa* for this purpose. The benefit or *maṣlaḥa* the law preserves may also be its *ratio legis*. Therefore, for Ghazālī, identifying the benefits behind a law mentioned in revelation can also lead to uncovering its *ratio legis*.

---

[54] Ahmed El Shamsy, 'The Wisdom of God's Law: Two Theories', in *Islamic Law in Theory*, ed. A. Kevin Reinhart and Robert Gleave (Leiden: Brill, 2014), 24–7.

[55] El Shamsy, 'Wisdom of God's Law', 27.

[56] El Shamsy, 'Wisdom of God's Law', 33.

[57] El Shamsy, 'Wisdom of God's Law', 30–1.

El Shamsy underlines Ghazālī's heavy use of *maṣlaḥa* to deduce *rationes legis*. He then notes that '[w]e thus arrive at the counterintuitive conclusion that the Ashʿarī decoupling of ethics from law coincided with the transformation of benefit considerations from mere theological postulate to a tool of legal reasoning'.[58] El Shamsy uses the word 'counterintuitive' to emphasize the paradox between Ghazālī's Ashʿarī theology and his use of benefit in qiyās . Consequently, for El Shamsy, it would have been more 'intuitive' to find the early Shāfiʿī jurists, who adopt a moral theory similar to that of Muʿtazilīs, allowing *maṣlaḥa* a larger role in *qiyās*. For understandable reasons, El Shamsy expects the adoption of Muʿtazilī theology to allow more use of *maṣlaḥa* to deduce *rationes legis* in legal theory. He also expects the adoption of an Ashʿarī theology to limit the use of *maṣlaḥa* for this purpose. When the jurists he studies do not realize his expectations, he assumes, again for recognizable reasons, that this is a case in which legal theory contradicts the jurists' adopted theology. However, he does not actually examine the possibility that the jurists he studies may not accept his interpretation of the legal theory consequences of their moral theory.

Another modern scholar who underlines some form of a 'tension' between Shāfiʿī legal theory and Ashʿarī theology is Christian Lange. Chapter five of Lange's book *Justice, Punishment, and the Medieval Muslim Imagination*, examines the Shāfiʿī-Ḥanafī debate on the use of *qiyās* in extending the decreed numerical objects (*muqaddarāt*).[59] The latter are specific rules (often numerical) explicitly mentioned in the Qur'ān or Sunna. Among those are, for example, the expiation (*kaffāra*) for breaking an oath, namely to cloth and feed ten poor individuals, free one slave, or fast three days. Can legal theory, for instance, extend the same expiation to cases other than breaking the oath? An important part of the *muqaddarāt* is the

---

[58] El Shamsy, 'Wisdom of God's Law', 33–4. For a similar comment, see Felicitas Opwis, *Maṣlaḥa and the Purpose of the Law: Islamic Discourse on Legal Change from the 4th/10th to the 8th/14th Century* (Leiden: Brill, 2010), 30–2.

[59] Here, I borrow Lange's translation of *muqaddarāt*, see Christian Lange, *Justice, Punishment, and the Medieval Muslim Imagination* (Cambridge: Cambridge University Press, 2008), 184.

divinely ordained punishments (*ḥudūd*).[60] The debate around the applicability of *qiyās* in the *ḥudūd* is particularly intense. Ḥanafīs and members of other Sunnī schools of law, especially Shāfiʿīs, debate whether *qiyās* can extend those punishments to cover cases not mentioned in revelation? For example, the Qurʾān mentions a specific punishment for extramarital heterosexual intercourse. Can *qiyās* be used to extend and apply the same punishment to homosexual intercourse? Shāfiʿī jurists accept the use of *qiyās* to extend the divinely ordained punishments to cases not explicitly mentioned in revelation whereas Ḥanafīs often reject it.[61]

Lange comments on the relationship between this legal theory debate and other theological doctrines. He writes that Ashʿarīs (the theological school of many Shāfiʿīs) adopt a theology that greatly undermines human freewill and largely denies natural causality. The Māturīdī School of theology, which attracts many Ḥanafīs, have a position on natural causality that is not categorically different. However, Māturīdīs adopt a milder form of predestination if compared to Ashʿarīs. Moreover, notes Lange, Māturīdīs and even more the Ashʿarīs undermine the ability of human reason to understand the purpose behind many divine actions and laws. The idea of *qiyās*, on the other hand, is primarily based on some notion of causality and recognizing the 'purpose' behind the law. Given their theological convictions, limiting the applicability of *qiyās* would appear more akin to Māturīdī and, in particular, Ashʿarī doctrines. Lange argues that the Ḥanafī position to disallow *qiyās* in *muqaddarāt* is logical, if not a deliberate choice motivated by their theology. Given that Ashʿarīs share the same Māturīdī rejection of natural causality and adopt a stricter form of predestination, Lange remarks

---

60 Translation of *ḥudūd* as divinely ordained punishments is also borrowed from Lange. The *ḥudūd* (sg. *ḥadd*) are specific punishments mentioned in the Qurʾān for specific transgressions. Those would include, for instance, one hundred lashes for extramarital sex and hand amputation for theft. The application of those *ḥudūd* requires stringent conditions. For example, for a couple to receive the *ḥadd* punishment for extramarital intercourse, four eye witnesses are required to testify in court and present an identical account of the event.

61 For his complete chapter, see Lange, *Justice*, 179–214.

that there is some form of tension between Ashʿarī theology and the Shāfiʿī acceptance of *qiyās* in *muqaddarāt*. Since many Shāfiʿīs are Ashʿarī, therefore 'one would expect the Shāfiʿītes to be more cautious in specifying a cause, or *ratio legis* (*ʿilla*), for the *muqaddarāt*. Surprisingly, however, it is precisely the Shāfiʿīs who embraced analogy [i.e. legal theory] in the *muqaddarāt*'.[62]

El Shamsy and Lange both hold that speculative theology significantly influence the formation of legal theory. Their studies, nonetheless, shed light on what they believe to be tensions between some aspects of legal theory and particular theological positions. Yet, they do not really utilize their findings to explore the nature of the relationship between both disciplines. They do not explain why there might appear to be 'tensions' between a jurist's legal theory and his theology. Again, they perceive the relationship between theology and legal theory as one of cause and effect, where a theological doctrine (cause) consistently leads to the adoption of the same position in legal theory (effect). They assume that there is one logical legal theory outcome for each of the theological doctrines they examine. When a jurist adopts a legal theory position, other than the 'logical' outcome of his theology, this would be a case of contradiction between his legal theory and his theology.

This study tries to explore the relationship between theology and legal theory beyond the cause and effect model. Jurists disagree on the legal theory implications of the same theological doctrine. Adopting Ashʿarī theology and using *maṣlaḥa* to deduce *rationes legis* might appear contradictory to some scholars. For others, there would be no contradiction between both positions. Therefore, this study pays special attention to the arguments each jurist puts forward to support his legal theory choice. Jurists often utilize theological arguments to justify legal theory positions. They use such arguments to show the harmony between their creed and their legal

[62] Lange, *Justice*, 189. One the same page he adds that 'this is in some tension with their adherence to Ashʿarī theology was duly pointed out to them by their opponents, for how could Shāfiʿītes espouse a theology that denied causality while at the same time claim that they would apprehend the causal logics of legal statutes, especially of the *muqaddarāt*'. For the whole discussion, see Lange, *Justice*, 187–9.

theory. Such arguments are often directed to jurists of the same theological school who embrace a different legal theory opinion. Each jurist uses theological arguments to prove that his legal theory choice is the one in harmony with their common theology. Analysing such arguments gives pre-modern authors more agency; it allows us to see how jurists themselves saw the legal repercussions of their doctrines. Furthermore, what may appear to be a contradiction between theology and legal theory might be the result of the jurists' attempts to keep some of the most controversial aspects of theology at some distance from legal theory. Jurists seem aware that distancing theology from legal theory may create some tensions between both disciplines. Therefore, they employ a number of methods trying to harmonize their legal and theological stands. Examining and analysing those methods constitute an important part of the chapter on *qiyās* in this study.

CONCLUSION

In this chapter we have surveyed modern studies on the relationship between speculative theology and legal theory. Makdisi and Sānū picture legal theory, in the classical period, as dominated by theology and theologians. Johansen and Fazlur Rahman take almost the opposite position; they underestimate the interconnections between *ʿilm al-kalām* and *uṣūl al-fiqh*. This study tries to take a more nuanced position on the nature of the relationship between both disciplines. Speculative theology certainly informs the legal theory decisions of individual jurists. However, the impact of theology on legal theory is not consistent on group level. Jurists often debate the legal entailments of the same theological doctrine. Therefore, the adoption of a common theology does not always lead to favouring the same legal theory positions. One should not rush to see contradictions between a jurist's creed and his legal theory, but carefully read his supporting arguments trying to understand how he perceives the legal implications of his theology. Furthermore, this study tries to also examine aspects of the relationship between both disciplines that go beyond the cause and effect narrative. Therefore, it does not only explore the impact of theology on a jurist's legal theory choices but also on the arguments he utilizes to support these choices. In the next chapter we will survey the intellectual context of the fifth/eleventh century, the timeframe of this study. This survey will put the four Shāfiʿī scholars, the focus of the current research, and their texts in their wider context. This should allow us to better understand the historical and intellectual developments that might have influenced a jurist's perception of the relationship between speculative theology and legal theory.

CHAPTER TWO: THE CONTEXT

INTRODUCTION

This chapter will attempt to describe the political and the intellectual context in which our four Shāfiʿī jurists lived and produced their ideas. It is primarily concerned with surveying the forces that might have influenced the four jurists' ideas and writings, particularly their perception of the relationship between speculative theology and legal theory. It appears that the ascendance of 'traditionalism' placed some pressures on speculative theologians to distance (but not separate) their theology from their legal theory. This distance is an attempt to limit the legal theory discrepancies caused by theological disagreements. It should also facilitate the theologians' membership in Sunnī schools of law, help them avoid accusations of deviancy, legitimize their law and allow them better employment opportunities. Creating some distinctions between theology and legal theory is also crucial for maintaining conformity within Sunnī legal schools and facilitate tolerance among them. Despite pressures on speculative theologians, theology flourished in the fifth/eleventh century and enjoyed a strong presence in legal theory literature.

The first section of this chapter is a brief account of some of the primary political developments in fourth/tenth-fifth/eleventh century Iraq and Iran, the period and the geographical locations where the four Shāfiʿī jurists spent most of their lives. The second section is a survey of the major intellectual developments, especially in law and theology that influenced the legal thought of the four scholars. The third includes brief biographical information on each of the four jurists. When possible, I try to underline the developments and events in their lives that might have influenced their legal writings. Yet, this task will always remain incomplete due to the limited amount of biographical information available on most of them. The final section is a conclusion and summary of the findings.

POLITICAL CONTEXT

The ʿAbbāsid Caliphate (132/750–656/1258) once controlled huge territories from Ifrīqiyya (eastern parts of the Maghreb) in the west well into Central Asia in the east. By the fourth/tenth century, the heyday of the Abbasid Caliphate was over. It turned into a highly decentralized and fragmented entity. For the most part, the Abbasid caliph enjoyed only limited political authority, even in his capital Baghdad. Practical political control of the provinces fell into the hands of local rulers and dynasties. Iraq, Iran and the eastern ʿAbbāsid provinces were still nominally part of the Abbasid Caliphate. However, during most of the fourth/tenth-fifth/eleventh centuries, two dynasties dominated these regions, namely the Būyids (or Būwayhids r. 320/932–454/1062) and the Saljūqs (in Iraq and Iran r. 429/1037–590/1194). The Būyids controlled Baghdad from 334/946 until the Saljūqs seized it in 447/1055. It remained in their possession until 547/1152. Afterwards, it was largely controlled by the ʿAbbāsid caliphs,[1] until the Mongol invasion of Baghdad practically ended the ʿAbbāsid Caliphate in 656/1258.[2] Although the Būyids and the Saljūqs were the *de facto* rulers of Baghdad, they did not abolish the ʿAbbāsid Caliphate. They, however, turned the caliph into a titular figure deprived of almost any practical authority, especially outside of his capital. Nonetheless, the caliph retained his prestigious position as the spiritual leader of the Sunnī community.[3]

---

[1] *EI²*, s.v. 'Saldjūḳs' (C. E. Bosworth).

[2] For more details on the disintegration of the ʿAbbāsid Caliphate, see Hugh Kennedy, *The Court of the Caliphs* (London: Weidenfeld and Nicolson, 2004), 261–96.

[3] In brief phases, some caliphs were capable of negotiating more practical power within Baghdad. For more details on the relations between the Būyid princes and the ʿAbbāsid caliphs, see Heribert Busse, 'The Revival of Persian Kingship under the Būyids', in *Islamic Civilization 950–1150* ed. D. S. Richards (London: B. Cassirer, 1973): 47–70; Mafizullah Kabir, *The Buwayhid Dynasty of Baghdad* (Calcutta: Iran Society,

John Donohue and Joel Kraemer note that Būyid reign, from a political and a social perspective, was a very unstable period of time.[4] The Būyid state rarely enjoyed a prosperous economy, excluding probably the reign of ʿAḍud al-Dawla (r. 365/976–372/983).[5] Insecurity was a constant problem; rioting and sectarian violence were common,[6] soldiers in the service of Būyid princes frequently revolted against late payment and debased currency,[7] and local governments could not constantly deter gangs and thugs in urban centres.[8] Trade routes were often left unprotected; travellers and merchants were vulnerable to brigandage and highway

---

1964), 186–200. For the Saljūq period, see Muḥammad ʿAbd al-ʿAẓīm Abū al-Naṣr, *al-Salājiqa: Tārīkhahum al-siyāsī wa-l-ʿaskarī* (Giza, Egypt: ʿEin [sic] for Human and Social Studies, 2001), 120–8; Vanessa Van Renterghem, 'Controlling and Developing Baghdad: Caliphs, Sultans, and the Balance of Power in the Abbasid Capital', in *The Seljuqs: Politics Society and Culture* ed. Christian Lange and Songül Mecit (Edinburgh: Edinburgh University Press, 2011): 117–38. For both the Būyid and Saljūq periods, see Eric Hanne, *Putting the Caliph in his Place* (Madison, NJ : Fairleigh Dickinson University Press, 2007), 55–141. These sources also provide a good survey of the political history of Iraq and Iran during the Būyid and Saljūq periods.

[4] John J. Donohue, *The Buwayhid Dynasty in Iraq 334H./945 to 403H./1012: Shaping Institutions for the Future* (Leiden: Brill, 2003), 351; Joel Kraemer, *Humanism in the Renaissance of Islam: The Cultural Revival during the Būyid Age* (Leiden: Brill, 1986), 21, 23.

[5] Kabir, *Buwayhid Dynasty*, 146–50. Also, see Heribert Busse, *Chalif und Großkönig: Die Buyiden im Iraq* (Wiesbaden: Franz Steiner Verlag, 1969), 608.

[6] For examples of such incidents, see Abū al-Faraj ʿAbd al-Raḥmān b. al-Jawzī (d. 597/1200), *al-Muntaẓam fī tārīkh al-mulūk wa-l-umam*, 18 vols ed. Muḥammad ʿAbd al-Qādir ʿAṭā and others (Beirut: Dār al-Kutub al-ʿIlmiyya, 1412/1992), 15:58–9, 120; ʿIzz al-Dīn Abū al-Ḥasan ʿAlī b. Abī al-Karam al-Maʿrūf bi-Ibn al-Athīr, *al-Kāmil fī-l-tārīkh*, 13 vols ed. Carolus J. Tornberg (Beirut: Dār Ṣādir, 1966), 9: 295, 305, 331, 336, 410, 418–20.

[7] See for example Ibn al-Jawzī, *Muntaẓam*, 14:361–2, 15:256, 273; Ibn al-Athīr, *Kāmil*, 9:100, 136, 393, 446.

[8] See Ibn al-Jawzī, *Muntaẓam*, 14:344, 369, 15:33, 170–1, 197, 239, 245; Ibn al-Athīr, *Kāmil*, 9:432; Donohue, *Buwayhid*, 338–4.

robbery.[9] It is, therefore, natural to see the economy deteriorating and people suffering from inflating prices.[10]

The first decades of the fifth/eleventh century witnessed the advent of the Saljūqs as a new power in the eastern ʿAbbāsid domains of Khurasān and Transoxania. Sweeping westwards capturing new lands in Iran and Iraq, the Saljūqs were taking over Būyid lands, until finally capturing Baghdad in 447/1055, putting an end, practically, to the Būyid dynasty. The first years of Saljūq rule were probably not very different from the final decades of Būyid reign, when their state was suffering the most, and the Saljūqs were still going through the formation phase. However, the Saljūqs reached their peak and their greatest geographical expansion during the reign of Alp Arslān (r. 455/1063–465/1072) and his son Mālik Shāh (r. 465/1072–485/1092).[11] Both sultans, supported by the skills of their talented wazīr Niẓām al-Mulk (d. 485/1092), managed to relatively improve security in most of their dominions. This certainly had positive influence on the economy: trade routes were more secure, tax revenues increased, more resources were allocated to infrastructure, and prices were relatively low throughout Saljūq lands.[12]

The Saljūq defeat of the Būyids and their capture of Baghdād marked the beginning of many intellectual developments. Saljūq victory over Būyids was, *rightly or wrongly*, seen as a Sunnī victory that eventually led to ending the dominance of Shīʿī dynasties in the Middle East. Furthermore, the new rulers of Baghdād were Ḥanafīs. They attempted to turn their school of law into the official legal school of their new state. They particularly favoured Ḥanafī

---

[9] *EI²*, s.v. 'Buwayhids or Būyids' (C. Cahen); Busse, *Chalif und Großkönig*, 608 (also see p. 393–8).

[10] Busse, *Chalif und Großkönig*, 377–92.

[11] C. Edmund Bosworth, 'The Political and Dynastic History of the Iranian World (A.D. 1000–1217)', in *The Cambridge History of Iran*, ed. John Andrew Boyle, vol 5, *The Saljuq and Mongol Periods* (Cambridge: Cambridge University Press, 1968), 55, 66.

[12] Bosworth, 'Political and Dynastic History', 55–6, 61, 85–7. For a brief survey of Saljūq history, see *EI²*, s.v. 'Sald̲j̲ūḳids' (Bosworth and others).

scholars from eastern Turkish origin who often followed Māturīdī theology and were part of the Transoxanian Ḥanafī sub-school (*Ḥanafiyyat Samarqand*). Those scholars received the largest share of religious and official appointments in the newly conquered Saljūq lands. Their policy encouraged the migration of eastern Ḥanafī jurists westwards towards western Iran, Iraq and Syria. Moreover, it also led to the eventual dominance of the Transoxanian Ḥanafī sub-school and Māturīdī theology within the Ḥanafī School of law.[13]

Favouring one particular legal school, especially in official appointments, might lead to the alienation of others. In the case of the Saljūqs, the Shāfiʿī School of law paid the greatest price for the advancement of Ḥanafīs. Especially that, as Wilferd Madelung notes, Saljūqs had a distinct hostility towards Shafiʿīs and Ashʿarīs.[14] This was particularly true during the reign of Ṭughril Beg (r. 431/1040–455/1063) who took drastic measures against Ashʿarīs. He ordered the cursing of Abū al-Ḥasan al-Ashʿarī from pulpits, arrested and exiled Ashʿarī scholars from Khurasān, and replaced Shāfiʿī judges with Ḥanafī ones. Ashʿarī-Shāfiʿī scholars remained relatively under pressure until the late sixth/twelfth century. However, the most extreme measures of persecution ended with the death of Ṭughril Beg.[15]

Alp Arslān (r. 455/1063–465–72), Ṭughril Beg's successor, appointed a staunchly Ashʿarī-Shāfiʿī wazīr, namely the famous Niẓām al-Mulk (d. 485/1092). He started to gradually adopt pro-

---

[13] For more details on the development of the Ḥanafī legal school during Saljūq rule, see Wilferd Madelung, 'The Spread of Māturīdism and the Turks', in *Actos do IV Congresso de Estudos Árabes e Islâmicos, Coimbra-Lisboa 1968* (Ledien: Brill, 1971), 140–5; Wilferd Madelung, *Religious Trends in Early Islamic Iran* (Albany, N.Y.,; The Persian Heritage Foundation, 1988), 32, 37–8; *EI²*, s.v. 'Saldjūḳs' (C. E. Bosworth and others).

[14] Madelung, 'Spread of Māturīdism', 126.

[15] For more details on Saljūq policies towards Shāfiʿī and Ashʿarī scholars, see Richard W. Bulliet, 'The Political-Religious History of Nishapur in the Eleventh Century' in *Islamic Civilization* 950–1150, ed. D. S. Richards (Oxford: Cassirer, 1973), 81–7; Madelung, *Religious Trends*, 32–8; Madelung, 'Spread of Māturīdism', 126–37.

Shāfiʿī and pro-Ashʿarī policies while still holding a balanced relationship with Ḥanafīs.[16] Nonetheless, he could not become openly pro-Shāfiʿī until the death of Alp Arslān. The latter favoured Ḥanafī jurists and had some reservations on Shāfiʿīs,[17] probably because of their earlier association with Būyids. Nonetheless, the presence of Niẓām al-Mulk eased some of the pressures on Shāfiʿīs allowing some of the exiled scholars, including Juwaynī, to return to Iran and practice teaching in their home towns.[18]

Before moving to the next section, one must point to a phenomenon that was widespread during Būyid and Saljūq reigns. Despite the policy of religious tolerance adopted by the Būyids, their reign was plagued with sectarian violence and tensions among the followers of legal and theological schools.[19] The appearance of the Saljūqs did not improve the situation. On the contrary, Bulliet notes that their pro-Ḥanafī and anti Ashʿarī-Shāfiʿī policies disrupted the delicate balance between both groups. He adds that the fifth/eleventh century, the timeframe of this study, witnessed the height of the Shāfiʿī-Ḥanafī rivalry.[20] Madelung writes that factionalism, during Saljūq reign, pervaded all aspects of life as never before and that their pro-Ḥanafī and anti Shāfiʿī-Ashʿarī measures caused unprecedented sectarian violence and rioting.[21] The violence was sometimes severe that it ruined many major Iranian cities well before the arrival of the Mongols, as Madelung remarks.[22] It is, therefore, important to realize that our four jurists lived in an environment simmering with sectarian tensions.

---

[16] Richard W. Bulliet. *The Patricians of Nishapur: A Study in Medieval Islamic Social History* (Cambridge, M.A.: Harvard University Press, 1972), 45.

[17] Madelung, 'Spread of Māturīdism', 130–1.

[18] Makdisi, 'Sunnī Revival', 157; Madelung, *Religious Trends*, 33.

[19] Donohue, *Buwayhid Dynasty*, 338; Kraemer, *Humanism*, 22–3, 40–3; Mafizullah, *Buwayhid Dynasty*, 201–13.

[20] Bulliet, *Patricians of Nishapur*, 33.

[21] Madelung, *Religious Trends*, 32, 35; Madelung, 'Spread of Māturīdism', 138–9; *EI*^{2}, s.v. 'Saldjūk' (C. Bosworth and others).

[22] Madelung, *Religious Trends*, 37.

INTELLECTUAL CONTEXT

Since the early decades of Muslim history there existed two major competing intellectual trends. The first maximized the use of allegorical and rational interpretations of the Qurʾān and Sunna to reach legal and theological conclusions. The second was a trend that did not refuse but minimized the use of such interpretations and adopted methods that maximized a scholar's dependence on religious texts for deducing and supporting legal and theological findings. In the second century, the rivalry between both trends can be noticed in the contention between the rationalistic jurists (*ahl al-raʾy*)[23] and the speculative theologians (*mutakallimūn*), on one hand, and the traditionalist scholars (*ahl al-ḥadīth*), on the other. The latter preferred laws and dogmas based on literalist readings of the Qurʾān and Prophetic Sunna. They therefore avoided discussing theological, metaphysical, and philosophical questions that were not raised in these sources, whereas speculative theologians delved deep into such issues and allowed reason a greater role in shaping their creed. Rationalistic jurists, likewise, assumed methods that awarded reason a larger role in reaching legal decisions when compared to their traditionalist counterparts.[24]

Traditionalism and Rationalism: Competition and Rivalry

The rivalry between both trends peaked during the fifteen years (218/833–233/848) of the famous inquisition (*miḥna*) initiated by the ʿAbbāsid Caliph al-Maʾmūn (r. 198/813–218/833). During those years, Maʾmūn and two of his successors attempted to force scholars to adopt the doctrine of the created Qurʾān (*khalq al-Qurʾān*), a doctrine associated with Muʿtazilī speculative theology.

---

[23] Translation borrowed from Christopher Melchert, 'Traditionist-Jurisprudents and the Framing of Islamic law', *Islamic Law and Society* 8 (2001): 383–406.

[24] The difference between *ahl al-raʾy* and *ahl al-ḥadīth* is certainly far more complicated. A proper treatment of this difference is beyond the scope of the current study. For a good and brief explanation of this difference, see Muḥammad Aḥmad Sirāj, *Madkhal li-dirāsat tārīkh al-fiqh al-Islāmī* (Cairo: Saʿd Samak lil-Naskh wal-Ṭibāʿa, 1995), 100–4.

Those who refused to publicly adopt this doctrine and renounce the belief in the eternal nature of the Qurʾān (*qidam al-Qurʾān*, a doctrine associated with traditionalist thought) where removed from public positions, prisoned and sometimes tortured. Traditionalist forces showed great opposition. The leader and symbol of their resistance was the eponym of the Ḥanbalī School of law Aḥmad b. Ḥanbal (d. 241/855). Despite facing prison, torture and losing some of his comrades, he uncompromisingly refused to recognize the Muʿtazilī doctrine of the created Qurʾān. Pressures on traditionalist scholars remained until the ʿAbbāsid Caliph al-Mutawakkil (r. 232/847–247/861) decided to end the inquisition and relax (at least some of) the pressures placed on the traditionalists.[25]

Since the inquisition failed to impose the doctrine of the created Qurʾān and eradicate opposing beliefs, modern historians often note that traditionalist forces emerged victorious from the inquisition.[26] Makdisi notes that the way the inquisition ended decided, for centuries to come, the relationship between rationalists and traditionalists. Since the end of the inquisition, traditionalist forces gained ascendency over rationalist ones.[27] The events of the inquisition, moreover, pictured the ʿAbbāsid Caliphate and its rationalist allies as oppressive whereas traditionalists emerged as heroic challengers of repressive rulers. Such an image undermined the popularity of the rationalists and allowed traditionalists to gain popular support, especially that the theology they offered was simpler than

---

[25] Mutawakkil is usually considered the Caliph who ended the *miḥna.* However, Christopher Melchert argues that ending the *miḥna* was a longer and gradual process; anti-traditionalist policies were abandoned around five decades after Mutawakkil's death. For Melchert's argument see his 'Religious Policies of the Caliphs from al-Mutawakkil to al-Muqtadir A H 232–295/A D 847–908', *Islamic Law and Society* (1996): 316–42. For more information on the *miḥna*, see *EI*², s.v. 'Miḥna' (M. Hinds).

[26] See for instance, George Makdisi, *The Rise of Colleges: Institutions of Learning in Islam and the West* (Edinburgh: Edinburgh University Press, 1981), 282; Melchert, *Formation*, 1; Hallaq, *Sharīʿa*, 57.

[27] George Makdisi, 'Significance of Sunni Schools of Law in Islamic Religious History', *International Journal of Middle Eastern Studies* 10 (1979), 6.

the complicated speculative theology of the Muʿtazilīs (and later the Ashʿarīs). Moreover, since the eponym of the Ḥanbalī School was the leader of traditionalist resistance; Ḥanbalī scholars continued after him to lead traditionalist anti-rationalist efforts.

As noted above, the debate between traditionalist and speculative thought revolved around the extent to which it is possible to use rational methods to reach legal and theological conclusions. This is in addition to the aptness of discussing theological, philosophical and metaphysical topics not explicitly raised in the Scriptures. One must point out that, as repeatedly mentioned by Makdisi, the debate between traditionalist and speculative thought was not a debate between Muʿtazilīs and Ashʿarīs. It was rather a debate between traditionalist thought, on one hand, and rational speculative thought of all sorts, including Muʿtazilīs, Ashʿarīs and Māturīdīs, on the other.[28] It was a dialogue between a group of scholars who accept and another who reject the methods associated with speculative theology(ies). The traditionalist-rationalist debate, furthermore, was not mainly concerned with legal conclusions. Daphna Ephrat correctly writes that it was the 'theological-doctrinal perspectives, rather than legal interpretation, that constituted the source of animosity between the religiously defined factions'.[29] What confirms this understanding is that we often find more jurists ready to tolerate legal disagreements than theologians ready to tolerate theological disparities. Disagreements among legal schools are more tolerated than theological discrepancies amongst different theological trends.

Religious Educational Institutions and Schools of Law

Traditionalist ascendancy can be noticed from the end of the *miḥna* and even earlier. Makdisi, rightly or wrongly, argues that the fifth/eleventh century witnessed a traditionalist revival in which traditionalism overwhelmed rationalist and speculative trends of all

---

[28] Makdisi, *The Rise of Humanism*, 42; Makdisi, 'Ashʿarī and the Ashʿarites I', 47–8; Makdisi, 'Significance of Sunnī Schools', 5.

[29] Daphna Ephrat, *A Learned Society in a Period of Transition: The Sunni 'Ulama' of Eleventh-Century Baghdad* (Albany, New York: State University of New York Press, 2000), 92.

shades.[30] He explains that among the main features representative of this ascendance is the traditionalist dominance of religious educational institutions.[31] Religious education took place mainly in mosques and private homes. During the fifth/eleventh century there was a surge in the number of *madrasa*s. The latter are colleges of law established by politicians and wealthy patrons, each dedicated to the instruction of law according to the teachings of one of the four Sunnī legal schools.[32] Teaching at a mosque or a *madrasa* was usually a paid position, unlike teaching in one's private home. Teaching in a *madrasa* was also a source of social prestige. Unfortunately, we do not have enough information about the educational institutions of Iraq and Iran as a whole (where the four jurists spent most of their lives); most of the information available about the educational institutions of the fifth/eleventh century concerns Baghdad.

Nonetheless, it is generally accepted, among modern historians, that in mosques and *madrasa*s the teaching of speculative theology, philosophy and mysticism (i.e. the rational sciences) was, to

---

[30] For Makdisi's full argument, see his 'Sunnī Revival', 155–68. He even chooses to name the fifth/eleventh century as the 'traditionalist century', see his, *Ibn ʿAqīl*, 257. However, I prefer Adam Mez's earlier description of the fourth/tenth century as one that witnessed a renaissance of Islam. In the fourth/tenth-fifth/eleventh century, various theological and legal schools flourished and not only the traditionalist. See Adam Mez, *The Renaissance of Islam*, trans. Khuda Bakhsh and D. S. Margoliouth (Patna: The Jubilee Printing and Publishing House, 1937).

[31] Makdisi describes educational institutions as ones of traditionalist learning and notes that it was created to, among other reasons, resist rational and speculative theology, see his *Rise of Humanism*, 2–3. He even claims that the emergence of the *madrasa* system can be in itself a sign of traditionalist victory over rationalism, see his *Rise of Colleges*, 282. Along the same lines, Éric Chaumont argues that *salafī* (i.e. traditionalist) thought was dominant in Baghdad and its educational institutions see his 'Encore au sujet de l'Ash'arisme d'Abû Isḥâq Ash-Shîrâzî', *Studia Islamica* 74 (1991), 167–8.

[32] For a brief survey of the emergence of *madrasa*s, see Makdisi, *Rise of Colleges*, 27–32.

some extent, restricted; teaching mainly focused on law and its auxiliary disciplines such as Prophetic Sunna (*ḥadīth*) and Qurʾānic interpretation (*tafsīr*). The teaching of the rational sciences usually took place in private homes.[33] This posed a significant problem for speculative theologians. As mentioned before, colleges of law provided jurists with a stable income and social prestige. Limiting the teaching of speculative theology in *madrasa*s might have prevented theologians from making use of the opportunities a teaching position would provide. Nonetheless, we know that theologians were often allowed to teach law and legal theory in *madrasa*s. However, it appears that they found it difficult to teach speculative theology or include explicit theological discussions in their legal lectures. Those who discussed speculative theology or openly criticised traditionalist doctrines risked losing their jobs and were sometimes harassed by their traditionalist colleagues and their followers.[34] Traditionalist presence in educational institutions was probably strongest in Baghdad, whereas in Iran the traditionalist presence appears to have been relatively weaker.

---

[33] Donohue, *Buwayhid Dynasty*, 334; Bulliet, *Patricians of Nishapur*, 37; Kraemer, *Humanism*, 56; Makdisi, *Rise of Colleges*, 283–5; Makdisi, 'Sunnī Revival', 158–61; Makdisi, *Rise of Humanism*, 2–3. However, Daphna Ephrat doubts that there was a systematic exclusion of the rational sciences from *madrasa*s. She writes that although 'the *madrasa* was founded for the teaching of the traditional religious and legal sciences (to the exclusion of the so-called ancient rational sciences), what a professor taught was not closely regulated; he would teach what he knew. Nor are there any examples of a trustee (*mutawalli* or *naẓir*, i.e. the administrator of the *waqf* on which the *madrasa* was founded) complaining about the study content, or reprimanding or dismissing a teacher because he taught the 'wrong books' or in the 'wrong way'. Concerned with public order, political rulers tried to influence the curricula of the *madrasa* only when the preaching of Ashʿari theology through the popular or academic sermon (*waʿẓ*) led to strong objections of the Hanbalis, who headed the movement of the 'people of hadith', see her, *A Learned Society*, 126–7.

[34] For examples of such incidents, see for instance Ibn al-Jawzī, *Muntaẓam*, 16:105–6, 181–2, 241.

One should not conclude that speculative theology witnessed a decline in the fourth/tenth-fifth/eleventh century. On the contrary, during both centuries Muʿtazilī, Ashʿarī and Māturīdī theology flourished. Both centuries also witnessed the emergence of some of the most prominent speculative theologians in Islam. Furthermore, as just mentioned, speculative theologians were not banned from teaching in educational institutions altogether. There are numerous examples of theologians who taught and headed *madrasa*s, including two of the scholars studied here, namely Juwaynī and Shīrāzī. However, in *madrasa*s, theologians primarily taught law and other legal disciplines. Their lectures on speculative theology had to be mostly confined to their private homes. Christopher Melchert mentions that theologians were pressured not to 'make parade of their theology but rather teach it only in private'.[35] Theologians, therefore, could access educational institutions primarily in their capacity as jurists but not so much as theologians.

However, for a jurist to teach law or legal theory, he is expected to be a member in a particular legal school and show that he has received education according to its teachings. This was particularly true since the *madrasa*s and the teaching circles (sg. *ḥalqa*) in mosques were divided along legal school lines. There were *madrasa*s and teaching circles dedicated to each of the four Sunnī schools of law. Therefore, a jurist can teach law or legal theory only after showing expertise in the legal tradition of one particular school. Legal education and membership in a school of law was also important for securing official jobs. Political authorities often hired jurists as judges, notaries and supervisors of religious endowments (sg. *waqf*). These positions required legal expertise and association with a school of law. Theologians rarely occupied public posts in their capacity as theologians or as a result of their theological education and knowledge. Theologians who were also jurists received public appointments thanks to their legal education and expertise.

---

[35] Melchert, *Formation*, 1, 200. Additionally, Kraemer notes that being a Muʿtazilī 'did not affect the status of the jurists in the eyes of the populace unless they overtly taught offensive Muʿtazilī doctrines'. See Kraemer, *Humanism*, 74–5.

Moreover, Bulliet, rightly, points out that legal schools were 'formally constituted and recognized by the state ... [whereas theological schools] exist as intellectual currents without concrete form of official recognition'.[36] Makdisi argues that speculative theologians joined Sunnī schools of law in an attempt to gain legitimacy and, to use his own term, as a bid for 'orthodoxy'.[37] More recently, Melchert writes that speculative theologians and mystics often joined legal schools to avoid accusations of deviancy and persecution. Among the reasons he gives for why some Muʿtazilī scholars joined the Shāfiʿī School of law was that 'rationalists began to press in under pressure of persecution. Membership in the [Shāfiʿī] School had been useful as a badge of orthodoxy, to fend off persecution'.[38] It seems, then, that membership in a legal school was a scholar's gateway for acceptance and legitimacy within the intellectual community. It was also important for determining the identity of any scholar among his peers. This identity would, in turn, enhance his employability, social and intellectual standing.

It was, therefore, crucial for any speculative theologian, or in fact any Muslim scholar, to be recognized as a member within a school of law. After all, this identification was a natural part of his education. It is important to note that the concept of a legal school required some form of conformity to shared legal principles that distinguished and united each school. Therefore, to be identified as a member in a particular legal school, a scholar was expected to conform, at least, to some of the principal legal theory positions that characterized the school of his choice. Excluding the Ḥanbalī School, all other Sunnī schools of law included jurists from various theological backgrounds. If theological differences were allowed to cause major legal discrepancies, this might undermine the common legal doctrines that united and distinguished each school of law. Therefore, to preserve conformity within a legal school, jurists (both speculative theologians and traditionalists) had an invested

---

[36] Bulliet, *Patricians of Nishapur*, 34.

[37] George Makdisi, 'Juridical Theology', 26, 43; Makdisi, *Rise of Humanism*, 8, 39–4; Makdisi, 'Ashʿarī and the Ashʿarites I', 45; Makdisi, *Rise of Colleges*, 281, 284.

[38] Melchert, *Formation*, 85.

interest not to allow their significant theological disagreements to cause equally significant legal discrepancies that may ruin the common foundations of their common legal school. Therefore, a jurist's legal theory was not only informed by his theology; it was also informed and influenced by the accepted legal norms within his school.[39]

Traditionalization of Legal Theory

The role of the Qur'ān and the Prophetic Sunna in the legislation process during the first fifteen decades of Muslim history was the topic of huge debates that cannot be covered here. What scholars seem to have agreed upon is that by the end of the second/eighth century, if not slightly earlier, Muslim jurists started to base their laws more closely and more structurally on the Qur'ān and on traditions attributed to the Prophet.[40] The use of rational methods to

---

[39] Daphna Ephrat argues that since the fifth/eleventh century there was a tendency to conformity and uniformity and that the establishment of the *madrasa*s was one step towards this direction. She admits that disagreement and variety still existed however the 'range of knowledge which would have been accepted in earlier centuries was probably narrowed'. She argues that this tendency started in the fifth/eleventh century and became more obvious in the sixth/twelfth. See Ephrat, *A Learned Society*, 2–6.

[40] The debate mainly concerns the period before the end of the second/eighth century. Following the studies of I. Goldziher and J. Schacht, the dominant position among western scholarship of Islam assumes that neither the Qur'ān nor the Prophetic Sunna play a major role in the formation of Islamic law in the first fifteen decades of Muslim history. Islamic law, for Schacht, Goldziher and many others, is mainly derived from pre-Islamic and early Islamic government practices in addition to the jurists' personal opinions. Starting from the first half of the second/eighth century Prophetic traditions were fabricated and projected backwards to justify the laws that have been already formed. Therefore, most, if not all, extant Prophetic traditions are nothing but later fabrications created to justify existing laws. See Ignaz Goldziher, *Muslim Studies*, 2 vols ed. M. Stern trans. C. R. Barber and M. Stern (Albany: State University of New York, 1971), 2:17–254; Joseph Schacht, *The Origins of Muhammadan Juris-*

deduce (or create) new laws were *never* abandoned, but were regulated and structured to make the deduced laws (or at sometimes make them appear to be) in harmony with the Qur'ān and Sunna. Western academics usually call the process that led to this development 'traditionalization'. This process led to the dominance of the legal theory methods that were mainly associated with *ahl al-ḥadīth* or the traditionalists.

Wael Hallaq has a slightly different position. He explains that this 'traditionalization' process was not a one-way process in which rationalists presented concessions to traditionalists. The latter also had to meet rationalists in a middle point. Hallaq acknowledges that traditionalism emerged victorious from the *miḥna*; its legal theory also became dominant. Yet, most religious and intellectual

---

prudence, 3rd ed. (1950; repr., Oxford: Clarendon Press, 1967). Increasingly more western academics challenge this theory not by denying it completely but by noting that Islamic law started to be based on Prophetic Sunna from a slightly earlier date. Some also consider Schacht's and Goldziher's conclusions that the whole body of Prophetic traditions as mere fabrications to be an exaggeration. See for instance G.H.A. Juynboll, *Muslim Tradition: Studies in Chronology, Provenance, and Authority of Early ḥadīth* (Cambridge: Cambridge University Press, 1983); Harald Motzki, *The Origins of Islamic Jurisprudence: Meccan Fiqh before the Classical Schools*, trans. Marion H. Katz (Leiden: Brill, 2002). Modern Muslim religious scholars certainly have serious reservations on Schacht's and Goldziher's conclusions. For most of them, the Qur'ān and the Prophetic Sunna were from the very beginning seen as normative sources of law. They admit that there was considerable amount of traditions falsely attributed to the Prophet. However, most Muslims scholars agree that the six 'canonical' *ḥadith* collections can serve as, more or less, a reliable source of Prophetic traditions. The position I favor here is one between Motzki's and Juynboll's and the position common among most Muslim religious scholars. The Qur'ān and the Sunna were considered normative sources of legislations far before the middle of the second/eighth century. However, the authenticity of many of the available 'Prophetic' traditions remains questionable regardless of where they have been recorded. Yet, Goldziher's and Schacht's assumptions that extant traditions attributed to the Prophet are nothing but later fabrications seems to be an unwarranted exaggeration.

elites were not willing to adopt an extreme form of traditionalism or rationalism; the latter was seen as too libertarian, the former as rigid and austere. Following the *miḥna*, argues Hallaq, jurists preferred to combine elements of rationalism and traditionalism. After the third/ninth century, rarely was any jurist characterized as belonging exclusively to one trend. Rationalist scholars became more willing to ground their law on Prophetic traditions while traditionalists started to gradually accept *qiyās* and sometimes even legal preference (*istiḥsān*). Hallaq prefers to call this process of traditionalization the 'great rationalist-traditionalist synthesis', in which a third middle position between both trends was created. Hallaq holds that this middle position was reached in the fourth/tenth century. Legal theory, notes Hallaq, was created and defined by this synthesis. It became the discipline that managed to combine rational and traditionalist methods to reach and support legal conclusions. However, despite this synthesis, traditionalist methods had relatively the upper hand.[41]

This new middle position required rationalist jurists to traditionalize some aspects of their legal theory. Christopher Melchert traces this traditionalization process within the Ḥanafī School of law. He notes that Ḥanafīs started this process during the third/ninth century. Their traditionalization process includes basing their legal opinions on Prophetic traditions, modifying their legal theory to agree with traditionalist legal theory, and dissociating themselves from 'dubious' theological doctrines.[42] Those 'dubious'

---

[41] For Wael Hallaq's complete argument, see his *The Origins and Evolution of Islamic Law* (Cambridge: Cambridge University Press, 2005), 122–8; *Sharīʿa*, 55–69.

[42] Melchert, *Formation*, 48. The whole third chapter of Melchert's book is an explanation of the traditionalization of the Ḥanafī legal school, see p. 48–67. He accepts Schacht's conclusion that Muslim jurists, in the first fifteen decades of Muslim history, did not see the Qur'ān or the Prophetic Sunna as sources of law. Traditionalization, for Melchert, is a process that turned the Qur'ān and the Prophetic Sunna into law-making tools. My reference to Melchert's argument here does not assume accepting his and Schacht's conclusion. As mentioned above, my position assumes that the Qur'ān and the Prophetic Sunna were already seen by ju-

doctrines include the 'creation of the Qur'ān' and *irjā'*.[43] Both are doctrines associated with speculative theology. The Ḥanafī traditionalization process is an attempt to make its law and legal theory more acceptable to traditionalist eyes, gain legitimacy and avoid accusations of deviancy from their traditionalist counterparts.

Melchert adds that Ḥanafīs, by the late third/ninth century,

> did not exactly repudiate such doctrines as the created Qur'an and *irjā'*, but rather pushed them to the side, divorcing their theological interests and their jurisprudential.[44]

---

rists as normative texts well before the middle of the second/eighth century. However, during the first fifteen decades of Muslim history the use of reason, common sense, social customs and other non-textual methods to produce laws was less regulated when compared to the use of the same methods in later centuries. For me, the process of 'traditionalization' did not actually turn the Qur'ān and the Sunna into normative sources. It was rather a process that produced theoretical regulations for the use of extra-textual and rational methods to produce laws. It is a process that created rules to make sure that rational methods will produce laws that are in harmony with revelation or at least appear to be so. A good example is *qiyās*. Instead of using the old concept of legal preference (*istiḥsān*) to create new laws, jurists became required to create a link between their reasoning and Scriptures. This link, in the case of *qiyās*, is established by showing that the result of this rational effort is in fact inspired by the *ratio legis* mentioned in the Qur'ān or a particular Prophetic tradition (for brief remarks on the development of *qiyās* into a tool based on Scriptures, see Bernard Weiss, *The Spirit of Islamic Law* (1998; repr., Athens, G.A.: University of Georgia Press, 2006), 68–70. The rules of *ijtihād* mentioned in legal theory literature are mainly efforts in this direction (for examples of these rules, see for instance Muḥammad Maʿrūf al-Dawālībī, *al-Madkhal ilā ʿilm uṣūl al-fiqh*, 5th ed. (Beirut: Dār al-ʿIlm li-l-Malāyīn, 1385/1965), 380–91). For me, 'traditionalization' does not entail rejecting reason. It rather entails creating a theoretical structure that would legitimize and 'Islamicize' the result of a jurist's rational effort. The legal theory that became dominant since the third/ninth century is traditionalist in the sense that it does not accept any legal effort unless they are based, somehow, on revelation.

43 Melchert, *Formation*, 54.

44 Melchert, *Formation*, 59.

Elsewhere Melchert mentions that it 'was the essence of the *madhhab* system that law and theology were pursued separately'.[45] It appears then that distancing speculative theology from legal theory was a step in the Ḥanafī process of traditionalization. One might even argue that creating this distance was necessary in other schools of law and not only that of the Ḥanafī. The dominance of traditionalism pressured speculative theologians, from different legal backgrounds, to base their law on the now widely accepted traditionalist foundations. To gain acceptance and legitimacy, speculative theologians had to traditionalize their law by basing their legal doctrines more closely on textual evidence and adopt traditionalist legal theory. However, theologians appear to have been unwilling to undermine the rational character of their theology. Although they adopted traditionalist methods in legal theory, their theology remained speculative. Keeping their speculative theology at some distance from legal theory was an essential step, allowing speculative theologians to meet traditionalists in a middle position without traditionalizing their speculative theology. It allowed them to borrow the traditionalists' methods in reaching and supporting legal conclusions without undermining the rationalist character of their dogma. This distance is also necessary to avoid associating their legal doctrines with their theology; a theology that was considered 'dubious' by their traditionalist counterparts.

Traditionalists, as Melchert shows, were also keen to take some steps towards rationalists and their legal theory. He explains that traditionalists adopted methods of education common among rationalists, namely receiving instruction in law from only one teacher. Moreover, traditionalists relied less on traditions attributed to the Companions (*ṣaḥāba*) and the Successors (*tābiʿūn*) to deduce laws and rather based their law primarily on traditions attributed to the Prophet.[46] Melchert notes that traditionalists felt a need to close ranks with what he calls the semi-rationalist theologians (i.e. those who use the methods of speculative theology to defend traditional-

---

[45] Melchert, *Formation*, 129. In fact, this is also one of Murteza Bedir's major conclusions. He argues that the Ḥanafī School of law tends to separate theology from legal theory, see his 'Early Development'.

[46] Melchert, *Formation*, 199, 201.

ist doctrines, mainly Ashʿarīs and Māturīdīs). Melchert argues that traditionalists took this step in an attempt to resist the spread of Shīʿī Islam and the more radical trends among rational jurists and theologians.[47] Both groups, speculative theologians and traditionalists, therefore, seem to have had an interest in finding common grounds at least in law and legal theory.

Standardization of Legal Theory

Both traditionalist jurists and speculative theologians were making an effort to reach a compromise in law and legal theory. It is interesting to note that schools of law, such as the Ẓāhrīs, who refused to adopt some rationalist methods gradually disappeared. Speculative theologians, on the other hand, needed to traditionalize their legal theory to be accepted as members within Sunnī schools of law and legitimize the laws *(fiqh)* deduced via their legal theory. A good example of this traditionalization process is the transformation of the Muʿtazilī criteria for evaluating the probative value of Prophetic traditions.

Early Muʿtazilīs tend to adopt very strict criteria for identifying the Prophetic traditions valid for use in law and speculative theology. Traditionalist scholars utilize more relaxed criteria which allowed them to accept more traditions as valid to produce legal conclusions. George Hourani and Joseph Schacht note that the dominance of the traditionalists' evaluation criteria pressured Muʿtazilīs to relax their own criteria.[48] In a previous study, I have shown that the Muʿtazilī Abū al-Qāsim al-Balkhī (d. 319/931) adopted evaluation criteria that were less strict than earlier Muʿtazilīs and were almost identical to the criteria of the traditionalists. This is also true about ʿAbd al-Jabbār al-Hamadhānī and his student Abū al-Ḥusayn al-Baṣrī. In legal matters, they adopt almost the identical criteria common among traditionalist jurists. This development allows Muʿtazilīs to accept Prophetic traditions which would have been disallowed if the strict criteria of earlier Muʿtazilīs

---

[47] Melchert, *Formation*, 201; Melchert, 'Traditionist-Jurisprudents', 404.

[48] Hourani, *Islamic Rationalism*, 259.

have been applied.[49] The more relaxed authentication methods of later Muʿtazilīs allow them to share common legal theories with Sunnīs, adopt similar legal positions, and thus comfortably fit within a Sunnī school of law.

ʿAbd al-Jabbār and Abū al-Ḥusayn are among the few Muʿtazilī jurists whose legal theory literature has been (albeit partially) discovered. The similarity between their legal thought and that of other Sunnīs is not limited to their use of Prophetic traditions in law. This study will show that their use of *qiyās* in law is similar to that of any other contemporary Sunnī jurist,[50] unlike in theology where disagreements remain to be significant. This is also certainly true for the numerous Ashʿarī theologians who joined the Shāfiʿī or the Mālikī schools of law. The legal theory of speculative theologians is very close to that of traditionalist jurists. It is certainly not identical; though their legal differences are not as significant as their theological disagreements.

It is very important to note that this similarity remained limited to the field of law and legal theory. Speculative theologians managed to 'traditionalize' their legal theories without compromising their commitment to a rational and a speculative theology. Despite relaxing the authentication criteria of Prophetic traditions in law, speculative theologians continue to adopt strict criteria for identifying the traditions valid for use in theology. Theologians remain committed to rationalist and speculative methods in theology unlike the traditionalists who insist on keeping their dogma closely reliant on Scriptures. Despite the speculative theologians' and the traditionalists' attempts to create common grounds in legal

---

[49] Mohamed Ahmed Abdelrahman, 'The Muʿtazilī Criteria for Evaluating Prophetic Traditions with Special Reference to Uṣūl al-Fiqh', (M.A. diss., The American University in Cairo, 2008).

[50] Furthermore, Marie Bernand notes that Abū al-Ḥusayn and ʿAbd al-Jabbār embraced the Sunnī concept of consensus (*ijmāʿ*), see her *L'accord unanime de la communauté comme fondement des statuts légaux de l'Islam* (Paris: J. Vrin, 1970), 128. Robert Brunschvig writes that ʿAbd al-Jabbār and Abū al-Ḥusayn drew 'very near' to Sunnī Islam, see his 'Logic and Law in Classical Islam', in *Logic in Classical Islamic Culture*, ed. G. E. von Grunebaum (Wiesbaden: Otto Harrassowitz, 1970), 17.

theory and law, in theology they remain poles apart. This 'traditionalization' or 'synthesis', to use Hallaq's terms, does not cross the boundaries from law and legal theory to theology. The fact that traditionalist jurists and speculative theologians managed to adopt similar (certainly not identical) legal theory positions without compromising on their different theologies shows that they both managed to, largely, prevent their theological disagreements from causing significant variations in legal theory. Theologians also managed to draw some distinctions between theology and legal theory allowing them to adopt some of the traditionalist methods in law but not in speculative theology. These distinctions are necessary to allow them to be identified with Sunnī schools of law without traditionalizing their theology.

FOUR BIOGRAPHIES

The previous part of this chapter drew a brief sketch of the political and intellectual context in which the four scholars under study lived and produced their ideas. It also attempted to describe some of the developments that might have informed a jurist's perception of the relationship between speculative theology and legal theory. The remaining part of the chapter presents brief biographical information on the four jurists who lie at the centre of the current study. When possible, this part uses information from the previous sections to better understand how some of the developments explained above left a mark on the four jurists' legal theory.

ʿAbd al-Jabbār al-Hamadhānī

ʿAbd al-Jabbār b. Aḥmad al-Hamadhānī, often designated as the 'Chief Judge' (*Qāḍī al-Quḍāt*), was born ca. 325/937 in Asadābād, Iran. He was a Shāfiʿī who, initially, followed Ashʿarī theology before embracing Muʿtazilī doctrines.[51] He moved from Asadābād to Basra in 342/954 where he studied with the Muʿtazilī Abū Isḥāq b.

[51] Heemskerk seems to be implicitly doubting the claim that ʿAbd al-Jabbār was initially an Ashʿarī; she notes that there is no evidence that he was versed in ʿAshʿarī theology. See *EI*[3], s.v. "ʿAbd al-Jabbār b. Aḥmad al-Hamadhānī" (Margaretha T. Heemskerk).

ʿAyyāsh. The Zaydī scholar and biographer al-Ḥākim al-Jushamī (d. 484/1101) says that ʿAbd al-Jabbār embraced Muʿtazilī theology during his stay in Basra and before his move to Baghdad.[52] ʿAbd al-Jabbār's prominence within the Muʿtazilī School is attested by most of his biographers who often describe him as the leader of his contemporaneous Muʿtazilīs.

In 360/970, the Būyid wazīr and patron of arts, al-Ṣāḥib b. ʿAbbād, himself a Muʿtazilī and Shāfiʿī, invited ʿAbd al-Jabbār to Rayy. He appointed ʿAbd al-Jabbār as a judge in more than one city before promoting him to the position of chief judge of Rayy in 367/977. After the death of Ibn ʿAbbād, the Būyid ruler Fakhr al-Dawla (d. 387/997) dismissed ʿAbd al-Jabbār from his position and confiscated his property. As Heemskerk notes, this was not for sectarian reasons as he was replaced by another chief judge who followed Shāfiʿī law and Muʿtazilī theology.[53] Nothing much is known about ʿAbd al-Jabbār's life after his dismissal from his public post.[54] However, we know that he remained in Rayy for the rest of his life teaching and writing books, where, according to most of his medieval biographers, he died in 415/1024.[55]

---

[52] Abū Saʿd al-Muḥsin b. Muḥammad Karāma al-Ḥākim al-Jushamī (d. 484/1101), *Sharḥ al-ʿUyūn* in *Faḍl al-iʿtizāl wa-ṭabaqāt al-muʿtazila*, ed. Fu'ād Sayyid (Tunis: al-Dār al-Tūnisiyya lil-Nashr, 1974), 366.

[53] Margaretha T. Heemskerk, *Suffering in Mu'tazilite Theology: Abd al-Jabbar's Teaching on Pain and Divine Justice* (Leiden: Brill, 2000), 48–9.

[54] Hourani, *Islamic Rationalism*, 7.

[55] This brief biography is based on the following sources: Tāj al-Dīn b. ʿAlī b. ʿAbd al-Kāfī al-Subkī (d. 771/1370), *Ṭabaqāt al-Shāfiʿiyya al-kubrā*, 10 vols , 2nd ed., ed. Maḥmūd Muḥammad al-Ṭanāḥī and ʿAbd al-Fattāḥ Muḥammad al-Ḥulw (N.p.: Hajr lil-Ṭibāʿa wa-l-Nashr, 1413/[1993]), 5:97 in CD-ROM *al-Jāmiʿ al-kabīr li-kutub al-turāth al-ʿArabī wa-l-Islāmī* 5th ed. (Amman: Markaz al-Turāth li-l-Barmajiyyāt, 2012) [hereafter I refer to this database as CD-ROM *al-Jāmiʿ al-kabīr*]; Abū Bakr b. Aḥmad b. Muḥammad b. ʿUmar b. Qāḍī Shuhba (d. 851/1448), *Ṭabaqāt al-Shāfiʿiyya*, 4 vols , ed. al-Ḥāfiẓ ʿAbd al-ʿAlīm Khān (Beirut: ʿĀlam al-Kutub, 1407/[1987]), 1:184, in CD-ROM *al-Jāmiʿ al-kabīr*; ʿAbd al-Karīm b. Muḥammad al-Rāfiʿī al-Qazwīnī (d. 623/1226), *al-Tadwīn fī akhbār Qazwīn*, 4 vols , ed. ʿAzīz Allāh al-ʿAṭṭārī (Beirut: Dār al-Kutub al-ʿIlmiyya, 1987),

Although most of his legal writings have not yet been discovered, ʿAbd al-Jabbār's legal legacy seems to have been quite influential. Until the ninth/fifteenth century we find leading Sunnī jurists praising his work. Among them is the Shāfiʿī Badr al-Dīn al-Zarkashī (d. 794/1392) who describes ʿAbd al-Jabbār's legal literature as a major milestone in the development of legal theory.[56] As I previously noted, the famous Mālikī scholar Ibn Khaldūn describes ʿAbd al-Jabbār's book on legal theory *al-ʿUmad* as one of the four pillars of the legal theory method of the theologians (*ṭarīqat al-mutakallimīn*).[57]

ʿAbd al-Jabbār spent all of his life under Būyid rule and in lands under their control. Būyids and many of their senior officials were generous patrons of the arts. ʿAbd al-Jabbār himself enjoyed the patronage of the Būyid wazīr al-Ṣāḥib b. ʿAbbād. Most importantly, Būyids were also sympathetic to Muʿtazilīs and Shāfiʿīs. Therefore, we might assume that ʿAbd al-Jabbār lived during times and in lands in which there was no systematic pressures on Muʿtazilīs from the political authorities.

3:125, in CD ROM *al-Jāmiʿ al-kabīr*; Abū ʿAmr ʿUthmān b. ʿAbd al-Raḥman b. al-Ṣalāḥ (d. 643/1245), *Ṭabaqāt al-fuqahāʾ al-Shāfiʿiyya*, 2 vols , ed. Muḥyī al-Dīn ʿAlī Najīb (Beirut: Dār al-Bashāʾir al-Islāmiyya, 1992), 1:523, in CD ROM *al-Jāmiʿ al-kabīr*; Aḥmad b. Yaḥyā b. al-Murtaḍā (d. 840/1437), *Kitāb Ṭabaqāt al-Muʿtazila*, ed. Susanna Diwald-Wilzer (Beirut: al-Maktaba al-Kāthūlīkiyya, 1407/1987), 112–3; al-Ḥākim al-Jushamī, *Sharḥ al-ʿUyūn*, 366; *EI*[3], s.v. "ʿAbd al-Jabbār b. Aḥmad al-Hamadhānī', (Margaretha T. Heemskerk); Heemskerk, *Muʿtazilite Theology*, 36–53. For a comprehensive biography of ʿAbd al-Jabbār, see ʿAbd al-Karīm ʿUthmān, *Qāḍī al-Quḍāt ʿAbd al-Jabbār b. Aḥmad al-Hamadhānī* (Beirut: Dār al-ʿArabiyya, 1968).

[56] Badr al-Dīn Muḥammad b. Bahādur al-Zarkashī (d. 794/1392), *al-Baḥr al-muḥīṭ fī uṣūl al-fiqh*, 6 vols ed. ʿAbd al-Qādir ʿAbd Allāh al-ʿĀnī (Kuwait: Wizārat al-Awqāf wa-l-Shuʾūn al-Islāmiyya, 1413/1992), 1:6.

[57] Ibn Khaldūn, *Muqaddima*, 3:18. The other three pillars are Abū al-Ḥusayn al-Baṣrī's commentary on ʿAbd al-Jabbār's *Kitāb al-ʿUmad* (hitherto undiscovered), Juwaynī's *Burhān* and Ghazālī's *Mustaṣfā*. Abū al-Ḥusayn's commentary has not yet been discovered.

In light of what has been explained before, ʿAbd al-Jabbar's membership in the Shāfiʿī School and his profession as a judge probably encouraged him to adopt legal positions that were not highly distinguishable from his fellow Shāfiʿīs. Moreover, creating a legal theory that was explicitly grounded in his Muʿtazilī doctrines might have undermined his status among his fellow non-Muʿtazilī Shāfiʿīs. Furthermore, it would have been uncommon for a Muʿtazilī to join the Shāfiʿī legal school that was largely dominated by Ashʿarīs and traditionalists.[58] This probably placed even more pressure on ʿAbd al-Jabbār not to appear as a non-conformist. It is therefore not surprising to see the striking similarity between ʿAbd al-Jabbār's legal theory and that of other non-Muʿtazilī Shāfiʿīs, including traditionalists. Although his theology remained categorically different from any other Sunnī jurist or theologian, his legal theory is hardly distinguishable from any Sunnī in general. This similarity is a product of what Hallaq calls the great rationalist-traditionalist synthesis in addition to the speculative theologians' efforts to be associated with a Sunnī school of law. Furthermore, as I will argue all through this study, jurists managed to limit the legal discrepancies caused by their theological disagreements.

Abū Isḥāq al-Shīrāzī

Abū Isḥāq Ibrāhīm b. ʿAlī b. Yūsuf al-Fīrūzabādī al-Shīrāzī was born between 393/1003 and 396/1006 in Fīrūzābād in South Iran. He received his education in his home town in addition to Shiraz, Basra and Baghdad. In 430/1038, he started teaching law in his own study circle in several mosques in Baghdad. Three decades later, the Saljūq wazīr Niẓām al-Mulk appointed him as the first professor in the newly founded Niẓāmiyya *madrasa* in Baghdad where he taught until his death in 476/1083. Shīrāzī's biographers are unanimous on his prominence among his peers and influence

[58] Makdisi points out that traditionalist Shāfiʿī jurists viewed Ashʿarīs joining the Shāfiʿī School as parasites, see Makdisi, 'Ash'arī and the Ash'ariates II', 37. It is likely that traditionalists would be even more critical of Muʿtazilīs joining their school.

within the Shāfiʿī legal school.[59] Modern scholars share the same view; Daphna Ephrat describes him as one of the greatest Shāfiʿīs of Baghdad.[60] Éric Chaumont considers him an 'eminent jurist whose work constitutes one of the major reference sources of the Shāfiʿī school'.[61]

Although modern scholars are unanimous that Shīrāzī was part of the Shāfiʿī legal tradition, they disagree on his theological orientation. Zakariyyā al-Miṣrī, Henri Laoust and George Makdisi believe that he followed the theology of *ahl al-ḥadīth* and preferred a traditionalist oriented dogma rather than a speculative one.[62] On

---

[59] This brief biographical account is based on the following sources: Muḥammad Maẓhar Baqā, *Muʿjam al-uṣūliyyīn* (Mecca: Jāmiʿat Umm al-Qurā, 1414/[1993]), 1:39–43; Muḥammad b. Aḥmad b. ʿUthmān al-Dhahabī (d. 748/1348 or 753/1352–3). *Siyar aʿlām al-nubalāʾ*, 23 vols , ed. Shuʿayb al-Arnāʾūṭ and Muḥammad al-ʿIrqisūsī (Beirut: Muʾassasat al-Risala, 1413[/1992]), 18:452–64 in CD-ROM *al-Jāmiʿ al-kabīr*; Shams al-Dīn Aḥmad b. Khallikān (d. 681/1282), *Wafayāt al-Aʿyān wa-anbāʾ abnāʾ al-zamān*, 7 vols ed. Iḥsān ʿAbbās (Lebanon: Dar al-Thaqāfa, no date), 1:28–31 in CD-ROM *al-Jāmiʿ al-kabīr*; Ibn Qāḍī Shuhba, *Ṭabaqāt al-Shāfiʿiyya*, 1:238–40; Subkī, *Ṭabaqāt al-Shāfiʿiyya al-kubrā*, 4:215–56; *EI*[2], s.v. 'al-Shīrāzī, al-Shaykh al-Imām Abū Isḥāq Ibrāhīm b. ʿAlī b. Yūsuf al-Fīrūzabādī', (E. Chaumont).

[60] Ephrat, *A Learned Society*, 79.

[61] *EI*[2], s.v. 'al-Shīrāzī' (E. Chaumont). Makdisi, Melchert and Devin Stewart all use similar terms to describe Shīrāzī's status among Shāfiʿīs. See Makdisi, 'Sunnī Revival', 159; Christopert Melchert, review of *Kitāb al-Lumaʿ fī uṣūl al-fiqh, Le Livre des Rais illuminant les fondements de la compréhension de la Loi*, by Abū Isḥāq Ibrāhīm al-Shīrāzī, trans. Éric Chaumont, *Islamic Law and Society* 9 (2002), 116; Devin Stewart, review of *Kitāb al-Lumaʿ fī uṣūl al-fiqh* (*Le Livre des Rais illuminant les fondements de la compréhension de la Loi*) by Abū Isḥāq Ibrāhīm al-Shīrāzī, trans. Éric Chaumont, *Journal of the American Oriental Society* 123 (2003), 246.

[62] Henri Laoust, *La Politique de Gazali* (Paris: P. Geuthner, 1970), 30; Henri Laoust, *Les Schismes dans l'Islam* (Paris: Payot, 1965), 128–30 both quoted in ʿAbd al-Majīd Turkī introduction to Abū Isḥāq Ibrāhīm al-Shīrāzī (d. 476/10832), *Sharḥ al-Lumaʿ fī uṣūl al-fiqh*, 2 vols ed. ʿAbd al-Majīd Turkī (Tunis: Dār al-Gharb al-Islāmī, 1429/2008), 1:85; Makdisi,

the other hand, Muḥammad Ḥasan Hītū, ʿAbd al-Majīd Turkī, C. Gilliot and Marie Bernand argue that Shīrāzī was in fact an Ashʿarī speculative theologian.[63] The second position has now been confirmed after the publication of two of Shīrāzī's theological epistles.[64] The first is *ʿAqīdat al-salaf* in which he expressed himself in the language and terminology of a speculative theologian rather than a traditionalist. He also discussed issues such as the substance (*jawhar*), accident (*ʿaraḍ*), existent (*mawjūd*) and *maʿdūm* (non-existent). Those are topics that typically appear in speculative theology manuals and are usually avoided by traditionalist authors.[65] In his other epistle *al-Ishāra ilā madhhab ahl al-ḥaqq*, Shīrāzī is more explicit about his Ashʿarī doctrine.[66] For example, he warns that anyone who adopts beliefs other than those of the Ashʿarīs is an infi-

---

'The Sunnī Revival',159; Makdisi, *Ibn ʿAqīl*, 81; al-Maṣrī, *al-Imām al-Shīrāzī*, 87–100.

63 C. Gilliot, 'Deux professions de foi du juriste théologien aš'arite Abū Isḥāq aš-Šīrāzī', *Studia Islamica* 68 (1988): 170–196; Marie Bernand, *La Profession de foi d'Abū Isḥāq al-Šīrāzī* (Cairo: Institut français d'archéologie orientale, 1987), 3–16; ʿAbd al-Majīd Turkī introduction to Abū Isḥāq Ibrāhīm b. ʿAlī b. Yūsuf al-Fīrūzabādī al-Shīrāzī, *Kitāb al-Maʿūna fi-l-jadal*, ed. ʿAbd al-Majīd Turkī (Beirut: Dār al-Gharb al-Islāmī, 1988/1408), 71–89; Hītū, *al-Imām al-Shīrāzī*, 121; Turkī, introduction to al-Shīrāzī, *Sharḥ al-Lumaʿ*, 73–87.

64 Both are published in Bernand, *La Profession de foi d'Abū Isḥāq al-Šīrāzī*. One must note here that Chaumont is skeptical about the attribution of both treatises to Shīrāzī. He notes that none of his biographers mentions them among his list of works, see *EI*^{2}, s.v. 'al-Shīrāzī', (E. Chaumont).

65 For the text of *ʿAqīdat al-salaf* see Bernand, *La Profession de foi d'Abū Isḥāq al-Šīrāzī*, 63–72.

66 For the text of *Ishāra*, see Bernand, *La Profession de foi d'Abū Isḥāq al-Šīrāzī*, 17–48. This treatise was also published in Turkī, introduction to Shīrāzī, *Sharḥ al-Lumaʿ*, 91–116. It was also published by the Egyptian Ministry of Endowments, see Abū Isḥāq al-Shīrāzī, *al-Ishāra ilā madhhab ahl al-ḥaqq* ed. Muḥammad al-Sayyid al-Jalaynad (Cairo: Wizārat al-Awqāf, 1420/1999). All of the following references are to the latter edition.

del (*kāfir*).[67] He adds, elsewhere, that Ashʿarīs should be proud of their name, since it is the name of the tribe to which Abū Mūsā al-Ashʿarī (d. 42/662), a famous companion of the Prophet, belongs.[68] He boasts that Abū al-Ḥasan al-Ashʿarī is a descendant of Abū Mūsā and quotes a Qurʾānic verse and a tradition attributed to the Prophetic supposedly praising the descendants of this companion.[69] At the end of the epistle, he mentions four verses of poetry lauding those who follow Shāfiʿī law and Ashʿarī theology.[70] Unless one chooses to doubt the authorship of *Ishāra*, Shīrāzī's statements leave no room for doubt concerning his Ashʿarī creed.[71]

As mentioned above, the question of Shīrāzī's theological affiliation was not settled until the discovery of two of his theological epistles. The fact that Shīrāzī's legal literature is not sufficient for modern scholars to unanimously agree on his creed entails that this literature is neither explicit nor unequivocal enough about its author's theological orientation.[72] Shīrāzī might have been attempting, consciously or not, to limit the presence of theology in his legal theory literature. Modern scholars had to wait until some of

---

[67] Shīrāzī, *Ishāra*, 191.

[68] Shīrāzī, *Ishāra*, 196–7.

[69] Shīrāzī, *Ishāra*, 197–8.

[70] Shīrāzī, *Ishāra*, 199.

[71] E. Chaumont refuses to take an explicit position from the debate concerning Shīrāzī's creed, see his 'Encore au sujet de l'Ashʿarisme d'Abû Isḥâq', 177 where he notes that 'On voit ainsi qu'à la question Shîrâzî était-il ashʿarite? je serais tenté de répondre oui et non'. In his *EI²*, article on Shīrāzī, Chaumont notes that the debate around Shīrāzī's theological affiliation seems to have been settled in favor of Ashʿarism after the publication of the above mentioned theological epistles. However, Chaumont doubt's Shīrāzī's authorship of both epistles and, thus, remains undecided. See *EI²*, s.v. 'al-Shīrāzī' (E. Chaumont).

[72] A good example is ʿAbd al-Majīd Turkī, editor of Shīrāzī's *Sharḥ al-Lumaʿ*. In his introduction to the first edition, Turkī holds the opinion that Shīrāzī is a traditionalist. However, after the publication of Shīrāzī's theological treatises and in his introduction to the second edition of *Sharḥ al-Lumaʿ*, Turkī changes his position noting that the newly published material reveals Shīrāzī's Ashʿarī creed.

Shīrāzī's theological treatises were finally published to have more concrete evidence revealing his theological background. Éric Chaumont argues that '[f]undamentally, the legal thinking of al-Shīrāzī expresses a radical insistence on the autonomy of the sphere of the legal sciences in relation to theology'.[73] Failing to uncover Shīrāzī's theological background from his legal theory writings reveals his attempts to distance his theology from his writings on legal theory.

Abū al-Maʿālī al-Juwaynī

Abū al-Maʿālī ʿAbd al-Malik b. ʿAbd Allāh b. Yūsuf al-Juwaynī was born, according to most biographers, in 419/1028, in a village near the Iranian city of Nishapur. He followed Ashʿarī theology and Shāfiʿī law. He spent most of his life teaching in Nishapur. He was forced, temporarily, to leave the city in the face of the anti-Ashʿarī policies of Ṭughril Beg (r. 431/1040–455/1063) and his Muʿtazilī wazīr ʿAmīd al-Mulk al-Kundurī. Both ordered the cursing of Abū al-Ḥasan al-Ashʿarī from pulpits, Ashʿarīs and Shāfiʿīs were prohibited from teaching, some of the leading Ashʿarī scholars were arrested and exiled, and Ḥanafīs replaced Shāfiʿī jurists in public posts.[74] Faced with these pressures, Juwaynī left Nishapur in 445/1053 to Baghdad. Around five years later he moved to the Ḥijāz where he taught in Mecca and Medina (hence his nickname Imām al-Ḥaramayn).

---

[73] *EI²*, s.v. 'al-Shīrāzī' (E. Chaumont).

[74] The reasons behind this particular wave of anti-Ashʿarī campaign are not entirely clear to me. Medieval biographers often note that 'some people' falsely informed Ṭughril Beg that Abū al-Ḥasan al-Ashʿarī taught deviant doctrines and therefore he took these measures. Zuḥaylī and Dīb suggest that the wazīr Kundurī saw the leader of the Shāfiʿīs in Nishapur, Abū Sahl b. al-Muwaffaq, as a rival for the wizarate. Attempting to exclude his rival, Kundurī encouraged Ṭughril Beg to take these measures and thus exclude any Shāfiʿī as a possible alternative. See Muḥammad al-Zuḥaylī, *al-Imām al-Juwaynī: Imām al-Ḥaramayn*, 2nd ed. (Damascus: Dār al-Qalam, 1412/1992), 70; ʿAbd al-ʿAẓīm al-Dīb, *Fiqh Imām al-Ḥaramayn* (n.p,: n.p., 1405/1985), 45.

Juwaynī returned to Nishapur shortly after the death of Ṭughril Beg and at the beginning of his successor's reign Alp Arslān (r. 455/1063–465/1072). Although the new sultan was staunchly Ḥanafī, he appointed Niẓām al-Mulk, a man with Ashʿarī-Shāfiʿī sympathies, as his wazīr. The latter's appointment certainly helped to ease pressures on Ashʿarīs and Shāfiʿīs. Niẓām al-Mulk gradually ended the anti-Ashʿarī measures which eventually allowed Juwaynī to return to his home town. Upon his return, Niẓām al-Mulk appointed Juwaynī in the Niẓāmiyya *madrasa* of Nishapur and invited him to join his court. Many of his biographers note that Juwaynī became very close to Niẓām al-Mulk which enabled him to accumulate influence, power and assume many official posts, including the supervisor of all endowments within the city. Juwaynī remained in Nishapur teaching at the Niẓāmiyya *madrasa* until his death in 478/1085.[75]

Juwaynī holds a prominent place among Ashʿarī theologians and Shāfiʿī jurists. Alessandro Bausani describes him as the greatest

[75] This brief biography is based on Ibrāhīm b. Muḥammad b. al-Azhar al-Ṣarīfīnī (d. 641/1243), *al-Muntakhab min al-Siyāq l-tārīkh Naysābūr*, ed. Muḥammd Aḥmad ʿAbd al-ʿAzīz (Beirut: Dār al-Kutub al-ʿIlmiyya, 1409/1989), 330–1; Abū Muḥammd ʿAbd Allāh b. Asʿad b. ʿAlī b. Sulaymān al-Yāfiʿī (d. 768/1367), *Mirʾāt al-janān wa-ʿibrat al-yuqẓān*, 4 vols (Cairo: Dār al-Kitāb al-Islāmī, 1413/1993), 3:124–31; Dhahabī, *Siyar aʿlām al-nubalāʾ*, 18:468–77; al-Subkī, *Ṭabaqāt al-Shāfiʿiyya al-kubrā*, 5:165–222 (his entry includes a verbatim quotation of Juwaynī 's entry in *Siyāq Naysābūr* by ʿAbd al-Ghaffār al-Fārisī (d. 529/1135) who was a student of Juwaynī. The latter book, as far as I know, has not been discovered); Ibn Khallikān, *Wafayāt al-aʿyān*, 3:167–70; Ibn Qāḍī Shuhba, *Ṭabaqāt al-Shāfiʿiyya*, 1:255–6; *EI*[2], s.v. 'al-Djuwaynī, Abū al-Maʿālī ʿAbd al-Malik', (C. Brockelmann and L. Gardet). Many modern authors have written biographies of Juwaynī, see for instance Fawqiyya Ḥusayn Maḥmūd, *al-Juwaynī Imām al-Ḥaramayn* (Cairo: al-Muʾassasa al-Miṣriyya al-ʿĀmma li-l-Taʾlīf wa-l-Anbāʾ wa-l-Nashr, 1970), esp. part one; Dīb, *Imām al-Ḥaramayn*, 17–45; Zuḥaylī, *al-Imām al-Juwaynī*, 1–92.

Ashʿarī-Shāfiʿī scholar in Khurasan in his times.[76] The modern Egyptian scholar Yūsuf al-Qaraḍāwī considers Juwaynī to be the second founder of the Ashʿarī School.[77] Pre-modern biographers of Juwaynī often describe him as the leader of his contemporaneous Shāfiʿīs.[78] Ibn Khaldūn, as previously noted, considers Juwaynī's book *al-Burhān fī uṣūl al-fiqh* as one of the four pillars for the legal theory method of the theologians.[79] Most importantly, Juwaynī is known for his innovations in legal theory and theology. In his *Giyāthī*, he blames authors for being repetitive and lacking creativity and boasts that he does not fear adopting novel legal positions that no one ever favoured.[80] Furthermore, despite being an Ashʿarī theologian and a Shāfiʿī jurist, Juwaynī often challenges the opinions of Muḥammad b. Idrīs al-Shāfiʿī and Abū al-Ḥasan al-Ashʿarī.[81] He is also often credited with introducing new innova-

---

[76] A. Bausani, 'Religion in the Saljuq Period', in *The Cambridge History of Iran*, ed. John Andrew Boyle and others, vol. 5, *The Saljuq and Mongol Periods* (Cambridge: Cambridge University Press, 1968), 287.

[77] Yūsuf al-Qaraḍāwī, 'Tarjamat al-Imām al-Juwaynī bayna al-muʾarrikhīn: al-Dhahabī wa-l-Subkī', in *al-Dhikrā al-alfiyya li-Imām al-Ḥaramayn al-Juwaynī*, ed. ʿAbd al-ʿAẓīm al-Dīb and Muḥammad Ṣāliḥ al-Shīb (Doha: University of Qatar, 2000), 106. This article is part of an anthology composed of the papers presented at a conference held in Doha (April 1999). Almost all articles point to Juwaynī's central role in Ashʿarī theology and Shāfiʿī law.

[78] See for instance Dhahabī, *Siyar aʿlām al-nubalāʾ*, 2574; Subkī, *Ṭabaqāt al-Shāfiʿiyya*, 5:174 .

[79] See also Bernard G. Weiss, *The Search for God's Law: Islamic Jurisprudence in the Writings of Sayf al-Dīn al-Āmidī* (Salt Lake City: University of Utah Press, 1992), 19–20 where he describes Juwaynī's *Burhan* as the first great classical legal theory work in the speculative-theological tradition.

[80] Imām al-Ḥaramayn ʿAbd al-Malik ʿAbd Allāh al-Juwaynī, *al-Ghiyāthī: Ghiyāth al-umam fi-l-tiyāth al-ẓulam*, 2nd ed. ed. ʿAbd Al-ʿAẓīm al-Dīb (n.p: n.p., 1401/1981), 39, 164–5, 266–7.

[81] In his edition of Juwaynī's *Burhān*, ʿAbd al-ʿAẓīm al-Dīb attached two appendices. The first is a list of the legal theory differences between Juwaynī and Muḥammad b. Idrīs al-Shāfiʿī, see *Burhān*, 1443–4. The sec-

tions within the Ashʿarī school of theology that were not always in line with the thought of previous Ashʿarī figures, including his own teacher Abū Bakr al-Bāqillānī.[82] Juwaynī, in sum, enjoys an independent spirit that favours innovation to imitation.[83]

Abū al-Muẓaffar al-Samʿānī

Abū al-Muẓaffar Manṣūr b. Muḥammad al-Samʿānī was born in 426/1035 in Marv within the historical region of Khurāsān (within the modern borders of Turkmenistan). His father was a Ḥanafī

---

ond is a list of three legal theory differences between Juwaynī and Abū al-Ḥasan al-Ashʿarī, see *Burhān*, 1445.

[82] For examples of Juwaynī's innovations in Ashʿarī theology, see Muḥammad ʿAbd al-Faḍīl al-Qūṣī, 'Malāmiḥ al-madhhab al-kalāmī ʿinda al-Juwaynī', in *al-Dhikrā al-alfiyya li-Imām al-Ḥaramayn al-Juwaynī* , ed. ʿAbd al-ʿAẓīm al-Dīb and Muḥammad Ṣāliḥ al-Shīb (Doha: University of Qatar, 2000): 355–78; Aḥmad b. ʿAbd al-Laṭīf b. ʿAbd Allāh Āl ʿAbd al-Laṭīf, *Manhaj Imām al-Ḥaramayn fī dirāsat al-ʿaqīda* (Riyadh: Markaz al-Malik Fayṣal li-l-Buḥūth wa-l-Dirāsāt al-Islāmiyya, 1414/1993), 75–82; Helmut Klopfer, *Das Dogma des Imâm al-Ḥaramain al-Djuwainî* (Cairo: al-Arab Salaheddine Boustany, 1958), 9–23.

[83] Subkī quotes Juwaynī's student ʿAbd al-Ghaffār al-Fārisī noting that Juwaynī was involved in Ṣūfī sciences (*takallam fī-l aḥwāl wa-khāḍ fī-ʿulūm al-ṣūfiyya*, see Subkī, *Ṭabaqāt al-Shāfiʿiyya*, 5:180. Probably following Fārisī, other biographers also note that Juwaynī was involved in Ṣūfism, see for instance Ibn Khallikān, *Wafāyāt al-ʿayān*, 3:169; Dhahabī, *Siyar aʿlām al-nubalāʾ*, 2576. The modern scholars Ḥarfūsh and Maḥmūd note that Juwaynī was in fact a Ṣūfī, see Ashraf Ḥarfūsh, *Falsafat al-kalām ʿind Imām al-Ḥaramayn al-Juwaynī* (Damascus: al-Ḥikma, 1415/1994), 98–9; Fawqiyya Ḥusayn Maḥmūd introduction to Imām al-Ḥaramayn Abū al-Maʿālī ʿAbd al-Malik al-Juwaynī, *Lumaʿ al-adilla fi-qawāʿid ʿaqāʾid ahl al-sunna wa-l-jamāʿa*, ed. Fawqiyya Ḥusayn Maḥmūd (Cairo: al-Dār al-Miṣriyya li-l-Taʾlīf wa-l-Tarjama, 1385/1965), 36. I did not come across obvious Ṣūfī signs in Juwaynī's examined literature. Yet, one doubts that his student Fārisī would attribute Ṣūfism to Juwaynī without him adopting some mystic ideas of some sort. Furthermore, Maḥmūd notes that Juwaynī was also versant in philosophy. She writes that his book *Shāmil* includes discussions with philosophers that show an acute knowledge of this discipline, see Maḥmūd, introduction to *Lumaʿ al-adilla*, 37.

jurist and Samʿānī grew up following the same school of law. Little is known about his life. His biographers note that, in 461/1069, he visited Baghdad where he met Abū Isḥāq al-Shīrāzī. He also visited Nishapur and took part in a debate in the presence of Juwaynī.[84] In 468/1076 a dramatic change in Samʿānī's career occurred. He abandoned the Ḥanafī School of law and adopted that of the Shāfiʿī. All of his biographers note that this change took place after his pilgrimage to Mecca. His decision caused much rioting in his home town of Marv; Ḥanafīs protested against his conversion. State officials pressured Samʿānī trying to dissuade him from his decision. Facing these pressures, Samʿānī, chose to leave the city to Ṭūs. He later moved to Nishapur where the Shāfiʿī scholars of the city and the Saljūq wazīr Niẓām al-Mulik are reported to have received him with great honour. Niẓām al-Mulk, furthermore, appointed him as a teacher in the Shāfiʿī *madrasa* of the city. Only in 479/ 1086 was Samʿānī able to return to Marv, where he taught Shāfiʿī law until his death in 489/1096.[85]

---

[84] It is interesting to note that three of the four jurists studied here met each other. In addition to Samʿānī meeting Shīrāzī, Ibn al-Athīr writes that, in 475/1082, Shīrāzī visited Nishapur where he met Juwaynī and both held disputations in the presence of Niẓām al-Mulk, see Ibn al-Athīr, *al-Kāmil fī-l-tārīkh*, 8:428. Subkī recorded the text of those disputations, see his *Ṭabaqāt al-Shāfiʿiyya*, 5:209–18.

[85] This brief biographical survey is based on the following sources: Shams al-Dīn Muḥammad b. Aḥmad b. ʿUthmān al-Dhahbī, *al-ʿIbar fī khabar man ghabar*, 5 vols, 2nd ed., ed. Ṣalāḥ al-Dīn al-Munjid (Kuwait: Maṭbaʿat Ḥukumat al-Kuwayt, 1984), 3:328, in CD ROM *al-Jāmiʿ al-kabīr*; Shams al-Dīn Muḥammad b. Aḥmad b. ʿUthmān al-Dhahabī, *Tarīkh al-Islām wa-wafayāt al-mashāhīr wa-l-aʿlām*, 52 vols ed. ʿUmar ʿAbd al-Salām Tadmūrī (Beirut: Dār al-Kitāb al-ʿArabī, 1987/1407), 33:321–8 in CD-ROM *al-Jāmiʿ al-kabīr*; ʿImād al-Dīn Ismāʿīl b. ʿUmar b. Kathīr (d. 774/1373), *al-Bidāya wa-l-nihāya*, 14 vols (Beirut: Dār al-Maʿārif, n.d.), 12:153–4, in CD ROM *al-Jāmiʿ al-kabīr*; al-Ṣarīfīnī, *Muntakhab*, 442–4; Dhahabī, *Siyar aʿlām al-nubalāʾ*, 19:114–9; Ibn Qāḍī Shuhba, *Ṭabaqāt al-Shāfiʿiyya*, 1:273–4; al-Qazwīnī, *al-Tadwīn fī akhbār Qazwīn*, 4:118–9. On al-Samʿānī's conversion to Shāfiʿī law and the events that followed, see Bulliet, 'Political History of Nishapur', 88; Madelung, *Religious Trends*, 35–6.

CONCLUSION

Ideas never exist in a vacuum; they are a product of a contemporaneous and a preceding context. Islamic law and theology are no exception. Their shape in the fifth/eleventh century is an outcome of the intellectual, social and political developments that took place in previous centuries. This chapter has been an attempt to highlight some of the major developments that might have influenced the legal writings of the four Shāfiʿī jurists examined here. The primary focus here is those developments relevant to the relationship between speculative theology and legal theory.

Among those developments is the ongoing debate between rationalism and traditionalism which dominated the Muslim intellectual scene especially in its first three or four centuries. Since the third/ninth century traditionalist forces had begun to have the upper hand and emerged as the dominant intellectual trend. Features of traditionalist dominance include placing restrictions on the teaching of speculative theology in religious educational institutions in addition to the traditionalization of legal theory. This dominance entailed that a largely traditionalist legal theory became the accepted legal norm. Therefore, to avoid accusations of deviancy and legitimize their law, speculative theologians could not but accept – at least some of – the traditionalist legal methods. However, at the same time, traditionalist jurists adopted methods that were associated with rationalists, such as *qiyās* and legal preference. As Hallaq explained, by the fourth/tenth centuries, a middle position was created that combined elements from rationalism and traditionalism. Within this middle position, there existed different trends, more are rational than others. However, all accept the Qurʾān and the Prophetic Sunna as sources of law in addition to extra-textual methods, such as *qiyās*.

Furthermore, speculative theologians were under pressure to join any of the Sunnī schools of law. Membership in such schools was required to access educational institutions, receive government appointments and was an important factor determining the identity of a scholar within the intellectual community. Association with a legal school was also vital for acquiring legitimacy and recognition for a jurist's legal knowledge and expertise. The need to become a member in a school of law placed limitations on how far a jurist can allow his theology to overtly influence his legal theory; a theology that would be considered deviant by his theological opponents within his own legal school. However, the presence of traditionalist jurists and speculative theologians in the same legal school was made easy by what Hallaq calls the 'rationalist-traditionalist synthesis'. Jurists of all types managed to create a middle position between rationalism and traditionalism allowing them to share similar legal theories despite their theological disagreements. In spite of this reproach in legal theory, speculative theologians retained their speculative theology and traditionalists remained committed to their relatively literalist methods in theology. The creation of a middle ground in legal theory, but not in theology, could not have been possible without creating some distinctions between both disciplines. These distinctions allowed speculative theologians to, at least in part, traditionalize their legal theory without traditionalizing their theology. Distinguishing between the methods valid in theology and those valid in legal theory allowed speculative theologians to legitimize their law and legal theory without compromising the speculative nature of their theology. Therefore, in legal theory, traditionalist jurists and speculative theologians managed to reach a middle position whereas in theology both remain at odds.

Distinguishing between both disciplines is also vital for maintaining conformity within the Sunnī schools of law. If theological disagreements were allowed to produce significant legal disparities, there would appear significantly different legal theories within the same legal school. This would ruin the legal theory foundations of each school of law and disrupt the common theoretical framework that keeps each of them intact. It is important to note that, excluding the Ḥanbalī School, all other Sunnī schools of law include jurists from various theological backgrounds, including ones that consider each other as unbelievers. The fact that these legal schools embrace jurists from various theological traditions entail that jurists have managed to reach a formula limiting the ability of theological disagreements to bring about considerable legal differences. Otherwise, jurists from divergent theological backgrounds could have hardly co-existed within the same legal tradition.

Furthermore, dialectical reasons required the recognition of some epistemological differences between theology and legal theory. For example, we often find theologians insisting on distinguishing between the evidence and methods valid for producing legal knowledge and those valid for producing theological knowledge. The validity of using solitary traditions (*khabar al-āḥād*) is an obvious example. As mentioned earlier, by the late third/ninth century we find speculative theologians using solitary traditions to reach legal conclusions but vehemently refusing such traditions to reach theological conclusions. On the other hand, most traditionalist scholars, at least until the fifth/eleventh century, refuse such a distinction. For them solitary traditions are valid sources of legal as well as theological knowledge.

In addition, speculative theologians often award unaided human reason wide authority in theology but they limit its authority in the field of law. Theologians of all sorts (Ashʿarīs, Muʿtazilīs and Māturīdīs), frequently argue that revelation cannot be a source of knowledge for the theological issues relevant for establishing the veracity of revelation. Those issues would include the existence of God, divine attributes, authenticity of prophets and many others. Reaching conclusions about such issues via revelation would rest the authority of revelation on a circular argument. In other words, one cannot trust revelation as a source of knowledge before first establishing the existence of God and knowing His attributes.[86] Theologians, however, admit that once the veracity of revelation has been established it becomes a valid source of knowledge for all aspects of law. This is because no aspect of law is relevant to establishing the veracity of revelation. On the contrary, most traditionalist jurists, at least until the fifth/eleventh century, often consider revelation a valid source of knowledge for all aspects of law and theology. For many of them, resting foundational theological doctrines on revelation would not constitute a dialectical fallacy.

What we notice here is that speculative theologians, often for convincing reasons, tend to differentiate between the methods and evidence valid for use in law and those valid for speculative theology. The theologians' distinction between both disciplines made it easier for them to adopt traditionalist methods in legal theory without traditionalizing their theology. Furthermore, recognizing

[86] For the Muʿtazilī position, see for instance ʿAbd al-Jabbār, *Mughnī*, 12:166, 14:151–2, 16:395, 17:93, 315, 393; Abū al-Ḥusayn, *Muʿtamad*, 886–7, 910. For the Ashʿarī position, see for instance Richard Frank, 'Knowledge and Taqlid: The Foundations of Religious Belief in Classical Ashʿarism', *Journal of the American Oriental Society* 109 (1989): 37–62.

methodological and epistemological differences between both disciplines aided the creation of a middle position between rationalism and traditionalism in legal theory, without the need to reach similar compromises in theology. Distinguishing between the methods valid for legal theory and those valid for speculative theology allowed jurists from diverse theological backgrounds to exist within the same legal school without their different theologies ruining their common legal positions.

Preventing, as much as possible, theological disparities from producing legal disagreements is important for maintaining the tolerance of legal plurality common among Sunnī schools of law. Jurists often accept the validity of different legal opinions within their school of law and beyond it. Theological disagreements are far less tolerated than legal ones. Theological disagreements, even within the same theological trend, can prompt accusations of infidelity (*kufr*). The creation of legal theories based on particular theological doctrines, especially controversial ones, might undermine the tolerance of legal plurality. If particular legal theories are based on certain theological beliefs, they will be invalidated by jurists and members of other theological trends. The creation of legal schools and legal theories based upon particular theological foundations might transfer the intolerance common in theology to law and legal theory. Legal schools might turn into different denominations, each considering the 'Muslim other' as an infidel (*kāfir*). As will be explained in the following chapters, we rarely find a major legal theory stand that was monopolized by a single theological trend. This allowed jurists from various theological backgrounds to accept similar positions in legal theory, regardless of their theological disagreements. They can still accept the legitimacy of various positions in legal theory, without compromising their commitment to their own theology. Since theological schools do not accept the legitimacy of each other's doctrines, keeping the most controversial theological disagreements at some distance from legal theory might prevent importing the intolerance of plurality common among theological schools to legal ones.

Creating distinctions between theology and legal theory did not only serve the interest of the religious elite, but it was a practical step that eased the everyday lives of average Muslims. Muslim law touches almost every aspect of a Muslim's everyday life. Diet, clothing, personal status, commercial transactions, death, rituals and many other details of daily life are regulated by law. The laws created by the four Sunnī schools of law are, thus, being practiced on a daily basis, in fact many times a day. Unlike speculative theology which hardly influences an average Muslim's daily routine. One wonders how many Muslims ever thought about the nature of the Qurʾān, whether created or eternal. How many Muslims ever thought about the nature of divine speech, divine attributes, freewill and predestination, in addition to the many head spinning theological debates? The intolerance common among theological schools will hardly leave an impact on the lives of Muslims. From a very pragmatic perspective, for the interest of all Muslims, the intolerance common among theological schools should be prevented from crossing to the realm of law and legal theory. The recognition of some differences between theology and legal theory functions as a barrier that prevents this from occurring.

Recognizing epistemological and methodological differences between theology and legal theory served the interests of all parties. It permitted speculative theologians to assimilate within Sunnī schools of law. It allows jurists from various theological backgrounds to set aside their theological disagreements and create a common legal framework. However, it is important to note that this study does not argue that speculative theology and legal theory are two mutually exclusive disciplines that exist in isolation. This chapter explained the pressures on jurists and theologians that might have encouraged them to distance theology from legal theory. Despite all these pressures, theological discussions are still strongly present in manuals of legal theory. Jurists often utilize their theological doctrines as justifications for adopting particular stands in legal theory. Scholars of all theological trends are usually keen to show that their legal theory is in harmony with their creed. Many jurists see strong connections between theology and legal theory. The following chapters examine the intricate relationship between both disciplines. I highlight the significant similarities among the legal theories of four Shāfiʿī jurists who belong to three different theological trends. These similarities in themselves are evidence that they managed, in many cases, to prevent their significant theological disagreements from producing equally significant legal discrepancies, without creating a legal theory that is insensitive to the requirements of their theology. Exploring how they managed to do this is one of the major concerns of the following chapter.

CHAPTER THREE: THE THEOLOGY OF *QIYĀS*

INTRODUCTION

This chapter compares the perceptions of *qiyās* adopted by the four Shāfiʿī jurists who are the focus of this study, namely ʿAbd al-Jabbār, Juwaynī, Samʿānī and Shīrāzī. It is important for our purpose here to understand the differences and similarities between the four jurists' perceptions of *qiyās*. How far do their different theologies inform their concepts of *qiyās* in general, and how did they perceive the *ratio legis* (*ʿilla*, i.e. the occasioning factor behind a law), its deduction process and its function in *qiyās*, in particular? I argue that their perceptions of *qiyās* and the *ratio legis* are, to some extent, similar. This indicates that theological disagreements do not always lead to discrepancies in their understanding of *qiyās* as a legal tool. Jurists from different theological backgrounds, who are members of the same school of law, do not often adopt categorically different concepts of *qiyās*. Moreover, theology certainly informs each individual jurist's concept of *qiyās*; however, on a group and legal school level, the influence of theology on *qiyās* is less than uniform and consistent. Jurists from the same theological background do not always favour similar concepts of legal theory. I suggest two reasons that hinder theology from having a uniform impact on legal school level. First, it seems that the four jurists under study adopt theories of *qiyās* that undermine the impact of the most controversial theological doctrines on this aspect of legal theory. Second, jurists who hold the same theological doctrines interpret the legal implications of their common doctrines differently. Therefore, in most cases, no theological doctrine consistently leads to the adoption of specific positions in *qiyās*.

This chapter is divided into eight sections in addition to the current introduction. In the second section, I define *qiyās*. In the third, I mention some of the theological doctrines that are *expected* to have an impact on a jurists' perception of *qiyās* and the function of the *ratio legis*. In the fourth section, I analyse the relationship between the theological debates around causality and their relevance to the *ratio legis*. The fifth section discusses the areas of law (*fiqh*) in which *qiyās* is disallowed. The sixth and the seventh sections investigate the tools the four jurists utilize to deduce the *rationes legis* behind the deontic qualifications (*aḥkām sharʿiyya*) mentioned in the Qur'ān or the Prophetic Sunna. In the eighth, I mention the methods of determining preponderance (*tarjīḥ*) between apparently contradicting *rationes legis*. The ninth, and final, section includes the concluding remarks. I selected those particular aspects of *qiyās* to study because those are the issues on which there is relatively more information than others. Furthermore, the aspects of *qiyās* that I decided to focus on in this chapter are all relevant to the *ratio legis*. The *ratio legis* is the aspect of *qiyās* that is most relevant to theological debates, as explained below in more detail. Therefore, examining the role of the *ratio legis* in *qiyās* provides a good opportunity for exploring the role of theology in legal theory in general and *qiyās* in particular.

The conclusions of this chapter are undermined by the fact that not all aspects of *qiyās* have been examined. I deliberately left out issues such as *qawāḍiḥ al-ʿilla* (what invalidates a *ratio legis*), the four jurists' typology of *qiyās*, the probative value of the different types of *qiyās*, determining preponderance between conflicting processes of *qiyās* (based on factors other than the *ratio legis*), juridical preference (*istiḥsān*) and I do not conduct a thorough analysis of the four jurists' definitions of the four pillars of *qiyās* (excluding the *ratio legis*), to mention only a few. Covering all aspects of *qiyās* in a comparative study of four jurists and examining the impact of their theological doctrines on all of these aspects would require far more time and space than possible. Whether or not my conclusions would have been different if more aspects of *qiyās* were included in the study is a question that I cannot answer with confidence. Therefore, I phrase my conclusions hesitantly, being aware of this shortcoming.

THE DEFINITION OF *QIYĀS*

Before attempting to define *qiyās*, one must note that finding an adequate English translation for it is an intricate task. The most common English translation for *qiyās* is 'analogy' or a phrase that includes the word analogy, such as 'analogical reasoning' and 'legal analogy'.[1] Wael Hallaq has pointed to the problems raised by using the term 'analogy' in a translation of *qiyās*. This translation excludes all the non-analogical methods that are often subsumed under *qiyās* by many jurists.[2] In his works, Hallaq usually translates *qiyās* as 'legal reasoning',[3] admitting that this term sometimes includes methods that go beyond *qiyās* to include ones usually subsumed under *istidlāl*, *istiḥsān* and *istiṣlāḥ*.[4] However, in his English translation of Abū al-Ḥusayn al-Baṣrī's treatise on *qiyās*, Hallaq says that due to the lack of an equivalent term in English he will not translate the term *qiyās* at all, keeping it in its Arabic original.[5] Given that this term is now very well known among specialists of Islamic law and legal theory within non-Arab academic circles, I follow Hallaq's example. I do not translate the term; *qiyās* is a very complicated and

---

[1] Among the authors who translate *qiyās* as analogy are: Weiss, *Search for God's Law*; Opwis, *Maṣlaḥa*. For authors who use analogical reasoning as the translation for *qiyās*, see for example Mohammad Hashim Kamali, *Principles of Islamic Jurisprudence*, 3rd ed. (1989; repr,. Cambridge: Islamic Texts Society, 2003); Ahmad Hasan, *Analogical Reasoning in Islamic Jurisprudence* (Islamabad: Islamic Research Institute, 1986); Bernard Weiss, *The Spirit of Islamic Law* (Athens, GA: University of Georgia Press, 1998); David Vishanoff, *Formation of Islamic Hermeneutics*). Opwis also translates *qiyās* as 'legal analogy', see her monograph *Maṣlaḥa*. Other translations of *qiyās* include, 'juridical reasoning by analogy' (see for example *EI*², s.v. "Ḳiyās"), 'reasoning by analogy' (e.g. Vishanoff, *Formation of Islamic Hermeneutics*; Bernard Weiss, "Interpretation in Islamic Law: Theory of *Ijtihād*," *The American Journal of Comparative Law* 26.2 (1977): 199–212), 'juridical *qiyās*' (e.g. Wael Hallaq, "A Tenth-Eleventh Century Treatise on Juridical dialectic," *Muslim World* 77 (1989): 197–228) and *qiyās* (e.g. Hallaq, *Sharīʿa*).

[2] For Wael Hallaq's detailed argument, see his 'Non-Analogical Arguments in Sunni Juridicual *Qiyās*', 36.3 *Arabica* (1989): 286–306; Hallaq, *Islamic Legal Theories*, 96–101.

[3] See for example, Hallaq, *Islamic Legal Theories*; Hallaq, *Sharīʿa*.

[4] Hallaq, *Islamic Legal Theories*, 83.

[5] Hallaq, "Tenth-Eleventh Century Treatise," 205–6.

highly contextualized term and I could not find a satisfying translation for it.

Defining *qiyās* is a no less difficult task. This difficulty stems from the fact that the term *qiyās* is a reference to various, 'inferential tools'[6] ranging from analogical, logical and linguistic methods to comparisons based on sheer resemblance or what is usually known as *qiyās al-shabah* (*argumentum a simile*).[7] It is therefore difficult to find a statement or two as a definition for *qiyās* that would be inclusive of all methods that medieval jurists subsume under it. Another difficulty in defining the term is that pre-modern jurists disagree on which of these methods are actually part of *qiyās*. For example, some of the linguistic methods that are subsumed under *qiyās* by some scholars are considered nothing more than interpretation by others.[8] This is why Hallaq rightly notes that *qiyās* 'should be regarded as a relative term whose definition and structure vary from one jurist to another'.[9]

Due to the highly problematic nature of defining *qiyās*, I refrain from mentioning a 'one statement' definition of it; instead I attempt to describe it.[10] The need for *qiyās* is initiated by the need for an encompassing source of legislation. Muslims face new questions every day; the texts of the Qurʾān and the Sunna are finite and cannot keep offering direct answers to the novel situations Muslims continuously encounter. Consensus rarely occurs. If it occurs; this happens slowly. Therefore, consensus can hardly match

---

[6] Hallaq, *Sharīʿa*, 75.

[7] Translation borrowed from Hallaq, 'Non-Analogical Arguments', 303. The concept of *qiyās al-shabah* is explained in more detail below.

[8] An example of those 'linguistic' methods is the *a fortiori* arguments. Jurists such as the Muʿtazilī ʿAbd al-Jabbār do not consider this method a type of *qiyās*, whereas others such as Juwaynī consider it one form of *qiyās*. See, ʿAbd al-Jabbār, *Mughnī*, 17:312; Juwaynī, *Burhān*, 786–8.

[9] Hallaq, 'Non-Analogical Arguments', 305.

[10] This decision is influenced by Knut Vikør's explanation of *qiyās*. He avoids mentioning a 'one statement' definition of the term. He rather, vividly, describes it in a few paragraphs, see his *Between God and the Sultan* (Oxford: Oxford University Press, 2006), 54–7.

the dynamic life Muslim generations have been facing since the first/seventh century. *Qiyās* is a set of methods that turns revelation from a finite into an 'infinite' source of religious guidance. Should a new question arises that the Qur'ān, Sunna, or consensus do not directly cover, a jurist, through the different processes of *qiyās*, identifies a similar case directly covered by these sources. The deontic qualification of the case covered by these sources, i.e. the original case (*aṣl*), is extended to the novel case (*farʿ*) not directly covered by revelation. Similarity between the original and the novel case can have many forms; the most common is a shared *ratio legis*. Jurists members in Sunnī schools of law argue that when two cases share a common *ratio legis*, it is then justifiable to assume that the deontic qualification of the original case must be also that of the novel case.

In legal theory literature, the archetypical case of *qiyās* is that of *khamr* and *nabīdh* (both are types of intoxicating drinks). The Qur'ān explicitly prohibits the consumption of *khamr*; however, it says nothing on the consumption of other intoxicants. Muslim jurists are unanimous that the *ratio legis* (i.e. the occasioning factor bringing about a law) behind the Qur'ānic prohibition of *khamr* is its intoxicating quality. Therefore, any other substance that causes intoxication (i.e. any other substance in which this *ratio legis* can be found, e.g. *nabīdh*) should share the same deontic qualification of *khamr*, namely prohibition (*taḥrīm*). What justifies sharing the same deontic qualification is the common *ratio legis*. This is true in most (if not all) types of *qiyās*. It is easy to notice here that the crux of *qiyās* is knowledge of the *ratio legis*; without it no *qiyās* can be complete. The *ratio legis* can sometimes be explicitly stated in the text of revelation. In this case, it is termed *ʿilla manṣūṣa* or what I translate as an 'explicit *ratio legis*'. Nevertheless, in most cases revelation does not disclose the *ratio legis* behind a deontic qualification. In these cases, the jurist resorts to specific methods designed to deduce (and/or verify) the *ratio legis*. These methods are usually called *masālik al-ʿilla*. A *ratio legis* that is known through any of these methods is called *ʿilla mustanbaṭa* or what I translate as a 'deduced *ratio legis*'.

SPECULATIVE THEOLOGY AND *QIYĀS*

It is the *ratio legis* and its deduction process that constitutes the most important part of *qiyās*. Both are also the two aspects of *qiyās* that one would expect to be greatly influenced by speculative theology. By definition, a *ratio legis* is the assumed rationale and motivation behind the deontic qualification of the original case. In other words, in theory, the *ratio legis* is assumed to be the 'cause' whereas the deontic qualification is its 'effect'. This opens the door for the theological debate around causality to influence *qiyās*. The Muʿtazilīs hold a position close to an acceptance of natural causality. In their view, events of this world are tied together in a chain of causes and effects. For Muʿtazilīs, a cause must necessarily lead to the occurrence of its effect. On the other hand, the Ashʿarīs reject natural causality. Rather, they have an atomistic view of the world; the universe is created and re-created every single moment. In this model, a 'cause' produces its 'effect' because God creates the universe again in a way that allows the cause to produce 'its' effect. For the Ashʿarīs, what humans believe to be a cause is not essentially effective in bringing about what they believe to be its effect. A 'cause', for the Ashʿarīs, does not necessarily have to lead to its 'effect'. It is God who creates the effect after the occurrence of the 'cause', and He can alter His creation at will.[11]

---

[11] This is a very brief survey of the debate that admittedly lacks nuance. The disagreement between the Muʿtazilī and the Ashʿarī position is more complicated. One must note that Ashʿarīs do not categorically deny natural causality nor Muʿtazilīs completely accept it. However, the Ashʿarī position can be described as being close to a partial denial of causality and the Muʿtazilī as being close to a partial acceptance of it. For surveys of this debate, see for instance Ilyās Balkā, *al-Wujūd bayna al-sababiyya wa-l-niẓām* (Herndon, Virginia: al-Maʿhad al-ʿĀlamī li-l-Fikr al-Islāmī, 2009); *EI*², s.v. (Allāh) section IIB; *EI*², s.v. (ʿIlla) section III. For surveys of the Muʿtazilī position, see Ibrāhīm Turkī, *al-Sababiyya ʿinda al-qāḍī ʿAbd al-Jabbār* (Alexandria: Dār al-Wafāʾ, 2004); Albīr Naṣrī Nādir, *Falsafat al-Muʿtazila*, 2 vols (Alexandria: Maṭbaʿat Dār Nashr al-Thaqāfa, 1950), 1:204–20; Samīḥ Dughaym, *Falsafat al-qudur fī fikr al-Muʿtazila*, 2nd ed. (Beirut: Dār al-Fikr al-Lubnānī, 1992), 115–48. For more information on the Ashʿarī position, see Richard Frank, 'The Structure of Created Causality According to al-Ašʿarî: An Analysis of the Kitâb al-Lumaʿ' *Studia Islamica* 25 (1966): 82–164; Mehmet Evkuran, 'The Problem of Causality in Islamic Thought', *Journal of Islamic Research* 2.2 (2009): 115–27.

One would expect to find the debates around natural causality mirrored in the debates around juridical causality.[12] The *ratio legis*, on which a *qiyās* is based, help answer the question why God proscribes or prescribes a particular action. This is another contentious debate. The Muʿtazilīs hold that God's actions have rational grounds behind them; those grounds are usually ascertainable by the human mind. Furthermore, the Muʿtazilīs believe that God will always, or must always, protect the optimal interest of humans; a doctrine known as optimism.[13] Ashʿarīs and traditionalists (*ahl al-*

---

[12] I use the term juridical causality in reference to accepting a causal relationship between the *ratio legis* and the deontic qualification, the former being the cause whereas the latter its necessary effect. A scholar who accepts juridical causality sees a logical and a deterministic relationship between the *ratio legis* and its deontic qualification; the occurrence of the former will inevitably lead to the occurrence of the latter. Jurists who refuse juridical causality would see no logical and deterministic causal relationship between both. For them there is nothing in the ontological being of the *ratio legis* that would necessitate the occurrence of the deontic qualification. The *ratio legis* is only a sign (*ʿalāma*) that revelation puts forward, when humans see it they know that the deontic qualification should occur. If revelation were to choose another *ratio legis* as a sign for the same deontic qualification this would make no difference for humans. This is because humans are not capable of understanding the causal connection between the *ratio legis* and the deontic qualification, therefore for them both appear not to be connected except via revelation. Therefore, in this model it is revelation that makes a deontic qualification appears as the effect of a *ratio legis*. Before revelation sets a *ratio legis* as a sign for a deontic qualification both were not linked.

[13] According to this Muʿtazilī doctrine, God's justice necessitates that He will always do what best serves the optimal benefit of humans in this life and the one to come. If God were to do what does not serve their optimal interest this, for Muʿtazilīs, would undermine His justice and wisdom. Another relevant Muʿtazilī doctrine is benevolence (*luṭf*). According to this tenet, God will always, or must always, facilitate human salvation in the afterlife and guarantee their wellbeing in this life. Benevolence entails that God will provide humans with what they need to obey Him. God's revelation to humans is part of His benevolence. Revelation facilitate humans' quest to salvation and guides them to their best interest in this life.

ḥadīth) refuse both tenets. For them, this understanding of the motivation behind God's actions makes Him accountable to human evaluations of His actions. Both accuse the Muʿtazilīs of restricting God's omnipotence by keeping Him bound to act according to causes, effects, reasons and motivations. Furthermore, if God is bound to protect optimal human interest, this would entail that His actions are finite; what God did the best He could have ever do; nothing exists after that. To safeguard their understanding of divine omnipotence, the Ashʿarīs and the traditionalists hold that laws of causality do not govern divine actions and that God is not bound to bring a revelation that would lead to human optimal interest in this life and one to come.[14]

The debate around human benefit as the motivation behind divine actions opens the door wide to the following theological questions: Does God prescribe an action because it is good (*ḥasan*) or an action becomes good because God prescribes it? Does God proscribe an action because it is evil (*qabīḥ*) or an action becomes evil because God proscribes it? Does the good or evil nature of an action determine whether it is useful or harmful? Does the moral character of an action determine its deontological status? These questions are a reflection of the debate around moral epistemology

---

Luṭf can also be a reference to the benefits (*maṣāliḥ*, sg. *maṣlaḥa*) that God intends to humans. For more information on the relationship between *luṭf* and *maṣlaḥa*, see ʿAbd al-Jabbār, *Mughnī*, 13:20–22; Aron Zysow, 'Two Theories of the Obligation to Obey God's Commands', in *The Law Applied: Contextualizing the Islamic Sharīʿa*, ed. Peri Bearman and others (London: I. B. Tauris, 2008), esp. p. 400. For more details on *luṭf* and *al-salāḥ wa-l-aslaḥ*, see Anver Emon, *Islamic Natural Law Theories* (Oxford: Oxford University Press, 2010), 58–62.

[14] For more details on the Ashʿarī position, see Abū Bakr Muḥammad b. al-Ḥasan Ibn Fūrak (d. 406/1015), *Mujarrad maqālāt abī al-Ḥasan al-Ashʿarī*, ed. Aḥmad ʿAbd al-Raḥīm al-Sāyaiḥ (Cairo: Maktabat al-Thaqāfa al-Dīniyya, 1425/2005), 126–31; Abū al-Maʿālī ʿAbd al-Malik b. ʿAbd Allāh b. Yūsuf al-Juwaynī, *Kitāb al-Irshād ilā qawāṭiʿ al-adilla fī uṣūl al-iʿtiqād*, ed. Muḥammad Yūsuf Mūsā and ʿAlī ʿAbd al-Munʿim ʿAbd al-Ḥamīd (Cairo: Maktabat al-Khānjī, 1369/1950), 287–301. For the traditionalist position, see for example Samʿānī, *Qawāṭiʿ al-adilla*, 4:61, 430, 433.

and deontology: Whether actions are ontologically good or evil or they just acquire their 'goodness' or 'evilness' after the advent of revelation. A Muʿtazilī who holds that God will, or must, guarantee optimal human interest will consider the ethical character of most actions to be part of their ontological being. An action's ontological ethical quality will influence its deontic status; good actions will be obligatory, recommended, or permissible whereas evil actions will be prohibited. Whereas Ashʿarī and traditionalist scholars will consider most actions to have no ontological ethical quality; their moral and deontic status are acquired after the advent of revelation.[15]

Modern and medieval jurists often see the *ratio legis*, not only as the 'cause' behind a deontic qualification, but also as a sign for the benefit (*maṣlaḥa*) that this deontic qualification is attempting to realize.[16] Being seen as the 'cause' behind a deontic qualification

---

[15] This debate can only be mentioned very briefly here. Presenting the debate, as I do, as one between mutually exclusive dichotomies is an over simplification. The positions of the Muʿtazilīs, the Ashʿarīs and the traditionalists are certainly different, but they overlap in some respects. However, going into the details of their debates is beyond the scope of this chapter. The following monograph include surveys of this debate and its relationship to the law-making process in Islam: Reinhart, *Before Revelation*. In addition, there is an extensive literature on Muslim moral thought, the following is only a sample that provides enough detail on the various positions adopted by different theological schools: Oliver Leaman, *An Introduction to Classical Islamic Philosophy*, 2nd ed. (Cambridge: Cambridge University Press, 2004), 147–173; Sophia Vasalou, *Moral Agents and their Deserts: The Character of Muʿtazilite Ethics* (Princeton: Princeton University Press, 2008); George Hourani, *Reason and Tradition in Islamic Ethics* (Cambridge: Cambridge University Press, 1985); Muḥammad al-Sayyid al-Jalaynad, *Qaḍiyyat al-khayr wa-l-sharr fi-l-fikr al-Islāmī*, 2nd ed. (Cairo: Maṭbaʿat al-Ḥalabī, 1981).

[16] Nādiya Sharīf al-ʿUmarī, *al-Qiyās fi-l-tashrīʿ al-Islāmī* (Giza, Egypt: Dār Hajr li-l-Ṭibāʿa wa-l-Nashr wa-l-Tawzīʿ, 1407/1987), 5; Shaʿbān Muḥammad Ismāʿīl, *Dirāsāt ḥawl al-ijmāʿ wa-l-qiyās* (Alexandria: Maktabat al-Nahḍa al-Miṣriyya, 1989), 200; Ahmad Hasan, 'Rationality of Islamic Legal Injunctions: The Problem of Valuation (*taʿlīl*)', *Islamic Studies* [Islamabad] 13 (1974): 101–2. For pre-modern scholars, see for instance Abū

should make the theological debates around causality relevant to determining the function of *rationes legis* in *qiyās*. The *ratio legis* being perceived as the motivation or benefit behind a deontic qualification should make the theological controversies around God's commitment to human benefit and moral epistemology relevant to debates around the use of the *ratio legis* and *qiyās* in law-making. Given that these theological debates are relevant to the task of the *ratio legis* in *qiyās*, one then assumes to find them informing those aspects of *qiyās* that are relevant to the *ratio legis*. Chiefly among those aspects are the debates around deducing the *ratio legis* and its role in *qiyās*.

By influencing the *ratio legis* and its deduction process (both being the crux of *qiyās*) the above theological debates should have the opportunity to leave an impact on the whole process of *qiyās*. If this assumption is accurate, one would expect to see Muʿtazilīs forming a unique theory of *qiyās* based on their theology, the Ashʿarīs forming a unique theory of *qiyās* that is in harmony with (or dictated by) their theology, and the same would apply to the traditionalists as well. The aim of the following sections is to examine to what extent is the four jurists' concepts of *qiyās* are similar or different and find out in what way, if ever, did the above theological debates inform their perceptions of *qiyās* as a legal tool.

CAUSALITY AND THE *RATIO LEGIS*

The *ratio legis* is unanimously seen as the most important component of *qiyās*. The majority of Muslim jurists, excluding some Ḥanafīs, hold that there are four pillars (*arkān*, sing. *rukn*) for any *qiyās*, namely: the original case, the deontic qualification, the *ratio legis* and the novel case. ʿAbd al-Ḥakīm al-Saʿdī notes that the majority of Ḥanafī scholars consider the *ratio legis* as the only pillar of

---

Isḥāq al-Shīrāzī, *al-Tabṣira fī uṣūl al-fiqh*, 2nd ed. ed. Muḥammad Ḥasan Hītū (Damascus: Dār al-Fikr, 1403/1983), 453, 481; Fakhr al-Dīn Muḥammad b. ʿUmar b. al-Ḥusayn al-Rāzī (d. 606/1209), *al-Maḥṣūl fī ʿilm uṣūl al-fiqh*, 2nd ed. 6vols ed. Ṭāhā Jābir Fayyāḍ al-ʿUlwānī (Beirut: Muʾassasat al-Risāla, 1412/1992), 5:284; ʿAbd al-Jabbār, *Mughnī*, 17:290–1, 314, 320, 330; Samʿānī, *Qawāṭiʿ al-adilla*, 4:63, 128, 131; Abū al-Ḥusayn, *Muʿtamad*, 714–5.

qiyās, whereas the remaining three components to be merely conditions (*shurūṭ*).[17] Al-Ghazālī describes the *ratio legis* as the greatest pillar (*al-rukn al-aʿẓam*) of *qiyās*.[18] Al-Shawkānī notes that no qiyās can take place in the absence of a *ratio legis*.[19] Many modern scholars, as well, consider the *ratio legis* as the most important pillar of *qiyās*.[20] Given the function of the *ratio legis*, this can hardly be an exaggeration. The *ratio legis* is what justifies extending the deontic qualification of the original case to the novel case; without the *ratio legis* no *qiyās* is possible. The previous section explained the intertwined relationship between the *ratio legis* and some of the most important theological debates in Islam. This section focuses on the relationship between the *ratio legis* and natural causality (*sababiyya*). How far, and in what way, did the concepts of causality embraced by the four jurists who are the under study informed their perceptions and definitions of the *ratio legis*? Did their disagreements over causality lead to discrepancies in their understandings of the *ratio*

---

[17] ʿAbd al-Ḥakīm ʿAbd al-Raḥmān Asʿd al-Saʿdī, *Mabāḥith al-ʿilla ʿinda al-uṣūliyyīn*, 2nd ed. (Beirut: Dār al-Bashāʾir al-Islāmiyya, 1421/2000), 64. Al-Saʿdī does not mention examples of Ḥanafī jurists who hold this position. Ahmad Hasan singles out Fakhr al-Islām al-Bazdawī (d. 482/1089) and Abū Bakr al-Sarakhsī (d. 490/1096), as among those Ḥanafīs, see his 'The Legal Cause in Islamic Jurisprudence: An Analysis of 'illat al-ḥukm', *Islamic Studies* [Islamabad] 19.4 (1980), 247.

[18] Abū Ḥāmid Muḥammad b. Muḥammad al-Ghazālī (d. 505/1111), *Shifāʾ al-ghalīl fī bayān al-shabah wa-l-mukhīl wa-masālik al-taʿlīl*, ed. Ḥamad al-Kabīsī (?) (Baghdad: Maṭbaʿat al-Irshād, 1390/1971), 20.

[19] Muḥammad b. ʿAlī al-Shawkānī (d. 1255/1839), *Irshād al-fuḥūl fī taḥqīq al-ḥaqq min ʿilm al-uṣūl*, ed. Abū Ḥafṣ Sāmī b. al-ʿArabī al-Atharī (Riyadh: Dār al-Faḍīla, 1421/2000), 870.

[20] For example, see Mohammad Hashim Kamali, *Principles of Islamic Jurisprudence*, 3rd ed. (Cambridge: Islamic Texts Societies, 2003), 265, 274; ʿĀdil al-Shūwaykh, *Taʿlīl al-aḥkām fi-l-sharīʿa al-Islāmiyya* (Tanta, Egypt: Dār al-Bashāʾir li-l-Thaqāfa wa-l-ʿUlūm, 1420/2000), 127; ʿAbd al-Wahhāb Khallāf, *ʿIlm uṣūl al-fiqh*, 8th ed. (n.p.: Maktabat al-Daʿwa al-Islāmiyya, 2002), 63; Muḥammad Maḥmūd Farghalī, *Buḥūth fi-l-qiyās* (Alexandria: Dār al-Kitāb al-Jāmiʿī, 1981), 27; al-Saʿdī, *Mabāḥith al-ʿilla*, 13, 64, 67; Vikør, *Between God and the Sultan*, 58; Hallaq, *Sharīa*, 101.

legis and their perception of its functions in *qiyās*? I now turn to these questions.

Defining the *Ratio Legis*

One expects those jurists who accept natural causality, i.e. natural causes (*ʿilal ʿaqliyya*) are essentially effective (*mūjiba*) regardless of divine intervention, to accept juridical causality, i.e. *rationes legis* (*ʿilal sharʿiyya*) are essentially effective in producing their deontic qualifications.[21] To harmonize their legal theory and theology, their perception and definition of the *ratio legis* should mirror their position on natural causality. On the other hand, one should not be surprised to see scholars who reject natural causality rejecting also juridical causality. A jurist who accepts natural causality but rejects juridical causality must explain why, or else there would be some tension between his legal theory and his theology.

I study each of the four Shāfiʿīs' perception of *rationes legis* through analysing their definitions of this term. Unfortunately, only

---

[21] Essentially effective is the translation I choose for *mūjiba bi-dhātihā*, *muʾaththira bi-dhātihā*, or simply *mūjiba* or *muʾaththira*. A *ratio legis* or a natural cause that is essentially effective is capable of independently producing and determining its effect without extra assistance. The effect will automatically occur whenever the *ratio legis* or the natural cause occurs. Jurists/theologians who accept natural and juridical causality see the *ratio legis* and the natural cause as essentially effective. For them, both types of causes ontologically include elements that will inevitably lead to the occurrence of their effects. Those who reject natural and juridical causality see them not as essentially effective (sg. *ghayr mūjiba*). In other words, the occurrence of the *ratio legis* or the natural cause in itself does not necessarily entail the occurrence of the 'effect'. There is nothing in the ontological being of the *ratio legis* or the natural cause that determines a particular 'effect'. In this model, a *ratio legis* or a natural cause needs extra assistance to produce what seems to be its effect. This extra assistance comes in the form of divine intervention; God creates the 'effect' each time the natural cause obtains. It is God who assigns a particular *ratio legis* as a sign for a particular deontic qualification without both being logically or causally connected. In this second understanding, there is no real causal or logical relationship between the 'cause' and the 'effect'.

Shīrāzī explicitly states his definition of the *ratio legis*. Samʿānī mentions two definitions that he attributes to unnamed scholars; he does not rebut them indicating that he accepts both.[22] ʿAbd al-Jabbār does not exactly define the term *ratio legis* in volume seventeen of his major work *Mughnī*.[23] However, he describes some of the characters of the *ratio legis* that are relevant to the question of causality. Juwaynī does not define the *ratio legis* in his legal theory literature, but he briefly discusses the relationship between causality and the *ratio legis*, which will allow us to deduce his position on the relationship between the two. Let me first start by presenting the available definitions and descriptions of the *ratio legis* in the table below.

Scholar	Definition or description of a *ratio legis*
ʿAbd al-Jabbār	'by a *ratio legis* we are referring to [something] that is relevant to the deontic qualification, without it the deontic qualification will not obtain'.[24] *'wa-l-ladhī yufīd qawlunā ʿilla anna lahu taʾthīr fi-l-ḥukm ḥattā lawlāhu kāna lā-yakūn dhālika al-ḥukm'*.
ʿAbd al-Jabbār	'a juridical *ratio legis* is one of two things: the reason behind an action becoming beneficial or the motive behind performing an action'.[25] *'inna al-ʿilla al-samʿiyya lā-takhruj ʿann hādhayn al-qismayn: aḥaduhumā mā-li-ajlihi ṣār al-fiʿil luṭfa^an^. Wa-l-thānī mā-li-ajlihi yufʿal al-fiʿl wa-tadʿū ilayhi al-dawāʿī'*.
Shīrāzī	'a *ratio legis* in religious law [i.e. the juridical *ratio legis*] is the quality that determines the deontic qualification'[26]

[22] In legal theory literature, it is common for authors to mention definitions (or opinions) only to refute them. An author who mentions a definition without objecting to it is a sign that he actually accepts it.

[23] In his compendium of ʿAbd al-Jabbār's technical terminology, Sāmiḥ Dughaym has an entry for '*ratio legis*' (*ʿilla sharʿiyya*) and another for '*rationes legis*' (*ʿilal sharʿiyya*), see his *Mawsūʿat muṣṭalaḥāt al-Ashʿarī wa-l-Qāḍī ʿAbd al-Jabbār* (Beirut: Maktabat Lubnān, 2002), 2:420, 422 respectively. Both entries contain quotations from ʿAbd al-Jabbār's literature in which both terms occur. None of these quotations is a definition of the term '*ratio legis*'.

[24] ʿAbd al-Jabbār, *Mughnī*, 17:285.

[25] ʿAbd al-Jabbār, *Mughnī*, 17:290.

	'al-ʿilla fi-l-sharʿ hiya al-maʿnā al-ladhī yaqtaḍī al-ḥukm'
Samʿānī	'As for the definition of the *ratio legis*, they say: it is the feature that brings about the deontic qualification. Others say it is the quality stimulating the deontic qualification'.[27] *'wa-ammā ḥadd al-ʿilla fa-qad qālū innahā al-ṣifa al-jāliba li-l-ḥukm. Wa-qīl: annahā al-maʿnā al-muthīr li-l-ḥukm'*.

At first sight, the above definitions of the *ratio legis* indicate that all four scholars see the *ratio legis* as essentially effective in producing the deontic qualification. None of them mentions divine intervention as a necessary factor in enabling the *ratio legis* to occasion a deontic qualification. ʿAbd al-Jabbār's first statement describes the *ratio legis* as something relevant in producing the deontic qualification. He adds that in its absence the deontic qualification will not occur. This entails that, for him, the *ratio legis* is the decisive factor brining about the deontic qualification. His second statement describes the *ratio legis* as the benefit (*luṭf*),[28] motive, and reason behind the deontic qualification. In other words, it is the *raison d'être* behind the deontic qualification. Without the *ratio legis* there would be no reason for the deontic qualification to exist.

Shīrāzī's definition of the *ratio legis* describes it as the quality that determines the deontic qualification. In other words, it is the decisive factor in determining and occasioning the deontic qualification. His use of the word 'determine' (*yaqtaḍī*) is demonstrative of this meaning. The word *yaqtaḍī* comes from the three letter root *q-ḍ-ā*, which is a strong verb denoting, among several meanings, ne-

---

[26] Abū Isḥāq Ibrāhīm b. ʿAlī b. Yūsuf al-Firūzabādī al-Shīrāzī, *al-Lumaʿ fī uṣūl al-fiqh*, ed. Muḥyī al-Dīn Mistū and Yūsuf ʿAlī Bidīwī (Beirut: Dār al-Kalim al-Ṭayyib, 1416/1995), 215. Similar definitions of the *ratio legis* are also repeated in Abū Isḥāq Ibrāhīm b. ʿAlī b. Yūsuf al-Shīrāzī, *al-Mulakhkhaṣ fi-l-jadal fī uṣūl al-fiqh* in Muḥammad Yūsuf Ākhindijān Niyāzī, '*al-Mulakhkhaṣ fi-l-jadal fī uṣūl al-fiqh*', (M.A. diss., University of Umm al-Qurā, 1987), 25; Shīrāzī, *Sharḥ al-Lumaʿ*, 833.

[27] Samʿānī, *Qawāṭiʿ al-adilla*, 4:187.

[28] The term *luṭf* is a unique Muʿtazilī term. As mentioned before, it is a reference to God's commitment to facilitate human salvation. However, it is also often a reference to benefit or *maṣlaḥa*. On this point, see Zysow, 'Two Theories of the Obligation', 400.

cessity and determinacy. From this three letter root we have the words *qāḍī* (judge), *qaḍā'* (judiciary), *qaḍā* (to judge or impose) and *qaḍā' wa-qadar* (predetermined destiny), all terms designating forceful imposition. The use of this root to describe the relationship between the *ratio legis* and the deontic qualification indicates that the former necessitates or determines the occurrence of the latter. Samʿānī's definitions are not very different. His first definition describes the *ratio legis* as the feature (*ṣifa*) that brings about the deontic qualification.[29] The second definition is similar. It pictures the *ratio legis* as the stimulating factor (*al-maʿnā al-muthīr*) behind the deontic qualification. Both definitions give the impression that the *ratio legis* is the 'cause' and the deontic qualification is its 'effect'.

All of the previously mentioned definitions are framing the relationship between the *ratio legis* and the deontic qualification in causal terms. They present the *ratio legis* as something like a 'cause' and the deontic qualification appears to be the 'effect'. None of the above definitions makes this apparently 'causal' relationship contingent on any factor other than the *ratio legis* itself. None of them award divine intervention or revelation a role in creating this 'causal' relationship.

This should not be a problem for ʿAbd al-Jabbār, since he accepts natural causality; one expects to see him acknowledging juridical causality as well. The Ḥanafī jurist Ṣadr al-Sharīʿa al-Maḥbūbī (d. 747/1346) argues that the Muʿtazilī acceptance of juridical causality is a product of their adoption of natural causality and their belief in God's commitment to optimal human benefit. He notes that those who hold that a natural cause is essentially effective, will also hold that a *ratio legis* is essentially effective. Ṣadr al-Sharīʿa adds that those who hold that a natural cause is not essentially effective will also hold that a *ratio legis* is not essentially effective.[30] A number

[29] The translation of *ṣifa* as feature is borrowed from Weiss, *Search for God's Law*, 546, 555.

[30] Ṣadr al-Sharīʿa ʿUayb Allāh b. Masʿūd al-Maḥbūbī (d. 747/1346), *al-Tawḍīḥ li-matn al-tanqīḥ fī uṣūl al-fiqh*, published in Saʿd al-Dīn Masʿūd b. ʿUmar al-Taftāzānī (d. 792/1390), *Sharḥ al-Talwīḥ ʿalā al-tawḍīḥ li-matn al-tanqīḥ fī uṣūl al-fiqh*, 2 vols ed. Zakariyyā ʿUmayrāt (Beirut: Dār al-Kutub al-ʿIlmiyya, 1416/1996), 2:132–5.

of modern scholars adopt a position similar to that of Ṣadr al-Sharīʿa al-Maḥabūbī. Ahmad Hasan, ʿAlī Sāmī al-Nashshār, Muḥammad Farghalī and ʿAbd al-Ḥakīm al-Saʿdī hold that the Muʿtazilī acceptance of juridical causality is the direct outcome of their acceptance of natural causality. For them, a jurist who accepts natural causality must also accept juridical causality; the latter legal position appears as the logical outcome of the former theological position; if causes are essentially effective in the natural universe why would not they be also essentially effective in the 'sharʿī universe'.[31]

Furthermore, Sayf al-Dīn al-Āmidī (d. 631/1233), Jamāl al-Dīn al-Asnawī (d. 772/1370), in addition to Muḥammad b. ʿAlī al-Shawkānī (d. 1255/1839) all argue that the Muʿtazilī acceptance of juridical causality is a consequence of their belief in a rational moral epistemology.[32] The modern jurists ʿAlī al-Ḍuwayḥī and Muḥammad Farghalī accept this analysis. They note that Muʿtazilīs believe that actions have an ontological moral quality, either good or evil. Their ontological goodness or evilness is the reason behind religion prescribing (in case of goodness) or proscribing (in case of evilness) them.[33] The deontic qualification attached to each action is a result of the ontological moral quality of its *ratio legis*. In other

---

[31] ʿAlī Sāmī al-Nashshār, *Manāhij al-baḥth ʿind mufakkirī al-Islām* (Beirut: Dār al-Nahḍa al-ʿArabiyya, 1404/1984), 44, 104; Hasan, 'The Legal Cause', 260; Farghalī, *Buḥūth fi-l-qiyās*, 133; al-Saʿdī, *Mabāḥith al-ʿilla*, 93. Farghalī is an Egyptian professor of legal theory at the Faculty of Sharīʿa and Law, al-Azhar University. ʿAlī Sāmī al-Nashshār was an Egyptian professor of Islamic Philosophy. He taught at the University of Alexandria and Muhammad the Fifth University, Rabat. ʿAbd al-Ḥakīm al-Saʿdī is a professor at the Faculty of Sharīʿa, University of Qatar.

[32] Jamāl al-Dīn ʿAbd al-Raḥīm b. al-Ḥasan al-Asnawī (d. 772/1370), *Nihāyat al-sūl fī sharḥ minhāj al-uṣūl*, 4 vols (Beirut (?): ʿĀlam al-Kutub, 1982(?)), 4:55; Shawkānī, *Irshād al-fuḥūl*, 870.

[33] ʿAlī b. Saʿd b. Ṣāliḥ al-Ḍuwayḥī, *Ārāʾ al-Muʿtazila al-uṣūliyya* (Riyadh: Maktabat al-Rushd, 1415/1995), 404; Farghalī, *Buḥūth fi-l-qiyās*, 129–31. Al-Ḍuwayḥī is a Ḥanbalī jurist from Saudi Arabia. He is a professor of legal theory at the Faculty of Sharīʿa, Muḥammad b. Saʿūd Islamic University branch in al-Ahsa.

words, divine intervention does not necessarily have to interfere to create a link between a *ratio legis* and its deontic qualification. Therefore, for the above jurists, the Muʿtazilī acceptance of juridical causality is the result of their acceptance of the existence of an ontological moral quality for acts and their adoption of rational moral epistemology.

Given the above explanations, one might then conclude that ʿAbd al-Jabbār's acceptance of juridical causality and his descriptions of the *ratio legis* as the 'cause' behind the deontic qualification are in harmony with his theology. This would entail that Shīrāzī's, Samʿānī's and Juwaynī's *apparent* acceptance of juridical causality runs against their theology. All three adopt a theology that rejects, to a great extent, natural causality, rational moral epistemology and undermines the ability of human reason to ascertain the purpose of divine legislations. The concept of *qiyās* rests on finding a cause and effect relationship between the deontic qualification and the *ratio legis* and recognizing the benefit behind deontic qualifications, therefore one *might be tempted* to assume that the Ashʿarī acceptance of *qiyās* as a legal tool, runs against their theology. This is a point that is noticed by pre-modern non-Ashʿarī jurists and theologians in addition to modern scholars such as Aron Zysow, Muḥammad al-Ṭāhir b. ʿĀshūr and Muḥammad Muṣṭafā Shalabī.[34]

---

[34] Zysow, *Economy of Certainty*, 198–201. Zysow mentions Ibn Taymiyya (d. 728/1328), Ibn Qayyim al-Jawziyya (d. 751/1350), the Twelver Muḥammad Bāqir al-Bihbihānī (d. 1205/1791) and the Zaydī Ibn al-Wazīr (d. 840/1434) as among those who saw a contradiction between Ashʿarī theology and their acceptance of the probative value of *qiyās*. Zysow's comments are part of his analysis of the method of suitability (*munāsaba*), a method used to deduce the *ratio legis* in *qiyās*. He argues that the use of this method seems to contradict Ashʿarī theology, see his *Economy of Certainty*, 199–200. See also, Muḥammad Muṣṭafā Shalabī, *Taʿlīl al-aḥkām*, 2nd ed. (Beirut: Dār al-Nahḍa al-ʿArabiyya, 1981), 105–6; Muḥammad al-Ṭāhir b. ʿĀshūr, *Tafsīr al-taḥrīr wa-l-tanwīr*, 2 vols (Tunis: al-Dār al-Tūnisiyya li-l-Nashr, n.d.), 1:380–1. Both sources quoted in al-Shtīwī, *ʿAlāqat ʿilm uṣūl al-fiqh bi-ʿilm al-kalām*, 660–1. See also al-Shtīwī's discussion of the connections between Ashʿarī theology and *qiyās*, p. 653–

Are Juridical Causes Truly Essentially Effective?

Let me start by saying that the oft-assumed position that there is a contradiction between aspects of Ashʿarī theology and their acceptance of *qiyās* seems to me inaccurate. Accepting this contradiction is based on the assumption that scholars who accept *qiyās* must also accept juridical causality.[35] It also takes for granted that *rationes legis* behave just like natural causes. Therefore, a jurist who holds that natural causes are essentially effective must also consider *rationes legis* to be essentially effective, and vice versa. It is also based on the assumption that Ashʿarī and traditionalist scholars see *rationes legis* as essentially effective. If these assumptions are wrong, there would be no contradiction between Ashʿarī moral epistemology and their rejection of natural causality, on one hand, and their acceptance of the probative value of *qiyās*, on the other.

All three assumptions are not entirely accurate. Although the above definitions/descriptions of the *ratio legis* imply that it plays a deterministic role in causing the occurrence of the deontic qualification, a closer look at the legal theory literature shows that all four Shāfiʿīs reject such a causal relationship. In other words, they reject juridical causality; for them a *ratio legis* is not essentially effective. Moreover, all four jurists make a clear distinction between natural causes and *rationes legis*, showing that the rules that apply to the former do not necessarily apply to the latter. One of the main differences between both types of 'causes' or *ʿilal* is that natural causes are essentially effective (Ashʿarīs would say they become essentially effective after divine intervention) whereas a *ratio legis* is never essentially effective. The latter is only a sign (*ʿalāma*); the occurrence of which God makes as an indication for the occurrence of the deontic qualification. The *ratio legis* becomes a 'cause' only *bi-jaʿl Jāʿil*, literally, it becomes a 'cause' with the doing of a Doer. However, there is nothing in the ontological being of the *ratio legis* that

64. Al-Shtīwī is a professor of law and legal theory at the High Institute of *Uṣūl al-din*, Ez-zitouna University.

[35] Al-Shtīwī suggests that it is better to accept causality in theology and legal theory or reject them in both disciplines, see his *ʿAlāqat ʿilm uṣūl al-fiqh bi-ʿilm al-kalām*, 663.

logically necessitates the occurrence of a particular deontic qualification.

ʿAbd al-Jabbār cannot be more explicit, he repeatedly states that *rationes legis* are not like natural causes, the latter are essentially effective whereas the former are only signs.[36] He adds that being essentially effective is not even a condition for the validity of a *ratio legis*.[37] For ʿAbd al-Jabbār, a *ratio legis* becomes a motive (*dāʿī*) for a particular deontic qualification only after the advent of revelation. There is nothing in the nature of the *ratio legis* that would lead to the occurrence of the deontic qualification before revelation. It is revelation that informs humans that a specific *ratio legis* is a sign for a particular deontic qualification, unlike fire that will always cause burning before or after revelation. ʿAbd al-Jabbār uses the example of the *ratio legis* behind the prohibition of *khamr* as an illustration. Before the advent of the Muslim revelation, *khamr* was not prohibited. If inebriation (*iskār*) were essentially effective in causing the prohibition of *khamr*, it would have been prohibited before and after revelation alike. However, *khamr* was prohibited only after the advent of revelation; therefore, inebriation became a *ratio legis* only after God made it a sign for prohibition in His revelation.[38] In other words, there is nothing in the nature of inebriation that would logically lead to the prohibition of inebriating beverages. Only via revelation do Muslims know of inebriation as a sign for prohibition.

ʿAbd al-Jabbār even argues that the idea of a *ratio legis* being essentially effective runs against foundational Muʿtazilī theological tenets. He argues that if *rationes legis* were essentially effective, this would indicate that humans are forced by the [logical] power of the essentially effective *ratio legis* to follow revelation, and this would threaten the concept of choice (*ikhtiyār*), i.e. humans freely choosing to follow revelation. If the choice factor is undermined then the concept of obligation (*taklīf*) would be, in turn, undermined. Hu-

---

[36] ʿAbd al-Jabbār, *Mughnī*, 17:282, 290, 335, 345–6. Elsewhere he mentions two more minor differences between natural causes and *rationes legis*, see his *Mughnī*, 17:342–3.

[37] ʿAbd al-Jabbār, *Mughnī*, 17:335.

[38] ʿAbd al-Jabbār, *Mughnī*, 17:292.

mans then would not deserve reward for voluntarily following revelation.[39] Furthermore, ʿAbd al-Jabbār argues that since divine legislations are based on benefits (*maṣāliḥ wa-alṭāf*), therefore no *ratio legis* can be essentially effective. Benefits change from one age to another; the same action can be useful before revelation (thus permitted), but harmful after revelation (thus proscribed). Thus, the immediate benefit resulting from an action/object is what determines its deontic qualification, rather than any essential [or rather ontological] character within an action/object.[40]

As mentioned above, a number of medieval and modern scholars argue that the Muʿtazilī acceptance of natural causality and rational moral epistemology led them to perceive *rationes legis* as essentially effective in producing their deontic qualifications. This understanding is probably a result of the confusing definitions/descriptions of the *ratio legis* that give the impression of a causal relationship between a *ratio legis* and a deontic qualification. It is important here to note that other Muʿtazilīs such as Abū Bakr al-Jaṣṣāṣ (d. 370/981), Ḥusayn b. ʿAlī al-Ṣaymarī (d. 436/1045), Abū al-Ḥusayn al-Baṣrī (d. 436/1044) and the Zaydī-Muʿtazilī Abū Ṭālib al-Nāṭiq bi-l-Ḥaqq (d. 424/1033) also share ʿAbd al-Jabbār's perception of the non-essentially effective nature of the *ratio legis*.[41]

---

[39] ʿAbd al-Jabbār, *Mughnī*, 17:282, 291–2.

[40] ʿAbd al-Jabbār, *Mughnī*, 17:282, 292, 345–6.

[41] Ḥusayn b. ʿAlī al-Ṣaymarī (d. 436/1045), *Kitāb Masāʾil al-khilāf fī uṣūl al-fiqh* in Abdelouahad Jahdani 'Les problems de divergences en méthodologie juridique: Presentation, analyse et edition critique' (PhD diss., Universite de Provence, 1991), 234, 254; Abū al-Ḥusayn al-Baṣrī Muḥammad b. ʿAlī b. al-Ṭayyib [pseudo, Abū Ṭālib Yaḥyā b. al-Ḥusayn al-Nāṭiq bi-l-Ḥaqq (d. 424/1033)], *Sharḥ al-ʿUmad*, 2 vols ed. ʿAbd al-Ḥamīd b. ʿAlī Abū Zunayd (Medina: Maktabat al-ʿUlūm wa-l-Ḥikam, 1410/[1990]), 2:17; Aḥmad b. ʿAlī al-Rāzī al-Jaṣṣāṣ (d. 370/981), *Uṣūl al-fiqh al-musammā al-fuṣūl fi-l-uṣūl*, 4 vols 2nd ed. ed. ʿUjayl Jāsim al-Nashmī (Kuwait: Wizārat al-Awqāf wa-l-Shuʾūn al-Islāmiyya, 1414/1994), 4:10; Abū al-Ḥusayn, *Muʿtamad*, 714–5. A note on *Sharḥ al-ʿUmad*: The book is an edition of MSS vat. ar. 1100, an untitled manuscript preserved at the Biblioteca Apostolica Vaticana. The editor identifies this manuscript as Abū al-Ḥusayn al-Baṣrī's *Sharḥ al-ʿUmad*. However, Wilferd Madelung

Therefore it is inaccurate to attribute this position to all Muʿtazilīs.[42]

The traditionalist Samʿānī and the Ashʿarīs Shīrāzī and Juwaynī have the same perception of the *ratio legis* just like ʿAbd al-Jabbār, despite their disagreements over natural causality. Shīrāzī holds that natural causes are essentially effective (*mūjiba bi-nafsihā*) whereas *rationes legis* are not.[43] For him, a *ratio legis* in itself is not the 'cause' for any deontic qualification. It is revelation that informs humans that a particular *ratio legis* is a sign or a 'cause' for a particular deontic qualification.[44]

Samʿānī is not as consistent as ʿAbd al-Jabbār and Shīrāzī. At one point in his *Qawāṭiʿ al-adilla*, he equates between natural causes and *rationes legis* saying that both become essentially effective after 'the doing of a Doer', i.e. after divine intervention. He writes that

> juridical *rationes legis* are essentially effective (*mūjiba*) just like natural causes (*ʿillal ʿaqliyya*). We see no difference between

---

argues that vat. ar. 1100 is rather *al-Mujzī fī uṣūl al-fiqh* authored by the Zaydī-Muʿtazilī Abū Ṭālib Yaḥyā b. al-Ḥusayn al-Nāṭiq bi-l-Ḥaqq. What supports Madelung's opinion is the discovery of further manuscripts of *Mujzī* (e.g. MSS. ar. E. 409 preserved in Biblioteca Ambrosiana) that are identical with the manuscript Abū Zunayd erroneously identifies as Abū al-Ḥusayn's *Sharḥ al-ʿUmad*. For Madelung's argument, see his *Der Imam al-Qasim b. Ibrahim*, 178–80. For Abū Zunayd's identification of the manuscript, see his introduction to *Sharḥ al-ʿUmad*, 1:22–5. It was Sabine Schmitdke who informed me of the Biblioteca Ambrosiana manuscript in a personal e-mail correspondence on the 20th of March 2010.

[42] Among the few modern scholars who reject attributing this position to all Muʿtazilīs is Khazna 'al-Ikhtilāfāt al-uṣūliyya', 241–2; al-Shtīwī, *ʿAlāqat ʿilm uṣūl al-fiqh bi-ʿilm al-kalām*, 642–3. Khazna is an associate professor at the Faculty of Sharīʿa and Law, Al-Asmarya University for Islamic Sciences, Libya.

[43] Shīrāzī, *Tabṣira*, 421; Shīrāzī, *Sharḥ al-Lumaʿ*, 763, 764, 834–5.

[44] Shīrāzī, *Tabṣira*, 421; Shīrāzī, *Sharḥ al-Lumaʿ*, 763–5, 790, 887, 946.

> them. A cause does not become a cause, only revelation turns it into a cause.[45]

This is perfectly fine, since, for him as a traditionalist scholar (as well as for Ashʿarīs), natural causes become effective also after divine intervention.[46] God has been creating (by custom or *ʿāda*) the same 'effect' each time the same 'cause' occurs since the beginning of creation.[47] However, God turned *rationes legis* into signs for particular deontic qualifications at a relatively very late stage, only after the advent of the Muslim revelation. Juwaynī and Shīrāzī would probably not object to Samʿānī's above statement. However, Samʿānī's statement is unique; the two other jurists, as far as I can discern, do not use the term essentially effective or *mūjiba* to describe *rationes legis.* Moreover, they are keen, for reasons discussed below, to consistently make a clear distinction between natural causes and *rationes legis.*

Despite the above quotation, earlier in the same book Samʿānī adopts a position identical to that of ʿAbd al-Jabbār, Shīrāzī and Juwaynī. Samʿānī's imaginary interlocutor argues against *qiyās* say-

---

[45] Samʿānī, *Qawāṭiʿ al-adilla*, 4: 320. Also see *Qawāṭiʿ al-adilla*, 4:401 where he says that a *ʿilla* is *mūjiba*, i.e. essentially effective.

[46] For his rejection of natural causality, see Samʿānī, *Qawāṭiʿ al-adilla*, 4:525–6.

[47] I borrow Wolfson's translation of *ʿāda* as custom. *ʿĀda* is a theological term usually, but not exclusively, used by Ashʿarī scholars to explain the regularity and predictability of events in this world without adopting causality. It refers to the fact that it is the customary habit of God to create the same 'effect' each time the same 'cause' occurs. For example, God always creates burning each time fire touches wood; He creates pain each time a sharp object penetrates a human body etc… Fire and sharp objects are not the actual causes for their effects. They only appear to humans as such because of the customary habit of God to create their 'effects' each time they occur. For more details on this term, see Harry A. Wolfson, *The Philosophy of the Kalām* (Cambridge: Harvard University Press, 1976), 544–58; Muhrā Ḥasan Abū Saʿda, *al-Ittijāh al-ʿaqlī fi mushkilat al-maʿrifa ʿinda al-Muʿtazila* (Cairo: Dār al-Fikr al-ʿArabī, 1993), 142; Sobhi Rayan 'Al-Ghazâlî's Use of the Terms Darûrah and ʿâdah in his Theory of Causality', *Islamic Culture* 78.3 (2004): 77–98.

ing that *rationes legis* cannot function as a reason or a cause behind a deontic qualification. If they were 'actual causes', they would have been just like natural ones, essentially effective before and after revelation. Samʿānī replies saying that

> natural causes are essentially effective, this is why they consistently accompany their effects. [On the other hand] revelation makes *rationes legis* effective (*al-ʿilal al-sharʿiyya mūjiba bi-l-sharʿ*). This is why they are extraneously imposed on their effects (*fa-ṣārat ṭāriʾa ʿalā maʿlūlahā*). Therefore, both [i.e. natural causes and *rationes legis*] are different. This is because religious laws are based on benefits (*al-sharāʾiʿ maṣāliḥ*). It may be that one thing is a benefit in one particular age (*zamān*) but not in another. This is why the laws of prophets, peace upon them, are not the same. Thus they [i.e. these laws] may be abrogated. Therefore, a *ratio legis* may be not essentially effective before revelation, because it brings about no benefit. After revelation it may [become] essentially effective, because it leads to a benefit. This is the answer of the speculative theologians.[48]

In the second quotation, Samʿānī is clearly distinguishing between natural causes and *rationes legis*. The former is essentially effective whereas the latter becomes effective only after revelation makes it effective in bringing about a certain deontic qualification. It is interesting to note here that Samʿānī is using ʿAbd al-Jabbār's argument of benefit (*maṣlaḥa*) to show that *rationes legis* cannot be essentially effective. He notes that revelation (*sharʿ*) aims at realizing benefit. Benefits change from time to time, what is beneficial in the age before revelation (thus permitted) might be harmful after revelation (thus prohibited). Thus, a *ratio legis* does not consistently lead to the same deontic qualification at all times. This shows that the ontological being of the *ratio legis* does not determine its deontic qualification. It is, rather, revelation that determines the deontic qualification that each *ratio legis* produces, according to the benefit or harms to which it will lead.

---

[48] Samʿānī, *Qawāṭiʿ al-adilla*, 4: 63. For other similar quotations, see *Qawāṭiʿ al-adilla*, 4:197, 392.

I have failed to find Juwaynī's definition of the *ratio legis*. However, there are strong signs showing that his perception of the *ratio legis* is very similar to that of the three other Shāfiʿīs. Again, Juwaynī, distinguishes between natural causes and *rationes legis*. In his *al-Kāfiya fi-l-jadal*, he makes a list of sixteen differences between both; the first three show that natural causes are essentially effective whereas *rationes legis* are not, they become effective only after the advent of revelation.[49] Nothing in the nature of a *ratio legis* causes the occurrence of a particular deontic qualification. It is revelation that turns it into a sign for the occurrence of a specific deontic qualification.[50] Just like the imaginary interlocutors of the previous three Shāfiʿīs, Juwaynī's interlocutor argues against the probative value of *qiyās* saying that if a *ratio legis* were the real reason behind the occurrence of a deontic qualification, it would have been essentially effective just like a natural cause. Juwaynī rejects natural causality and, at the same time, refuses to compare natural causes to *rationes legis* saying that

> *rationes legis* behave in manner different from rational [causes]. Rational judgments are based on essential and ontological features. *Rationes legis* are based on impositions [i.e. what revelation imposes on them], and they do not essentially produce their effects. (*al-ʿillal al-sharʿiyya lā-tajrī majrā al-maʿqūlāt; fa-ʾinna al-aḥkām al-ʿaqliyya tastanid ilā ṣifāt al-anfus wa-l-dhawāt, wa-l-ʿllal al-sharʿiyya mustanaduhā al-naṣb, wa-hiya laysat muqtaḍiyya maʿlūlāthā li-anfusihā*).[51]

Juwaynī offers the same answer as all three previous Shāfiʿī scholars, namely natural causes and *rationes legis* are not the same. The first are essentially effective while the second are not. All four Shāfiʿī scholars are consistently refusing to equate between *rationes legis* and natural causes. They insist that the rules that apply to one do not necessarily apply to the other.

---

[49] Imām al-Ḥaramayn al-Juwaynī, *al-Kāfiya fi-l-jadal*, ed. Fawqiyya Ḥusayn Maḥmūd (Cairo: Maṭbaʿat ʿIsā al-Bābī al-Ḥalabī, 1979), 14–6.

[50] Juwaynī, *Burhān*, 837–8, 984–5, 1000, 1002.

[51] Juwaynī, *Burhān*, 1097.

Distancing Causality from *qiyās*

All four Shāfiʿī scholars I examined here have the same perception of the *ratio legis*, i.e. it is not essentially effective. It is rather revelation that determines its 'effect'.[52] One must ask why all four Shāfiʿī scholars, despite their profound theological disagreements (especially concerning causality), unanimously adopt the same position on *rationes legis*? As mentioned above, a number of medieval and modern scholars see that debates around natural causality, moral epistemology, moral ontology and God's commitment to human optimal benefit as theological issues that *should* influence a jurist's perception of the *ratio legis* and the probative value of *qiyās*. One would expect to find scholars who accept natural causality and rational moral epistemology to perceive *rationes legis* as essentially effective whereas those who hold the opposite theological positions to see *rationes legis* as essentially non-effective. Moreover, the whole process of *qiyās* itself assumes an acceptance of some form of causality and rational moral epistemology. It also assumes that humans can uncover the good God intends from His legislations. Therefore, there *seems* to be an *apparent* 'elective affinity' between accepting these theological positions and accepting the probative value of *qiyās*.[53] There appears also to be an *apparent* 'elective affinity' be-

---

[52] This perception is common among the majority of scholars who accept *qiyās*. See for example Abū al-Thanāʾ Maḥmūd b. Zayd al-Lāmishī (died 6th/12th century), *Kitāb Fī Uṣūl al-fiqh*, ed. ʿAbd al-Majīd Turkī (Beirut: Dār al-Gharb al-Islāmī, 1995), 191; Ghazālī, *Mustaṣfā*, 4:721; Ibn Burhān, *al-Wuṣūl ilā al-uṣūl*, 2:267; Samarqandī, *Mīzān al-uṣūl*, 863; Shawkānī, *Irshād al-fuḥūl*, 871. This is why Weiss rightly comments on translating the term *ʿilla* as 'cause' saying 'the term 'cause' must here be understood somewhat loosely and not in terms of strict necessity or determinism. The intoxicating quality of wine does not in itself necessitate its being prohibited. Rather it is always the will of God that is the true necessitating factor, the real determinant of rules', see his *Spirit of Islamic Law*, 67.

[53] I borrow Christian Lange's use of this 'Weberian' term in reference to the possible connections between particular theological doctrines and specific positions in legal theory. For Lange's use of this term in a similar context, see his *Justice*, 188; Lange, 'Sins, Expiation', 143–75.

tween rejecting those theological positions and rejecting the probative value of *qiyās*.[54] However, none of these 'elective affinities' seem to be operative here; all four Shāfiʿī scholars despite their contradicting theological positions accept the probative value of *qiyās* and have the same perception of the *ratio legis*.

Now several questions arise here: How far did their theological doctrines inform their perceptions of the *ratio legis* and their positions from the probative value of *qiyās*? Is there a contradiction between their theologies and their acceptance of *qiyās* as many medieval and modern scholars argue?

All four scholars consistently differentiate between natural causes and *rationes legis*. They insist on refusing to compare both types of 'causes'. I have quoted above the attempts by their imaginary interlocutors to equate between *rationes legis* and natural causes, and I have quoted the four scholars' replies to these attempts. All four jurists refuse any argument against *qiyās* that is based on equating *rationes legis* and natural causes. All four scholars are keen to distinguish between both types of 'causes'. This distinction is supposed to function as a barrier that should limit the impact of theological controversies, especially ones around causality, on legal debates around the *ratio legis* and *qiyās*. If natural causes are different from *rationes legis*, it follows that a scholar's position on natural causes should not determine his position on *rationes legis*. Jurists (Sunnīs and Muʿtazilīs) who belong to Sunnī schools of law, by clearly distinguishing between natural causes and juridical causes (i.e. *rationes legis*), are creating for themselves a common ground on which they can create a common perception of *qiyās*, one that is not divided along the lines of their theological disagreements.

The *ratio legis* is made a sign or a 'cause' for a specific deontic qualification by revelation. It is revelation that awards the *ratio legis* its function in *qiyās* rather than an ontological quality within the *ratio legis*. Even those Muʿtazilī scholars who accept rational moral epistemology and hold that acts have an ontological moral quality, acknowledge that revelation may determine the moral value of human acts. Muʿtazilī scholars usually hold that once the veracity of

---

[54] See for example the debates in, al-Shtīwī, *ʿAlāqat ʿilm al-kalām bi-uṣūl al-fiqh*, 639–65.

revelation has been established, a believer can use revelation as a guide for benefits and moral knowledge.[55] The *ratio legis* being sanctioned by revelation assures Muʿtazilīs, Ashʿarīs, and all Muslims, that it is an indicator for benefits and good. For all four jurists it is revelation that makes *rationes legis* capable of producing their deontic qualification. This perception of the *ratio legis* distances it from the theological debates around causality, moral epistemology and moral ontology. Disagreements around those theological debates do not produce significant differences in the jurist's perception of the *ratio legis* and its function in law-making. This allows jurists from various theological backgrounds to share a common perception of the *ratio legis*, regardless of their doctrinal differences.

There is no contradiction between the acceptance of *qiyās*, the above explained perception of the *ratio legis*, on one hand, and any of the theological beliefs of the four Shāfiʿī jurists examined here. All four jurists seem to have, consciously or unconsciously, adopted a theory concerning the *ratio legis* that distances it, as much as possible, from their theological quarrels. This distance limits the discrepancies in their legal theory produced by their theological disagreements. This appears to be an attempt to protect *qiyās* from some of the most controversial theological debates. If these theological debates were left to cause significant discrepancies in each jurist's perception of the *ratio legis*, there could have been different concepts of *qiyās* each attached to a theological trend. It is impossible to have categorically different conceptions of *qiyās* within the

---

55 See for example, ʿAbd al-Jabbār, *Mughnī*, 6:177–99; Abū al-Ḥusayn, *Muʿtamad*, 78, 80–1, 178–80, 403–5, 710–3, 573–4, 908. On Abū al-Ḥusayn al-Baṣrī's moral epistemology, see Mohamed Ahmed Abdelrahman Eissa, 'Abū al-Ḥusayn al-Baṣrī's Use of Reason in *ʿilm al-kalām* and *uṣūl al-fiqh*', *al-Shajarah Journal of the International Institute of Islamic Thought and Civilization* 16.1 (2011), 31–7. There is a huge literature on ʿAbd al-Jabbār's moral epistemology the most famous is Hourani, *Islamic Rationalism.* A more recent publication that focuses on Muʿtazilī ethics with a special emphasis on ʿAbd al-Jabbār and Abū al-Ḥusayn is Sophia Vasalou, *Moral Agents and their Deserts: The Character of Muʿtazilite Ethics* (Princeton: Princeton University Press, 2008).

same legal school. This would not only lead to different theories of *qiyās*, but might also ruin the common legal theory and jurisprudential (*fiqhī*) foundations that distinguish the Shāfiʿī school of law and keeps it intact.[56]

JURISDICTION OF *QIYĀS*

I am not aware of any Muslim jurist who acknowledges the probative value (*ḥujiyya*) of *qiyās* in all aspects of law.[57] The jurists under discussion are not different; all four hold that any original case or deontic qualification whose *ratio legis* is unfathomable to the human mind cannot be the subject of *qiyās*.[58] Examples of such cases are

---

[56] Khazna notes that Irāqī Ḥanafīs –who are usually Muʿtazilī– make a distinction between natural causes and *rationes legis*. Whereas Samarqandī Ḥanafīs –who are usually Māturīdī– do not usually make this distinction. He concludes that the Samarqandī position opened the door for their theology to influence their perception of the *ratio legis* and its role in the process of *qiyās*. Whereas the Irāqī-Ḥanafī distinction between the two types of 'causes' allowed them to isolate their perception of the *ratio legis* from their theology. He adds that the fact that Samarqandī-Ḥanafīs allow their Māturīdī theology to influence this aspect of their legal theory creates disagreements in the use of the *ratio legis* in *qiyās* between both Ḥanafī sub-schools. For Khazna's argument, see his 'al-Ikhtilāfāt al-uṣūliyya', 235–263.

[57] *Ḥujiyya* comes from the three letter root ḥ-j-j. Like many Arabic roots, its derivatives denote very different meanings. Among them is *ḥujāj* (i.e. argument or disputation) and *ḥujja* (i.e. evidence or proof). The term *ḥujjiyya* is used by pre-modern authors in reference to the normative or law-making authority of the Qurʾān, Sunna, or the other non-textual methods of *qiyās*. For example, a scholar who acknowledges the *ḥujjiyya* of *qiyās* accepts it as a method to deduce new laws or a tool to ratify already existing ones. A source or a method that enjoys *ḥujiyya* entails that it can be used as evidence revealing the correct jurisprudential position. This section examines the aspects of law in which *qiyās* enjoys probative value or *ḥujjiyya*.

[58] ʿAbd al-Jabbār, *Mughnī*, 17:329; Juwaynī, *Burhān*, 960; Samʿānī, *Qawāṭiʿ al-adilla*, 4:119–20, 173; Shīrāzī, *Lumaʿ*, 213; Shīrāzī, *Sharḥ al-Lumaʿ*, 825.

the regulations of the five daily prayers, fasting Ramaḍān, and the *ḥajj* rituals.[59] Muslims cannot understand why they are required to pray five times a day and not six, why the first obligatory prayer in the day includes two inclinations (*rakʿa*s) rather than three and why Muslims are required to fast during Ramaḍān and not any other month.

This is not a position unique to the four jurists under study; the majority of Muslim jurists hold that deontic qualifications whose *rationes legis* are not discoverable fall outside the jurisdiction of *qiyās*. Disagreements start to appear when identifying those aspects of *fiqh* whose *rationes legis* cannot be known. The most contentious debates centre on the use of *qiyās* in what is called the *muqaddarāt*.[60] Christian Lange describes the *muqaddarāt* as 'things decreed by God' and he translates the term as 'decreed numerical objects'.[61] The diverse natures of the deontic qualifications subsumed under *muqaddarāt* complicate defining the term. However, there are some common factors among the decreed numerical objects; they are deontic qualifications (*aḥkām sharʿiyya*) explicitly mentioned in textual evidence (either Qur'ān or Sunna), the rationale behind them is not always easy to grasp. They are rather taken as 'givens'.[62] Examples of the *muqaddarāt* are expiations (*kaffārāt*), the divinely ordained punishments (*ḥudūd*), dispensations (*rukhaṣ*), in addition to most rituals (*ʿibādāt*). For example, the punishment for extra-marital sex for an unmarried couple is one hundred lashes (the punishment is contingent on the occurrence of other legal conditions). A traveller traveling more than (in modern measurements) approximately 85 kilometres is exempted from fasting in Ramaḍān. The expiation for breaking an oath is to feed and clothe ten of the poor, free a slave,

---

[59] Juwaynī, *Burhān*, 960; Shīrāzī, *Sharḥ al-Lumaʿ*, 825; Samʿānī, *Qawāṭiʿ al-adilla*, 4:173.

[60] For more details on this debate, see Muḥammad Manẓūr Iālhī, *al-Qiyās fi-l-ʿibādāt: ḥukmuh wa-atharuh* (Riyadh: Maktabat al-Rushd, 1424/2004), 313–644; Rāmī b. Muḥammad Salhab, *al-Qiyās fi-l-ʿibādāt wa-taṭbīqātuh fi-l-madhhab al-Shāfiʿī* (Beirut: Dār Ibn Ḥazm, 2010); Lange, *Justice*, 179–214; Lange, 'Sins, Expiation'.

[61] Lange, *Justice*, 184.

[62] Lange, *Justice*, 188.

or fast three days. Humans cannot exactly understand why God has stipulated these particular numerical values and not others.

Can *qiyās* extend the above *muqaddarāt* to novel cases mentioned neither in the Qur'ān or the Prophetic Sunna? For example, is the punishment for heterosexual extra-marital intercourse applicable to homosexual intercourse? The dispensation relieving a traveller from fasting, can it be extended, via *qiyās*, to someone whose job is excessively exhausting? Jurists who hold that the *rationes legis* behind those *muqaddarāt* are discoverable by the human mind allow extending them to other novel cases via *qiyās*, and vice versa. The majority of Muslim scholars, excluding the Ḥanafīs, accept the use of *qiyās* in the *muqaddarāt*.[63] Although scholars from the remaining three Sunnī schools of law debate against the Ḥanafī position, the debates between Shāfiʿīs and Ḥanafīs are particularly strong. This is a complicated debate and I am here only concerned with examining whether the adoption of particular theological dogmas necessitate a position on this debate or not.

Before surveying the possible influence of speculative theology on this debate, I will first very briefly mention the position of the four jurists under study from the use of *qiyās* in the *muqaddarāt*. Although this will cause some repetition, I will elaborate more on their positions as the argument unfolds. Juwaynī, Shīrāzī and Samʿānī hold that since the *ratio legis* behind the divinely ordained punishments, dispensations and expiations are fathomable, therefore *qiyās* is allowed to extend their deontic qualifications to novel cases.[64] ʿAbd al-Jabbār does not mention his position in enough detail. In volume seventeen of his *Mughnī*, he has two brief consecutive sections in which he mentions the aspects of law in which *qiyās* is disallowed.[65] The *muqaddarāt* as a category is not among them.[66] The only type of *muqaddarāt* that he excludes from the ju-

---

[63] ʿAbd al-Karīm b. ʿAlī b. Muḥammad al-Namla, *al-Muhaẓẓab fī ʿilm uṣūl al-fiqh al-muqāran* (Riyadh: Maktabat al-Rushd, 1999), 1939.

[64] Juwaynī, *Burhān*, 895–902; Samʿānī, *Qawāṭiʿ al-adilla*, 4:119–20.

[65] ʿAbd al-Jabbār, *Mughnī*, 17:324–9.

[66] However, ʿAbd al-Jabbār excludes a type of *muqaddarāt* that has to do with human nature (*khilqa* or *jibilla*), such as the minimum and maximum periods of menstruation and pregnancy. These *muqaddarāt* are im-

risdiction of *qiyās* is dispensations.[67] Although I have not come across a positive statement in which ʿAbd al-Jabbār states that the ordained punishments and expiations lie within the jurisdiction of *qiyās*, the fact that they are not mentioned among the jurisprudential issues excluded from *qiyās* indicate that, for him, they lie within the jurisdiction of *qiyās*. This is particularly the case since he ends one of those sections saying that all other jurisprudential issues, not mentioned, lie within the jurisdiction of *qiyās*.[68]

Speculative Theology and the *muqaddarāt*

In chapter five of his book *Justice, Punishment, and the Medieval Muslim Imagination*, Christian Lange examines the expected impact of some theological dogmas on the position taken on the debate around the probative value of *qiyās* in *muqaddarāt*. To understand his argument, one must remind the reader of few theological positions. The Ashʿarīs adopt a theology that greatly undermines freewill. They adopt a dogma not identical with but close to predestination. Furthermore, the majority of Sunnī scholars, including the Ashʿarīs, refuse natural causality. They adopt an atomistic view of the world in which God creates the effect of the cause, rather than the cause having a direct impact on producing its effect. The Māturīdī School of theology, which attracts many Ḥanafīs, have a position on natural causality that is not categorically different. However, Māturīdīs give humans more role in their choices, adopting only a milder form of 'predestination' if compared to the Ashʿarīs.

Given the above theological positions Lange notes that

> both Ashʿarīs and Māturīdīs maintained that ultimately 'the acts of man are created by God and subject to His will and decree'. This theology – postulating the human incapacity to understand the causes of God's sovereign imposition of life's

---

portant to settle legal cases such as alimony, inheritance, divorce and descent. There is no huge debate whether or not this type of *muqaddarāt* fall within the jurisdiction of *qiyās*, the majority of jurists keep them beyond *qiyās*, see ʿAbd al-Jabbār, *Mughnī*, 17:325.

[67] ʿAbd al-Jabbār, *Mughnī*, 17:328–9.

[68] ʿAbd al-Jabbār, *Mughnī*, 17:329.

> fundamental conditions – bears a certain resemblance, or elective affinity, with the Ḥanafī position that the *muqaddarāt* in the law are 'things whose purpose cannot be apprehended in order to infer judgments'... or things that 'escape the human mind'. The *muqaddarāt* are characterized by the simple imposition of a norm, without specification of either the concrete reason or the larger purpose (*ḥikma*) that lies behind the norm. Instead the *muqaddarāt* are, as it were, 'givens'. Analogical reasoning in the law, on the other hand, requires the jurist to explain, by a process of independent *qiyās*, why a certain factor (*ʿilla*) occasions the rule (*ḥukm al-aṣl*), and with what purpose, and then to investigate whether this occasioning factor also occurs in the case under examination, that is, the novel case. Consequently, the argument goes, the *muqaddarāt* fall outside analogy's scope...[69]

In the above quotation, Lange notes that, given their Māturīdī background that rejects natural causality and adopts a form of 'predestination', the Ḥanafī choice to disallow *qiyās* in *muqaddarāt* is logical if not a deliberate choice based on their dogma. Ashʿarīs share the Māturīdī rejection of natural causality and even adopt a stronger form of 'predestination. Therefore, Lange's above statement implies that the acceptance of *qiyās* in the *muqaddarāt* by Shāfiʿī jurists, who follow the Ashaʿrī creed, runs against the requirements of their theology. This implicit conclusion is explicit in Lange's following statement:

> it could be said that all legal regulations that came to be subsumed under the loose category of *muqaddarāt* have one important feature in common: they all illustrate God's unfathomable purpose in connecting what man calls 'cause' with what man calls 'result'...the denial of causality was first and foremost a character of Ashʿarite theology, traditionally the province of Shafiʿites. Consequently, one would expect the Shāfiʿītes to be more cautious in specifying a cause, or *ratio legis* (*ʿilla*), for the *muqaddarāt*. Surprisingly, however, it is precisely the Shāfiʿīs who embraced analogy in the *muqaddarāt*. That this

[69] Lange, *Justice*, 187–8.

> is in some tension with their adherence to Ashʿarī theology was duly pointed out to them by their opponents, for how could the Shāfiʿīs espouse a theology that denied causality while at the same time claiming that they could apprehend the causal logics of legal statutes, especially of the *muqaddarāt*?[70]

Although Lange does not use the terms 'contradict' or 'contradiction', his conclusion practically entails the presence of a contradiction (or 'tension' to use his terms) between Shāfiʿī-Ashʿarī theology and their acceptance of *qiyās* in *muqaddarāt*. The concept of *qiyās* seems to be based on accepting a form of 'causality' and the human apprehension of the divine purpose behind the law. Lange's conclusion, then, is understandable. The Shāfiʿī-Ashʿarī rejection of natural causality does not only contradict their acceptance of *qiyās* in *muqaddarāt*; it contradicts their acceptance of the probative value of *qiyās* altogether. Therefore, one would expect to see the Shāfiʿī-Ashʿarīs not only rejecting *qiyās* in *muqaddarāt*, but also, at least, reluctant to accept the probative value of *qiyās* in all aspects of law. The same may also apply to Māturīdīs, whose position on these theological issues not significantly different from the Ashʿarīs. Therefore, the Ḥanafī-Māturīdī acceptance of *qiyās* in areas other than the *muqaddarāt* seems to contradict their theology, as well. In fact, the Sunnī jurists' acceptance of the probative value of *qiyās* in general seems to contradict the theologies they usually adopt, theologies that, largely, deny natural causality and make it difficult for the human mind to apprehend the exact divine intention behind the law.[71] As Lange mentions above, opponents of the Ashʿarīs have noted to them the apparent 'contradiction' between their theology and their approval of qiyās. I also assume that Sunnī jurists in general were aware of these criticisms. The question now: how did Sunnī jurists resolve this apparent contradiction?

As mentioned in the section on the definitions of the *ratio legis*, medieval Muslim jurists are aware that their disagreements on natu-

---

[70] Lange, *Justice*, 189.

[71] One must say here that Lange does not conclude that speculative theology has no impact on legal theory. He probably holds the opposite, see for example his *Justice*, 186–7; Lange, 'Sins, Expiation'.

ral causality could or should influence their legal theory. Therefore, to distance their theological disagreements from *qiyās*, they insist that *rationes legis* are different from natural causes, both are two different 'species'. Statements to this effect appear numerous times in the chapters on *qiyās* in all Sunnī and Muʿtazilī legal theory works examined for this study. This entails that both types of 'causes' behave differently and rules that apply to one do not necessarily apply to the other. Therefore, there is no need to harmonize one's position on natural causality and one's position on *qiyās*, in general, and the function of the *ratio legis* in law-making in particular. Thus, theological positions on natural causality should not always influence positions on *rationes legis.* This way a theological position on natural causes does not have to dictate a particular position on *qiyās* or *rationes legis.* Whether differentiating between natural causes and *rationes legis* is a development that preceded the maturation of *qiyās*, or is a theory constructed in retrospect to solve a contradiction that appeared after the formation of *qiyās*, is – due to the paucity of early primary sources – a question that cannot be efficiently answered.

In all cases, distinguishing between both types of 'causes' allow jurists, belonging to the same legal school, to adopt relatively similar perceptions of *qiyās*, despite any doctrinal disagreements. For example, among the major Ḥanafī shibboleths is their rejection of *qiyās* in *muqaddarāt.* As Lange suggests, there seems to be an apparent 'elective affinity' between rejecting natural causality and freewill, on one hand, and disallowing *qiyās* in *muqaddarāt*, on the other. However, even Muʿtazilī-Ḥanafī scholars who adopt freewill and have a more favourable position on natural causality when compared to their Māturīdī counterparts, will still disallow *qiyās* in *muqaddarāt* just like their Ḥanafī-Māturīdī fellows. Among those Muʿtazilīs are Abū Bakr al-Jaṣṣāṣ and Ḥusayn al-Ṣaymarī, both disallow *qiyās* in *muqaddarāt.*[72] Abū al-Ḥusayn al-Baṣrī writes that Abū al-Ḥasan [al-Karkhī], a famous Muʿtazilī-Ḥanafī authority, disallows *qiyās* in *ḥudūd* and implies that he refuses *qiyās* in all *muqaddarāt.*[73] The only Muʿtazilī-Ḥanafī known to me who does not disallow *qiyās* in all *muqaddarāt* is Abū al-Ḥusayn al-Baṣrī himself. He notes

[72] Jaṣṣāṣ, *Fuṣūl*, 4:105–6; Ṣaymarī, *Masāʾil al-khilāf*, 263–5.

[73] Abū al-Ḥusayn, *Muʿtamad*, 794–5.

that *muqaddarāt* should be examined on a case by case basis: and if their *rationes legis* are fathomable the case will lie within the jurisdiction of *qiyās*, but otherwise not. He adds that expiations are among the *muqaddarāt* that lie within the jurisdiction of *qiyās* whereas dispensations are not.[74] This relatively uniform position on this debate is also observable within the Shāfiʿī School. Despite their theological differences, all four Shāfiʿīs under examination accept the probative value of *qiyās* in *muqaddarāt*. The only exception is ʿAbd al-Jabbār who disallows *qiyās* only in dispensations.

If theological debates around causality and the ability of the human mind to ascertain the divine intent from legislations were to have a crucial impact on this debate, there would be no uniform position on it within each single legal school. Positions on the use of *qiyās* in *muqaddarāt* would be divided along theological school lines rather than legal school lines. It is not possible to have categorically different perceptions of *qiyās* and the *ratio legis* within the same school of law. Therefore, jurists have to limit, as much as possible, the impact of theological disagreements on their legal theory, *especially* on those legal theory issues that function as distinguishing marks for legal schools. Otherwise, Sunnī legal schools will not maintain their unity and split into smaller schools, each attaching itself to a theological trend.

DEDUCING THE *RATIO LEGIS*: THE FORMAL METHODS

The term *masālik* is the plural of the singular *maslak*. One of its meanings is a road or a path towards something; it can also denote the method of performing a particular task. The phrase *masālik al-ʿilla* is a reference to the methods (or sources) through which the

---

[74] Abū al-Ḥusayn, *Muʿtamad*, 796. There are other Muʿtazilī scholars who disallow *qiyās* in the *muqaddarāt* or at least in some of them, e.g. ʿAbd al-Jabbār and Abū al-Ḥusayn al-Baṣrī say that Abū ʿAlī al-Jubbāʾī disallows it in *ḥudūd*, see ʿAbd al-Jabbār, *Mughnī*, 17: 324; Abū al-Ḥusayn, *Muʿtamad*, 794. The Zaydī-Muʿtazilī Abū Ṭālib al-Nāṭiq bi-l-Ḥaqq holds the same opinion, see his Abū al-Ḥusayn al-Baṣrī [pseudo], *Sharḥ al-ʿUmad*, 2:118, 125–6. Al-Nāṭiq bi-l-Ḥaqq also mentions that the Muʿtazilī-Ḥanafī Abū ʿAbd Allāh al-Baṣrī (d. 369/980) disallows *qiyās* in *ḥudūd* and expiations, see p. 204–5.

ratio legis behind the deontic qualification of an original case can be known or a putative *ratio legis* may be verified. Simply put, *masālik al-ʿilla* are methods that deduce and/or verify the *ratio legis* behind a particular deontic qualification.[75] The process of deducing the *ratio legis* via these methods is called *taʿlīl* or *istinbāṭ*. This process, as Bernard Weiss rightly notes, is the most important (and I would add controversial) step in *qiyās*.[76]

There are several methods to deduce and verify a *ratio legis*; all are subject to controversy and disagreement.[77] However, there are two main broad types of deduction methods under which all the rest are subsumed, namely textual and non-textual methods. The textual methods can be, more accurately, described as textual sources for the *ratio legis*, namely the Qurʾān, Prophetic Sunna and consensus. As previously noted, a *ratio legis* that is explicitly mentioned in one of the textual evidence is termed an explicit *ratio legis* (*ʿilla manṣūṣa*). In few cases a Qurʾānic verse or a Prophetic tradition would explicitly state the *ratio legis* behind the deontic qualification they mention. A jurist search for a consensus about a *ratio legis* or reads and interprets Qurʾānic verses and Prophetic traditions to understand the *ratio legis* behind a specific deontic qualification these sources mention. Using explicit *rationes legis* in *qiyās* is quite straightforward and unanimously accepted among analogist scholars (i.e. jurists who accept the probative value of *qiyās*). Therefore, it receives little space and attention in legal theory literature when compared to other methods of *taʿlīl*. Accordingly, I do not discuss it here. It is enough to know that all four jurists who are the focus

---

[75] Zysow argues that *masālik al-ʿilla* are methods for validating putative *rationes legis* rather than deducing unknown ones, see his *Economy of Certainty*, 196–7. Hallaq, on the other hand, holds that they are methods of, both, validation and deduction, see his *Islamic Legal Theories*, 89. I am not aware of any pre-modern Muslim jurist who explicitly refers to these methods as ones only for verifying putative *rationes legis*. Therefore, Hallaq's opinion appears to me more convincing. Bernard Weiss seems also to be adopting an opinion similar to Hallaq's, see his *Search for God's Law*, 585–8.

[76] Wiess, *Search for God's Law*, 584.

[77] Hallaq, *Islamic Legal Theories*, 88.

of this study (and probably most analogist scholars as well) consider an explicit *ratio legis* as the strongest and most reliable of all types of *rationes legis*.[78] This should not be surprising since explicit *rationes legis* are to some extent unequivocal and leave little room for doubt and speculation.[79]

The second type of methods that reveal the *ratio legis* are the non-textual methods. Aron Zysow divides them into two categories. The first is what he calls the formal methods and those 'require only that the cause (*ʿilla*) and the deontic qualification (*ḥukm*) appear together without exception'.[80] The formal methods I discuss here are *al-ṭard wa-l-ʿaks* (concomitance) and *al-sabr wa-l-taqsīm* (elimination of alternatives),[81] both are strongly related to logic (*manṭiq*) and dialectics (*jadal*). The second type of the non-textual methods is what Zysow calls material methods. He notes that those 'require some relation of substance between the cause and the rule of law from which it is drawn (*aṣl*)'.[82] For Zysow the material methods are suitability (*munāsaba*) and effectiveness (*ta'thīr*); each is discussed in an independent section below.[83] I adopt Zysow's typology of the non-textual methods. It is the non-textual methods that receive most attention in legal theory literature. They are also the methods that are the subject of most disagreements and controversies; therefore, I choose to focus on them here. This section compares the four Shāfiʿī scholars' use of the formal methods. The following section deals with their use of the material methods.

---

[78] ʿAbd al-Jabbār, *Mughnī*, 17:332; Juwaynī, *Burhān*, 806, 1259; Shīrāzī, *Sharḥ al-Lumaʿ*, 952; Samʿānī, *Qawāṭiʿ al-adilla*, 4:147.

[79] For a survey of these textual methods, see Weiss, *Search for God's Law*, 588–96.

[80] Zysow, *Economy of Certainty*, 197.

[81] The translations of *al-sabr wa-l-taqsīm* and *al-ṭarḍ wa-l-ʿaks* (which is also sometimes referred to as *dawarān*) is borrowed from Weiss, *Search for God's Law*.

[82] Zysow, *Economy of Certainty*, 197.

[83] I am here using Zysow's translations of both terms, see his *Economy of Certainty*, 196–215. Wael Hallaq considers the textual evidence that reveals explicit *rationes legis* to be among the material methods, see Hallaq, 'Non-Analogical Arguments', 287.

Elimination of Alternatives

The elimination of alternatives (*al-sabr wa-l-taqsīm*) is a method in which the jurist attempts to create a list of the possible *rationes legis* that are likely to be behind a particular deontic qualification. The jurist then proceeds to eliminate the ones s/he believes are least likely to be the correct *ratio legis*. At the end, the jurist will have only one remaining candidate; this would be, most probably, the correct *ratio legis*.[84] Shīrāzī mentions the common example of deducing the *ratio legis* behind the prohibition of usurious transactions in bread (*khubz*) via *taqsīm*. For Shāfiʿīs there are three possible candidates, namely measurability by weight (*wazn*), measurability by volume (*kayl*) and edibility (*ṭuʿm*).[85] Shīrāzī says that bread is neither weighed nor measured in volume. We are left only with edibility; it must be the *ratio legis* behind this deontic qualification.[86]

Excluding Samʿānī, the remaining three Shāfiʿīs accept the elimination of alternatives as a valid method to deduce the *ratio legis*. However, Shīrāzī is the only scholar who accepts it without any qualifications that would limit its use.[87] He even hints that it may lead to conclusive knowledge (*ʿilm*) of the *ratio legis* behind a deontic qualification.[88] ʿAbd al-Jabbār also places great trust in this method as a means to uncover *rationes legis*. He describes it as the strongest tool to ascertain a *ratio legis* and implies that it may produce conclusive knowledge of the correct *ratios legis*.[89] However, unlike Shīrāzī, he does not allow its use in all aspects of law. He accepts it only in those cases in which the jurist has a maximum of three putative *rationes legis*; a jurist can use the elimination of alternatives to ex-

---

[84] For more details on this method, see Weiss, *Search for God's Law*, 596–99.

[85] I am here using Hallaq's translations of *wazn*, *kayl* and *ṭuʿm*, see his *Islamic Legal Theories*, 92.

[86] Shīrāzī, *Sharḥ al-Lumaʿ*, 860.

[87] Shīrāzī, *Lumaʿ*, 211, 230; Shīrāzī, *Sharḥ al-Lumaʿ*, 860; Shīrāzī, *al-Mulakhkhaṣ fi-l-jadal*, 87–8.

[88] See Shīrāzī, *Lumaʿ*, 230; Shīrāzī, *Sharḥ al-Lumaʿ*, 860.

[89] ʿAbd al-Jabbār, *Mughnī*, 17:333.

clude two.[90] This automatically excludes those cases in which there are more than three potential *rationes legis*.

Juwaynī insists that the elimination of alternatives can only produce inconclusive knowledge of the *ratio legis*.[91] He also criticizes his Ashʿarī teacher Abū Bakr al-Bāqillānī for counting it among the most efficient tools to validate a *ratio legis*.[92] However, Juwaynī accepts the validity of this method. Yet, he mentions two necessary conditions in an original case in order to allow the elimination of alternatives to deduce the *ratio legis* behind its deontic qualification. First, the *ratio legis* behind the original case must be fathomable to the human mind. This is hardly a unique condition, since all jurists agree that *qiyās* is applicable only to those cases which humans can ascertain their *ratio legis*. The second condition is similar to ʿAbd al-Jabbār's; Juwaynī notes that for a jurist to use the elimination of alternatives method, he should be capable of preparing an exhaustive list of all the putative *rationes legis* that could be behind the deontic qualification in question.[93] After the realization of both conditions, the elimination of alternatives becomes a valid tool to uncover or validate *rationes legis*.

Shīrāzī's and ʿAbd al-Jabbār's use of the elimination of alternatives method in *qiyās* are similar. Juwaynī's is not drastically different. The only unique position is Samʿānī's. He utterly refuses to accept it as a tool to uncover *rationes legis*.[94] Unfortunately, his argument against it is quite terse. He argues that the invalidity of one *ratio legis* does not necessarily mean that another is valid, especially

---

[90] ʿAbd al-Jabbār, *Mughnī*, 17:333. It is noteworthy here that ʿAbd al-Jabbār does not use the term *al-sabr wa-l-taqsīm*. However, he explicitly discusses the concept of eliminating putative *rationes legis* to uncover the most probable one, which is nothing but *al-sabr wa-l-taqsīm*. This may indicate that the concept of *al-sabr wa-l-taqsīm* existed during ʿAbd al-Jabbār's time. However, a commonly accepted term for this concept may have not yet been widespread.

[91] Juwaynī, *Burhān*, 817–8; Juwaynī, *al-Kāfiya fi-l-jadal*, 283.

[92] Juwaynī, *Burhān*, 817.

[93] Juwaynī, *Burhān*, 816–8. In *al-Kāfiya fi-l-jadal*, 394 Juwaynī does not mention this condition.

[94] Samʿānī, *Qawāṭiʿ al-adilla*, 4:239, 341, 415.

that the list of putative *rationes legis* a jurist might be examining may all be wrong. He adds that a deontic qualification might have more than one *ratio legis*, whereas the elimination of alternatives assumes that any deontic qualification has only one *ratio legis*.[95] Samʿānī does not mention any theological arguments behind his rejection of the elimination of alternatives. However, let's remember that he is the only traditionalist jurist among the four scholars who are the focus of this study. The following sections will show that his traditionalist theology may have been a reason for rejecting the elimination of alternatives and other similar methods.

Co-Presence and Co-Absence

This and the following section continue discussing the formal methods to deduce and/or validate a *ratio legis*. I discuss here three different formal methods. The first is co-presence (*ṭard*) which is the occurrence of the deontic qualification whenever the *ratio legis* is present. The second is co-absence (*ʿaks*) which is the absence of the deontic qualification whenever the *ratio legis* is absent. Both methods are the topic of this section. Third, both methods can be fused together as one method to deduce the *ratio legis*. In this case, it is referred to as concomitance (*al-ṭard wa-l-ʿaks*, *dawarān*, or *jarayān*),[96] which can be defined as the occurrence of the deontic qualification whenever the *ratio legis* is present and the absence of the deontic qualification whenever the *ratio legis* is absent.[97] It is important to understand that concomitance, co-presence and co-absence are three different tools to deduce *rationes legis*. An acceptance of one method does not automatically entail accepting the validity of the other two.

---

[95] Samʿānī, *Qawāṭiʿ al-adilla*, 4:239.

[96] Saʿd b. Nāṣir b. ʿAbd al-ʿAzīz al-Shithrī, '*Qiyās al-ʿaks: ḥaqīqatuh wa-ḥukmuh*', *Majallat Umm al-Qurā li-ʿulūm al-Sharīʿa wa-l-lugha al-ʿArabiyya wa-ādābihā* 28 (1424[/2003]), 441; Nashshār, *Manāhij al- baḥth*, 97.

[97] For definitions of concomitance, see Hallaq, *Islamic Legal Theories*, 90; Zysow, *Economy of Certainty*, 216–8. My translations of *ṭard* as co-presence, *ʿaks* as co-absence are borrowed from Weiss, *Search for God's Law*.

Before surveying and comparing the four Shāfiʿī jurists' positions on the above three methods, one must first explain the difference between a condition of validity (*sharṭ al-ṣiḥḥa*) and an evidence of validity (*dalīl al-siḥḥa*). The following jurisprudential example should clarify this difference. Ritual purity (*ṭahāra*) is a condition for a valid prayer (*ṣalāt*), without which the prayer will be invalid. Therefore, before starting any prayer Muslims are required to perform one of the washing rituals that ends the state of ritual impurity, such as ablution (*wuḍūʾ*). However, ritual purity is not enough as evidence for the validity of one's prayer; there are other required conditions for that, such as facing Mecca, performing certain moves in a specific order, pronouncing certain phrases after each move, etc. The performance of all of these conditions (including ritual purity) are required to validate any prayer (i.e. all of them collectively are evidence of validity), and intentionally omitting any of them will invalidate any prayer. Ritual purity, then, is a necessary condition for a valid prayer but not enough evidence for proving the validity of prayer.

Three of the four Shāfiʿī scholars who are under study have a similar position on co-presence. Just like ritual purity, Juwaynī, Shīrāzī and Samʿānī all hold that co-presence is a necessary condition for any valid *ratio legis* but on its own it is not an efficient evidence proving its validity.[98] ʿAbd al-Jabbār agrees with the other three that co-presence is not sufficient evidence proving the validity of a *ratio legis*.[99] However, he does not explicitly mention his position whether co-presence is a necessary condition in a valid *ratio legis*. However, there are implicit indications that he does in fact consider co-presence a necessary condition in any valid *ratio legis*. ʿAbd al-Jabbār argues that *naqḍ* invalidates a *ratio legis*.[100] Co-presence is the occurrence of the deontic qualification whenever

---

[98] Imām al-Ḥaramayn al-Juwaynī, *Matn al-Waraqāt wa-yalīh naẓm al-waraqāt li-l-shaykh Sharaf al-Dīn al-ʿAmrīṭī* (Riyadh: Dār al-Ṣaymaʿī, 1416/1996), 16: Juwaynī, *Burhān*, 836, 857; Shīrāzī, *Sharḥ al-Lumaʿ*, 868; Shīrāzī, *Tabṣira*, 462; Samʿānī, *Qawāṭiʿ al-adilla*, 4:232, 248. On this debate, see Namla, *Muhadhdhab*, 2140–3.

[99] ʿAbd al-Jabbār, *Mughnī*, 17:313–4.

[100] ʿAbd al-Jabbār, *Mughnī*, 17:314.

the *ratio legis* is present, whereas *naqḍ* is the absence of the deontic qualification despite the presence of the *ratio legis*. *Naqḍ*, then, is the absence of co-presence. In other words, saying that *naqḍ* invalidates a *ratio legis* is the same as saying that the absence of co-presence invalidates a *ratio legis*. Accordingly, a scholar who considers *naqḍ* as sufficient grounds to invalidate a *ratio legis* must also hold that co-presence is a condition for its validity. Holding that *naqḍ* invalidates a *ratio legis* is an implicit statement that co-presence is a necessary condition in any valid *ratio legis*.

ʿAbd al-Jabbār's rejection of *naqḍ* raises the question of the particularization of the *ratio legis* (*takhṣīṣ al-ʿilla*). A particularized *ratio legis* is one that does not bring about its deontic qualification in specific cases. In other words, a particularized *ratio legis* is not co-present with its deontic qualification. Therefore, it is just another term for *naqḍ*. ʿAbd al-Jabbār explicitly notes that a particularized *ratio legis* cannot be a valid.[101] This is another indication that he considers co-presence a necessary condition to validate a *ratio legis*. Interestingly, some pre-modern authors consider accepting a 'particularized' *ratio legis* to be a Muʿtazilī shibboleth. Abū Bakr al-Sarakhsī (d. 483/1090), for instance, blames fellow Ḥanafīs and Māturīdīs for accepting such *rationes legis*. He explains that this position entails the adoption of Muʿtazilī theology.[102] Furthermore, the modern historian Haluk Songur notes that the validity of the particularized *ratio legis* is among the important differences between Central Asian Ḥanafīs, who are often Māturīdīs, and Irāqī Ḥanafīs, who are often Muʿtazilī. He argues that the latter's acceptance of this type of *rationes legis* is a product of their Muʿtazilī theology.[103] Accepting par-

---

[101] ʿAbd al-Jabbār, *Mughnī*, 337–9.

[102] Aḥmad b. Abī Sahl al-Sarakhsī (d. 490/1097). *Uṣūl al-sarakhsī*, 2 vols ed. Abū al-Wafā al-Afghānī (Beirut: Dar al-Kutub al-ʿIlmiyya, 1414/[1993]), 2:208. On the Māturīdī reservations on this position in legal theory, see Zysow, 'Muʿtazilism and Māturidism', 250; Zysow, *Economy of Certainty*, 248–9.

[103] Haluk Songur, 'Two Approaches to the Particularization of Effective Cause (takhsis al-ʿillah) in Islamic Legal Theory', *Süleyman Demirel Üniversitesi İlahiyat Fakültesi Dergisi* 17 (2006): 15–26. Songur is an associate

ticularized *rationes legis* is probably the position of most Muʿtazilīs, but certainly not all of them. I have already mentioned ʿAbd al-Jabbār's rejection of this type of *ratio legis*. Abū al-Ḥusayn al-Baṣrī, a Muʿtazilī theologian and Ḥanafī jurist, also shares the same view of his teacher ʿAbd al-Jabbār.[104]

Moreover, this position is not a Muʿtazilī hallmark. We know that some Ḥanbalīs and Shāfiʿīs accept particularized *rationes legis*. Mālikīs also often accept and defend them.[105] Furthermore, Zysow has shown that the Central Asian attitude towards the particularized *ratio legis* is not unanimous. Despite being an Irāqī-Ḥanafī, Abū Zayd al-Dabūsī (d. 430/1039) adopts Māturīdī theology. Yet, he accepts the validity of a particularized *ratio legis*. Zysow adds that the Māturīdī-Ḥanafīs Abū al-Yusr al-Bazdawī (d. 493/1100) and ʿAbd Al-Azīz al-Bukhārī (d. 730/1329) both refuse this type of *rationes legis*. Nonetheless, they note that accepting it does not entail accepting Muʿtazilī doctrines. Zysow further argues that after the eighth/fourteenth century, the connection between the particularization of the *ratio legis* and Muʿtazilī doctrines fades away and the standard Ḥanafī position became to accept this form of *rationes legis*.[106] What is important to note here is that Māturīdī jurists disagree on the theological implications of this legal theory position.

---

professor of Islamic Law at the Faculty of Divinity, University of Suleyman Demirel.

[104] Abū al-Ḥusayn, *Muʿtamad*, 821–34. In chapter four of his doctoral dissertation, Haytham Khazna studies the inter-Ḥanafī debate around the validity of the particularized *ratio legis*. He argues against modern and premodern authors who suggest that Muʿtazilī theology is the reason behind the dominance of this doctrine among Muʿtazilī-Ḥanafīs. He notes that accepting this type of *rationes legis* is not the product of any particular Muʿtazilī doctrine. I agree with his conclusion. However, I think he erroneously categorized ʿAbd al-Jabbār among those Muʿtazilīs who accept the particularized *ratio legis*. For his argument, see Khazna, 'al-Ikhtilāfāt al-uṣūliyya',264–92.

[105] Zysow, *Economy of Certainty*, 244. For a survey of the different positions on the particularization of the *rationes legis*, see Māzin Haniyya, 'Takhṣīṣ al-ʿilla', *Majallat al-Jāmiʿa al-Islāmiyya* [Gaza] 12.2 (2004): 343–66.

[106] Zysow, 'Muʿtazilism and Māturīdism', 248–251.

Those who consider it a product of Muʿtazilī theology refuse it. Others who see no connection between it and any 'deviant' doctrine either accept it or refrain from condemning those who accept it as heretics.

After this detour, I will now return to the formal methods used to deduce or validate *rationes legis*. Co-absence is another formal method. ʿAbd al-Jabbār does not comment on the efficiency of this method. Therefore, I can only examine the opinion of the other three Shāfiʿī scholars. All three hold that co-absence, unlike co-presence, is not a necessary condition (*sharṭ*) for the validity of a *ratio legis*.[107] Put differently, the fact that a *ratio legis* is not, constantly, absent when a particular deontic qualification is absent does not disqualify it from being actually the *ratio legis* of this deontic qualification in some cases. For example, temporary consecration (*iḥrām*)[108] is one possible *ratio legis* for the prohibition of sexual intercourse between a married couple. If co-absence were a necessary condition for a valid *ratio legis*, temporary consecration would be an invalid *ratio legis* for this deontic qualification. This is because the same deontic qualification can be found even in cases when temporary consecration is absent. For example, Muslim scholars are unanimous that fasting (*ṣawm*) and menstruation also lead to the prohibition of sexual intercourse.[109] Here we find the same deontic qualification (prohibition of intercourse) despite the absence of temporary consecration which itself is considered a valid *ratio legis* for the prohibition of intercourse in certain cases. Therefore, for

---

[107] Abū Isḥāq Ibrāhīm b. ʿAlī b. Yūsuf al-Shīrāzī, *al-Maʿūna fi-l-jadal*, ed. ʿAlī ʿAbd al-ʿAzīz al-ʿAmrīnī (Kuwait: Jamʿiyyat Iḥyāʾ al-Turāth al-Islāmī, 1407/[1987]), 102; Shīrāzī, *Sharḥ al-Lumaʿ*, 834–5; Juwaynī, *Burhān*, 855–7; Juwaynī, *al-Kāfiya fi-l-jadal*, 15, 177; Samʿānī, *Qawāṭiʿ al-adilla*, 4:235–6, 248, 393.

[108] Translation borrowed from *EI*[2], s.v. 'Iḥrām' (A. J. Wensinck and J. Jomier).

[109] If the deontic qualification has only one *ratio legis*, the whole question of co-absence will become, in this context, superfluous. In this situation co-absence becomes a necessary condition. See Āmidī, *Iḥkām*, 3:294; Ghazālī, *Mustaṣfā*, 3:728.

Juwaynī, Shīrāzī and Samʿānī the lack of co-absence in itself is not sufficient evidence to invalidate a putative *ratio legis*.

However, all three Shāfiʿīs are not unanimous on using co-absence to validate a putative *ratio legis*. Samʿānī refuses to use it as a tool to deduce or validate *rationes legis*.[110] On the other hand, Juwaynī and Shīrāzī accept it as evidence for the validity of a putative *ratio legis*.[111] For example, if a jurist notices that a *ratio legis* is always absent whenever the deontic qualification is absent, this is enough evidence that the *ratio legis* being examined is the one behind the occurrence of the deontic qualification in question. Here we have two Ashʿarī scholars who accept the use of co-absence in their endeavour to discover *rationes legis*, whereas the traditionalist Samʿānī rejects it altogether. One must ask, is Samʿānī's position a product of his traditionalist theology? Unfortunately, Samʿānī does not mention his argument against co-absence; therefore, answering this question with certainty is impossible. However, for the time being, let us keep in mind that Samʿānī is the only jurist, among the four being examined, who consistently refuses to use the formal methods as tools to uncover *rationes legis*.

Concomitance

I have so far spoken about co-presence and co-absence as two independent tools to deduce and/or verify a *ratio legis*. A third formal method combines both co-presence and co-absence together in what is called concomitance. A feature is described as concomitant if it is always present when the deontic qualification is present (co-presence) *and* is always absent whenever the deontic qualification is absent (co-absence).[112] This proves that the feature being examined is probably the *ratio legis* behind the deontic qualification in question. Excluding Samʿānī, the remaining three Shāfiʿīs accept concomitance as sufficient evidence for the validity of a *ratio legis*.[113]

---

[110] Samʿānī, *Qawāṭiʿ al-adilla*, 4:236, 248–52.

[111] Juwaynī, *Burhān*, 856; Shīrāzī, *Sharḥ al-Lumaʿ*, 819–20.

[112] Hallaq, *Islamic Legal Theories*, 90; Weiss, *Search for God's Law*, 623.

[113] Samʿānī, *Qawāṭiʿ al-adilla*, 4:231; Juwaynī, *Burhān*, 839, 840–1, 1261; Juwaynī, *al-Kāfiya fi-l-jadal*, 303; Shīrāzī, *Sharḥ al-Lumaʿ*, 820; ʿAbd al-Jabbār, *Mughnī*, 17:333.

For Samʿānī, concomitance can only determine preponderance (*tarjīḥ*) between two conflicting *rationes legis*; the one that is concomitant overrules the one that is not.[114] Otherwise, Samʿānī awards concomitance no role in ascertaining *rationes legis*. He presents two main arguments against concomitance. First, he says that referring to concomitance as evidence for the validity of a *ratio legis* is nothing but a circular argument. As an example, Samʿānī notes that Ḥanafīs resort to concomitance to prove that measurability by volume (*kayl*) is the *ratio legis* behind the prohibition of usurious transactions in wheat. When challenged about the validity of concomitance, Ḥanafīs would refer to measurability by volume as an example of a valid *ratio legis* that is concomitant with the prohibition of this type of transactions. Samʿānī concludes that this is a circular argument that proves nothing.[115] Second, Samʿānī argues that concomitance does not preclude the possibility that there might be other factors or evidence invalidating the examined *ratio legis*. This being the case, the jurist might not be aware of the presence of evidence invalidating the putative *ratio legis* despite its concomitance with the deontic qualification. Samʿānī concludes that there should be evidence additional to concomitance proving the validity of the putative *ratio legis*. For Samʿānī, concomitance alone is not sufficient for this task.[116]

Samʿānī's account against concomitance seems not well structured. However, those are Samʿānī's two main arguments against it; all others are derivatives of these two. Unfortunately, his argument does not reveal much about his theoretical grounds for rejecting concomitance. What we can notice here, nonetheless, is the absence of any apparent theological motivations for disallowing concomitance. In isolation, Samʿānī's rejection of concomitance is not worthy of attention. However, when placed beside his rejection of the elimination of alternatives and co-absence, we notice that he is

---

[114] Samʿānī, *Qawāṭiʿ al-adilla*, 4:394, 432. Juwaynī and Shīrāzī also use concomitance to determine preponderance between conflicting *rationes legis*, see Juwaynī, 303; Shīrāzī, *Sharḥ al-Lumaʿ*, 959.

[115] Samʿanī, *Qawāṭiʿ al-adilla*, 4:232.

[116] Samʿanī, *Qawāṭiʿ al-adilla*, 4:233–6.

consistently reluctant to acknowledge the validity of formal methods to uncover *rationes legis.*

Logic, Causality and the *ratio legis*

Three of the four Shāfiʿī jurists under examination here have very similar positions from the use of formal methods to deduce and/or validate putative *rationes legis.* Juwaynī, Shīrāzī and ʿAbd al-Jabbār, with few variations, accept using elimination of alternatives, co-presence, co-absence and concomitance to uncover the *ratio legis* behind a particular deontic qualification. The jurist with the unique position from these formal methods is Samʿānī. He consistently refuses to accept any of the formal methods as tools to deduce or validate *rationes legis.* The only formalist method Samʿānī accepts only as a condition, but not as an evidence, for a valid *ratio legis* is co-presence. He insists that appropriateness (explained in the following section) is the only valid method to deduce a *ratio legis.*[117] Samʿānī does not explicitly reveal his reasons for refusing any of the formal methods. One must note here that all the formal methods Samʿānī rejects are somehow associated with logic (*manṭiq*), dialectics (*jadal*) and their practitioners. Juwaynī writes that debates around the validity of co-absence as a condition for a valid *ratio legis* mix religion with dialectics.[118] Elsewhere, he adds that dialecticians hold that concomitance is the strongest method to deduce a *ratio legis.*[119] Like many traditionalist scholars, Samʿānī is very critical of dialecticians and logicians. Therefore, his rejection of the formal methods is likely to be an outcome of his traditionalist reluctance to mix logic and dialectics with legal theory. Juwaynī and Shīrāzī have a very different position. Both accept mixing dialectics with legal theory. Both wrote at least one work on juridical dialectics (Shīrāzī wrote at least two).[120] Therefore, unlike Samʿānī, they see no problem in bringing logical and dialectical elements (such as the formal methods) into their legal theory.

---

[117] Shīrāzī, *Qawāṭiʿ al-adilla*, 4:251.

[118] Juwaynī, *Burhān*, 856.

[119] Juwaynī, *Burhān*, 835.

[120] Juwaynī, *al-Kāfiya fi-l-jadal*; Shīrāzī, *al-Maʿūna fi-l-jadal*; Shīrāzī, *al-Mulakhkhaṣ fi-l-jadal.*

Knut Vikør notes that jurists might invalidate a method of deducing *rationes legis* because it depends too much on logic.[121] Wael Hallaq says that a Muslim jurist resists some aspects of logic because its unconditional acceptance into law implies an 'acceptance of metaphysical conclusions which run against the fundamentals of his belief as a Muslim. Only when logic is stripped from its theological implications and used merely as a tool does the Islamic lawyer considers it legitimate'.[122] One might then assume that traditionalist jurists remain aloof from logic and dialectics for theological considerations. On the other hand, it seems that the Ashʿarīs Juwaynī and Shīrāzī, who both wrote on dialectics, are not troubled by any theological implications and felt comfortable to utilize dialectical methods in their legal theory.

Samʿānī's traditionalist mentality, which undermines the use of reason in law, legal theory and theology, probably makes him reluctant to bring logic and dialectics into legal theory. Traditionalist scholars refuse speculative theology because of (among other reasons) its speculative nature. Dialectics and logic also share a similar speculative nature. It is only natural to find those who are repulsed by the speculative nature of *ʿilm al-kalām* to be equally repulsed by the speculative nature of dialectics and logic and resist introducing them into law and legal theory. Shīrāzī, ʿAbd al-Jabbār and Juwaynī all wrote on speculative theology (specially the latter two); in principal, they have no theoretical objections on the methods used in *ʿilm al-kalām*. This might have made it easier for them to accept the introduction of logical and dialectical methods in legal theory.

Finally, one expects to see the disagreements over natural causality between the four jurists under study mirrored in their debates around the formal methods discussed above. Zysow rightly notes that formal methods 'rest on the assumption that the methods of the rational sciences are suitable for law. The causes of the natural world are consistent and convertible, and this standard is applicable

[121] Vikør, *Between God and the Sultan*, 63.

[122] Wael Hallaq, 'The Logic of Legal Reasoning in Religious and non-Religious Cultures: The Case of Islamic Law and the Common Law', *Cleveland State Law Review* 34 (1985), 80.

to the causes of the law'.[123] The fact that these formal methods rest on the concept of causality entails that accepting or rejecting them should be contingent on the position taken from causality. However, discussions of natural causality do not form a prominent part of the sections dedicated to the formal methods in the four jurists' legal theory literature. Interestingly, Samʿānī rarely refers to his refusal of causality as a reason behind his rejection of the formal methods. The Ashʿarīs Juwaynī and Shīrāzī do not consider their rejection of natural causality to be in contradiction with their acceptance of the formal methods. ʿAbd al-Jabbār who accepts some form of natural causality rarely refers to it as evidence supporting the formal methods. As previously mentioned, all four jurists (and many others) insist that natural causes and *rationes legis* are different. Therefore, the laws that apply to one are not always applicable to the other. This distinction undermines the relevance of natural causality to *qiyās* and the *ratio legis*. The marginalization of natural causality saves the four jurist's perceptions of *qiyās* from being divided along theological lines, thus helping to maintaining some form of coherence within the Shāfiʿī School of law.

DEDUCING THE RATIO LEGIS: THE MATERIAL METHODS

Suitability (*munāsaba*), as Hallaq notes, is considered by many jurists as the 'single most important method' to deduce a *ratio legis*.[124] It is a method that, more or less, equates the *ratio legis* with the benefit (*maṣlaḥa*) the deontic qualification intends to bring about or the harm (*mafsada*) it intends to avert. It assumes that the goal of all deontic qualifications is to realize human benefit.[125] Suitability is based on ascertaining the benefit behind the deontic qualification of the original case. Once the benefit is identified, a jurist then tries to isolate the feature (*waṣf*) in the original case that is *munāsib* or

[123] Zysow, *Economy of Certainty*, 220.

[124] The translation of suitability as *munāsaba* is widely accepted, see for instance Hallaq, *Islamic Legal Theories*, 88; Weiss, *Search for God's Law*, 599–600; Opwis, *Maṣlaḥa*, 96–113. Zysow, on the other hand, prefers appropriateness, see *Economy of Certainty*, 196–204.

[125] Weiss makes a similar comment in reference to Āmidī's use of *munāsaba* in *qiyās*, see his *Search for God's Law*, 607, 620.

most suitable to realizing the benefit intended from the deontic qualification.[126] For example, it is assumed that the Qur'ānic prohibition of *khamr* aims at maintaining human rationality (*ʿaql*). The feature in *khamr* that is most suitable to realizing this aim is intoxication; therefore, it must be the *ratio legis* rather than other features in *khamr* irrelevant to this aim, such as smell, taste, or colour. Excluding Shīrāzī, the remaining three Shāfiʿīs accept suitability (or a similar method) as a valid tool to deduce the *ratio legis*. Nonetheless, they disagree on the framework that regulates using it as a method to deduce *rationes legis*. The following sections compare the four scholars' positions on suitability (and similar concepts) and assess how far their theological dogmas inform their positions on this important aspect of *qiyās*.

Juwaynī's Concept of Suitability

Juwaynī refers to suitability sometimes as *munāsaba*, at others as suggestiveness (*ikhāla*)[127] or effectiveness (*ta'thīr*). Unfortunately, as Felicitas Opwis rightly notes, Juwaynī does not define any of these terms.[128] However, she writes that he

> indirectly tells us that a suitable *ratio legis* is connected to the *maṣlaḥa* that the ruling entails. He states that the suitability of a meaning can be established, even when no source mentions it, by looking at the universal *maṣlaḥa*s (*maṣāliḥ kulliyya*).[129]

Wael Hallaq explains the concept of suitability saying that its 'goal is to offer 'relevant' ways of rational reasoning that serve the public interest (*maṣlaḥa*) as defined through the fundamental principles of the law'.[130] Suitability in itself, adds Hallaq, is a rational method to

---

[126] My definition is influenced by Zysow's explanation of the term *munasāba*, see his *Economy of Certainty*, 198–200, 214. For more definitions and explanations of this term, see Hallaq, *Islamic Legal Theories*, 88; Weiss, *Search for God's Law*, 607, 620.

[127] I here adopt Zysow's translation of the term, see his *Economy of Certainty*, 205–6.

[128] Opwis, *Maṣlaḥa*, 47–8, 55, 57.

[129] Opwis, *Maṣlaḥa*, 47.

[130] Hallaq, *Sharīʿa*, 104.

deduce a *ratio legis*, however 'it must conform to what may be called the spirit of the law, a spirit that dictates to what extent and in what circumstances suitability is to be accepted or not'.[131] This is exactly Juwaynī's only condition to accept suitability as a valid means to ascertain a *ratio legis*. Juwaynī makes it clear that not all benefits are suitable (*munāsib*) indicators for the correct *rationes legis*.[132] Only those benefits we know are acknowledged by the Lawgiver are suitable indicators for the *rationes legis* behind divine legislations.

The question becomes now, how can the benefits that the Lawgiver takes into account in legislation be identified? Juwaynī would probably answer saying that benefits that are in conformity with the principles of Sharīʿa (*uṣūl al-sharīʿa*) are the ones we know are acknowledged by the Lawgiver.[133] By the principles of Sharīʿa, Juwaynī is referring to Qur'ānic verses and Prophetic traditions. When a jurist notices that a Qur'ānic verse(s) or a Prophetic tradition(s) create laws to promote a particular benefit, this is enough evidence that God acknowledges this particular benefit as a foundation for law-making. This is a process of inductive reading where jurists scan the Qur'ān and Sunna searching for the acknowledged benefits. As Opwis explains, by 'investigating the meanings and implications of the divinely revealed rulings, jurists apprehend the *maṣlaḥa*s that these rulings aim at'.[134]

For example, Q 2:178 prescribes execution as the punishment for murder. The following verse adds that 'Fair retribution saves life for you…'. Juwaynī explains that both verses clearly state that the benefit behind this deontic qualification (execution of murderers) is the protection of human lives (*ṣiyānat al-dimā'*). Therefore, we know that among the benefits that the Lawgiver acknowledges is preserving human lives.[135] We are, thus, justified to assume that other Qur'ānic verses (or Prophetic traditions) that mention punishments for murders or punishments for offensive physical harm inflicted upon other humans must be motivated by God's will to

[131] Hallaq, *Islamic Legal Theories*, 90.
[132] Juwaynī, *Burhān*, 1204.
[133] Juwaynī, *Burhān*, 1203.
[134] Opwis, *Maṣlaḥa*, 55.
[135] Juwaynī, *Burhān*, 1208.

protect human lives. Even if these verses do not explicitly say so as Q 2:179 does. Moreover, commenting on intoxication, Q 4:52 says 'You who believe, do not come anywhere near the prayer if you are intoxicated, not until you know what you are saying…'. Therefore, we know that the benefit intended from the prohibition of intoxicants has to do with maintaining consciousness and rationality. Since this benefit is acknowledged in a Qur'ānic verse, it must then be one of those universal benefits acknowledged by the Lawgiver. Therefore, humans can assume that God may issue other legislations that maintain the same benefit, even if He does not explicitly repeat the rationale behind these laws.

Juwaynī is very keen to make his use of suitability to deduce the *ratio legis* as faithful as possible to benefits mentioned or deduced from textual evidence. For example, Q 5:38 informs Muslims of the *ḥadd* punishment for theft which is hand amputation. We also know via traditions attributed to the Prophet that for this punishment to be applied, the object stolen must be taken from a safe place (*ḥirz*), in addition to other conditions. For example, someone who steels a valuable object left on the back seat of an unlocked car will not receive the *ḥadd* punishment because the backseat of an unlocked car is not a safe place. However, if the valuable object is stolen from a wardrobe in a locked apartment, then the thief might deserve the *ḥadd* punishment because a locked apartment is a safe place. Juwaynī says that the benefit behind the *ḥadd* punishment is the protection of property and the deterrence of thieves (*ṣawn al-amwāl wa-zajr al-sāriqīn*), however the application of this *ḥadd* is a punishment for stealing objects from safe places only. Juwaynī explains that the benefit acknowledged by the Lawgiver in the application of the *ḥadd* for theft is limited only to deterring thefts from safe places. This acknowledged benefit is not found in other types of thefts.

To clarify his point, Juwaynī mentions a hypothetical example in which two separate thieves (not accomplices) stole a treasure hidden underground. One thief dug the whole and left the scene, the other came and picked it up and left. This is certainly theft, but Juwaynī argues that this theft does not deserve the *ḥadd* punishment because the first 'thief' did not yet steal anything, whereas the other stole an object that is not in a safe place anymore.[136] Juwaynī concludes that jurists should not utilize suitability and *qiyās* to apply the *ḥadd* punishment of theft to these hypothetical thieves. This is due to the fact that applying this divinely stipulated punishment, and the benefit expected from it, is limited by conditions not present in this hypothetical case [the thief may be punished by *taʿzīr*, but not the *ḥadd*]. The benefit that the Lawgiver acknowledges in this punishment is limited to thefts from safe places. Although it might appear that punishing those hypothetical thieves would realize the benefit intended from the *ḥadd* punishment (i.e. protecting property), Juwaynī insists that 'the application of this punishment [i.e. hand amputation] leads to the protection of property only when applied to thefts from safe places (*al-sariqa min-l-ḥirz*)'. He adds that humans should not assume that the same benefit would happen when applied to cases other than the one mentioned in Q 5:38. He ends this statement saying that jurists have no right to create new rationales and new benefits (*laysa ilaynā waḍʿ al-ḥikam wa-l-maṣāliḥ*); they should only follow the benefits that the Lawgiver acknowledges.[137]

Elsewhere, Juwaynī writes that only benefits acknowledged by revelation (sg. *ḥikma marʿiyya*) can be used to extend a deontic qualification to a novel case. Nonetheless, no other rationale or benefit should be used in *qiyās* even if it is similar to the one acknowledged in revelation. He argues that depending on benefits or rationales that are similar to ones mentioned in revelation open the door to an infinite regression of similar benefits and this will lead to the disintegration (*inḥilāl*) of Sharīʿa.[138] Opwis, rightly, notes that Juwaynī's concept of suitability aims at preventing the 'unrestricted use of *maṣlaḥa*'.[139] For Juwaynī, suitability's main aim is to make sure that the benefit being used to deduce the *ratio legis* has grounds in revelation. A jurist reads all the textual evidence (i.e. Qurʾān and the Sunna). From this survey, he deduces a number of benefits the Lawgiver acknowledges in His legislations. Only those benefits can

---

[136] Juwaynī, *Burhān*, 1220–1.

[137] Juwaynī, *Burhān*, 1221.

[138] Juwaynī, *Burhān*, 1219.

[139] Opwis, *Maṣlaḥa*, 57. Also see, p. 55–6.

be used to uncover the intended benefit and the *ratio legis* behind the deontic qualifications whose rationale have not been disclosed by the Lawgiver. Most importantly, suitability assumes that divine legislations are not only beneficial but that humans can, with the aid of revelation, uncover and appreciate those benefits; a point to which I will return later.

Shīrāzī's Concept of Effectiveness

Shīrāzī's concept of effectiveness is categorically different from that of Juwaynī's suitability. Shīrāzī explains that there are two methods to discover and/or validate a *ratio legis* behind a particular deontic qualification. The first is via textual evidence, i.e. a jurist might know a *ratio legis* if it is explicitly mentioned either in the Qur'ān or in a Prophetic tradition. The second is deduction (*istinbāṭ*). He notes that there are two types of deduction, the first is *shahādat al-uṣūl* and this is reserved for a particular type of *qiyās* often termed *qiyās al-dalāla* or what Wael Hallaq translates as indicative inferences.[140] The second is effectiveness. Shīrāzī uses this method in another type of *qiyās*, namely *qiyās al-ʿilla* (or *qiyās al-maʿnā*).[141] It is

---

[140] See for example, Hallaq, *Sharīʿa*, 101.

[141] Shīrāzī, *Lumaʿ*, 223–31; Shīrāzī, *Sharḥ al-Lumaʿ*, 857–62. The best way to explain the difference between *qiyās al-ʿilla* and *qiyās al-dalāla* is by putting them in juxtaposition. *Qiyās al-ʿilla* is based on the knowledge of the *ratio legis*, the fact that a jurist sees a novel case sharing the *ratio legis* of the original case justifies concluding that the former shares the deontic qualification of the latter. On the other hand, *qiyās al-dalāla* is not based on knowledge of a *ratio legis*. It takes place when the *ratio legis* is unknown. It is rather based on the presence of a common feature in the original and the novel case. This common feature indicates that the original and the novel case share the unknown *ratio legis* that led to the occurrence of the deontic qualification in the original case. Therefore both share the same deontic qualification. The following hypothetical example should clarify the difference between both types of *qiyās*: *Khamr* has smell *x*; *khamr* is prohibited; all substances with smell *x* are prohibited. This is a case of *qiyās al-dalāla*, because smell *x* in itself cannot be a *ratio legis*. There is no logical connection between the smell of a drink and its prohibition. Smell *x* is only an indication that all substances with this smell share the same un-

important to note that Shīrāzī explicitly states that those are the only legitimate methods to deduce a *ratio legis*; all other methods are invalid.[142] It is the second type of deduction that I am interested in here. Shīrāzī defines effectiveness as the occurrence of the deontic qualification whenever the *maʿnā* (i.e. the *ratio legis*) occurs. This mutually inclusive relationship entails that the *ratio legis* in question is *probably* the 'reason' behind the occurrence of the deontic qualification.[143] Shīrāzī's definition of effectiveness is exactly the same as the definition of co-presence. However, as mentioned above, Shīrāzī rejects using co-presence to ascertain a *ratio legis*.[144]

A closer look at the example that Shīrāzī mentions for deducing a *ratio legis* via effectiveness will reveal that by effectiveness he is not actually referring to co-presence. He says that effectiveness can be proven via two methods, first by *al-salb wa-l-wujūd* and by the elimination of alternatives. The latter has been already discussed; therefore, I focus here on the former. He explains *al-salb wa-l-wujūd* as the occurrence of the *ratio legis* whenever the deontic qualification occurs, and the absence of the *ratio legis* whenever the deontic

---

known *ratio legis* (presumably intoxication) that led to the prohibition of consuming *khamr*. The jurist using this type of *qiyās* does not know the *ratio legis*. He bases his *qiyās* on a feature that signifies the presence of an unknown, but common, *ratio legis*. The following, on the other hand, is a *qiyās ʿilla*: *Khamr* is prohibited; *khamr* is intoxicant; therefore all intoxicants are prohibited. In the second example we directly know the *ratio legis* that led to the prohibition of *khamr*. The jurist bases his *qiyās* on the *ratio legis* itself rather than a common feature indicating the presence of a common *ratio legis*. Intoxication is a feature that can be logically linked to the prohibition of consuming a substance unlike its smell or colour. This example is borrowed from Muḥammad Muḥammad ʿAbd al-Laṭīf Jamāl al-Dīn, *Qiyās al-uṣūliyyīn bayn al-Muthbitīn wa-l-nāfīn* (Alexandria: Muʾassasat al-Thaqāfa al-Jāmiʿiyya, 1985), 98. For more details on *qiyās al-dalāla*. For Shīrāzī's explanations of *qiyās al-ʿilla* and *qiyās al-dalāla*, see his *Sharḥ al-Lumaʿ*, 799–814.

[142] Shīrāzī, *Lumaʿ*, 230; Shīrāzī, *Sharḥ al-Lumaʿ*, 863.

[143] Shīrāzī, *Lumaʿ*, 229; Shīrāzī, *Sharḥ al-Lumaʿ*, 858.

[144] See for example his strong refutation of co-presence as a method to deduce the *ratio legis* in Shīrāzī, *Sharḥ al-Lumaʿ*, 864–870.

qualification is absent. This is nothing but the definition of concomitance (*dawarān*). As an example of *al-salb wa-l-wujūd* Shīrāzī mentions the prohibition of *nabīdh*. He states that before the juice acquires its intoxicating quality (i.e. before fermentation), it is permitted. When the juice acquires the feature of intoxication it becomes prohibited just like *khamr*. If this feature of intoxication disappears from the juice [by turning it into vinegar after oxidation] the juice will be permissible once again. So here we notice that the prohibition occurs whenever intoxication occurs and is omitted whenever intoxication is absent. Shīrāzī concludes that the feature of intoxication must be the *ratio legis* behind the prohibition of *khamr* and *nabīdh*.[145]

We notice here that *al-salb wa-l-wujūd* is not only co-presence. It is rather concomitance, i.e. co-presence and co-absence put together. For Shīrāzī, neither co-presence nor co-absence on their own is enough evidence to prove that a particular feature is the *ratio legis* behind a deontic qualification. To prove this relationship, the feature in question must be concomitant with the deontic qualification. Most importantly, it is obvious here that Shīrāzī makes no reference to the benefit behind the deontic qualification as an indication for the *ratio legis*. Benefits, for him, play no role in his endeavours to ascertain *rationes legis*.

To make sure that all methods Shīrāzī considers as legitimate tools to deduce *rationes legis* are covered, I mention a brief explanation of *shahādat al-uṣūl* (the method reserved of indicative inferences or *qiyās al-dalāla*). *Shahādat al-uṣūl* is a reference to the treatment of Sharīʿa to a specific genus (*jins*) of original cases (*uṣūl*); all members of this genus should receive the same deontic qualification. For example, Shāfiʿī jurists hold that laughter before or during performing prayers (*ṣalāt*) does not invalidate ritual purity. Other jurists agree, but add that laughing *during* prayers would invalidate ritual purity. Shīrāzī, as a Shāfiʿī, argues that revelation equates all actions that invalidate ritual purity (all belong to the genus of actions that invalidate ritual purity); anything that invalidates ritual purity out of prayer will also invalidate ritual purity during prayer.

---

145 Shīrāzī, *al-Maʿūna fi-l-jadal*, 99; Shīrāzī, *Lumaʿ*, 299; Shīrāzī, *Sharḥ al-Lumaʿ*, 858–9.

On the other hand, actions that do not invalidate ritual purity outside of prayer will not invalidate ritual purity during prayer. Shīrāzī concludes saying that since laughter does not invalidate ritual purity outside of prayer therefore it cannot invalidate ritual purity during prayer. This is a case of *qiyās* based on *shahādat al-uṣūl.*

Another example of *shahādat al-uṣūl*: Muslim jurists agree that the payment of alms (*zakāt*) on livestock, regardless of the sex of each animal, is obligatory. Accordingly, Shīrāzī says that revelation equates between the sex of the animals on which alms is obligatory. There is a debate among some Muslim scholars whether alms is obligatory on mares, whereas the majority of scholars say that alms is not obligatory on stallions. Al-Shīrāzī says that revelation equates between the sex of those animals on which alms is imposed (all belong to the same genus). Therefore, he performs the following *qiyās*: since *zakāt* is not obligatory on stallions, therefore it cannot be obligatory on mares.[146] Again, al-Shīrāzī makes no reference to benefit or *maṣlaḥa* in this type of *qiyās*. He depends on what he calls *shahādat al-uṣūl*, assuming that actions or objects that belong to the same genus must share the same deontic qualification. He does not endeavour to find the rationale or the *ratio legis* behind the deontic qualification in this type of *qiyās*.

In sum, for Shīrāzī there are only two valid methods to deduce a *ratio legis*. First, via textual evidence and the second is what he calls *istinbāṭ* (deduction). There are two types of the latter, the first is effectiveness (which is of two types, namely elimination of alternatives and concomitance) and the second is *shahādat al-uṣūl.* As mentioned above, Shīrāzī says that those are the *only* valid methods to deduce or validate a *ratio legis*. In other words, he rejects all other methods. Shīrāzī's methods of deducing *rationes legis* are categorically different from Juwaynī's. Shīrāzī does not utilize benefit as means to uncover *rationes legis*. This is surprising since he believes that a *ratio legis* might be an indication for the benefit behind its deontic qualification.[147] Here we have two Ashʿarī-Shāfiʿī

---

[146] Shīrāzī, *Sharḥ al-Lumaʿ*, 860–1.

[147] Shīrāzī, *Tabṣira*, 453. He makes this comment in reference to the deduced intransitive *ratio legis* (*ʿilla qāṣira* or *ʿilla wāqifa*). This is a type of *rationes legis* that cannot be transferred to any novel case, therefore it can-

scholars with similar positions from theological debates concerning the purposefulness of God's acts, God's commitment to human optimal benefit, moral epistemology and moral ontology. Nonetheless, we have two very different methods of deducing the *ratio legis*, Juwaynī's method heavily depends on benefit, whereas Shīrāzī's methods disregard benefit as an indicator for the *ratio legis*. The fact that both Ashʿarī scholars share common theological grounds does not motivate them to adopt similar methods to deduce and validate *rationes legis*. This phenomenon is present not only among Ashʿarīs, but, as we see in the following section, among Muʿtazilīs as well.

ʿAbd al-Jabbār's Concept of Effectiveness

ʿAbd al-Jabbār does not use the term suitable (*munāsib*), but rather uses the term effective (*muʾaththir*) in reference to using benefit as an indicator for the *ratio legis*.[148] Understanding ʿAbd al-Jabbār's concept of effectiveness is not easy. Unfortunately, in volume seventeen of *Mughnī* (the one dedicated to legal theory), he does not discuss methods of deducing the *rationes legis* in sufficient detail; the chapter he dedicates to this topic does not exceed two pages.[149] Furthermore, nowhere in the same volume does he explicitly define effectiveness. However, I have collected a number of statements in which ʿAbd al-Jabbār refers to effectiveness and/or the process of deducing *rationes legis*; an analysis of those statements may help re-

---

not be used in *qiyās*. Jurists often debate whether it is useful to deduce an intransitive *ratio legis*. Shīrāzī believes that it is. He argues that it can, at least, explain the benefit behind the deontic qualification of the original case.

[148] It seems that until the late fifth/eleventh century the technical terms used in reference to the processes of deducing the *ratio legis* were not standardized. For example, Zysow quotes Ghazālī saying that scholars from different geographical locations used different terms in reference to the concepts of *munāsaba* and *taʾthīr*, in Samarqand they use *taʾthīr*, in Iraq they use *dalāla*, in Nishapur they use *shabah*, see Zysow, *Economy of Certainty*, 211. For Ghazālī's comment, see his *Shifāʾ al-ghalīl*, 318. See also Zysow, *Economy of Certainty*, 205–6; Ghazālī, *Shifāʾ al-ghalīl*, 144.

[149] ʿAbd al-Jabbār, *Mughnī*, 17:332–3.

veal ʿAbd al-Jabbār's concept of effectiveness as a method to deduce the *ratio legis*.

ʿAbd al-Jabbār explains that a *ratio legis* is one of two things: either the *luṭf* (i.e. benefit) resulting from an action or the motive (*dāʿī*) behind performing it.[150] Elsewhere he writes that a *ratio legis* functions just like a motive for performing an action or the factor revealing the benefit resulting from its occurrence (*al-ʿilla fi-l-sharʿiyyāt tajrī majrā al-dawāʿī wa mā yakshif ʿan kawn al-fiʿl luṭfan*).[151] Furthermore, he notes that the process of deducing *rationes legis* is impossible without uncovering the benefits and motives behind actions (*taʿlīl al-uṣūl al-sharʿiyya lā yakūn illā bi-bayān mā yakshif ʿan al-dawāʿī wa-ʿan kawn al-fiʿl ṣalāḥan*).[152] He adds that *qiyās* 'follows' the feature (i.e. the *ratio legis*) that uncovers the benefit and the motive [behind an action].[153] In addition, he describes *qiyās* as an indicator for the motive and the benefit behind performing an action or its omission (*al-qiyās yakūn ishāra ilā mā-lahu yadʿū al-dāʿī ilā al-fiʿl aw-l-tark aw-yakūn ishāra ilā mā-yakūn luṭfan*).[154] Here, we see that ʿAbd al-Jabbār considers benefit as a major component not only of the *ratio legis* but of the whole process of *qiyās*. A *ratio legis* is the benefit expected from the imposition of a deontic qualification and the motivation behind its imposition. This should not be surprising, since for ʿAbd al-Jabbār, as Anver Emon notes, it is benefit that makes religious obligation justified and meaningful.[155]

The above statements still do not exactly uncover ʿAbd al-Jabbār's definition of effectiveness. The following quote should clarify his understanding of this term. ʿAbd al-Jabbār's explains that

> among the conditions for a valid *ratio legis* is that it should be relevant to the deontic qualification of the original case (*an yakūn lahā taʿlluq bi-ḥukm al-aṣl*). Therefore, it is not allowed to consider a name (*laqab*), and similar things, as *rationes legis*.

---

[150] ʿAbd al-Jabbār, *Mughnī*, 17:290.
[151] ʿAbd al-Jabbār, *Mughnī*, 17:330.
[152] ʿAbd al-Jabbār, *Mughnī*, 17:314.
[153] ʿAbd al-Jabbār, *Mughnī*, 17:320.
[154] ʿAbd al-Jabbār, *Mughnī*, 17:291.
[155] Emon, *Islamic Natural Law*, 61.

> However, features (*ṣifāt*) may be considered as *rationes legis*. [However,] it is better to say that a feature cannot become a *ratio legis* unless it is relevant to the motive or the benefit, as we argued before. Some people consider the *ratio legis* a sign for the deontic qualification. Therefore, they accept all features as possible *rationes legis*. However, the first position is the correct one. This is because a *ratio legis* must have an effect (*lā-budda min an-yakūn lahā taʾthīr*). The effect of the *ratio legis* cannot realize except through one of the two aspects we [just] mentioned (*wa-taʾthīrahā lā-yakūn ilā min aḥad al-wajhayn al-ladhayn dhakarnāhumā*).[156]

At the end of the quote, ʿAbd al-Jabbār remarks that being effective is a necessary condition for a valid *ratio legis*. He adds that the effect of the *ratio legis* can be felt or known via two aspects that he mentioned at the beginning of the quote. An analysis of those aspects reveals his concept of effectiveness. First, the *ratio legis* must be relevant to the deontic qualification of the original case. This would exclude features such as the name, color, smell, or taste of wine and carcasses, for instance, as possible *rationes legis* behind the prohibition of consuming both. None of these is relevant to the prohibition of consuming wine or carcasses. A valid *ratio legis* must, rather, be logically relevant to the deontic qualification in question.[157] Second, the *ratio legis* must be relevant to the good/benefit (*luṭf*) intended from the deontic qualification. For example, the name, colour, or smell of wine brings about neither benefits nor harms, whereas intoxication is a feature with harmful consequences. Therefore, intoxication is a feature that can function as the *ratio legis* behind the prohibition of wine. ʿAbd al-Jabbār notes that those are the only two signs for an effective *ratio legis*. Effectiveness then for ʿAbd al-Jabbār is based on identifying the benefit and/or the relevant motive for the deontic qualification in question. Therefore, benefits and motives behind deontic qualifications, for ʿAbd al-Jabbār, are signs of effectiveness. This effectiveness or *taʾthīr* is a

---

[156] ʿAbd al-Jabbār, *Mughnī*, 17:334. For another similar passage, see p. 17:333.

[157] On this condition, see ʿAbd al-Jabbār, *Mughnī*, 17:333.

valid tool for uncovering the *ratio legis* behind a deontic qualification. The relevant feature that reveals the benefit intended from and the motive behind a deontic qualification is the *ratio legis* 'causing' the imposition of this particular legislation.

For both ʿAbd al-Jabbār and Juwaynī benefit plays a crucial role in deducing the *ratio legis*. However, there is a major difference between the methods used by both jurists. Juwaynī does not automatically consider any benefit as a path to uncover the *ratio legis*; only those benefits acknowledged in textual evidence are legitimate tools to ascertain the *ratio legis*. This limitation is not evident at all in ʿAbd al-Jabbār's discussion of effectiveness. Nowhere does he put limitations allowing only the use of textually acknowledged benefits as the only valid indicators for *rationes legis*. For ʿAbd al-Jabbār it is enough to know that a feature in the original case leads to *any* benefit and/or averts *any* harm and that this feature is concomitant with the deontic qualification. This is sufficient evidence that this feature is the correct *ratio legis*. The disagreement between ʿAbd al-Jabbār and Juwaynī may be motivated by their theological disagreements. I will come back to this point after discussing Samʿānī's concept of appropriateness and effectiveness.

Samʿānī's Concept of Suitability and Effectiveness

Samʿānī considers suggestiveness (*ikhāla*) and suitability as the only valid means to ascertain a *ratio legis*.[158] Unfortunately, he does not offer an explicit definition for any of them. Nonetheless, his concept of effectiveness must be very different from Shīrāzī's. Shīrāzī's effectiveness depends on concomitance, whereas Samʿānī, as previously explained, is a vehement opponent of concomitance and co-presence as methods to deduce a *ratio legis*. Samʿānī names Shīrāzī as one of those jurists who depend on concomitance in their deductions of the *ratio legis*. Samʿānī's rebuttal of co-presence will help reveal his understanding of effectiveness.

Samʿānī argues that there are no reports showing the Prophet's Companions using co-presence in their processes of *qiyās*. 'Instead, they look at the features (*maʿānī*), follow the path of wisdom

[158] Samʿānī, *Qawāṭiʿ al-adilla*, 4:194–5, 244, 245, 246, 251, 329.

(*marāshid*) and benefits (*maṣāliḥ*) that uncover the beauties of Sharīʿa (*maḥāsin al-sharīʿa*)'. He concludes saying that if co-presence was a valid tool in *qiyās*, the Companions would not have abandoned it.[159] Unfortunately, al-Samʿānī does not define benefits, wisdom, or the beauties of Sharīʿa. Yet, one may assume that they are references to the good intended from and the motive behind deontic qualifications. Moreover, he does not clarify the role benefit plays in deducing a *ratio legis*. He does not, furthermore, explain which types of benefits are allowed to play this role. Is Samʿānī referring to the free use of benefit in agreement with ʿAbd al-Jabbār? Or is he referring to the textually acknowledged benefit on Juwaynī's style?

Samʿānī's concept of effectiveness, appropriateness and suggestiveness seems to be closer to Juwaynī's than ʿAbd al-Jabbār's. His reference to the beauties of Sharīʿa (in addition to benefit and wisdom) indicates that, like Juwaynī, he is trying to limit the use of benefit as indicators to *rationes legis* to those benefits acknowledged in revelation. Later in his *Qawāṭiʿ al-adilla*, he explains that

> the crux of suggestiveness and appropriateness is to say: The evidence that can prove the validity of a *ratio legis* is the presence of a feature that is known to be effective and suggestive in prescribing a deontic qualification. We know that a feature is effective and suggestive if it conforms to the laws, regulations, and principles of revelation (*Sharʿ*)... The validity of a *ratio legis* cannot be proven by arrogant and stubborn arguments (*al-mukābarāt wa-l-muʿānadāt*). It can be proven by resorting to the basics and regulations of revelation (*uṣūl al-sharʿ wa-qawāʿiduh*) ... By effectiveness we mean, feeling in the heart that there is evidence in revelation that the deontic qualification [in question] is brought about by the *ratio legis* [under examination].[160]

Samʿānī does not elucidate much on his theory of appropriateness and effectiveness. However, it is evident that he accepts benefit as a tool to discover *rationes legis*. It is also clear that Samʿānī, like Juwaynī, places some restrictions on the benefits that can be used as indicators for a *ratio legis*. Samʿānī accepts only those benefits men-

---

159 Samʿānī, *Qawāṭiʿ al-adilla*, 4:194.

160 Samʿānī, *Qawāṭiʿ al-adilla*, 4:246.

tioned in revelation as indicators for *rationes legis*. For him, benefits not acknowledged in revelation cannot be used to ascertain *rationes legis*. Among the three scholars who accept benefit as an indicator for valid *rationes legis*, only ʿAbd al-Jabbār does not place textual limitations. Is ʿAbd al-Jabbār's unique position theologically motivated? Is Juwaynī's and Samʿānī's insistence to place textual limitations on their theories of appropriateness theologically motivated? The following section attempts to answer these questions.

Theology and the Material Methods

We have above four Shāfiʿī scholars with three different positions from the use of benefit as a tool to deduce and/or validate *rationes legis*. The Muʿtazilī ʿAbd al-Jabbār allows benefit a leading role without many, if any, restrictions. The Ashʿarī Juwaynī and the traditionalist Samʿānī are on the same side of the fence. Both allow benefit a role in the process of deducing the *ratio legis*; however, they only award this role to those benefits acknowledged by revelation. On the other hand, the Ashʿarī Shīrāzī allows benefit no role at all in deducing the *ratio legis*. Whether benefit plays a role in the process of deducing *rationes legis* (and the whole process of legislation), or not, is a topic that is relevant to a number of theological debates, such as the ones around the purposefulness of divine actions, God's commitment to the optimal benefit of humans, moral epistemology, moral ontology and causality. An examination of the relationship between benefit, the *ratio legis* and *qiyās* is an important gateway to investigate the relationship between those theological debates and legal theory in general, and *qiyās* in particular.

Muʿtazilī theology holds that God will always guarantee optimal human benefit. It also holds that independent human reason can, in most cases, assess the moral quality of human actions. Most importantly, for the Muʿtazilīs, reason is capable of uncovering the benefits and the harms that human actions prompt. Therefore, it makes sense to expect Muʿtazilī jurists to allow the free use of benefits, not just ones acknowledged in revelation, to discern *rationes legis*. On the other hand, Ashʿarī scholars do not hold that God is obliged to guarantee optimal human benefit. Ashʿarīs, when compared to Muʿtazilīs, undermine the ability of human reason to morally evaluate human actions. Furthermore, for them, most actions do not have an ontological moral quality. Therefore, Ashʿarīs are expected to put restrictions on the use of benefits in their endeavour to uncover *rationes legis*. They need to ground benefits in revelation, because for them, independent human reason is not fully capable of identifying those benefits that are taken into consideration by the Lawgiver.

The above explanation assumes that theological beliefs shape legal theory choices on group and school levels. In other words, common theological beliefs among a particular theological school consistently lead jurists, members of the same school of theology, to favour similar positions in legal theory. If these assumptions were accurate, one should then find consistent positions on the use of benefit within the same theological school. However, this is far from the case. We already saw that the Ashʿarīs Juwaynī and Shīrāzī are at odds when it comes to the use of benefit to discern *rationes legis*. A similar phenomenon is noticeable within Muʿtazilī circles. ʿAbd al-Jabbār allows a relatively free use of benefit to uncover *rationes legis*. However, as Felicitas Opwis notes, Abū Bakr al-Jaṣṣāṣ (who at least had Muʿtazilī tendencies) and ʿAbd al-Jabbār's Muʿtazilī student Abū al-Ḥusayn al-Baṣrī limit the use of benefit in law-making to those only acknowledged in revelation.[161] In fact, Opwis writes that Ashʿarī scholars such as Juwaynī, Ghazālī and Fakhr al-Dīn al-Rāzī award *maṣlaḥa* a wider role in law-making than Jaṣṣāṣ and Abū al-Ḥusayn al-Baṣrī. She explains that

> [a]lthough rationalist objectivism corresponds loosely with the Muʿtazilī school of theology and theistic subjectivism with the Ashʿarī school of thought, this dichotomy does not necessarily hold when assessing a scholar's stand toward human ability to know and employ *maṣlaḥa* in law-finding. Al-Jaṣṣāṣ, who is considered to belong to the Muʿtazila, clearly does not understand *maṣlaḥa* as a tool of law-finding, although he gives the intellect the ability to assess what is good and bad in matters that the law leaves neutral (*mubāḥāt*). A similar approach is espoused by the Muʿtazilī al-Basri [...] In contrast, the Ashʿarī scholars al-Juwaynī, al-Ghazālī, and Fakhr al-Dīn al-Rāzī are

---

[161] For Opwis' comments on Jaṣṣāṣ, see her *Maṣlaḥa*, 16–27. For her explanation of Abū al-Ḥusayn's position, see *Maṣlaḥa*, 34–41. See also Jaṣṣāṣ, *Fuṣūl*, 4:141–7; Abū al-Ḥusayn, *Muʿtamad*, 403–5, 888–9.

> among the main proponents of using *maṣlaḥa* for unprecedented cases within the procedure of analogy (*qiyās*).[162]

The question now is: Why does the sharing of common theological doctrines not lead to favouring similar positions in legal theory? Why do scholars who have the same theological background adopt, sometimes, contradicting positions on the aspect of legal theory discussed in the previous paragraph? Opwis does not argue that theology has no impact on legal theory; in fact, she holds the opposite. Neither do I hold that theology has no impact on this particular legal debate. I contend that theology informed the legal theory choices on individual level. However, jurists, who share the same theological background, interpret the legal theory consequences of their common theological doctrines differently. Therefore, theology does not always have a consistent and uniform impact on group and school level. For example, Abū al-Ḥusayn al-Baṣrī use the Muʿtazilī doctrine of optimism (*al-ṣalāḥ wa-l-aṣlaḥ*) *against* the use of the benefits, not acknowledged by revelation, in the process of deducing *rationes legis*. Abū al-Ḥusayn argues that since God is omniscient, just and committed to guarantee optimal human interest, therefore God will always uncover all benefits in His revelation.[163] Any 'benefit' not acknowledged in revelation cannot be beneficial; thus, it cannot be a basis for law-making. For Abū al-Ḥusayn, if God were not to disclose all benefits in revelation, this would undermine His just character and would contradict His commitment to guaranteeing optimal human benefit. Such a situation would entail that God has left humans without sufficient guidance; a conclusion that no Muʿtazilī would accept. Consequently, those benefits not recognised by revelation cannot be benefits in the first place and thus cannot be used in the process of law-making.

ʿAbd al-Jabbār has a different position. He uses the same Muʿtazilī theological tenet to argue that benefits should have a wide role in formulating new laws. For ʿAbd al-Jabbār, divine revelation

---

[162] Opwis, *Maṣlaḥa*, 30–1.

[163] Abū al-Ḥusayn, *Muʿtamad*, 80–1, 574, 908–10. It was Opwis' remarks that drew my attention to Abū al-Ḥusayn's argument, see her *Maṣlaḥa*, 41.

aims at maintaining optimal human benefit. ʿAbd al-Jabbār also believes that God is always committed to rational and objective criteria for identifying benefits and harms. Furthermore, for him, humans can rationally recognize beneficial actions. Given these positions, ʿAbd al-Jabbār concludes that what humans rationally identify as beneficial will always be in harmony with the teachings of revelation. Therefore, he concludes that the use of benefits to ascertain a *ratio legis* should not be limited to those explicitly expressed in revelation; rationally ascertained benefits are also suitable for this task.

Both ʿAbd al-Jabbār and Abū al-Ḥusayn share a very similar theology and both equally accept the Muʿtazilī understanding of 'optimism'. However, they interpret the legal theory consequences of their common theological doctrines differently. For Abū al-Ḥusayn, optimism puts restrictions on the use of benefit in the process of deducing *rationes legis*. For ʿAbd al-Jabbār, the same doctrine allows benefit a free role in the same legal process. It is clear that theology informs the legal theory choices of the two scholars. However, they disagree on the legal theory implications of their common theological tenet. This disagreement prevents their common doctrines from having a consistent and standardising impact on their legal theory. A common theology, therefore, does not necessarily guarantee the adoption of a common legal theory.

Just like their Muʿtazilī counterparts, the Ashʿarī scholars examined here disagree on the use of benefit to deduce *rationes legis*. As explained earlier, Juwaynī allows benefits acknowledged in revelation to function as a tool to uncover *rationes legis*. Shīrāzī, on the other hand, awards benefit no role in this process. Instead, he depends on formal methods, mainly concomitance. Here we see two Ashʿarī jurists adopting very different methods to deduce *rationes legis*. Each of them believes that his methods are in harmony with his Ashʿarī theology. The traditionalist Samʿānī shares many of the Ashʿarī doctrines that are relevant to *qiyās* and the *ratio legis*. Like Ashʿarīs, he undermines the ability of human reason to uncover moral assessments and discern the purposes behind divine legislations. Yet, like Juwaynī and unlike Shīrāzī, he accepts the use of benefit to deduce *rationes legis*. Again, sharing a common theology does not necessarily lead to sharing a common position in legal theory. Jurists who share similar theological beliefs might deduce different legal theory positions from their shared doctrines. Therefore, it is not surprising to find contradicting positions from the use of benefit in *qiyās* within the Ashʿarī School of theology, just like the Muʿtazilī. Modern students (and scholars) of Islamic law should appreciate the fact that pre-modern jurists disagree on the legal theory implications of their theology. Hastily accusing pre-modern scholars of adopting positions in legal theory that contradict their theology assumes the presence of only one possible (or logical) legal theory outcome for each theological doctrine.

CONCLUSION

The nature of *qiyās* as a legislative tool brings it close to several foundational theological doctrines. *Qiyās* is based on finding a 'causal link' between a particular *ratio legis* and a particular deontic qualification. Pre-modern jurists often see the *ratio legis* as the rationale, benefit, or motive behind deontic qualifications. This understanding of *qiyās* and the *ratio legis* appears relevant to theological debates such as the ones around natural causality, the purposefulness of divine actions, God's commitment to human optimal benefit, and moral epistemology, to mention only a few. In this chapter, I have explored the nature of the relationship between those theological doctrines and *qiyās*, in general, and the *ratio legis* in particular. The four Shāfiʿī jurists, who are at the centre of this study, belong to three different theological trends. Each trend favours different positions on these theological debates. Despite their theological disagreements, the four jurists' conceptions of *qiyās* are not significantly different. Although they disagree on the issue of natural causality, they share a common perception of the *ratio legis* as non-essentially effective (*ghayr muʾaththira*) in producing its deontic qualification. Excluding Samʿānī, the other three Shāfiʿīs adopt similar positions on the use of formal methods to deduce *rationes legis.*

This does not mean that theological disagreements do not prompt discrepancies in their legal theory. A good example of such a discrepancy is Samʿānī's unique position on the formal methods of deducing *rationes legis.* Those methods, as explained before, are often associated with logic (*manṭiq*) and dialectics (*jadal*). Traditionalist jurists are characterized with an aloofness towards methods associated with logic and dialectics; this is probably a product of their theology that restricts speculative and rational methods in reaching theological and sometimes even legal conclusions. The influence of theological disagreements is also noticeable in the use of the material methods to deduce *rationes legis*. ʿAbd al-Jabbār allows benefit almost an unchecked role in ascertaining *rationes legis*. Juwaynī and Samʿānī, on the other hand, only accept benefits acknowledged in revelation as indicators for correct *rationes legis*. This might have been a theologically motivated disagreement. ʿAbd al-Jabbār's Muʿtazilī theology allows him to trust rational methods in the process of law-making. The Ashʿarī and traditionalist theologies of Juwaynī and Samʿanī undermine the ability of human reason to reach moral judgments, recognize benefits and harms and appreciate the purpose behind revelation. Their theology, therefore, does not allow a free use of benefit in the process of ascertaining the *rationes legis* behind divine laws.

The impact of theology on *qiyās* is therefore quite clear; however, this impact is far from consistent. I explained above that neither Ashʿarī nor Muʿtazilī jurists are unanimous on the legal theory implications of their common theological doctrines. The same theological tenet is sometimes used to argue for two contradicting positions in legal theory. Therefore, embracing the same theology does not always lead to favouring similar stands in legal theory. It is also interesting to note that theological disagreements do not always prompt discrepancies in legal theory. For example, the rejection of *qiyās* is a well-known hallmark of Twelver Shīʿī legal theory. The Akhbārī legal school, a Twelver Shīʿī sub-school, is split over the validity of Ṣūfī and mystical knowledge. Like most Shīʿīs, Akhbārīs reject the validity of *qiyās* as a tool for law-making. Robert Gleave shows that Akhbārī jurists, who are anti-Ṣūfī, only use traditions attributed to the Shīʿī Imāms in their arguments against *qiyās*. Those Akhbārī jurists who accept Ṣūfism use philosophical and mystical arguments, never used by anti-Ṣūfī Akhbārīs, in their refutations of *qiyās*.[164] Both groups have very different philosophical and theological orientations, yet they share a rejection of *qiyās*. Each group uses methods, that would be refused by the other group, to vindicate a common position in legal theory.

The Ẓāhirī School of law provides another similar example. Aron Zysow explains that Ẓāhirīs are divided over moral epistemology; a group accepts rational moral epistemology; another

[164] Gleave, 'Scriptural Sufism', 170–2.

group undermines the ability of human reason to ascertain moral judgments, and depends mainly on revelation for this purpose. However, Ẓāhirīs are unanimous on their rejection of *qiyās*. Those who favour a rational moral theory use their doctrines as evidence against the use of *qiyās* as a tool for law-making. Ẓāhirīs who favour a less rational moral theory use their moral theory to support the same position on *qiyās*. Both groups are utilizing contradicting theological tenets to support the same position in legal theory.[165] This shows that jurists, members of the same legal school, sometimes disagree on the theological foundations of their common positions in legal theory. Each group probably believes that its own theology is the proper theological premises for the legal theory they share. Furthermore, the examples from the Akhbārī and the Ẓāhirī schools of law show that theological disagreements do not always prompt discrepancies in legal theory. This is also clear in most Sunnī legal schools. Excluding the Ḥanbalī, Sunnī legal schools host jurists from various theological backgrounds. Their theological disagreements do not prevent them from membership in the same legal school and do not stop them from sharing similar positions in legal theory.

This raises the question of uniformity and conformity within schools of law. The concept of a school of law requires different jurists to share some common legal positions. Rejecting *qiyās* is an important Ẓāhirī and Twelver Shīʿī pillar. It is difficult for any jurist to comfortably fit and be accepted within a Ẓāhirī or a Shīʿī school of law despite accepting *qiyās*. Therefore, contradicting theological doctrines adopted by Twelver and Ẓāhirī jurists must all be interpreted as evidence against *qiyās* or at least as tenets that do not lead to vindicating it. Accepting *qiyās* and consensus (*ijmāʿ*) are hallmarks of the four major Sunnī schools of law. A jurist member of a Sunnī school of law cannot reach a conclusion that his theology requires the rejection of *qiyās* or consensus (*ijmāʿ*). Such positions would deprive his legal thought of legitimacy among his peers and would lead to his ostracization. A school of law, like the Shāfiʿī, that includes jurists from diverse theological trends, assumes that theological and philosophical disagreements do not necessarily ruin

---

165 Zysow, *Economy of Certainty*, 182.

the common legal grounds that it shares. This may imply that the foundational legal tenets of a jurist's school of law may play a role in interpreting the legal consequences of his theological beliefs. Out of conviction or convenience, a jurist will interpret the legal consequences of his theology in a manner that would not deprive him of his membership in his school of law. This membership, as explained in chapter two, is crucial for his employability, access to legal educational institutions and social prestige.

It appears to me that Sunnī jurists were aware that allowing theological disagreements to significantly shape legal theory could have been detrimental to the common framework that unites each of the Sunnī schools of law. Therefore, jurists might have been keen to limit the impact of the *most* controversial theological debates on essential aspects of *qiyās*. Or at least adopt methods that would minimize the discrepancies in legal theory caused by their theological disagreements. This may be noticed in the tendency among the four jurists, who are under study, and many others, to differentiate between *rationes legis* (*al-ʿilal al-sharʿiyya*) and natural causes (*al-ʿilal al-ʿaqliyya*). Muslim jurists unanimously consider the *ratio legis* as the cornerstone of *qiyās*; distancing it from controversial theological debates seems to be an attempt to undermine the impact of theological disagreements on *qiyās*. All four jurists insist that *rationes legis* are different from natural causes, therefore rules that apply to the latter do not influence the former. A theological disagreement on natural causality will then have less influence on debates around the function of the *ratio legis* in *qiyās*. This distinction between the two types of 'causes' allow jurists, from diverse theological backgrounds, to form a common perception of *qiyās* within the legal school they share, regardless of theological disagreements.

If theological debates were left to influence the perception of the *ratio legis* there could have been different theories of *qiyās* each attached to one theological school. It is difficult to have fundamentally different conceptions of *qiyās* within the same school of law. This would not only ruin the legal theory foundations of each legal school, but would also ruin their adoption of the common jurisprudential positions that distinguish each school of law. To maintain conformity within the Shāfiʿī School, there had to be some limitations on the impact of theological disagreements on *qiyās* and on legal theory in general. Otherwise, legal schools may split along theological lines. Theological schools will themselves become legal schools and existing *madhhabs* would split into different legal schools after jurists realize the impact of their diverse theologies. Therefore, either from the beginning of the formation of legal schools or in retrospect, there had to be a bridle limiting the impact of theology on legal theory. This bridle created the shape of legal divisions as we know them today and help maintain the unity of each of the four Sunnī schools of law.

CHAPTER FOUR: THE RULE OF LAW BEFORE THE LAW

INTRODUCTION

In this chapter, I will analyse and compare the answers of the four Shāfiʿī jurists under study to the following question: What is the deontic qualification (*ḥukm sharʿī*)[1] of actions (*afʿāl*) and things (*ashyāʾ* or *aʿyān*) before the advent of revelation?[2] Are they permitted (*mubāḥa*), proscribed (*maḥẓūra*), or should deontic qualifications be suspended (*mawqūfa*) until the advent of revelation?[3] I call this

[1] Let me remind the reader that within Islamic law there are five main deontic qualifications, namely obligatory (*wājib*), recommended (*mandūb*), permitted (*mubāḥ*), disapproved (*makrūh*) and proscribed (*maḥẓūr* or *ḥarām*). Following the example of Zysow in his *Economy of Certainty*, I use the term deontic qualifications in reference to these five qualifications. I use the terms moral qualifications and moral knowledge as a reference to the ethical values of good (*ḥasan*) and evil (*qabīḥ*).

[2] In pre-modern literature, this question is usually phrased using one of the following statements: *ḥukm al-ashyāʾ qabla wurūd al-sharʿ*, *ḥukm al-aʿyān qabla wurūd al-sharʿ*, or *ḥukm al-afʿāl qabla wurūd al-sharʿ*. I translate *ashyāʾ* and *aʿyān* as things. The terms *ashyāʾ* and *aʿyān*, in Muslim legal literature, are often used in reference to objects or beings that humans either use or consume, such as beef, pork, water, wine, gold and silver etc. I translate *afʿāl* as actions, by this term pre-modern jurists are usually referring not to objects but to the action of using or consuming these objects such as eating beef or pork, drinking water or wine, wearing silver or gold etc. Things cover all objects or beings that humans can use or consume; actions cover every possible human action.

[3] Scholars who hold that actions and things prior to revelation are permitted will be referred to as 'permitters' (*ahl al-ibāḥa*). Those who hold

group of enquiries the 'before revelation question'. This chapter is primarily an analysis of the four jurists' answers to this question, their arguments in support of their answers and their rebuttals of their opponents. The main aim of this analysis is to understand how far the theological doctrines of the four Shāfiʿīs inform their answers to this question and shape their supporting arguments.

The analysis of the four Shāfiʿīs' discussions of the before revelation question reveals that their theological doctrines significantly inform their positions on this debate. Theology, moreover, determines how a jurist justifies his position on this legal question. Jurists often refer to their theological doctrines to justify their position on the before revelation controversy. The theological debates that appear to have the greatest impact on this aspect of legal theory are the ones around moral epistemology (*al-taḥsīn wa-l-taqbīḥ*), divine justice (*ʿadl*) and divine wisdom (*ḥikma*). However, consulting a wider sample of literature shows that the influence of theology is inconsistent at group and theological school level. As is the case in *qiyās*, jurists disagree on how exactly their theology should influence their answers to the before revelation question. In other words, disagreements on the legal theory implications of common theological doctrines prevent jurists – holding the same beliefs – from offering similar answers to the before revelation question. Therefore, theology does not function as a 'standardizing factor' in this aspect of legal theory. What appear to have a more consistent impact here is the jurists' positions on various hermeneutical questions, such as the interpretation of doubt and the legal implication of the absence of revelational evidence (*adilla sharʿiyya*).[4] Jurists, regardless of their theological backgrounds, who offer similar answers to these hermeneutical questions tend to favour similar positions on the before revelation debate.

This chapter is divided into four sections. The first is the introduction which includes information on the importance of the

---

that actions and things before revelation are proscribed will be referred to as 'proscribers' (*ahl al-ḥaẓr*).

[4] Revelational evidence is the sources and tools Muslim jurists consider normative. The major revelational evidence is the Qurʾān, Prophetic Sunna, consensus and *qiyās*.

before revelation question and a review of some of the modern studies that examined this debate. The second is an analysis of the four jurists' arguments in support of their answers to the before revelation question and their refutations of opposing positions. None of the four Shāfiʿīs examined here holds that actions and things before revelation are proscribed. A thorough understanding of 'permission' and 'suspension', as answers to the before revelation question, is not possible without examining and understanding proscription. The third section focuses on those jurists who embrace proscription and analyses how the four jurists under study, and others, refute their arguments in favour of proscription. The fourth, and final, section is the conclusion.

A number of factors might challenge the conclusions of this chapter. First, due to space and time restraints, this chapter chooses only to focus on the relationship between speculative theology and the before revelation question and will not examine the impact of the before revelation debate on other aspects of legal theory. This examination could have provided valuable information on the motives that drive a jurist to select one position on the before revelation debate and not another. Second, the lack of primary sources necessary for the topic of this chapter is another challenge. The Shāfiʿī legal theory literature, of which I am aware, mainly consists of texts authored by jurists who adopt suspension. Excluding volume seventeen of ʿAbd al-Jabbār's *Mughnī*, I am not aware of further Shāfiʿī legal literature authored by jurists who promote permission. This prevents understanding how other Shāfiʿīs from different theological backgrounds justified permission and refuted suspension. Furthermore, as far as I know, there is only one available legal theory work authored by a jurist who advocates proscription, namely *al-ʿUdda fī uṣūl al-fiqh* by the Ḥanbalī Abū Yaʿlā b. al-Farrāʾ (d. 458/1066).[5] A solid understanding of permission and suspension, as positions on the before revelation question, is not feasible without a thorough understanding of proscription. The paucity of legal theory works favouring the proscription position makes un-

[5] Abū Yaʿlā Muḥammad b. al-Ḥusayn al-Farrāʾ (d. 458/1066), *al-ʿUdda fī uṣūl al-fiqh*, 2nd ed. ed. Aḥmad b. ʿAlī Sīr al-Mubārkī (1400/1980; repr., Riyadh: Muʾassasat al-Risāla, 1410/1990).

derstanding permission and suspension incomplete and prevents us from appreciating the theoretical, hermeneutical and theological foundations of all three positions. These factors, nonetheless, should not stop modern historians from examining the before revelation debate; however, such factors should remind them not to be too certain about any conclusions reached.

Before going into the details, we should first clarify the subject matter of the before revelation controversy. Jurists discussing the deontic qualification of actions before revelation are not actually pondering upon the deontic assessments of all actions. Most jurists only wonder about the deontic evaluation of useful actions (*al-afʿāl* or *al-aʿyān al-muntafaʿ bihā*) which entail the exclusion of actions and things known to be harmful.[6] In addition, the debate is not concerned with the deontic appraisals of actions necessary for human survival (*al-afʿāl al-iḍṭirāriyya*), such as breathing, eating and drinking. The majority of jurists see that such actions must be permitted before, as well as after, the advent of revelation.[7] Therefore, the before revelation debate, for most jurists, is concerned with examining the deontic qualification of useful and harmless actions and things; ones that are not necessary for human survival.

---

[6] Among those who explicitly note that this debate is concerned with useful actions only are Abū Bakr Aḥmad b. ʿAlī al-Khaṭīb al-Baghdādī (d. 463/1071), *Kitāb al-Faqīh wa-l-mutafaqqih*, 2 vols ed. ʿĀdil b. Yūsuf al-ʿAzāzī (Riyadh: Dār Ibn al-Jawzī, 1417/1996), 1:528; Samʿānī, *Qawāṭiʿ al-adilla*, 3:408; Shīrāzī, *Sharḥ al-Lumaʿ*, 977; Ṣaymarī, *Masāʾil al-khilāf*, 2:336; Jaṣṣāṣ, *Fuṣūl*, 3:247; Samarqandī, *Mīzān al-uṣūl*, 281; Abū Yaʿlā, *al-ʿUdda fī uṣūl al-fiqh*, 123. Neither Juwaynī nor ʿAbd al-Jabbār explicitly say whether they include harmful actions in their discussions of the before revelation debate or not.

[7] For scholars who explicitly exclude necessary actions from the debate, see Abū Zayd ʿUbayd Allāh b. ʿUmar b. ʿIsā al-Dabūsī (d. 430/1039), *Taqwīm al-adilla fī uṣūl al-fiqh*, ed. Khalīl Muḥyī al-Dīn al-Mīs (Beirut: Dār al-Kutub al-ʿIlmiyya, 1421/2001), 449; Rāzī, *Maḥṣūl*, 1:158; Samʿānī, *Qawāṭiʿ al-adilla*, 3:431. The later Shāfiʿī jurist Zarkashī (d. 794/1392) notes that few scholars make this question also applicable to necessary actions, see his *al-Baḥr al-Muḥīṭ*, 152–3. ʿAbd al-Jabbār, Shīrāzī and Juwaynī do not mention their position explicitly.

The debate asks whether, in a world in which humans did not yet receive any divine revelations, the deontic qualification of the actions they can perform and the things they can consume can in fact be discovered? If yes, what then is this deontic qualification? In pre-modern legal theory literature, there are three possible answers for these questions. The first two entail that humans can indeed disclose the deontic appraisals of actions and things prior to the arrival of divine revelation. First, permission (*ibāḥa*), actions and things before the advent of revelation are permitted until revelation arrives and declares some of them proscribed. In this case, humans can voluntarily choose which action to perform and which not, which thing to consume and which not. Permission also entails that the performance or the omission of any action deserves neither divine punishment nor reward. The second possible answer is proscription (*ḥaẓr*); actions and things are proscribed until revelation comes and declares some of them permitted. Humans are not allowed to perform any act unnecessary for their survival, until they receive an explicit permission from the Creator. In this case, the performance of any unnecessary act warrants divine blame and punishment. The third possible answer is suspension (*waqf*); prior to revelation humans cannot discern the deontic qualification of any action or thing. Therefore, humans should refrain from any deontic evaluations prior to divine revelation. Before revelation, all actions and things are neither permitted nor proscribed. Humans in this case remain in a state of confusion until they receive divine guidance.

Significance of the Before Revelation Question

The before revelation question seems, *prima facie*, a hypothetical question with little practical legal relevance. The Mālikī Abū al-Walīd al-Bājī (d. 474/1081) notes that occupying oneself with this question is an unnecessary contrivance (*takalluf*). Humans never existed prior to revelation; there is no need to occupy oneself with answering this question.[8] For Muslims, Adam is not only the first

---

[8] Abū al-Walīd Sulaymān b. Khalaf al-Bājī, *al-Ishāra fī uṣūl al-fiqh*, 2nd ed. ed. ʿĀdil ʿAbd al-Mawjūd and ʿAlī ʿAwaḍ (Riyadh: Maktabat Nizār

human, but also the first prophet. Nonetheless, this question is awarded at least one section in all of the legal theory literature examined for this study, including that of Bājī. In this literature, three reasons are usually mentioned explaining why this, seemingly hypothetical, question is important. First, finding an answer to the deontic qualification of actions prior to revelation will facilitate forming theories about uncovering the deontic qualifications of actions on which revelation does not comment.[9] In other words, creating a hypothetical situation in which humans existed prior to revelation will assist Muslim jurists to answer questions on which revelation is silent in the post-revelation era.

Second, answering the before revelation question helps to interpret the silence of revelation. Does the silence of revelation entail a particular deontic qualification? If yes, which? Permission or proscription? Can the silence of revelation, in itself, function as evidence supporting a particular deontic qualification? In other words, can a jurist support the permission of performing a specific action simply by noting that revelation does not comment on it, therefore it must be permitted? Can another jurist support the proscription of an action by noting that revelation does not comment on it, therefore it must be proscribed? Answering the last two questions will determine which jurist is required to put forward evidence in support of his argument, the one who claims an act is permitted, the opponent who claims that the same act is proscribed, or both.[10] Determining the deontic qualification of actions

---

Muṣṭafā al-Bāz, 1418/1997), 299. For another similar comment, see Abū al-Wafā᾽ ʿAlī b. ʿAqīl (d. 513/1119), *al-Wāḍiḥ fī uṣūl al-fiqh*, 5 vols ed. ʿAbd Allāh b. ʿAbd al-Muḥsin al-Turkī (Beirut: Mu᾽assasat al-Risāla, 1420/1998), 2:317.

[9] See for example, Maḥfūẓ b. Aḥmad b. al-Ḥasan Abū al-Khaṭṭāb al-Kalwadhānī (d. 510/1117), *al-Tamhīd fī uṣūl al-fiqh*, 4 vols ed. Mufīd Muḥammad Abū ʿAmsha (Mecca: Umm al-Qurā University, 1406/1985), 4:271; Zarkashī, *al-Baḥr al-muḥīṭ*, 1:160–1; Abū Yaʿlā, *al-ʿUdda fī uṣūl al-fiqh*, 1250–1.

[10] Among those who mention the relevance of these questions to the before revelation debate are: al-Khaṭīb al-Baghdādī, *al-Faqīh wa-l-*

prior to revelation might help answer some of these dialectical and hermeneutical questions.

The third issue usually mentioned by medieval legal theoreticians to justify investigating the before revelation question is often framed in the following manner: The before revelation question is important to know whether humans living on the peak of mountains (*qimam al-jibāl*) or on isolated islands (*juzur*) [i.e. and thus never encountered revelation] are obliged to embrace the correct faith and practice it or not.[11] Said differently, are humans, who never had access to revelation, obliged to believe in God and obey His legislations? Are these humans culpable should they fail to discover the correct faith and practice? This is an allusion to an ancient theological and philosophical debate: Can the human mind become aware of the Creator without the assistance of revelation? Are humans required to search for the 'true' faith regardless of access to revelation? How far can reason uncover the correct moral and deontic regulations humans are expected to follow without the help of revelation? These are all important questions with serious legal consequences that go beyond legal theory to theology, philosophy and mysticism. The before revelation debate can provide a theoretical framework for theorizing and contemplating about these philosophical and theological questions and uncover their consequences in legal theory and law.

Some modern historians of Islam have also recognized the importance of this legal theory debate. Ahmad Aṭif Ahmad, for instance, writes that the before revelation question is actually a debate over the interpretation of doubt. If there is uncertainty about the deontic qualification revelation awards to a particular action, should jurists adopt permission or proscription?[12] Furthermore, Kevin Reinhart explains that the most significant reasons why this

---

mutafaqqih, 1:531; Kalwadhānī, *al-Tamhīd fī uṣūl al-fiqh*, 4:271, 285; Abū Yaʿlā, *al-ʿUdda fī uṣūl al-fiqh*, 1251.

[11] See for example, Ibn ʿAqīl, *al-Wāḍiḥ fī uṣūl al-fiqh*, 5:261; Kalwadhānī, *al-Tamhīd fī uṣūl al-fiqh*, 4:272; Abū Yaʿlā, *al-ʿUdda fī uṣūl al-fiqh*, 1243.

[12] Ahmad, *Structural Interrelations*, 170.

debate is important are rarely explicitly mentioned. He adds that some of the legal theory questions raised by medieval jurists are

> 'things to think with,' or *camerae obscurae* by means of which a delicate or sensitive matter could be regarded indirectly, and without fear of injury. Muslim scholars cultivated these controversies like special strains of plants bred to study some anomaly or disease.[13]

The before revelation question is one such strain of plant bred not for its own sake but for the sake of examining other legal and theological questions. Jurists are not essentially interested in finding the deontic qualification of actions before the advent of revelation. In fact, Muslims believe that humans never existed prior to revelation. By asking this hypothetical question, jurists are rather indirectly raising other questions. Among those questions, notes Reinhart, are ones around moral epistemology and ontology, relationship between reason and revelation, definition of religious knowledge, relationship between morality and culture,[14] and minimalist and maximalist interpretations of revelation.[15] Reinhart argues that those are the real issues being examined when a jurist asks the before revelation question.

Anver Emon objects that this was far from a hypothetical question. Jurists, argues Emon, were not trying to avoid thorny controversies. Rather, they were 'theorizing the foundation for the use of juristic discretion to address those situations where no scrip-

---

[13] Reinhart, *Before Revelation*, 3–4.

[14] Reinhart clarifies this point saying that among the questions the before revelation debate examines is whether morality 'to be understood as something innate within humans, and so, universal across denominational lines, or were humans so corrupted by individual and collective interest as to be incapable of dispassionate moral knowledge? Were the moral commands of Islam congruent with human capacity to know the good from the detestable, or were the commands of God utterly transcendent of human capacity, and therefore reliably true and objective?' See his, *Before Revelation*, 5.

[15] Reinhart, *Before Revelation*, 3–5, 127, 132–7.

ture addresses a given issue'.[16] In all cases, modern scholars often agree that pre-modern jurists are not actually trying to find the deontic qualification of actions in a pre-revelation existence. They are rather struggling to answer questions in a post-revelation world. Therefore, knowing a jurist's position on this debate will not reveal much about his theology and legal theory. What is more revealing are the methods used and arguments raised during a jurist's attempt to answer this question. These methods and arguments are attempts to answer the questions being actually, but implicitly, asked when a jurist wonders about the deontic evaluation of actions in a pre-revelation world. A world, for Muslims, that humans never witnessed.

Modern Discussions of the Debate

Few modern scholars have attempted to study the before revelation debate in detail. I am only aware of one monograph that makes this legal theory controversy its main research question, namely Kevin Reinhart's *Before Revelation: The Boundaries of Muslim Moral Thought*, discussed in the following section in detail. Other scholars discuss the before revelation question in a chapter or a section of a work that examines a broader legal theory topic.[17] The best of those is

---

[16] Anver Emon, 'Natural Law and Natural Rights in Islamic Law', *Journal of Law and Religion* 20.2 (2004–5), 355.

[17] See for example, ʿĀyiḍ b. ʿAbd Allāh b. ʿAbd al-ʿAzīz al-Shahrānī, *al-Taḥsīn wa-l-taqbīḥ al-ʿaqliyyān wa-atharahumā fī masāʾil uṣūl al-fiqh*, 3 vols (Riyadh: Kunūz Ishbīliyya, 1429/2008), 2:98–122; Shtīwī, *ʿAlāqat ʿilm uṣūl al-fiqh bi-ʿilm al-kalām*, 247–259; Namla, *al-Muhadhdhab fī ʿilm uṣūl al-fiqh*, 262–9; ʿAbd al-Qādir, *al-Masāʾil al-mushtaraka*, 84–5. Emon also discusses some aspects of the before revelation question in his studies of the relationship between reason and revelation in law-making, see for example Emon, *Islamic Natural Law*; Emon, 'Natural Law and Natural Rights'. He shows that Muʿtazilī jurists who adopt permission reach this conclusion based on their theology that allows them to 'fuse fact and value'. In other words, their theology allows them to use teleological assessments of actions and things to reach normative values. Their understanding of optimism, divine justice and wisdom allows them to assume that God will

Haytham Khazna's PhD dissertation in which he compares the legal theory of Irāqī-Ḥanafīs, whom are usually Muʿtazilī, to Samarqandī-Ḥanafīs, whom are usually Māturīdī. In his chapter on the before revelation debate, he argues that permission is dominant among Irāqī-Ḥanafīs whereas suspension is dominant among Samarqandī-Ḥanafīs. Khazna concludes that this inter-Ḥanafī disagreement is mainly a result of the Māturīdī rejection of two Muʿtazilī theological doctrines, namely optimism (*al-ṣalāḥ wa-l-aṣlaḥ*) and the purposefulness of divine actions (*taʿlīl afʿāl Allāh*).

Khazna explains his conclusion saying that both Muʿtazilī tenets entail that God's actions are always motivated by maintaining optimal human benefit. God's revelation, therefore, *must* bring legislations that will guarantee humanity's best interest. For Muʿtazilīs, this means that revelation will always prohibit evil and harmful actions and permit good and harmless ones. Khazna concludes that Irāqī-Ḥanafīs embrace theological positions allowing them to assume that all harmless, useful and good actions must be permitted, both before and after the advent of revelation.

Khazna continues, noting that Māturīdīs refuse optimism and the purposefulness of divine actions. They hold that God cannot be conditioned to behave in a certain manner; nothing can stop God from imposing laws that do not preserve optimal human benefit. Therefore, Māturīdī theology does not guarantee that God will permit good and harmless actions and does not preclude the possibility of God permitting evil and harmful ones. This theology makes humans, before revelation, incapable of predicting which actions revelation would permit and which ones it would proscribe. Khazna concludes that Māturīdī theology offers Samarqandī-Ḥanafī jurists no other option but to suspend moral and deontic appraisals until the arrival of revelation, whereas Muʿtazilī theology encourages Irāqī-Ḥanafīs to choose permission.[18] Khazna's conclusion entails that theology plays an important role in determining a jurist's answer to the before revelation. It also demonstrates that

---

always allow useful and harmless actions and things and prohibit harmful actions and things, regardless of the presence or absence of revelation.

[18] For Khazna's complete argument, see his 'al-Ikhtilāfāt al-uṣūliyya', 170–92.

theological disagreements among jurists, even within the same school of law, may lead to discrepancies in legal theory.

Muḥammad al-Shtīwī's *ʿAlāqat ʿilm uṣūl al-fiqh bi-ʿilm al-kalām* has a section dedicated to discussing the before revelation question. He starts his section with a descriptive survey of the different positions on this question and the supporting evidence each party puts forward justifying its stand. In the final pages, he mentions his own opinion, noting that this is mainly a hypothetical question that has no practical benefit; it is neither relevant to legal theory nor law. He believes that jurists were actually pondering about deontic evaluations in a pre-revelation world and since we live in a post-revelation world this question becomes futile. Al-Shtīwī identifies some theological doctrines as relevant to this debate, such as moral epistemology, optimism and the eternity of divine speech. He considers the before revelation question to be an extension of the theological debate around moral epistemology. He remarks that jurists raise this question again in their legal works to reaffirm their position on moral knowledge. He is critical of those jurists who dedicate much space to this question in their legal theory writings, noting that the details of this debate should remain in works on theology.[19] Al-Shtīwī fails to recognize the significance of the before revelation question. He does not appreciate the important legal and philosophical questions being asked implicitly when wondering about deontic appraisals prior to divine revelations.

Another two works that include a chapter dedicated to the before question are ʿĀyiḍ al-Shahrānī's *al-Taḥsīn wa-l-taqbīḥ fī uṣūl al-fiqh* and ʿAbd al-Karīm al-Namla's *al-Muhdhdhab fī ʿilm uṣūl al-fiqh al-muqāran.*[20] Shahrānī's is a three volume work which investigates the impact of the moral theory debate on modern trends in legal theory. Namla's work is a five volume reference work in which he attempts to, exhaustively, collect the opinions of pre-modern schol-

---

[19] Shtīwī, *ʿAlāqat ʿilm uṣūl al-fiqh bi-ʿilm al-kalām*, 247–259.

[20] Shahrānī, *al-Taḥsīn wa-l-taqbīḥ*, 2:98–122; Namla, *al-Muhadhdhab fī ʿilm uṣūl al-fiqh*, 262–9. At the time of authoring the book, al-Shahrānī was a faculty member at the Department of Uṣūl al-Fiqh, Faculty of Sharīʿa, Imām Muḥammad b. Saʿūd Islamic University, Riyadh. Al-Namla is a professor at the same department.

ars towards all legal theory questions and debates. Shahrānī's and Namla's discussion of the before revelation question are mainly doxographical, descriptive, and includes no serious efforts to analyse the complexities of this question. The two authors mainly mention the different answers offered to the before revelation question, names of pre-modern jurists who prefer each answer and a brief account of the evidence each party offers to justify its position. They do not analyse any of this evidence. They do not attempt to deconstruct the debate and understand the motivations behind choosing any particular position. Namla does not discuss the theological significance of the before revelation question; Shahrānī, on the other hand, discusses it briefly. He, like many others, argues that embracing a revelational moral theory should lead to accepting suspension, whereas embracing a rational moral theory should lead to accepting either permission or proscription. Shahrānī notes that jurists who hold a revelational moral theory and yet who endorse either permission or proscription are being inconsistent.[21]

Kevin Reinhart's *Before Revelation*

The only monograph, of which I am aware, that focuses on the before revelation debate is Reinhart's *Before Revelation.* It is also, probably, the most profound study of this legal theory question hitherto offered. It is, therefore, worth spending some time exploring the author's arguments especially as this chapter will refer to them rather frequently. The book is formed of five parts. The first part (chapters one and two) is a historical and a doxographical survey of the before revelation question, showing which pre-modern scholars held which position on this debate.[22] Reinhart notices that, until the fifth/eleventh century, permission was widespread among

---

[21] Shahrānī, *al-Taḥsīn wa-l-taqbīḥ*, 2:119–22. By rational moral theory I am referring to the belief that human reason, without the aid of revelation, can discern moral knowledge. A revelational moral theory is one that does not totally reject the ability of reason to discern moral knowledge, but it greatly undermines it. Revelation is, rather, seen as the primary and most reliable source of moral values.

[22] Reinhart, *Before Revelation*, 1–28.

all schools of law and theology, excluding the Ḥanbalī who, for the most part, espouse proscription.

In the second part (chapters three, four, five and an appendix), Reinhart analyses each of the three possible answers to the before revelation question and the supporting evidence used to support every position. He concludes that suspension is mainly based on adopting a revelational moral theory; one that makes revelation the major source of moral knowledge. This moral theory is predominant among Ashʿarīs which explains, according to Reinhart, the popularity of suspension among them. On the other hand, he writes that permission and proscription is mainly grounded in embracing a rational moral theory, which depends more on unaided reason to acquire moral knowledge. His most important finding in this part is that starting from the fifth/eleventh century, suspension replaced permission as the dominant position among all schools of law, excluding the Ḥanafīs who, for the most part, keep favouring permission.[23]

Parts three and four of Reinhart's book analyse theological controversies relevant to, or influenced by, the before revelation debate. Part three (chapter six) focuses on the debate around the obligation to thank the benefactor (*shukr al-munʿim*), whether humans become aware of this obligation via their unaided reason or via revelation.[24] Part four (chapters seven to ten) focuses on moral epistemology and ontology. Reinhart examines the two main moral theories within Islam; the first is what he calls a 'low view of revelation', usually associated with Muʿtazilīs. This view sees actions and things as either ontologically good or evil and that human reason is capable of uncovering an act's moral quality, even in the absence of revelation. The second is what he calls the 'high view of revelation', often associated with Ashʿarī and traditionalist jurists and theologians. Moral qualities (i.e. goodness and evilness), according to this understanding, are not part of an act's ontological being. Things and actions acquire their moral status via revelation. The high view

---

[23] Reinhart, *Before Revelation*, 29–104.

[24] Reinhart, *Before Revelation*, 105–23.

of revelation, thus, makes moral assessments mainly the domain of revelation rather than reason.[25]

Part five is Reinhart's conclusion; here I do not only discuss conclusions mentioned in part five but also those raised in the conclusions of his previous chapters. Reinhart notes that none of the three positions on the before revelation question is monopolized by a particular legal or theological school. All three positions are found among various schools, especially before the fifth/eleventh century.[26] He observes that before the fifth/eleventh century the rational moral theory was widespread among most schools of law, excluding the Ḥanbalī where a revelational moral theory was prevailing.[27] The prevalence of the rational moral theory allowed permission to become a popular position among many jurists. Reinhart notes that after the fifth/eleventh century the revelational moral theory became the most dominant position among all schools of law (excluding the Ḥanafī); this dominance allowed suspension to replace permission as the most popular position on the before revelation debate.

Reinhart's most interesting remarks come in his explanation of this shift, why is rational moral theory more popular before the fifth/eleventh century whereas after this century the revelational moral theory takes its position of dominance? Reinhart argues that before the fifth/eleventh century, although Muslims were the dominant political power, they were still a minority living among and ruling a non-Muslim majority population. Islam, continues Reinhart, was a 'proselytizing missionary' religion trying to appeal to the non-Muslim majority. This socio-political context encouraged the creation of a religious ideology designed to allure not only the Muslim minority but the non-Muslim majority as well. This religious ideology aimed at winning the non-believing majority by creating common ground with them. This common ground is supposed to have been created by upholding the ability of the 'common' human rationality to determine moral and deontic evaluations. In this case, the Muslim revelation can be seen as supplementary knowledge

---

[25] Reinhart, *Before Revelation*, 125–75.

[26] Reinhart, *Before Revelation*, 180.

[27] Reinhart, *Before Revelation*, 21–5.

that confirms the moral values already held by all rational humans. Moreover, Islam needed to appear compatible with reason; this should award it legitimacy and persuasiveness. In such an environment, argues Reinhart, Muʿtazilī doctrines were formed. Their rational moral theory is an archaic position shaped in response to the early phases of Muslim political, social and intellectual history.

Reinhart argues that this social, political and intellectual situation lasted until conversion gained momentum in the fourth-fifth/tenth-eleventh century. The success of the gradual process of conversion changed the political and social environment in which Islam existed; Muslims became the majority of the population. Islam became a well-established religion, not a new faith trying to find a place among ancient religions. The new majoritarian position of Muslims and the well-established state of Islam made it the standard religion of the Middle East. Now, explains Reinhart, there was less need to form an Islam that would appeal to non-Muslims as well as Muslims. The majority position of Muslims made the legitimacy of Islam obvious. Muslims no longer had a need to prove the harmony between Islam and human reason.

Despite the new confident position of Muslims, the political situation of the *umma* was becoming less stable. By the fourth-fifth/tenth-eleventh century, the Abbasid Caliphate was politically fragmented and new Muslim sects were appearing. Some of the new sects became politically dominant over the Sunnī majority. The Muslim *umma* is a majority, but a fragmented majority. Reinhart argues that religious scholars saw the unity of Islam being jeopardized. They see, says Reinhart, the 'excessive' use of human reason as among the causes for the appearance of new religious groups that shredded the Muslim community. To safeguard the unity of the *umma*, Sunnī scholars advised holding fast to revelation and limiting the use of reason in religious interpretation. Reinhart argues that these political, social and intellectual conditions allowed the revelational moral theory to gain more ground and become the most popular moral theory among Sunnī Muslims.

Reinhart contends that the dominance of rational moral theory before the fifth/eleventh century made permission and proscription (specially the former) more popular answers to the before revelation question (rather than suspension). Reinhart writes that the political and social changes that took place during the fourth-fifth/tenth-eleventh centuries facilitated the dissemination of a religious ideology that had a 'high view of revelation', one that limits the role of reason in religious interpretation including in moral assessments. The popularity of this moral theory, after the fifth/eleventh century, allowed suspension to replace permission as the most popular answer to the before revelation question.

Reinhart's conclusions are well argued; however, they are not without shortcomings. In his review of *Before Revelation*, Oliver Leaman praises the book and accepts the political and social explanations Reinhart presents for the dissemination of permission before the fifth/eleventh century and the popularity of suspension after this century. Nonetheless, Leaman notes that it is possible that the firm establishment of Islam as a majoritarian religion of an empire would encourage rational thought as scholars would feel more confident about the status of their own faith. He adds that to understand the intellectual impact of the socio-political changes Reinhart discusses, one would have to study similar conditions that faced other religions and analyse their response to these changes, something that Reinhart does not attempt to do.[28] Eric Ormsby's review of *Before Revelation* includes harsh critical remarks. The most important of those is that Reinhart gives the impression that the first five centuries of Islam witnessed no serious schisms and that divisions became a problem only after the fifth/eleventh century. Ormsby argues that political schisms occurred before the fifth/eleventh century as well as after it, therefore they cannot be considered a new development that triggered the dissemination of a scripturalist understanding of Islam and in turn the popularity of the revelational moral theory.[29]

The above criticisms are valid; still, Reinhart's work is certainly a remarkable work. He manages, largely, to penetrate the lan-

---

[28] Oliver Leaman, review of *Before Revelation: The Boundaries of Muslim Moral Thought* by A. K. Reinhart *British Journal of Middle Eastern Studies* 22.1/2 (1995), 141.

[29] Eric Ormsby, 'Review of *Before Revelation: The Boundaries of Muslim Moral Thought* by A. K. Reinhart', *Islamic Law and Society* 5.1 (1998), 121. See also A. Kevin Reinhart, 'Response to Eric Ormsby's review of *Before Revelation: The Boundaries of Muslim Moral Thought* by A. K. Reinhart', *Islamic Law and Society* 6.3 (1999): 419–20.

guage of medieval jurists and understand the tools they use in argumentation. This allows him to recognize the practical relevance of the before revelation debate. As previously mentioned, he notices that the before revelation question is not important in itself; it is rather a tool to address other legal and philosophical concerns. Many debates raised in pre-modern legal theory literature seem, *prima facie*, hypothetical and with little practical relevance to law. Therefore, to the untrained eye, these debates might appear useless and not worthy of attention.[30] Reinhart is among the few scholars who have managed to understand the real points of contention behind the before revelation debate. This has allowed him to appreciate the practical consequences of this, seemingly, hair-splitting legal theory question.

SUSPENSION AND PERMISSION

Juwaynī, Shīrāzī and Samʿānī all adopt suspension. For them, humans should refrain from moral and deontic assessments prior to the advance of revelation.[31] ʿAbd al-Jabbār chooses permission; he

---

[30] For the functions of hypothetical questions in Muslim legal theory, see Ahmad, *Structural Interrelations*, 178–82.

[31] Abū al-Maʿālī ʿAbd al-Malik b. ʿAbd Allāh al-Juwaynī [pseudo], *Kitāb al-Talkhīṣ fī uṣūl al-fiqh*, 3 vols ed. ʿAbd Allāh Jawlam al-Nibālī and Bashīr Aḥmad al-ʿUmarī. (Beirut: Dār al-Bashāʾir al-Islāmiyya, 1428[/2007]), 3:473; Juwaynī, *Burhān*, 99–101; Shīrāzī, *Lumaʿ*, 246; Shīrāzī, *Tabṣira*, 532–7; Shīrāzī, *Sharḥ al-Lumaʿ*, 978–85; Samʿānī, *Qawāṭiʿ al-adilla*, 3:419–33. There is a debate over the authorship of *al-Talkhīṣ fī uṣūl al-fiqh*. Ibrāḥim Donmez and Fawqiyya Maḥmūd argue that *Talkhīṣ* might not be Juwaynī's independent work. They note that it is probably Juwaynī's abridgement of Abū Bakr al-Bāqillānī's book on legal theory titled *al-Taqrīb wa-l-irshād*, see Ibrāhīm Kāfī Donmez, 'Makānat Imām al-Ḥaramayn fī uṣūl al-fiqh', in *al-Dhikrā al-alfiyya li-Imām al-Ḥaramayn*, ed. ʿAbd al-Aẓīm al-Dīb and Muḥammad Ṣāliḥ al-Shīb (Doha: University of Qatar, 2000), 512; Maḥmūd, *al-Juwaynī*, 63. Muḥammad al-Zuḥaylī writes that *Talkhīṣ* is similar to another book titled *al-Irshād fī uṣūl al-fiqh*. The identity of the author of the latter book is not clear whether it is Juwaynī or Bāqillānī. Zuḥaylī also adds that *al-Taqrīb wa-l-irshād* is abridged by Bāqillānī and might have been also abridged by Jūwaynī, see Zuḥaylī, *al-Imām al-Jūwaynī*,

holds that all useful and harmless actions and things are permissible until revelation comes and declares the opposite.[32] Is it a coincidence that the only Muʿtazilī jurist, in the sample of scholars examined here, advocates permission whereas the Ashʿarīs and the traditionalist favour suspension? Is this inter-Shāfiʿī legal theory disagreement theologically motivated? These are the questions this section tries to answer. The current section analyses and dissects the arguments each jurist puts forward in support of his position. This analysis should, hopefully, uncover the motivations behind each scholar's decision to choose permission or suspension. I am mainly interested in identifying the theological foundations of permission and suspension in addition to understanding how far theological discrepancies contribute to this Shāfiʿī debate.

Arguments for Suspension: Shīrāzī and Samʿānī

Shīrāzī's and Samʿānī's arguments in support of suspension are, to some extent, similar. I discuss their arguments, first, then move to Juwaynī's.[33] Their argument for suspension is primarily based on rebutting rational moral epistemology. To justify suspension, they begin by stating their definitions of a permitted 'thing' (*mubāḥ*) and a proscribed one (*maḥẓūr*). The two scholars define the former as what revelation permits and the latter as what revelation proscribes. They conclude that should revelation neither permit nor proscribe a thing, humans must suspend the deontic assessment of this thing until revelation reveals its assessment.[34] Shīrāzī's and Samʿānī's definitions of the proscribed and the permitted are a product of their revelational moral theory, a theory that makes deontic qualifica-

---

168. Therefore, for information on Juwaynī's legal theory, I mainly depend on his famous *Burhān*. I only refer to *Talkhīṣ* when it is clear that it is in agreement with *Burhān*. In all cases, I avoid basing my arguments on information only found in *Talkhīṣ*.

[32] ʿAbd al-Jabbār, *Mughnī*, 17:145–9.

[33] For space restraints, I only discuss those arguments that include references to theological doctrines and thus useful for uncovering the theological motivations for espousing suspension. I leave out discussions that include no obvious references to speculative theology.

[34] Shīrāzī, *Sharḥ al-Lumaʿ*, 978; Samʿānī, *Qawāṭiʿ al-adilla*, 3:420.

tions almost entirely contingent upon revelation. Samʿānī explicitly states that his answer to the before revelation question is based on his belief that unaided reason cannot ascertain moral and deontic knowledge. This type of knowledge, he adds, must all be based on revelation (*kullu dhālika mawkūl ilā al-sharʿ*).[35] Given their definitions of the permitted and the proscribed, only revelation can describe a thing as permitted or proscribed; reason is not fit for this task. Therefore, deontic qualifications cannot be known in the absence of revelation.

Second, Shīrāzī and Samʿānī argue that God owns all things created. The Creator has the absolute right to declare any of His created objects, permitted, proscribed, or even obligatory. Both argue that in the absence of revelation humans cannot predict God's decisions. Therefore, humans have no other option but to suspend moral and deontic assessments until God reveals them.[36] This argument is based on the Ashʿarī and traditionalist eagerness not to place any limitations on God's omnipotence. God has unqualified powers to issue whatever deontic qualification to any action or thing He wishes. Given this principle, nothing before revelation, can help humans predict divine deontic assessments. Nothing in their creed allows unaided human reason to predict which actions God's revelation would prohibit and which it would permit. In this case, humans cannot but suspend all moral and deontic assessments until they receive divine guidance.

Third, Shīrāzī and Samʿānī quote a number of Qurʾānic verses to justify their adoption of suspension. Samʿānī cites, for example, Q 17:15 'We [do not] punish until We have sent a messenger', and Q 4:165 'They were messengers bearing news and warning, so that mankind would have no excuse before God'. Samʿānī comments on these verses saying that [divine] punishment is contingent upon receiving revelation rather than being contingent on humans acquiring rational faculties. He concludes that reason places no responsibility on humans; humans are held responsible for their

---

[35] Samʿānī, *Qawāṭiʿ al-adilla*, 3:420.

[36] Shīrāzī, *Sharḥ al-Lumaʿ*, 978; Samʿānī, *Qawāṭiʿ al-adilla*, 3:424.

deeds only after the advent of revelation.[37] Shīrāzī quotes only one verse, Q 16:116 'Do not say falsely, 'This is lawful, and that is forbidden' inventing a lie about God'. Commenting on this verse, he says the Qur'ān prohibits humans from passing judgments about things and ascribing these judgments to God. Judgments should only originate from revelation. Otherwise, this would be a false ascription to God.[38] The choice of the above verses as evidence in support of suspension indicate that Shīrāzī's and Samʿānī's position on the before revelation question is informed by (or a product of) their revelational moral theory. Both quote Qur'ānic verses emphasizing that deontic qualifications fall within the jurisdiction of revelation rather than reason. Therefore, deontic qualifications are unknowable before the advent of revelation.

Juwaynī's Evidence for Suspension

Juwaynī's discussion of the before revelation debate in *Burhān* and *Talkhīṣ* is quite terse.[39] In both texts, he does not present a well articulate argument in support of suspension.[40] He mainly presents

---

[37] Samʿānī, *Qawāṭiʿ al-adilla*, 3:403. He also cites other Qur'ānic verses with similar connotations, namely 5:19, 6:130, 67:8.

[38] Shīrāzī, *Sharḥ al-Lumaʿ*, 981–2; Shīrāzī, *Tabṣira*, 535.

[39] Juwaynī, *Burhān*, 99–101; Juwaynī [pseudo], *Talkhīṣ*, 3:461–81.

[40] This is also true about his discussion of the before revelation question in other books. See for example Abū al-Maʿālī ʿAbd al-Malik b. ʿAbd Allāh b. Yūsuf Juwaynī, *Kitāb al-Irshād ilā qawāṭiʿ al-adilla fī uṣūl al-iʿtiqād*, ed. Muḥammad Yūsuf Mūsā and ʿAlī ʿAbd al-Munʿim ʿAbd al-Ḥamīd (Cairo: Maktabat al-Khānjī, 1369/1950), 266–7. Juwaynī's *al-Shāmil fī uṣūl al-dīn* and *al-ʿAqīda al-niẓāmiyya*, both are theological works, include almost no reference to the before revelation question. See Abū al-Maʿālī ʿAbd al-Malik b. ʿAbd Allāh b. Yūsuf al-Juwaynī, *al-Shāmil fī uṣūl al-dīn*, ed. ʿAlī Sāmī al-Nashshār and others (Alexandria: Munsha'at al-Maʿārif, 1969) and his *al-ʿAqīda al-niẓāmiyya fi-l-arkān al-Islāmiyya*, ed. Muḥammad Zāhid al-Kawtharī (Cairo: al-Maktaba al-Azhariyya li-l-Turāth, 1412/1992). This is also true about Juwaynī's short treatise on theology *Lumaʿ al-adilla fī qawāʿid ahl al-Sunna wa-l-jamāʿa*, ed. Fawqiyya Ḥusayn Maḥmūd (Cairo: al-Mu'assasa al-Miṣriyya al-ʿĀma li-l-Ta'līf wa-l-Anbā' wa-l-Nashr, 1385/1965) and his short treatise on legal theory *Matn al-Waraqāt.*

arguments rebutting permission and proscription rather than presenting positive evidence justifying his acceptance of suspension. Furthermore, his argument is disjointed and poorly organized.[41] There are in fact only two statements that can be considered positive evidence vindicating suspension. The first is his introductory statement to his before revelation chapter in *Talkhīṣ* in which he confirms that reason has no role in moral assessments and that only revelation can make something good or evil.[42] Although Juwaynī does not mention an explicit conclusion to this statement, the only logical conclusion is that moral assessments are unfeasible before revelation. The fact that Juwaynī chooses to start his before revelation chapter by confirming his revelational moral theory indicates that his adoption of suspension is a greatly influenced by this theory.

The second positive argument Juwaynī presents in support of suspension is another introductory statement, this time to his short section on the before revelation debate in *Burhān*. He starts this section noting that 'rational people are not responsible [for their deeds] before the advent of revelation. This is based on [the belief that] deontic qualifications are identical with revelations and that deontic qualifications are not attributes of actions'.[43] Juwaynī starts his discussion of the before revelation debate noting that, in the absence of revelation, humans will not be held responsible for their deeds. Obligation and responsibility are contingent on receiving the divine message. He adds that this conclusion is based on the following: first, deontic qualifications (*aḥkām*) are identical with revelations (*sharāʾiʿ*). Second, deontic qualifications are not attributes (*ṣifāt*) of actions.

Juwaynī's remark that deontic qualifications are identical with revelations is a reference to a legal theory debate over the definition

---

[41] Reinhart rightly describes Juwaynī's argument as 'so unpolished, so inarticulate at times' and difficult to represent, see Reinhart, *Before Revelation*, 68.

[42] Juwaynī [pseudo], *Talkhīṣ*, 3:469–71.

[43] Juwaynī, *Burhān*, 99. (*lā-ḥukm ʿalā al-ʿuqalāʾ qabala wurūd al-sharʿ, bināʾan ʿalā ann al-aḥkām hiya al-sharāʾiʿ bi-aʿyānihā, wa-laysat al-aḥkām ṣifāt li-l-afʿāl*)

of the deontic qualification, whether it is identical with revelation or it is something independent and different from it. Juwaynī here embraces the first view, deontic qualifications and revelation are one and the same thing, therefore both are inseparable.[44] No deontic [and moral] assessment is possible in the absence of revelation. For Juwaynī, those assessments are completely dependent on access to revelation. If revelation is not present, deontic qualifications cannot be present as well. The second remark (deontic qualifications are not attributes of actions) is a reference to the moral ontology debate. Here, Juwaynī is confirming that deontic qualifications are not an essential part of an actions' ontological being. In other words, no action is ontologically permitted or proscribed. No action is created with an embedded deontic and moral qualification. For Juwaynī, revelation awards things and actions their deontic qualifications. Therefore, it is impossible for humans to discern deontic knowledge before accessing revelation.[45] Juwaynī's arguments here are obviously based on his revelational moral theory. He justifies his adoption of suspension by noting that reason is incapable of acquiring moral and deontic knowledge; this task must await the advent of revelation.

The above arguments are enough to show that Juwaynī's revelational moral theory is fundamental to his argument backing suspension. The rest of his section on the before revelation debate, both in *Burhān* and *Talkhīṣ*, consists of evidence rebutting permission and proscription rather than vindicating suspension; going through his refutation of both positions will not add new infor-

---

[44] The other position on this debate holds that revelation and deontic qualifications are two distinct entities. A Qurānic verse is part of revelation, however it cannot, in itself, be a deontic qualification. The latter is rather the legal impact of the verse. In other words, deontic qualifications are the regulations jurists deduce from Scriptures rather than Scriptures themselves. An example of a deontic qualification would be the obligation to fast during Ramaḍān rather than the Qurānic verses informing humans of this obligation. For a brief survey of this debate see, ʿAbd al-Karīm b. ʿAlī b. Muḥammad al-Namla, *al-Khilāf al-lafẓī ʿinda al-uṣūliyyīn*, 2 vols (1417/1996; repr., Riyadh: Maktabat al-Rushd, 1420/1999), 1:80–2.

[45] For a similar statement, see Juwaynī [pseudo], *Talkhīṣ*, 3:474.

mation. It is enough to know that his refutation is based on his belief that unaided reason is incapable of acquiring moral and deontic knowledge. He then argues that permission and proscription are based on the 'false' assumption that human reason can acquire this knowledge without the aid of revelation.[46] Since both positions are based on a false assumption, it follows that both must be false as well. Juwaynī's vindication of suspension and his refutation of permission and proscription, like that of Shīrāzī and Samʿānī, are primarily based on the rejection of rational moral knowledge. The fact that this theme is the linchpin of Juwaynī's argument indicates that his moral theory plays a major role in determining his answer to the before revelation question.

Justifying Permission: ʿAbd al-Jabbār al-Hamadhānī

This section analyses ʿAbd al-Jabbār's argument for permission. This analysis will not only uncover the theological foundations of his answer to the before revelation question, but it also discusses possible theological motivations for adopting suspension and proscription. ʿAbd al-Jabbār's argument is long and complicated, therefore more space will be dedicated to it here. His argument in support of permission has two stages. The first is a rebuttal of suspension in which he attempts to show that any action, even before revelation, must have a particular moral or deontic qualification. In the second stage, he argues that the only plausible deontic qualification for actions before the advent of revelation is permission. Surveying ʿAbd al-Jabbār's argument demonstrates that his rational moral theory in addition to his Muʿtazilī understanding of divine justice and wisdom (and derivative doctrines) play a crucial role motivating him to choose permission.

Necessary and Acquired Knowledge

To understand ʿAbd al-Jabbār's argument one must first define two terms, necessary knowledge (*ʿilm ḍarūrī*) and acquired knowledge

[46] See Juwaynī, *Burhān*, 99–101; Juwaynī [pseudo], *Talkhīṣ*, 3:474–81. For an analysis of Juwaynī's argument for suspension, see also Reinhart, *Before Revelation*, 67–70.

(*ʿilm muktasab*). In his recension of ʿAbd al-Jabbār's *Sharḥ al-Uṣūl al-khamsa*, ʿAbd al-Jabbār's student Mānkdīm (or Mānakdīm) Shashdīw (d. 425/1034)[47] notes that his teacher defines necessary knowledge as 'irrefutable knowledge that happens in us; one that is not a result of our effort'.[48] In *Mughnī*, ʿAbd al-Jabbār writes that necessary knowledge requires no further evidence to prove its validity.[49] Necessary knowledge, in other words, is the type of knowledge that imposes itself on the human mind; one that humans are compelled to accept (hence the name *iḍṭirār* i.e. compulsion). It is self-evident knowledge that does not require rational reflection; no sane human would doubt the validity of necessary knowledge or even require evidence proving its validity. Examples of such knowledge include; one is half of two, a body cannot be in two places at the same time and bread quenches hunger and water quenches thirst.

On the other hand, ʿAbd al-Jabbār describes acquired knowledge as one that is produced after rational reflection and contemplation (*naẓar wa-tafakkur*).[50] It is the product of human intellec-

---

[47] *EI²*, s.v. 'Muʿtazila' (D. Gimaret).

[48] ʿAbd al-Jabbār b. Aḥmad al-Hamadhānī [/Mānkdīm Shashdīw (d. 425/1034)], *Sharḥ al-Uṣūl al-khamsa* ed. ʿAbd al-Karīm ʿUthmān (Cairo: Maktabat Wahba, 1416/1996), 48–9. A short note on *Sharḥ al-Uṣūl al-khamsa*: It is now widely accepted that the published *Sharḥ al-Uṣūl al-khamsa* is not ʿAbd al-Jabbār's but, as noted by D. Gimaret, is a commentary on the text and paraphrastic reproduction of it by his Muʿtazilī student Mānkdīm Shashdīw. For more details, see D. Gimaret, 'Les Usul al-Hamsa du Qadi Abd al-Jabbar et leurs Commentaires', *Annales Islamologiques* 15 (1979): 47–96; George Hourani, 'The Rationalist Ethics of ʿAbd al-Jabbar', in *Reason and Tradition in Islamic Ethics*, ed. George Hourani (Cambridge: Cambridge University Press, 1985), 107–8; Heemskerk, *Suffering in the Muʿtazilite Theology*, 3–8.

[49] ʿAbd al-Jabbār, *Mughnī*, 14:152.

[50] ʿAbd al-Jabbār b. Aḥmad al-Hamadhānī [/Abū Muḥammad al-Ḥasan b. Aḥmad b. Mattawayh (fl. fifth/eleventh century)], *Kitāb al-Majmūʿ fi-l-muḥīṭ bi-l-taklīf*, 3 vols ed. Jan Peters (Beirut: Dār al-Mashriq, 1999), 2:260; ʿAbd al-Jabbār, *Mughnī*, 12:67–8, 15:402. Ibn Mattawahy's death date is not accurately known. However, Madelung and Schmidtke

tual effort. This type of knowledge is neither beyond doubt nor self-evident; it requires the support of rational effort and the presentation of evidence supporting its validity. Supporting evidence can come in the form of rational or revelational evidence. Examples of such knowledge would include existence of God, unity of God (i.e. monotheism), divine attributes and the veracity of revelation. Acquired knowledge is not compelling; it is rather debatable. Sane individuals can refuse to accept any acquired knowledge that is accepted by others and present rational evidence against it without being accused of insanity.[51]

If acquired knowledge is gained via rational reflection, how do humans 'gain' necessary knowledge? Let's remember that ʿAbd al-Jabbār holds that necessary knowledge happens in the knower and is not a product of the knower's intellectual efforts.[52] In other words, the knower plays no role in 'gaining' necessary knowledge. Who then is the source of this knowledge? ʿAbd al-Jabbār notes that there are two paths for necessary knowledge, first, divine crea-

---

note that Ibn Mattuwayh survived his teacher ʿAbd al-Jabbār who died in 415/1024. For more information on Ibn Mattawayh, see *EI²*, s.v. 'Ibn Mattawayh' (by W. Madelung); *EI³*, s.v. 'Ibn Mattawayh' (by Sabine Schmidtke). Ibn Mattawayh is one of ʿAbd al-Jabbār's students. He collected parts of ʿAbd al-Jabbār's book *al-Muḥīt bi-l-taklīf* and probably added his comments as well in the book that he titled *al-Majmūʿ fi-l-muḥīṭ bi-l-taklīf*.

[51] For more details on ʿAbd al-Jabbār's concept of necessary and acquired knowledge, see ʿAbd al-Jabbār, *Mughnī*, 8:6, 9–10, 123, 12: 59–68, 14:151–4, 15:402; ʿAbd al-Jabbār [/Mānkdīm], *Sharḥ al-Uṣūl al-khamsa*, 48–51; Ḥusnī Zayna, *al-ʿAql ʿinda al-Muʿtazila: Taṣawwur al-ʿaql ʿinda al-Qāḍī ʿAbd al-Jabbār* (Beirut: Dār al-Āfāq al-Jadīda, 1978), 59–74. For more information on the concept of necessary and acquired knowledge in general, see *EI²*, s.v. 'Iḍṭirār' (by L. Gardet); Weiss, *Search for God's Law*, 36–40; Binyamin Abrahamov, 'Necessary knowledge in Islamic Theology – Some Notes', *British Journal of Middle Eastern Studies* 20.1 (1993): 20–32; J. R. T. M. Peters, *God's Created Speech* (Leiden: E. J. Brill, 1976), 52–5 qtd. in Reinhart, *Before Revelation*, 41 f.n. 12.

[52] ʿAbd al-Jabbār [/Ibn Mattawayh], *al-Majmūʿfi-l-muḥīṭ bi-l-taklīf*, 1:3, 2:123, 126; ʿAbd al-Jabbār [/Mānkdīm], *Sharḥ al-Uṣūl al-khamsa*, 48–51.

tion, second, custom and experience (*al-ʿāda wa-l-tajriba*).[53] ʿAbd al-Jabbār's student Ibn Mattawayh (or Mattūya fl. fifth/eleventh century)[54] notes that his teacher describes necessary knowledge as knowledge that God creates (*yafʿal*, literally makes) in humans.[55] Mānkdīm Shashdīw writes that ʿAbd al-Jabbār has a twofold division for necessary knowledge. The first is innate knowledge (*mā yaḥṣul fīnā mubtadaʾ*) and the second is sense perception.[56] Therefore, for ʿAbd al-Jabbār there are only two paths to necessary knowledge. First, sense perception: for example humans know via visual perception and custom that the sun rises from the east and sets in the west. Second, divine creation: God creates necessary knowledge in humans, and this second path makes innate knowledge a type of necessary knowledge. It is the latter path to necessary knowledge that concerns us more here.

---

[53] ʿAbd al-Jabbār, *Mughnī*, 8:6. By experience (*tajriba*) ʿAbd al-Jabbār is probably referring to knowledge humans 'gain' via repeated sensual encounters. For example, experience teaches humans that fire is always hot, ice is always cold and water always quenches thirst etc… Since this type of knowledge is unrefusable, therefore it is necessary. The term custom (ʿ *āda*) has been defined before. To remind the reader, custom is a concept used by many speculative theologians to explain the regularity and predictability of events in this world. For example, it is the custom of God to create burning when fire touches wood. It is the custom of God to make the sun always rise from the east and sets in the west. Only in highly exceptional cases would God interfere to interrupt the custom of the world, usually in the form of miracles. For ʿAbd al-Jabbār's detailed discussion of this term see his *Mughnī*, 15:182–235, 335–82. See also Wael Hallaq, 'On the Authoritativeness of Sunni Consensus', *International Journal of Middle East Studies* 18 (1986), 436–8.

[54] *EI*³, s.v. 'Ibn Mattawayh' (by Sabina Schmidtke).

[55] ʿAbd al-Jabbār [/Ibn Mattawayh], *al-Majmūʿ fi-l-muḥīṭ bi-l-taklīf*, 1:3, also see p. 1:19; ʿAbd al-Jabbār [/Mānkdīm], *Sharḥ al-Uṣūl al-khamsa*, 50 where he says God can create necessary knowledge in us.

[56] ʿAbd al-Jabbār [/Mānkdīm], *Sharḥ al-Uṣūl al-khamsa*, 50.

Stage One: Refuting Suspension

Having the above definitions in mind, we can now turn to ʿAbd al-Jabbār's first stage of his argument in support of permission. The main aim of this stage is to disprove suspension by showing that actions and things are never void of a moral or a deontic qualification. He argues that permission

> assumes that rational evidence is prior to evidence from revelation … Once we agree that reason and its evidence can precede [in time] the advent of revelation, then what we have mentioned [i.e. permission] must be correct. Because we rationally know that actions must be permitted, proscribed, recommended, or obligatory. Each [of these deontic qualifications] has grounds in reason that we necessarily know either in general or in detail (*wa-li-kull dhālika aṣl fi-l-ʿuqūl yuʿlam bi-iḍṭirār immā ʿalā ṭarīq al-tafṣīl aw ʿalā ṭarīq al-jumla*). Therefore, [we] necessarily know the evilness of injustice and the evilness of lying, as we explained. This is also true about many obligations (*wājibāt*) and the recommendation [of performing] many good actions (*wa-kawn kathīr min al-muḥassināt nadba[an]*).[57]

ʿAbd al-Jabbār starts by saying that embracing permission presumes that rational evidence precedes revelational evidence [in chronological order]. In other words, humans already possess rational moral knowledge before they receive any divine revelations. He continues saying that we rationally know that every action must have a particular deontic qualification, either permitted, proscribed, recommended, or obligatory. No action is void of such qualifications. He remarks that the deontic qualification of every action is rationally known by necessity (*bi-iḍṭirār*), either in general (*ʿalā ṭarīq al-jumla* or what I translate as basic moral knowledge) or in detail (*ʿalā ṭarīq al-tafṣīl* which I translate as detailed moral knowledge).

What is the difference between basic and general moral knowledge? For ʿAbd al-Jabbār the former is a type of necessary knowledge that is used to acquire detailed moral knowledge. Without basic moral knowledge, acquiring detailed moral knowledge is

---

[57] ʿAbd al-Jabbār, *Mughnī*, 17:145–6.

impossible. The evilness of injustice is basic moral knowledge, but identifying a particular act as unjust and thus evil is detailed moral knowledge. The obligatory nature of thanking the benefactor is basic moral knowledge, but identifying which grace and which benefactor deserves gratitude is detailed moral knowledge. Basic moral knowledge is abstract while the detailed moral knowledge identifies particular actions (*aʿyān al-afʿāl*) as either good, evil, obligatory, or recommended.[58] Although the above quote may imply that both basic and general moral knowledge are known by necessity, elsewhere ʿAbd al-Jabbār makes it clear that only general moral knowledge is necessary. Detailed moral knowledge is known after rational reflection, therefore it is one form of acquired rather than necessary knowledge.[59]

Let us recall that, for ʿAbd al-Jabbār, there are two paths to obtain necessary knowledge, first innate information that God creates in humans, second, sense perception. Since one cannot 'gain' moral and deontic knowledge via any of the five senses, therefore moral knowledge must be of the first type; innate knowledge that God creates in humans. ʿAbd al-Jabbār notes that the divine process of creating human reason (*ʿaql*) includes the creation of innate knowledge within reason; this type of knowledge is necessary for the functioning of human reason. This innate knowledge (that is also necessary knowledge) includes basic moral information. Without God installing this innate knowledge in reason, its creation process will not be complete and it will not reach maturity (*kamāl al-ʿaql*). Without the maturity of reason, a human can be neither rational (*ʿāqil*) nor responsible (*mukallaf*).[60] Therefore, for ʿAbd al-

---

[58] For more information on ʿAbd al-Jabbār's distinction between basic and detailed moral knowledge see, ʿAbd al-Jabbār, *Mughnī*, 6:63–4, 12:357, 13:305–6, 14:154, 160; ʿAbd al-Jabbār [/Ibn Mattawayh], *al-Majmūʿ fi-l- muḥīṭ bi-l-taklīf*, 1:69, 103.

[59] ʿAbd al-Jabbār explicitly rejects the opinion of Abū Hāshim al-Jubbāʾī (d. 321/933) that detailed moral knowledge is necessary. See ʿAbd al-Jabbār, *Mughnī*, 12:305–6. Ibn Mattawayh attributes the same opinion to his teacher ʿAbd al-Jabbār. See ʿAbd al-Jabbār [/Ibn Mattawayh], *al-Majmūʿ fi-l- muḥīṭ bi-l-taklīf*, 1:3.

[60] ʿAbd al-Jabbār, *Mughnī*, 11:384, 12:417, 14:166.

Jabbār, any human with a mature reason will automatically possess basic moral knowledge. In other words, all humans, with a mature reason share common basic moral information. This is why ʿAbd al-Jabbār notes that no sane human would ever consider injustice and useless lying as good or doubt the obligation to thank the benefactor.[61]

ʿAbd al-Jabbār's Muʿtazilī theology allows him to assume that God must create basic moral information in humans' minds. The Muʿtazilī doctrines of divine justice, optimism and benevolence assume that God will always facilitate salvation for humans. There are two reasons explaining why the facilitation of salvation requires God to create basic moral knowledge in human reason. First, humans cannot choose to follow revelation before knowing that the god who sent this revelation is just and the content of his revelation is good. Before demonstrating these beliefs, humans cannot trust revelation as a source of moral guidance. Therefore, humans must, independent from revelation, already have moral knowledge (as an objective yardstick) that will allow them to realize the just nature of God and appreciate the goodness of His revelation and, thus, recognize that this revelation is worthy of being followed.[62]

---

[61] ʿAbd al-Jabbār, *Mughnī*, 6:63–4, 66, 14:154.

[62] ʿAbd al-Jabbār notes that humans will not be certain that revelation is trustworthy and infallible until they first know that God Himself is infallible, just and does not need to commit evil. Before establishing these divine attributes, revelation has no authority. Therefore, ʿAbd al-Jabbār argues that humans are left only with unaided reason to investigate the nature of God and His attributes. He adds that since the divine attributes are necessary to establish the authority of revelation, referring to revelation to ascertain the attributes of God would rest the authority of revelation on a *petitio principii.* ʿAbd al-Jabbār notes that, from a dialectical perspective, it does not make sense to refer to revelation to discover the divine attributes and then later use the divine attributes to establish the authority of revelation. Furthermore, it does not make sense to refer to God's words to prove His good and just attributes. ʿAbd al-Jabbār suggests that in order to avoid this logical fallacy, one should use reason, instead of revelation, to investigate any theological issue that is necessary to

ʿAbd al-Jabbār argues that without unaided reason having the ability to discern moral knowledge, one cannot prove the veracity of revelation. Without having an objective moral 'yardstick' humans will not be able to appreciate the goodness of revelation, and therefore will not choose to follow it. Second, as previously mentioned, necessary knowledge including basic moral information, is indispensable for the maturity of reason. Without the maturity of reason humans will not be responsible for their deeds. Innate necessary knowledge allows humans to choose to avoid evil and do good,[63] and thus be held responsible if they do not. For those two reasons, ʿAbd al-Jabbār holds that God is required to create in humans all the information they need to realize the worthiness of following revelation. God is also expected to create in humans the information that will make them responsible for their deeds.[64]

I went into this detour to show that ʿAbd al-Jabbār's Muʿtazilī theology allows him to assume that humans already have some fundamental moral knowledge prior to the advent of revelation. In fact, human moral awareness, prior to revelation, is an integral part of the Muʿtazilī argument establishing the justice and wisdom of God. If God were to hold humans responsible for their deeds without first giving them the means to distinguish between good and evil, He would be an evil and unjust god. If we accept ʿAbd al-Jabbār's rationale, then one must assume that humans have innate basic moral knowledge. Therefore, there is no need to suspend deontic assessments until the arrival of revelation.[65]

establishing the authority and veracity of revelation. See ʿAbd al-Jabbār, *Mughnī*, 12:166, 14:151–2; 16:395, 17:9, 93, 315, 393.

[63] ʿAbd al-Jabbār, *Mughnī*, 12:417–9.

[64] ʿAbd al-Jabbār, *Mughnī*, 11:371–5.

[65] Reinhart comments on this argument saying that the 'linchpin of the Permitter theory of moral epistemology is that this knowledge is not in the first place deduced or inferred, but it is incontestable spontaneous (*ḍarūrī*) knowledge, common to all humans by virtue of being *compotes mentis*'.

Stage Two: Refuting Proscription

ʿAbd al-Jabbār's above argument entails disproving suspension. However, it does not preclude proscription as a possible answer to the before revelation question. This is the intended task of the second stage of his argument. This stage includes eight arguments rebutting proscription and justifying permission. I mention only three; the ones relevant to uncovering the theological doctrines that inform ʿAbd al-Jabbār's answer to the before revelation question. The first of those is based on the information he mentions in the first stage of his argument. The first stage, supposedly, proves that all rational humans are created with innate basic moral knowledge. Therefore, ʿAbd al-Jabbār concludes that 'rational humans (*ahl al-ʿuqūl*) [must] know that a permitted action is nothing but an action they know or suspect to be useful and harmless'. In other words, actions that seem useful and harmless must be permitted.[66] Elsewhere he notes that it is even enough to doubt that an action is useful and harmless to *certainly* know that it is permitted.[67] ʿAbd al-Jabbār, here, is arguing that since rational humans have an innate ability to distinguish between good and evil, if they should see no evidence that a particular useful action is harmful, it must be permitted.

There is an important point worth highlighting here. ʿAbd al-Jabbār is using teleological information to uncover deontic conclusions. He argues that harmless useful actions (teleological information) must be permitted (deontic conclusion). One might assume that ʿAbd al-Jabbār would also accept the opposite argument: harmful or useless actions must be proscribed.[68] Using teleological premises to reach deontic conclusions is common in ʿAbd al-Jabbār's literature. For example, he notes that

---

[66] ʿAbd al-Jabbār, *Mughnī*, 17:146.

[67] ʿAbd al-Jabbār, *Mughnī*, 6:75.

[68] Elsewhere, ʿAbd al-Jabbār notes that the reason (*ʿilla*) behind an act being permitted, is the fact that it is useful and includes no harm. He adds that necessary knowledge indicating that an act is permitted entails that this act includes no corruption (*fasād*), see ʿAbd al-Jabbār, *Mughnī*, 17:146, 147. This might indicate that for him the knowledge that an act is proscribed entails that this act includes an aspect of corruption.

> any useful action performed by a responsible [human], that is not an obligation and brings about no harm to him and others… must be permitted by reason. Such an action remains permissible until there is evidence proving otherwise. This is what they mean when they say that all actions are permitted. They do not [actually] mean that all actions are permitted. Because we rationally know that some actions are evil, obligatory, and recommended.[69]

ʿAbd al-Jabbār here, again, mentions teleological information that leads to a deontic conclusion: harmless useful actions (teleological information), that are not obligations, must be permitted (deontic conclusion). He then, abruptly, says this is what they [i.e. Baṣrian Muʿtazilī figureheads] mean when 'they' say that all actions are permitted. 'They' do not exactly mean that all actions are permitted because we rationally know that some are evil. In other words, since some actions are evil, all actions cannot be permitted. This rationale indicates that, for ʿAbd al-Jabbār, actions known to be evil (moral information) cannot be permitted (i.e. they are proscribed which is a deontic conclusion). This implies that ʿAbd al-Jabbār, also, accepts the use of moral information to uncover deontic qualifications.

In his first quote at the beginning of this section, ʿAbd al-Jabbār uses deontic information to uncover a moral conclusion. As previously mentioned, ʿAbd al-Jabbār notes that humans have innate knowledge of basic deontic information that come in the form of necessary knowledge. Therefore, he concludes that humans must necessarily know the evilness of injustice and lying.[70] Here, ʿAbd al-Jabbār appears to be arguing that knowledge of deontic qualifications leads to knowing the evilness of injustice and lying. This signifies that, for him, knowledge of an action's deontic qualification (permission, proscription, obligation, or recommendation) leads to uncovering its moral qualification (good or evil). Proscribed actions are automatically known to be evil. Although he

---

[69] ʿAbd al-Jabbār, *Mughnī*, 17:145. For a similar quote see, ʿAbd al-Jabbār, *Mughnī*, 17:146.

[70] ʿAbd al-Jabbār, *Mughnī*, 17:145–6.

does not explicitly make the opposite argument, one might safely assume that ʿAbd al-Jabbār also holds that permitted actions are automatically known to be good. The quote in the previous paragraph shows that, for ʿAbd al-Jabbār, teleological information can uncover deontic conclusions. Here, I show that he holds that deontic qualifications uncover moral qualifications and moral qualifications uncover deontic qualifications as well. This reveals that for ʿAbd al-Jabbār knowing either the deontic, moral, or teleological qualification of any action or thing will lead to uncovering the other two qualifications, see figures below.

ʿAbd al-Jabbār's use of teleological information to reach deontic conclusions is made possible (or easier) by his Muʿtazilī doctrines of optimism and the purposefulness of divine actions. The latter entails that a wise and just god does not commit futile acts; all his actions and legislations have a meaningful motive; this motive is the wellbeing of his creatures.[71] Optimism teaches that God will (or

[71] Shīrāzī's and Juwaynī's imaginary permitter interlocutors mention arguments similar to ʿAbd al-Jabbār's. Shīrāzī and Juwaynī refuse these arguments saying that they are based on the 'corrupt' belief in the purposefulness of divine actions, see Shīrāzī, *Sharḥ al-Lumaʿ*, 982–3; Shīrāzī, *Tabṣira*, 536; Juwaynī [pseudo], *Talkhīṣ*, 3:478–9.

must) guarantee the optimal benefit for humans in this life and the next. Since Muʿtazilīs hold that God always guarantees the optimal benefit for humans, ʿAbd al-Jabbār, as a Muʿtazilī, rules out the possibility that God would prohibit a useful action or permit a harmful one. He assumes that God will always permit the former and proscribe the latter. Without both Muʿtazilī doctrines it would have been difficult for ʿAbd al-Jabbār to use teleological information to uncover deontic qualifications.[72]

Moreover, ʿAbd al-Jabbār's use of moral information to uncover deontic conclusions is made easier by what Hourani calls theistic objectivism. Theistic objectivism is a term Hourani uses to describe the Muʿtazilī belief that God adheres to objective moral criteria. God prohibits an act because it is evil; an act is not evil because God prohibits it. Given this belief, the Muʿtazilīs are certain that God prohibits only evil actions and permits only good ones, He does not (or cannot) do the opposite. Therefore, knowledge of an act's moral quality (either good or evil) will uncover its deontic qualification (proscribed or not). Without theistic objectivism it would have been difficult for ʿAbd al-Jabbār to use moral information to uncover deontic conclusions. Therefore, ʿAbd al-Jabbār does not need to suspend deontic qualifications until the advent of revelation; knowledge of an act's teleological qualification or an act's moral status can uncover its deontic qualification. An action that humans know or even suspect to be harmless, useful, or good must automatically be permitted. Any action known to be permitted is, also, automatically, known to be good and harmless. Therefore, for ʿAbd al-Jabbār, all actions are permitted until humans notice aspects of harm or evilness in this act.

ʿAbd al-Jabbār's second argument for suspension depends on the Muʿtazilī understanding of divine wisdom and the purposefulness of divine actions. He borrows this argument from unnamed

---

[72] Anver Emon describes this idea as 'fusing fact and value'. He explains that Muʿtazilī jurists like ʿAbd al-Jabbār, Abū al-Ḥusayn and Jaṣṣāṣ use empirical facts of nature to reach normative values. In other words, what appears in nature to be useful and harmless must be good and permissible. Whereas what seems to be harmful must be evil and proscribed. See Emon, *Islamic Natural Law*, 25–6, 62–6.

teachers of his. They argue that God has created creatures beneficial to humans. This act of creation entails that God allows humans to benefit from His useful creatures. If God would create creatures beneficial to humans and then prohibit humans from making use of them, His act of creation would be futile.[73] As explained before, the Muʿtazilī understanding of divine wisdom entails that God does not (or cannot) commit futile acts. If God were to commit a purposeless act this would entail that He is not wise. An unwise god is not worthy of worship and his revelations cannot be a reliable source of knowledge. ʿAbd al-Jabbār is arguing here that proscription entails that God is not wise; any Muslim would refuse this conclusion. Therefore, the beneficial (i.e. useful and harmless) creatures that God has created must all be permitted. Otherwise, the wisdom and the divinity of God and the value of His revelation would be compromised.

ʿAbd al-Jabbār's third, and final, argument is mainly aimed at proscription and is based on the Muʿtazilī belief that God does not impose on humans obligations impossible to fulfil (*ʿadam taklīf mā lā yuṭāq*). Speaking to his imaginary 'proscriber' interlocutor, ʿAbd al-Jabbār argues that we rationally know that humans should be allowed to avoid evil. Therefore, all actions cannot be evil. He adds that if we do not accept this conclusion, this would amount to imposing an impossible obligation on humans. Accepting it, on the other hand, would prove the goodness of breathing, moving, and other [necessary] actions.[74]

ʿAbd al-Jabbār here is arguing that proscription puts humans in a difficult situation. If all actions are proscribed; it becomes impossible for humans to avoid the performance of proscribed actions. The avoidance of evil becomes an obligation impossible to fulfil. Proscription, for ʿAbd al-Jabbār, makes the performance of evil through proscribed actions unavoidable. In this case, obeying God's laws becomes impossible. He adds that what makes things even worse for 'proscribers' are the actions necessary for survival,

---

[73] ʿAbd al-Jabbār, *Mughnī*, 146–7.
[74] ʿAbd al-Jabbār, *Mughnī*, 17:146.

e.g. breathing, moving and eating.[75] Proscription entails proscribing such actions. This would constitute, as well, an unachievable obligation; it is impossible for humans to survive without these and other similar actions. For ʿAbd al-Jabbār, proscription entails the imposition of impossible obligations. Only an unjust and unwise god would impose such obligations. Since God is neither unjust nor unwise, He will never impose an obligation on humans He knows they cannot accomplish.

Although ʿAbd al-Jabbār here does not explicitly note that proscription contradicts the Muʿtazilī doctrine of benevolence, however one cannot but see this conclusion between the lines of his argument. For Muʿtazilīs, benevolence entails that God will (or must) provide humans with the assistance they need to reach salvation and obey His legislations. God will not (or cannot) obstruct the human path to salvation. ʿAbd al-Jabbār argues that proscription makes disobeying God unavoidable. If God were to place humans in a situation in which disobeying His laws is inescapable, He would neither be a benevolent nor a just god. An unjust god cannot be worthy of worship and his revelation cannot be good.

Theoretical and Theological Foundations

ʿAbd al-Jabbār's argument for permission draws heavily on his Muʿtazilī theology. His adoption of permission appears to be a product of (or at least in harmony with) his Muʿtazilī doctrines of optimism, divine justice and his rational moral theory. The other three Shāfiʿīs, Juwaynī, Shīrāzī and Samʿānī, refuse the Muʿtazilī doctrines ʿAbd al-Jabbār uses to support permission. Their refusal of these doctrines and the alternative doctrines they embrace seem to be the theological beliefs that bring about suspension as their answer to the before revelation question. Their justifications of suspension are entirely based on their revelational moral theory.

---

[75] I have already mentioned above that actions necessary for survival are usually excluded from the before revelation debate. Most, if not all, scholars consider them permitted. However, ʿAbd al-Jabbār forms this argument assuming that jurists who embrace proscription consider actions necessary for survival to be proscribed before revelation, which is unlikely to be true.

The starting point of their supporting arguments is their insistence on keeping moral knowledge dependant on revelation. For them, moral and deontic knowledge are inaccessible prior to revelation. Therefore, the only plausible answer to the before revelation question would be suspension rather than permission or proscription.

Moral epistemology is perhaps the major point of contention between those who select suspension as their position and those who prefer permission or proscription. The nature of the before revelation question itself makes it relevant to debates around the source of moral knowledge. It asks whether humans can reach moral and deontic evaluations before the advent of revelation. This is just another formulation of the question as to whether reason, independent from revelation, can discern moral and deontic knowledge. Therefore, it is understandable to see numerous premodern and modern jurists suggest that an answer to the moral epistemology debate decides a jurist's answer to the before revelation question. The adoption of a rational moral theory might entail forsaking suspension and favouring either permission or proscription, whereas adopting a revelational moral theory might lead to upholding suspension.[76]

---

[76] For example, Abū Ḥāmid al-Ghazālī (d. 505/1111) notes that permission is based on the acceptance of a rational moral theory, see his *al-Mustaṣfā min ʿilm al-uṣūl*, 1:204. The Ẓāhirī jurist Ibn Ḥazm (d. 456/1064) says that all evidence disproving permission can be used to argue against the rational moral theory, see Abū Muḥammad ʿAlī b. Aḥmad b. Saʿīd b. Ḥazm, *al-Iḥkām fī uṣūl al-aḥkām*, 8 vols ed. Aḥmad Muḥammad Shākir (Cairo: Maktabat al-Khanjī, 1345–7/1926–9), 1:56. The Zaydī al-Amīr al-Ṣanʿānī (d. 1182/1768), Asnawī and Zarkashī all note that adopting a rational moral theory leads to forsaking suspension, see Muḥammad b. Ismāʿīl al-Ṣanʿānī [known as al-Amīr al- Ṣanʿānī] (d. 1182/1769), *Subul al-salām sharḥ Bulūgh al-marām min adillat al-aḥkām*, 4th ed. ed. Muḥammad b. ʿAbd al-ʿAzīz al-khūlī (Beirut: Dār Iḥyāʾ al-Turāth al-ʿArabī, 1379[/1959]), 4:172 in CD-ROM *al-Jāmiʿ al-kābīr*, Zarkashī, *al-Baḥr al-muḥīṭ*, 1:157–8; Asnawī, *Nihāyat al-sūl*, 1:276. The Ashʿarī-Shāfiʿī ʿAḍud al-Dīn al-Ījī (d. 756/1355) writes that once it has been established that good and evil are known only via revelation, we can then conclude that assessments must be suspended before the advent of revelation, see

Moral epistemology is not the only topic a jurist examines while answering the before revelation question. This question, as previously noted, is a testing ground for many legal theory questions. Among those is the predictability of divine legislations. ʿAbd al-Jabbār's rational moral theory allows him to assume that even, before revelation, God's judgments are predictable. Central to this view is what Hourani calls theistic objectivism; one of the doctrines that allows ʿAbd al-Jabbār to preclude the possibility that God would permit evil actions and prohibit good ones. Ashʿarī and traditionalist theology do not guarantee a particular pattern for divine laws. Juwaynī, Shīrāzī and Samʿānī adopt what Hourani calls theistic subjectivism; i.e. God does not conform to objective criteria for His deontic qualifications; He prohibits and permits any action as He wishes. Although Ashʿarīs and traditionalists would argue that God always permits good actions and proscribes evil ones, they would say that this is known only after the advent of revelation; prior to revelation it cannot be taken for granted. Accordingly, before revelation, there are no objective moral criteria allowing humans to predict God's deontic qualifications; humans should suspend all assessments until they receive the divine message.

Moreover, Ashʿarīs and traditionalists do not accept the Muʿtazilī understanding of divine justice and wisdom. Both doctrines are the source of other Muʿtazilī principles such as the purposefulness of God's actions, optimism, benevolence and the pro-

---

ʿAḍud al-Dīn ʿAbd al-Raḥmān b. Aḥmad al-Ījī, *Kitāb al-Mawāqif*, 3 vols ed. ʿAbd al-Raḥmān ʿUmayra (Beirut: Dār al-Jabal, 1417/1997), 3:276 in CD-ROM *al-Jāmiʿ al-kabīr*. In our modern times, Kevin Reinhart writes that suspension is based on two pre-requisites one of them is the adoption of a revelational moral theory, whereas permission and proscription are based on accepting a rational moral theory. See Reinhart, *Before Revelation*, 63. For another similar comment, see Hallaq, *Islamic Legal Theories*, 115. Muḥammad al-ʿArūsī ʿAbd al-Qādir says that maintaining permission or proscription is only possible if one embraces a rational moral theory, see his *al-Masāʾil al-mushtaraka*, 83–4. Muḥammad al-Shtīwī, as mentioned before, writes that the before revelation debate is just an extension of the controversy over moral epistemology, see his *ʿAlāqat ʿilm uṣūl al-fiqh bi-ʿilm al-kalām*, 259.

hibition of imposing impossible obligations. Ashʿarīs and traditionalists consider these Muʿtazilī doctrines as constraints on God's omnipotence. For them, God must have the freedom to perform aimless actions and impose obligations impossible to fulfil. God can impose laws that do not maintain the optimal interest of humans. For Ashʿarī and traditionalists, suggesting otherwise may compromise God's divine sovereignty and omnipotence. To safeguard God's ultimate omnipotence and perfection, Ashʿarīs and traditionalists do not preclude the possibility that God might do actions that may appear to humans unreasonable, unjust, or evil.

This Ashʿarī/traditionalist view of God's omnipotence makes His actions and legislations unpredictable. There is nothing in Ashʿarī and traditionalist theology that rules out the possibility that God would prohibit a useful action, obligate a harmful one, or impose an obligation that is impossible to fulfil. Nothing in their theology requires God to permit good and harmless actions and things. Before revelation, Ashʿarīs and traditionalists sever all links between teleological assessments, on one hand, and moral/deontic conclusions on the other. This makes the use of teleological information as a means to predict divine legislations very difficult.[77] Ashʿarī and traditionalist theology does not allow the prediction of divine legislations prior to revelation. In this case, humans have no other option but to suspend moral and deontic assessments until the reception of divine guidance.

ʿAbd al-Jabbār has a different perception of divine laws. For him, the predictability of these laws is central for establishing the divinity of God and the good nature of His revelation. Only after humans rationally know that God is just and wise will they appreciate the goodness of worshipping Him and following His revelation. Therefore, argues ʿAbd al-Jabbār, God created in humans basic moral knowledge allowing them to rationally realize His just nature and the goodness of His revelation. A by-product of this basic moral knowledge is that humans are also capable of discerning

---

[77] See Reinhart, *Before Revelation*, 73 where the author notes that Ghazālī, in his argument against rational moral theory, severs the relationship between good/evil (i.e. moral) assessments and the obligatory/prohibited (i.e. deontic) assessments.

moral and deontic values in the absence of revelation. Moreover, ʿAbd al-Jabbār argues that the Muʿtazilī understandings of benevolence, optimism, purposefulness of divine actions, are all central to establishing the divinity of God and the benefit of following His laws. Those same doctrines also allow humans to predict divine laws. A just and wise god does not impose impossible obligations, always permits useful, good, and harmless actions and only proscribes evil, harmful, and useless ones. ʿAbd al-Jabbār's Muʿtazilī theology allows humans to predict divine laws even before receiving any divine revelations. The ability of humans to predict divine actions and laws is also crucial for the Muʿtazilī argument justifying worshipping God and obeying His laws. Suspension entails the unpredictability of divine legislations, and this, for ʿAbd al-Jabbār, would be detrimental for both arguments. Whereas for the other three Shāfiʿīs, making God submit to objective moral criteria – which would in turn allow humans to predict His legislations – would undermine the divinity and the omnipotence of God.

PROSCRIPTION

I have so far discussed permission and suspension, but I have not sufficiently discussed proscription. One will not sufficiently understand the theoretical and theological foundations of permission and suspension until the foundations of proscription are examined and juxtaposed with them. This section examines these foundations by analysing arguments promoting proscription. This analysis attempts to identify the theological and theoretical presumptions of proscription and reveal the major points of contention between those who promote proscription and those who endorse permission or suspension as an answer to the before revelation question.

Reinhart notes that proscription, as well as the other two positions, is to be found in almost all theological and legal schools. However, pre-modern literature usually singles out particular groups as those who typically adopt proscription. Among those groups are the Baghdādī-Muʿtazilīs[78] and the Twelver Shīʿīs.[79] Ibn

[78] See for example, ʿAbd Allāh b. ʿUmar al-Bayḍāwī (d. 685/1286?), *Minhāj al-wuṣūl ilā ʿilm al-uṣūl*, ed. Muṣṭafā Shaykh Muṣṭafā (Damascus:

ʿAqīl (d. 513/1119) states that all three positions (including proscription) are to be found among the Ḥanbalīs and the Shāfiʿīs.[80] Badr al-Dīn al-Zarkashī (d. 794/1392) notes that Mālikīs adopt proscription, while the Mālikī Abū al-Walīd al-Bājī, more realistically, says some of them do.[81] Zarkashī, again, states that some Ḥanafīs adopt proscription, ʿĀlāʾ al-Dīn al-Samarqandī (d. 539/1144?)[82] attributes the same position to some traditionalists (*aṣḥāb al-ḥadīth*).[83] It is important to note here that no one legal or theological school monopolized proscription; this position is adopted by jurists from diverse theological and legal backgrounds.

The Muʿtazilī position on the before revelation debate is particularly important for this study. As mentioned above, several premodern sources inform us that Baghdādī-Muʿtazilīs favour proscription. This becomes more interesting when we note that premodern authors often mention that Baṣrian-Muʿtazilīs embrace permission.[84] ʿAbd al-Jabbār and his student Abū al-Ḥusayn al-

---

Muʾassasat al-Risāla, 2006), 25; Shīrāzī, *Sharḥ al-Lumaʿ*, 977; Shīrāzī, *Tabṣira*, 532–3; Ibn ʿAqīl, *al-Wāḍiḥ fī uṣūl al-fiqh*, 2:317, 5:260; Kalwadhānī, *al-Tamhīd fī uṣūl al-fiqh*, 4:270; Asnawī, *Nihāyat al-sūl*, 1:275; Abū Yaʿlā, *al-ʿUdda fī uṣūl al-fiqh*, 1240; Zarkashī, *al-Baḥr al-muḥīṭ*, 1:154; Rāzī, *al-Maḥṣūl fī ʿilm uṣūl al-fiqh*, 1:158; Samʿānī, *Qawāṭiʿ al-adilla*, 3:409.

79 Ibn ʿAqīl, *al-Wāḍiḥ fī uṣūl al-fiqh*, 5:260; Abū Yaʿlā, *al-ʿUdda fī uṣūl al-fiqh*, 1240; Rāzī, *al-Maḥṣūl fī ʿilm uṣūl al-fiqh*, 1:158; Asnawī, *Nihāyat al-sūl*, 1:275.

80 Ibn ʿAqīl, *al-Wāḍiḥ fī uṣūl al-fiqh*, 2:317.

81 Zarkashī, *al-Baḥr al-muḥīṭ*, 1:155; Bājī, *al-Ishāra fī uṣūl al-fiqh*, 299.

82 Samarqandī's death date is not known with certainty. Other possible dates include 538/1143, 540/1145 and 553/1148. However, Angelika Brodersen favors 539/1144 as his probable death date, see her *EI*[3], s.v. 'ʿAlāʾ al-Dīn al-Samarqandī'.

83 Zarkashī, *al-Baḥr al-muḥīṭ*, 1:155; Samarqandī, *Mīzān al-uṣūl*, 285.

84 See for example, Shīrāzī, *Tabṣira*, 533; Ibn ʿAqīl, *al-Wāḍiḥ*, 5:260; al-Zarkashī, *al-Baḥr al-muḥīṭ*, 1:154–5 (Zarkashī notes that Abū Hāshim al-Jubbāʾī says that Baṣrian Muʿtazilīs adopt permission whereas Baghdādī Muʿtazilīs prefer proscription, including Abū al-Qāsim al-Kaʿbī and his followers); Abū Yaʿlā, *al-ʿUdda fī uṣūl al-fiqh*, 1240; Bayḍāwī, *Minhāj al-*

Baṣrī (d. 436/1044), both Baṣrian-Muʿtazilīs, adopt permission. Their literature can serve as primary sources of information on their school's position in the fifth/eleventh century.[85] However, as far as I know, no Baghdādī-Muʿtazilī legal theory literature is available that includes information relevant to their stance on the before revelation debate.[86] This lack of primary sources on the Baghdādī-Muʿtazilī position makes examining and understanding their motives for adopting proscription a difficult and highly speculative task.

Reinhart does not seem concerned with this problem. He writes a section on Baghdādī-Muʿtazilī proscription that depends on Abū al-Ḥusayn al-Baṣrī's account of his interlocutor's argument in support of proscription.[87] Abū al-Ḥusayn mentions the argument of his 'proscriber' opponent without naming him or mentioning his theological affiliation. Reinhart ascribes this argument to the

---

wuṣūl, 25; ʿAbd al-Jabbār notes that his masters (*shuyūkh*) uphold permission and some of them adopt proscription, see his *Mughnī*, 17:145.

[85] For their chapters on the before revelation debate, see ʿAbd al-Jabbār, *Mughnī*, 17:145–8; Abū al-Ḥusayn, *Muʿtamad*, 868–79.

[86] The only legal text by a Baghdādī-Muʿtazilī, I am aware of, is Abū al-Qāsim ʿAbd Allāh al-Kaʿbī al-Balkhī (d. 319/931), *Qabūl al-akhbār wa-maʿrifat al-rijāl*, 2 vols ed. Abū ʿAmr al-Ḥusaynī ʿAmr b. ʿAbd al-Raḥīm (Beirut: Dār al-Kutub al-ʿIlmiyya, 2000). This is a text mainly in the discipline of *ʿilm al-rijāl* (the assessment of the probity (*ʿadāla*) and reliability (*ḍabṭ*) of transmitters of traditions). It does not include information relevant to the before revelation debate. Another text by a Baghdādī-Muʿtazilī with some legal information is Abū al-Ḥusayn ʿAbd al-Raḥīm b. Muḥammad b. ʿUthmān al-Khayyāṭ (d. ca. 300/913), *Kitāb al-Intiṣār wa-l-radd ʿalā Ibn al-Rāwandī al-mulḥid*, 2nd ed. ed. H. Y. Nyberg (repr., 1344/1925; Beirut: Awrāq Sharqiyya, 1423/1993). This book is mainly a rebuttal of the criticisms of Ibn al-Rāwandī (d. middle or end of 4th/10th century) against Muʿtazilī scholars and their doctrines. It includes discussions of some legal topics. Unfortunately, none of them are relevant to the concerns of this chapter. I am not aware of other legal works by Baghdādī-Muʿtazilī author that includes information relevant to their position on the before revelation question.

[87] Reinhart, *Before Revelation*, 31–3.

Baghdādī-Muʿtazilī Abū al-Qāsim al-Kaʿbī al-Balkhī (d. 319/931) saying that

> as for the identity of the opponent, it seems likely that Abū l-Ḥusayn al-Baṣrī would be arguing with a Baghdādī Muʿtazilī, since intramural argumentation seems more important to the Muʿtazilah than intermural. While it is clear that there were others than Abū l-Qāsim al-Kaʿbī who held the Proscribed position, for convenience, and lacking a more direct witness, we will ascribe the Proscribed arguments in the *Muʿtamad* to him.[88]

Reinhart does not conclusively claim that this argument is Balkhī's. However, the fact that he chooses to attribute it to him for no reason other than convenience is precarious. Most importantly, Reinhart does not present enough evidence demonstrating that Abū al-Ḥusayn's interlocutor is actually a Baghdādī-Muʿtazilī and not a scholar from another theological background. Nothing in Abū al-Ḥusayn's account of proscription uncovers the theological affiliation of his 'proscriber' interlocutor. Therefore, there is no good reason to accept Reinhart's attribution. All that we can do with this argument is to consider it an argument put forward by a 'proscriber' without presuming his identity and theological affiliation. Moreover, Abū al-Ḥusayn presents his 'proscriber' interlocutor's argument in a largely polemical context; he mentions it only to refute it. Depending on polemical accounts as sources of information is, needless to say, quite problematic.[89]

What further complicates our understanding of proscription is the lack of legal theory literature authored by scholars who accept it. Reinhart, rightly, notes that the only legal theory text authored

---

[88] Reinhart, *Before Revelation*, 32. For Abū al-Ḥusayn al-Baṣrī's account, see his *Muʿtamad*, 868–79.

[89] The main difference, here, between this study and Reinhart's *Before Revelation* is that Reinhart uses Abū al-Ḥusayn al-Baṣrī's polemical refutation of proscription to gain more information on proscription. Whereas this study uses the same polemical refutations (and other ones) to gain more information on the polemicist's position (either permission or suspension).

by a 'proscriber' jurist hitherto discovered is *al-ʿUdda fī uṣūl al-fiqh* by the Ḥanbalī Abū Yaʿlā b. al-Farrāʾ (d. 458/1066).[90] This seems to hold true today, therefore this study has no other option but to primarily depend on Abū Yaʿlā's book as the major source of information on proscription. In their literature, many opponents of proscription usually imagine the presence of a 'proscriber' interlocutor attempting to justify proscription. They attribute arguments in supportive of proscription to this interlocutor and then attempt to refute them and show their fallacy. In most cases, they neither name their interlocutor nor mention his theological affiliation. This section will not depend on these polemical refutations as a reliable source of information for proscription. However, polemical refutations of proscription might help uncover more information on permission and suspension and highlight the theological points of contention between all three positions. One must note here that given the paucity of first-hand information on proscription, the

[90] Reinhart, *Before Revelation*, 31. Reinhart observes that it is not absolutely clear whether Abū Yaʿlā upholds permission or proscription. Nonetheless, he favours the latter option and deals with Abū Yaʿlā as a proscriber jurist all through his book. It is true that Abū Yaʿlā's position is not crystal clear. However, there are indications that he accepts proscription rather than any other position. Although Abū Yaʿlā remarks that permission and suspension are possible answers to the before revelation question, he explicitly states that proscription is more probably to be the correct (*aẓhar*) one. See his *al-ʿUdda fī uṣūl al-fiqh*, 1249. Moreover, Abū Yaʿlā holds that after the advent of revelation, things that revelation does not comment on are proscribed, see pp. 1250. This might indicate that, *a fortiori*, before revelation things are proscribed. It is also interesting to note that Abū Yaʿlā seems to have changed his position on the before revelation debate. The later Ḥanbalī jurist ʿAlāʾ al-Dīn al-Mardāwī (d. 885/1480) notes that Abū Yaʿlā promotes permission in his, hitherto undiscovered, text *al-Mujarrad* whereas in *al-ʿUdda fī uṣūl al-fiqh* he endorses proscription, see Abū al-Ḥasan ʿAlāʾ al-Dīn ʿAlī b. Sulaymān al-Mardāwī (d. 885/1480), *al-Taḥbīr sharḥ al-Taḥrīr fī uṣūl al-fiqh*, ed. ʿAbd al-Raḥmān b. ʿAbd Allāh al-Jibrīn and others (Riyadh: Maktabat al-Rushd, 1421/2000), 766 (for his comment on *al-Mujarrad*), 768 (for his comment on *al-ʿUdda fī uṣūl al-fiqh*).

conclusions of this section can only be hesitant and sometimes speculative.

Legal Prudence: Abū Yaʿlā b. al-Farrāʾ

This sub-section mainly analyses Abū Yaʿlā's argument for proscription. It also examines refutations of his arguments by jurists who adopt permission or suspension. Abū Yaʿlā mentions three arguments in support of proscription. The first is the following: all creatures are owned by God. No human is allowed to use the property of another human without the owner's consent.[91] Abū Yaʿlā, abruptly, stops here, probably assuming that the rest can be easily deduced. The logical conclusion of Abū Yaʿlā's statement would be, since no human is allowed to the use the property of another human without the owner's consent, no human should be allowed to use God's property before His consent. God's consent is communicated to humans via revelation. As long as humans do not receive revelation, they are not allowed to use or consume any of God's creatures. This is the most often cited argument in support of proscription, numerous pre-modern authors, ones who hold suspension or permission, attribute it to their 'proscriber' interlocutors.[92]

ʿAbd al-Jabbār, Shīrāzī and Samʿānī rebut this argument saying that what prohibits consuming the property of another is not the fact that someone else owns this property. This prohibition is rather contingent on the owner suffering harm resulting from the illegitimate use of his property. They clarify their argument saying that sitting in the shade of a house owned by someone else, looking into his mirror, or walking in the light of his torch is not prohibited because the owner suffers no harm in these cases. They conclude that since nothing can harm God, therefore the fact that He owns all created things in the universe cannot serve as a justification for

---

[91] Abū Yaʿlā, *al-ʿUdda fī uṣūl al-fiqh*, 1243.

[92] See for example, Abū al-Ḥusayn, *Muʿtamad*, 874–5; Kalwadhānī, *al-Tamhīd fī uṣūl al-fiqh*, 4:281; Samʿānī, *Qawāṭiʿ al-adilla*, 3:419; Ibn Ḥazm, *al-Iḥkām fī uṣūl al-aḥkām*, 1:52; al-Khaṭīb al-Baghdādī, *Kitāb al-Faqīh*, 1:528.

proscription.[93] Just like the ownership of a torch does not entail prohibiting people from walking in its light. The Muʿtazilīs Abū Bakr al-Jaṣṣāṣ, Abū al-Ḥusayn al-Baṣrī and Ḥusayn b. ʿAlī al-Ṣaymarī mention very similar rebuttals to this proscriber's argument.[94] Many other non-Muʿtazilīs also utilize the same refutation for the same purpose.[95]

Abū Yaʿlā's argument in favour of proscription and the counter argument mentioned by his opponents both utilize a type of *qiyās* named *qiyās al-ghāʾib ʿalā al-shāhid*. This type of *qiyās* is often used by speculative theologians to establish the divine attributes,[96]

---

[93] ʿAbd al-Jabbār, *Mughnī*, 17:147; Shīrāzī, *Sharḥ al-Lumaʿ*, 980; Shīrāzī, *Tabṣira*, 534; Samʿānī, *Qawāṭiʿ al-adilla*, 3:413–4.

[94] Ṣaymarī, *Masāʾil al-khilāf*, 2:338; Abū al-Ḥusayn, *Muʿtamad*, 874–5; al-Jaṣṣāṣ, *al-Fuṣūl fī uṣūl al-fiqh*, 3:250.

[95] See for example, Muḥammad b. ʿAbd al-Ḥamīd al-Usmandī (d. 552/1158), *Badhl al-naẓar fī uṣūl al-fiqh*, ed. Muḥammad Zakī ʿAbd al-Barr (Cairo: Maktabat al-Turāth, 1412/1992), 665; Abū al-Walīd Sulaymān b. Khalaf al-Bājī (d. 474/1081), *Iḥkām al-fuṣūl fī aḥkām al-uṣūl*, ed. ʿAbd al-Majīd Turkī (Beirut: Dār al-Gharb al-Islāmī, 1995), 691–2; Ibn ʿAqīl, *al-Wāḍiḥ fī uṣūl al-fiqh*, 5:264–5; Kalwadhānī, *al-Tamhīd fī uṣūl al-fiqh*, 4:282–3; Asnawī, *Nihāyat al-sūl*, 1:294; Rāzī, *al-Maḥṣūl fī uṣūl al-fiqh*, 1:164; Ghazālī, *Mustaṣfā*, 1:208–9. Abū Yaʿlā rebuts this counterargument saying that what prohibits the use of the property of another is not the harm the owner suffers, but rather the harm the illegitimate user suffers in the hereafter as a result of this transgression. See Abū Yaʿlā, *al-ʿUdda fī uṣūl al-fiqh*, 1246. On this point, see also Reinhart, *Before Revelation*, 35.

[96] Bernard Weiss translates *qiyās al-ghāʾib ʿalā al-shāhid* as considering the absent analogous to the present. He defines *ghāʾib* as 'the numinous world beyond the reach of human sensory experience', and *shāhid* as 'the phenomenal, empirically available world', see Weiss, *Search for God's Law*, 53–4. In other words, the immanent world (*shāhid*) is the physical world humans live in; it is the world that they can see, feel and, touch. The transcendental world (*ghāʾib*) is the divine realm; a metaphysical world that is beyond human sensory experience. My translation of *ghāʾib* as the transcendental realm and *shāhid* as the immanent realm, is borrowed from Reinhart, *Before Revelation*, 69. For more information on theological *qiyās*, see Zakariyyā Bashīr ʿAlī Imām, 'Qiyās al-ghāʾib ʿalā al-shāhid', *Majallat al-Sharīʿa wa-l-Qānūn, Jāmiʿat al-Imārāt al-ʿArabiyya al-Muttaḥida* 8 (1415/1994):

therefore I translate it here as theological *qiyās*. The validity of this method is a point of contention between Ashʿarīs and Muʿtazilīs; the former usually reject it whereas the latter usually accept it.[97] Theological *qiyās* blurs the distinction between the transcendent metaphysical world (*al-ghāʾib*) of God and the immanent physical world (*al-shāhid*) of humans. It uses information from the immanent world to uncover information and reach conclusions about the transcendental world. Reinhart suggests that part of the debate between those who hold proscription or permission and those who adopt suspension concerns 'the continuity between the Hidden (*al-ghāʾib*) and the Manifest (*al-shāhid*) worlds'.[98] Elsewhere he writes that abstaining from deontic assessments before revelation is to be

---

143–202; Shāfiʿī, *al-Madkhal ilā dirāsat ʿilm al-kalām*, 163–71; Weiss, *Search for God's Law*, 53–6.

[97] One must note that the Ashʿarī position is not as straight forward. Ashʿarīs such as the school's eponym Abū al-Ḥasan al-Ashʿarī (d. 324/935–6) and Abū Bakr al-Bāqillānī (d. 403/1013) accept it as a valid method to reach and support theological conclusions, see Shāfiʿī, *al-Madkhal ilā dirāsat ʿilm al-kalām*, 166, 169. Whereas others such as Juwaynī, Ghazālī, Rāzī and Āmidī consider it invalid, see Ḥasan al-Khaṭṭāf, 'Qiyās al-Ghāʾib ʿalā al-shāhid wa-dawruh fī takwīn al-ʿaql al-Iʿtizālī', *Islāmiyyat al-Maʿrifa* 44 (2006): 91–128; Shāfiʿī, *al-Madkhal ilā dirāsat ʿilm al-kalām*, 165–71. Nonetheless, Ḥasan al-Khaṭṭāf, rightly, notes that the Ashʿarī rejection of theological *qiyās* is usually theoretical. In practice, the vast majority utilize it in their theological literature. Juwaynī is among the scholars who explicitly reject theological *qiyās* yet he still uses it to examine and establish the divine attributes. For Juwaynī's rejection of theological *qiyās*, see his *Burhān*, 129–30. For instances of Juwaynī's use of theological *qiyās* in his theological literature, see for example his *Irshād*, 31, 44, 61–2, 64–5, 82–4, 289. I became aware of Juwaynī use of theological *qiyās* from Āl ʿAbd al-Laṭīf, *Manhaj Imām al-Ḥaramayn*, 141–63. Reinhart's presentation of Juwaynī's position on the validity of theological *qiyās* lacks nuance. Based on his reading of *Burhān*, Reinhart concludes that Juwaynī does not accept theological *qiyās*, see his *Before Revelation*, 69–71, 75. Reinhart does not mention that in his theological literature, Juwaynī accepts this type of *qiyās*. It is noteworthy here that none of Juwaynī's theological works appear in the bibliography of Reinhart's *Before Revelation*.

[98] Reinhart, *Before Revelation*, 39.

'found earliest among those who distinguish most severely between this world's rules and those of the other world'.[99] What we can notice here is that Abū Yaʿlā is using theological *qiyās* to establish proscription. At the same time, jurists who accept both permission and suspension are using the same theological method to challenge proscription. Therefore, Reinhart's claim, although not completely wrong, lacks nuance.

The second argument Abū Yaʿlā mentions in support of proscription is the following:

> consuming [the property of God without His consent] is hazardous. This behaviour may be permitted; in this case, one is neither sinful nor deserves punishment. It may also be proscribed; in this case, one deserves blame and [becomes] sinful. Since both situations are possible, we rationally know that we must abstain from any action to avoid danger (*wajaba bi-dalīl al-ʿaql al-imtināʿ minhu li-ʾilla yarkab al-khaṭar wa-l-gharrar*). This is like someone being told that one road is safe and the other is dangerous. It is then a rational obligation to avoid the dangerous road, taking this road would be rationally repugnant (*wajaba bi-dalīl al-ʿaql tark al-mukhawwaf, wa-idhā rakabuh kāna qubḥ^an fi-l-ʿaql*). Therefore, precaution requires us to abstain [from any action before revelation].[100]

Abū Yaʿlā is noting that assuming things or actions to be permitted, before access to revelation, is a hazardous assumption. Actions performed (or things consumed) are either permitted or proscribed, if it is the latter the performer of this action will deserve blame. Prior to revelation, humans cannot be sure that the actions they perform bring about no divine blame. Therefore, argues Abū Yaʿlā, we *rationally* know that the most prudent option, which will rule out the possibility of divine blame, is refraining from performing all actions [until revelation uncover which ones are permitted and which ones are proscribed]. He concludes that, in the absence of revelation, siding with proscription is the safest option.

---

[99] Reinhart, *Before Revelation*, 62.

[100] Abū Yaʿlā, *al-ʿUdda fī uṣūl al-fiqh*, 1244.

I have so far mentioned two of Abū Yaʿlā's arguments supporting proscription. The first entails that, despite the absence of revelation, humans know that consuming the property of others without the owner's consent is prohibited. His second argument reveals that, for him, precaution (*iḥtiyāṭ*) and the avoidance of danger are *rational* obligations. Elsewhere, Abū Yaʿlā notes that although all actions before the advent of revelation are proscribed, we *rationally* realize that actions and 'things' necessary for human survival (e.g. eating and breathing) must be permitted.[101] These three comments might imply that Abū Yaʿlā considers unaided reason a reliable source of moral and deontic knowledge, at least in the absence of revelation.

Reinhart notes that to describe things as proscribed, prior to the advent of revelation, the ability of reason to discern moral knowledge must be accepted.[102] Otherwise there would be a contradiction between a jurist's moral theory and his answer to the before revelation question. However, and despite the above statements, Abū Yaʿlā is quite explicit: for him, reason plays no role in moral and deontic assessments.[103] Nonetheless, as noted by Reinhart, Abū Yaʿlā seems conscious of the theological consequences of proscription.[104] He is aware that without awarding reason some powers in moral/deontic assessments it would be difficult to justify embracing proscription. Therefore, Abū Yaʿlā presents an argument attempting to harmonize his promotion of proscription with his moral epistemology.

Being aware of Abū Yaʿlā's revelational moral theory, Abū Yaʿlā's interlocutor, who supports suspension, challenges him saying that since reason does not permit or proscribe actions (i.e. reason cannot discern deontic knowledge), therefore humans must suspend assessments until the advent of revelation. Abū Yaʿlā replies saying that

---

101 Abū Yaʿlā, *al-ʿUdda fī uṣūl al-fiqh*, 1247.

102 Reinhart, *Before Revelation*, 34.

103 Abū Yaʿlā Muḥammad b. al-Ḥusayn b. Muḥammad b. al-Farrāʾ, *Kitāb al-Muʿtamad fī uṣūl al-dīn*, ed. Wadīʿ Zaydān Ḥaddād (Beirut: Dār al-Mashriq, 1974), 21, 103; Abū Yaʿlā, *al-ʿUdda*, 88, 1257, 1259–60.

104 Reinhart, *Before Revelation*, 34.

> we knew that reason neither permits nor proscribes via revelation (*ʿalimnā anna al-ʿaql lā-yubīḥ wa-l-yaḥẓur bi-l-sharʿ*). Our discussion here concerns pre-revelation [times]. It is possible to say that reason permits and proscribes until the advent of revelation put an end to this. Nothing before revelation can prevent this.[105]

Abū Yaʿlā is saying that it was revelation that informed humans that reason is incapable of discerning deontic assessments. Before the advent of revelation, there is nothing that would prohibit reason from taking part in these assessments. In the absence of revelation, as noted by Reinhart, Abū Yaʿlā makes reason sovereign; the arrival of revelation puts an end to this sovereignty.[106] Only after revelation do humans realize the epistemological limitations of reason. However, since they are not aware of these limitations before revelation, they must, according to Abū Yaʿlā, act upon the rational moral knowledge they have.[107]

For good reasons, Reinhart describes Abū Yaʿlā as wanting to ride two horses, he wants to adopt a notion of natural knowledge and at the same time keep reason reliant on revelation for moral knowledge.[108] Abū Yaʿlā is aware that embracing proscription implies an acceptance of a rational moral theory. However, it appears that he is neither willing to submit to the theological implications of his legal theory position nor allow his revelational moral theory shape his answer to the before revelation question. He is neither ready to espouse a rational moral theory nor willing to forsake proscription. Therefore, he puts forward the above reply to harmonize his espousal of proscription with his revelational moral theory that he is not willing to undermine.

I have mentioned before that a rational moral theory makes it easier to justify permission or proscription, whereas a revelational

---

[105] Abū Yaʿlā, *al-ʿUdda fī uṣūl al-fiqh*, 1248. For another similar statement, see p. 1257.

[106] Reinhart, *Before Revelation*, 35.

[107] Reinhart, *Before Revelation*, 36. For Reinhart's explanation of and commentary on Abū Yaʿlā's argument see, his *Before Revelation*, 34–7.

[108] Reinhart, *Before Revelation*, 36.

one brings a jurist closer to embracing suspension. However, I also explained that jurists often disagree on the legal implications of their common theological doctrines. Abū Yaʿlā's above reply shows that he does not consider his revelational moral theory as requiring the acceptance of suspension. Proscription, as noted before, is a position found among all theological and legal schools. Some of those, like the Baghdādī-Muʿtazilīs, embrace a rational moral theory, whereas others, like Abū Yaʿlā, assume a revelational moral theory. Each of those groups and scholars certainly consider their selection of proscription to be in harmony with their theology and moral theory. I am not aware of other pre-modern legal theory works written by jurists who favour proscription. We cannot, therefore, here analyse and compare how jurists with different moral theories justify proscription.

There is another important aspect to Abū Yaʿlā's second argument for proscription that deserves attention. Let us remember that he prefers proscription because of the probability that an act might be proscribed. As long as this probability exists, the safest option, for him, would be to avoid performing any act or consuming anything. This reveals an important theoretical difference between jurists who adopt permission and those who adopt proscription, namely the interpretation of doubt. This difference becomes clearer in the argument Abū al-Ḥusayn al-Baṣrī attributes to his – unnamed – 'proscriber' interlocutor. His interlocutor argues that an action is either good or evil, permitted or proscribed. He adds that all actions before the advent of revelation might include an aspect of corruption (*mafsada*). Therefore, in the case of permission, humans *might* be performing an action that is corrupt, evil and harmful. His interlocutor argues that this probability, in itself, is an aspect (*wajh*) of evilness that warrants proscription. To avoid the risk of performing a possibly evil or harmful action, humans should abstain from committing all actions.[109] For Abū al-Ḥusayn's interlocutor, the doubt that an action is evil is enough evidence to know that this action is indeed evil and thus proscribed.

If Abū al-Ḥusayn's 'proscriber' interlocutor interprets doubt as a sign for proscription, jurists who embrace permission seem to

---

[109] Abu al-Ḥusayn, *Muʿtamad*, 869, 872–3.

prefer the opposite position. Abū al-Ḥusayn argues that the absence of aspects of evil in an action leads to *conclusively* knowing that evil is absent from this particular action.[110] His interlocutor refuses this rationale saying that having no evidence that an act is evil is not adequate evidence to preclude, conclusively, the possibility that this act *might* be evil. Abū al-Ḥusayn replies[111] saying that an action *might* be corrupt cannot be sufficient evidence proving its evilness.[112] In other words, the *doubt* that an act is evil cannot be sufficient as a proof for its evilness and thus its prohibition. For Abū al-Ḥusayn's 'proscriber' interlocutor, the doubt that an act might be evil is enough grounds for proscribing this act. For Abū al-Ḥusayn, doubt cannot serve as sufficient grounds for proscription.

Other jurists who adopt permission adopt positions similar to Abū al-Ḥusayn's. ʿAbd al-Jabbār, as previously mentioned, holds that a harmless action that is conclusively, or even inconclusively, known to be useful must be considered permitted.[113] Moreover, he adds that the fact that there are no evidence uncovering evil aspects within an action or a thing is enough evidence to *conclusively* know that this act is free from evil and is thus permitted. In other words, for him, the absence of evidence is evidence of absence. ʿAbd al-Jabbār, based on his Muʿtazilī doctrine of benevolence (*luṭf*), argues that God is required to make humans aware of evil actions either via evidence through which they will identify them or via necessary knowledge. Therefore, if humans notice no signs that a particular action is evil, this functions as enough evidence that this action is free from corruption and is, thus, permitted.[114]

---

110 Abū al-Ḥusayn, *Muʿtamad*, 868–9.

111 Abū al-Ḥusayn, *Muʿtamad*, 870.

112 Abū al-Ḥusayn, *Muʿtamad*, 872.

113 ʿAbd al-Jabbār, *Mughnī*, 17:145.

114 ʿAbd al-Jabbār, *Mughnī*, 17:148. Another Baṣrian-Muʿtazilī with a similar opinion is ʿAbd al-Jabbār's student Abū Rashīd al-Naysābūrī Saʿīd b. Muḥammad b. Saʿīd (d. after 415/1024), see his *al-Masāʾil fi-l-khilāf bayna al-Baṣriyyīn wa-l-Baghdādiyyīn*, ed. Maʿn Ziyāda and Riḍwān al-Sayyid (Tripoli, Libya: Maʿhad al-Inmāʾ al-ʿArabī, 1979), 356. Al-Naysābūrī's death date is not accurately known. However, we know that after ʿAbd al-Jabbār's death in 415/1024, Abū Rashīd assumed his place as the head of

Abū al-Khaṭṭāb al-Kalwadhānī (d. 510/1116), a Ḥanbalī jurist who supports permission, mentions a similar argument. He writes that the fact that an act includes no signs of evil or corruption is enough to prove that this act is good and useful.[115] He adds that the possibility that an act might be evil cannot be enough evidence to prove its evilness.[116] On a similar tone, Ḥusayn al-Ṣaymarī, a Muʿtazilī-Ḥanafī jurist who embraces permission, notes that the absence of revelational evidence informing us that a thing is harmful is enough evidence to prove that this thing brings about no harm in this life or the next.[117]

All four jurists who accept permission, ʿAbd al-Jabbār, Abū al-Ḥusayn al-Baṣrī, Ṣaymarī and Kalwadhānī, hold that the absence of evidence uncovering evil aspects within an act is enough evidence to prove that this act is free from evil, thus good and permitted. Abū Yaʿlā (and probably other 'proscribers') seems to be refusing this rationale. He rather holds that the absence of evidence that an act is evil is not enough to preclude the possibility that this act *might* be evil. For 'permitters' the absence of evidence is evidence of absence whereas for 'proscribers' the absence of evidence is not enough as evidence of absence.

The legal implication of doubt is a crucial difference between jurists who adopt permission and those who embrace proscription. For Abū Yaʿlā and Abū al-Ḥusayn's unnamed 'proscriber' interlocutor doubt is an aspect of evilness. Therefore, doubt is adequate evidence to proscribe an action. Consequently, the possibility that an action might be evil becomes enough evidence to consider it evil and proscribed. For the four jurists who accept permission, discussed in the previous paragraph, the possibility (or the doubt) that an act may be evil is not enough evidence to actually consider it evil and thus proscribed. Moreover, the absence of evidence creates doubt about the deontic qualification of an action. For 'permitters' this is not a problem, because, for them, the absence of evidence is

---

the Baṣrian-Muʿtazilīs, which indicates that he died after 415/1024. See *EI*², s.v. 'Abū Rashīd al-Naysābūrī' (by R. M. Frank).

115 Kalwadhānī, *al-Tamhīd fī uṣūl al-fiqh*, 4:273.

116 Kalwadhānī, *al-Tamhīd fī uṣūl al-fiqh*, 4:274.

117 Ṣaymarī, *Masāʾil al-khilāf*, 337–8.

evidence of absence. For 'proscribers', doubt and hesitance are aspects of evilness, and since the absence of evidence creates doubt it cannot be grounds for permission.

Now, we turn to Abū Yaʿlā's third, and final, argument in support of proscription. This argument has two stages: the first attempts to show that revelation and reason are a symbiotic phenomenon; the latter never existed without the former. The second stage uses this conclusion as an argument against permission. Let me first remind the reader that Abū Yaʿlā holds that in the absence of revelation, humans will never be certain which actions are proscribed and which are permitted. Therefore, before revelation the safest option would be not to perform any action at all. The first stage of Abū Yaʿlā's argument is based on this assumption. He argues that if reason exists without revelation, humans will still not be aware which actions are permitted and which are proscribed. In this case, consuming useful things and refraining from consuming useful things would be unacceptable; because both options might be wrong [i.e. both options might be proscribed]. Abū Yaʿlā is noting that in the absence of revelation humans would be in an absurd situation in which they are required to perform a useful action (because not performing it might be proscribed) and required not to perform the same action (because performing it might also be proscribed). He concludes that since the separation of revelation from reason (or the non-existence of revelation) would entail this absurdity, this separation could therefore never have happened in the first place. In other words, to avoid this absurdity, we must assume that revelation existed since the beginning of human life to assist them distinguish between permitted and proscribed actions.[118]

The second stage of his argument is based on the above conclusion. Having, supposedly, proven that revelation has been present since the beginning of human existence, the revelational prohibition of using the property of others without their consent must therefore have also been present since the start of human existence.

---

[118] Abū Yaʿlā, *al-ʿUdda fī uṣūl al-fiqh*, 1245. Abū Yaʿlā's argument is complicated and, at first, appears unclear. Reinhart's translation of this argument helped clarify Abū Yaʿlā's words, see Reinhart, *Before Revelation*, 35 footnote 18.

This entails that the prohibition against using God's creatures prior to His consent has been in operation since the earliest days of human lives in this universe. Therefore, Abū Yaʿlā concludes that those who adopt permission go against the dictates of revelation and allow humans to use the property of God without His consent.[119]

The Muʿtazilī theologian and Ḥanafī jurist Abū al-Ḥusayn al-Baṣrī (d. 436/1044) and the Ḥanbalī Abū al-Khaṭṭāb al-Kalwadhānī (who was a student of Abū Yaʿlā)[120] attribute a similar argument to their proscriber interlocutors.[121] Both refute this justification of proscription; two aspects of their refutations are relevant to uncovering the theological controversies with an impact on the before revelation debate. First, they remark that God is wise; a wise god does not oblige impossible obligations. The requirement on humans to perform and omit the same action is impossible to fulfil; God would never impose such obligations.[122] Therefore, humans will never be in the absurd situation Abū Yaʿlā imagines would result from the absence of revelation. Abū al-Ḥusayn's and Kalwadhānī's belief that God does not impose impossible obligations precludes the situation Abū Yaʿlā assumes will happen should revelation not co-exist with human existence.

Second, both jurists argue that since God is wise, He must inform humans, via rational or revelational evidence, of the actions that are good (thus permitted) and those that are evil (thus proscribed). If God does not provide such information, this would be

---

[119] Abū Yaʿlā, *al-ʿUdda fī uṣūl al-fiqh*, 1245.

[120] Abū al-Fidāʾ Ismāʿīl b. ʿUmar b. Kathīr (d. 774/1373), *al-Bidāya wa-l-nihāya*, 14 vols (Beirut: Maktabat al-Maʿārif, 1966), 12:180. CD-ROM *al-Jāmiʿ al-kābīr*; Burhān al-Dīn Ibrāhīm b. Muḥammad b. ʿAbd Allāh b. Muḥammad b. Mufliḥ (d. 884/1479), *al-Maqṣad al-arshad fī dhikr aṣḥāb al-Imām Aḥmad*, 3 vols ed. ʿAbd al-Raḥmān b. Sulaymān al-ʿUthaymīn (Riyadh: Maktabat al-Rushd, 1410/1990), 3:20. CD-ROM *al-Jāmiʿ al-kabīr*.

[121] See Abū al-Ḥusayn, *Muʿtamad*, 873–4; Kalwadhānī, *al-Tamhīd fī uṣūl al-fiqh*, 4:285–6.

[122] Abū al-Ḥusayn, *Muʿtamad*, 873–4; Kalwadhānī, *al-Tamhīd fī uṣūl al-fiqh*, 4:284.

evidence that performing or omitting the same action is good.[123] This argument is based on the Muʿtazilī doctrine of benevolence (*luṭf*). As previously mentioned, benevolence requires God to provide humans with the information they need to reach salvation, including information allowing them to obey divine laws. This entails that for humans to be able to avoid proscribed actions and escape divine blame, God must inform them of those proscribed actions. This is an obligation on God, and a just god never omits an obligation. Given this doctrine, the lack of signs from God indicating the proscription of performing a particular act or proscribing its omission, entails that both performing and omitting this act is permitted. If both actions are permitted, humans are, thus, free to perform or omit this act. For them, nothing is absurd about this situation.

Kalwadhānī's and Abū al-Ḥusayn's refutation of Abū Yaʿlā's third argument for proscription assumes an acceptance of the Muʿtazilī concepts of benevolence and the prohibition of imposing impossible obligations. Both are derivatives of the Muʿtazilī understanding of divine justice and wisdom. Although he is not a Muʿtazilī, Kalwadhānī shares some of their doctrines. For example, he adopts a rational moral theory,[124] accepts the purposefulness of divine actions,[125] and states that thanking the benefactor (*shukr al-munʿim*) and equity (*inṣāf*) are obligations known via reason.[126]

---

[123] Abū al-Ḥusayn, *Muʿtamad*, 874; Kalwadhānī, *al-Tamhīd fī uṣūl al-fiqh*, 4:285–6.

[124] Kalwadhānī, *al-Tamhīd fī uṣūl al-fiqh*, 4:294–306.

[125] Kalwadhānī, *al-Tamhīd fī uṣūl al-fiqh*, 4:280.

[126] Kalwadhānī, *al-Tamhīd fī uṣūl al-fiqh*, 4:291. Having said this, it is important to note that Kalwadhānī is not a Muʿtazilī. He is rather a Ḥanbalī jurist who embraces a relatively traditionalist theology. As far as I know, he did not leave any theological literature allowing modern students to thoroughly examine his dogma. However, he authored a short poem in which he states his creed. For his poem and a modern commentary on it, see ʿAbd al-Nāṣir b. Nāṣir al-Burāk and Yāsir b. Saʿd Badr al-ʿAskar, *Sharḥ al-Qaṣīda al-dāliyya* (Riyadh: Dār Ibn al-Jawzī, 1430/2009). His poem reveals his traditionalist creed. For example, in verses number 18, 19, 20, he accepts the *istiwāʾ* and the *nuzūl* without wondering about the *kayfiyya* (*bi-lā*

These doctrines allow Abū al-Ḥusayn and Kalwadhānī to predict divine legislations. They preclude the possibility that God will impose an impossible obligation. Benevolence allows them to assume that God will provide humans with the information they need to identify proscribed actions. Abū al-Ḥusayn's and Kalwadhānī's refutations of proscription are shaped by the theological doctrines they share. Their acceptance of permission appears also grounded in the same doctrines.

Despite belonging to the same legal school, Abū Yaʿlā and Kalwadhānī offer different answers to the before revelation question. Their disagreement is probably a reflection of their different understanding of divine justice and wisdom. In his *al-Muʿtamad fī uṣūl al-dīn*, Abū Yaʿlā explicitly rejects the Muʿtazilī understanding of benevolence; he notes that God is not required to make available for humans evidence [facilitating knowledge of His laws].[127] He also refutes the Muʿtazilī concept of divine justice. He holds that nothing is incumbent on God; justice and wisdom are whatever

---

kayf). *Istiwāʾ* is the term used to refer to the doctrine that God 'sat' on His thrown after creating the universe. *Nuzūl* is another doctrine referring to a tradition attributed to the Prophet in which he supposedly says that God descends to earth searching for 'repenters'. *Bi-lā kayf* is a doctrine that refuses to wonder about the modality of God's 'sitting' or 'descending', whether this is similar to the human mode of sitting and descending or God has His own divine 'way' of 'sitting' and 'descending'. The *bi-lā kayf* (literally without how or without further comment) doctrine is usually associated with traditionalist theologians who refuse Ashʿarī and Muʿtazilī speculative theology and their allegorical interpretations of theological Qurʾāic verses and traditions attributed to the Prophet. For more details on the *bi-lā kayf* doctrine, see Binyamin Abrahamov, 'The *bi-lā kayfa* Doctrine and its Foundations in Islamic Theology', *Arabica* 42 (1995): 365–79; *EI*[2], s.v. 'Bi-lā Kayf'. Moreover, in verse 22 of Kalwadhānī's poem, he accepts the beatific vision, in verse 25 he states that the Qurʾān is uncreated, and in verse 27 he notes that God creates the deeds of humans, which is a rejection of freewill. All three verses are, virtually, a rejection of Muʿtazilī theology. This is enough to prove that Kalwadhānī is not a Muʿtazilī.

[127] Abū Yaʿlā, *al-Muʿtamad fī uṣūl al-dīn*, 118.

God does. The Creator is not required to behave in a particular manner to confirm His justice and wisdom.[128] Therefore, Abū Yaʿlā's theology allows him neither to assume that God will not impose impossible obligations nor that He must assist humans to become aware of His laws. Abū Yaʿlā's vindication of proscription is shaped by his dogma. Without his rejection of the Muʿtazilī concepts of divine justice and wisdom, it would be very difficult for him to adopt any of the three arguments he puts forward in support of proscription. Moreover, Abū Yaʿlā's theology makes divine laws unpredictable. Therefore, before revelation, the safest option for him is to refrain from performing any action, fearing that it might bring about divine blame and punishment.

The Ascetic Attitude: Baghdādī-Muʿtazilīs

As discussed above, pre-modern legal theory literature frequently states that Baghdādī-Muʿtazilīs embrace proscription whereas Baṣrian-Muʿtazilīs prefer permission. ʿAbd al-Jabbār, a Baṣrian-Muʿtazilī, says some of his *shuyūkh* (i.e. teachers or school figureheads) favour permission whereas others side with proscription.[129] He does not clarify whether by *shuyūkh* he is referring to Baṣrians only or if he is also referring to major Baghdādī-Muʿtazilī figureheads as well. His student Abū al-Ḥusayn, another Baṣrian-Muʿtazilī, does not explicitly mention the position of Baṣrian-Muʿtazilīs. However, he notes that some (rather than all) Baghdādī-Muʿtazilīs accept proscription.[130] I have already mentioned that Baṣrian-Muʿtazilī legal theory literature is quite rare. Moreover, I am not aware of any Baghdādī-Muʿtazilī legal theory literature with information relevant to the before revelation debate. Given the paucity of primary sources, we cannot know the Baghdādī, or indeed the Baṣrian, Muʿtazilī position with certainty. However, one might argue that the fact that attributing proscription to Baghdādī-

---

[128] Abū Yaʿlā, *al-Muʿtamad fī uṣūl al-dīn*, 119, 213–4.

[129] ʿAbd al-Jabbār, *Mughnī*, 17:145.

[130] Abū al-Ḥusayn, *Muʿtamad*, 868. He also remarks that Abū ʿAlī al-Jubbāʾī (d. 303/915–6) and his son Abū Hāshim uphold permission; both are major figureheads within the Baṣrian-Muʿtazilī sub-school and the Muʿtazila in general.

Muʿtazilīs is quite widespread and not challenged by any Muʿtazilī or non-Muʿtazilī source indicates that proscription was common among them. This might also be true about Baṣrian-Muʿtazilīs; the fact that attributing permission to the Baṣrian sub-school is frequent and not challenged might indicate that permission is common among them.

If we are going to accept this attribution, this would raise an important question: why is proscription common among Baghdādī-Muʿtazilīs whereas permission is common among the Baṣrians? We know that the Baghdādī-Baṣrian split within the Muʿtazilī School is caused by theological and metaphysical disagreements. Can these disagreements be the reason behind their different positions on the before revelation debate? Kevin Reinhart presents an argument attempting to explain this inter-Muʿtazilī split. This section examines and evaluates his argument.

Reinhart suggests three reasons behind the Baghdādī-Baṣrian split over the before revelation question. First, permitters are usually scholars who have an optimistic view of the world whereas proscribers adopt a pessimistic outlook. He notes that 'permitters and No Assessors are optimists, believing that acts not obviously designated as harmful are likely to be harmless. The Proscribers are pessimistic, mistrusting all acts until Revelation permits them'.[131] Elsewhere, Reinhart notes that Baghdādī-Muʿtazilī proscription grows from a

> skepticism of the world and the means by which the world is known, a skepticism radical for the Mu'tazilah. It is only from the other world that knowledge of the virtues of acts and things can be obtained. Human capacities, including the *'aql*, are sufficient only to establish the likelihood that a particular deed is forbidden.[132]

Reinhart argues that the pessimism common among the Baghdādī-Muʿtazilīs motivates them to trust reason as a means to proscribe but not to permit actions before the advent of revelation. On the other hand, Baṣrian-Muʿtazilīs, motivated by their optimistic view

---

131 Reinhart, *Before Revelation*, 47–8.

132 Reinhart, *Before Revelation*, 33.

of the world, use their rational moral theory to permit actions before the arrival of revelation.

Reinhart's above argument might explain why a traditionist or a traditionalist scholar chooses proscription, however it does not seem a plausible explanation for the Baghdādī-Muʿtazilī espousal of proscription. Despite the theological disagreements between Baghdādī and Baṣrian Muʿtazilīs, both accept the Muʿtazilī concept of optimism. This doctrine assumes the presence of a benign God who must guarantee human optimal benefit in this world and the next. Both Muʿtazilī sub-schools also accept the doctrine of benevolence, which requires God to facilitate salvation to humans. Given that these doctrines make God always create the best for humans, facilitate salvation for humans and consider the universe as created for their benefit; I find it difficult to describe Baghdādī-Muʿtazilīs as pessimists who do not trust the world. Therefore, Reinhart's suggestion that Baghdādī-Muʿtazilī pessimism is the reason behind their espousal of proscription is unconvincing to me.

The second reason Reinhart proposes as an explanation for the Baghdādī Baṣrian split over the before revelation debate is their different views on moral ontology. He writes that Baghdādī-Muʿtazilīs have a strict moral ontology that makes the moral value of an act an integral part of its ontological being; for them, an act is ontologically and intrinsically either good or evil. Therefore, the moral assessment of an act can never changes regardless of the changing circumstances surrounding its occurrence. On the other hand, Baṣrian-Muʿtazilīs consider the aspect (*wajh*) of an act as the decisive factor in determining its moral qualification.[133] A brief explanation of the term *wajh* should clarify the difference between both moral ontologies.

Reinhart notes that Baṣrian-Muʿtazilīs believe that the *wajh* of an act 'was part of the ontological composite that constituted the

---

[133] I, here, borrow Hourani's and Reinhart's translation of *wajh* as aspect. See Hourani, *Islamic Rationalism*, 62–89, 104–8, 121–2; Reinhart, *Before Revelation*, esp. 146. Frank translates the term *wajh* as 'the manner of the act's occurrence'. See Richard M. Frank, *Beings and their Attributes: The Teachings of the Basrian School of the Muʿtazila in the Classical Period* (Albany: State University of New York, 1978), 126, 131–5.

nature of a thing or act; yet the *wajh* was only tenuously a part of the act's existence'.[134] He adds that the Baṣrian-Muʿtazilīs came up with the concept of *wajh* to mitigate the moral ontology of the Baghdādī-Muʿtazilīs who

> wished to lodge... [the act's] moral quality within its very being, to make the moral quality part of what made it what it was. For the Basrans, such a theory entailed too rigid a view of the act's moral qualities – since, consequently, similar acts could not differ in value though they differed in context. Yet the Basrans were unwilling to divorce the acts' being entirely, for this might entail the inability of the mind to perceive its qualities. [135]

The Baṣrians develop the concept of *wajh* to be able to contextualize each act. The *wajh* of an act can, roughly, be considered the context in which an act occurs. This context determines whether an act is good or evil. For example, lying to gain more profit is evil, whereas lying to save the life of a prophet is good. The *wajh* allows Baṣrian-Muʿtazilīs to evaluate an act as good in one context but evil in another. The little available information on Baghdādī-Muʿtazilī moral ontology gives the impression that they would refuse such a scheme. For them the moral character of an act is inseparable from its ontological being; an act is either always good or evil. Just as an orange is ontologically round, the context in which the orange is consumed will not affect its shape. For Baghdādī-Muʿtazilīs, the context in which an act occurs does not influence its moral assessment.[136] Having explained, albeit briefly, the difference between Baghdādī and Baṣrian moral ontology, the question now is: can this difference be among the reasons behind their different answers to the before revelation question?

Unfortunately, this question cannot be adequately answered in the absence of Baghdādī-Muʿtazilī primary sources with enough

---

[134] Reinhart, *Before Revelation*, 146.

[135] Reinhart, *Before Revelation*, 146.

[136] For more details on this disagreement, see Abū Rashīd al-Naysābūrī, *al-Masāʾil fi-l-khilāf*, 355–7; Reinhart, *Before Revelation*, 138–60; Eissa, 'Abū al-Ḥusayn al-Baṣrī's Use of Reason in *ʿIlm al-kalām*', 35–7.

relevant information. However, Reinhart hints to a positive answer; he explains that

> for the Muʿtazilah of the late 200s through the 300s, the 'aspect' (*wajh*) of the thing was understood to be a portion of its existence, its being. It was believed to be that part of a thing that signified an innate quality – its moral quality, for instance. For Abū l-Qāsim, one aspect of an otherwise useful thing is the perceptible possibility that it might be corrupt. For him, this outer sign indicated the inner fact of its detestability. In perceiving the act's aspect of possible corruption, one perceives the ontological quality that makes its performance detestable and hence Proscribed.[137]

Reinhart is noting that for Abū al-Qāsim al-Balkhī the possibility of an act being corrupt is, in itself, an aspect of evilness. Aspects of evilness for him are a sign for an inner ontological evil quality within an act. Doubt about the deontic status of an act becomes a reflection of the ontological evil status of this act. Doubt, in this case, becomes in itself an aspect of evilness. Again, the interpretation of doubt appears as a major disagreement between Baṣrian and Baghdādī Muʿtazilīs. The doubt that an act is evil, for Abū al-Qāsim al-Balkhī, is enough grounds to consider it evil. This moral theory encourages the creation of a strict hermeneutic that considers 'doubt' as enough evidence for proscription. Before revelation, the deontic status of all acts is doubtful, therefore all acts must be proscribed. Permitters, on the other hand, do not see doubt as an aspect of evilness. For them, suspecting that an act is evil is not enough to prove that this act is, actually, evil.

---

[137] Reinhart, *Before Revelation*, 32–3. Elsewhere, Reinhart further explains the difference between Baṣrian and Baghdādī-Muʿtazilī moral ontology saying that '[w]hile the Baghdādīs tried to defend the rigorist position that 'a lie is detestable and so is Proscribed', the Basrans developed a situational ontology that withheld assessment of an act until the time and circumstances of its actual occurrence. The Basrans forged an ontological theory that made the assessment dependent on the evanescent aspect (*wajh*) that arose at the coming –into- existence of the act', see his *Before Revelation*, 181.

Reinhart's conclusion appears plausible. The disagreement over moral ontology is probably among the reasons behind the Baghdādī-Baṣrian split over the before revelation question. However, one may note with surprise that the available Muʿtazilī discussions of the before revelation debate make no significant references to moral ontology. ʿAbd al-Jabbār's and Abū al-Ḥusayn's refutations of proscription and justifications of permission do not raise the issue of moral ontology. Moreover, none of the Muʿtazilī and non-Muʿtazilī sources studied here attribute an argument to their proscriber interlocutors that is based on Baghdādī-Muʿtazilī moral ontology. Furthermore, Abū Rashīd al-Naysābūrī (d. after 415/1024), a Baghdādī-Muʿtazilī convert to Baṣrian-Muʿtazilism, wrote a book recording the disagreements between Baṣrian and Baghdādī Muʿtazilīs. He discusses, albeit briefly, their debate over moral ontology. In his discussion of this debate, he does mention their disagreement on the before revelation question.[138] The fact that the Baghdādī-Baṣrian moral ontology debate is absent from discussions of the before revelation question (especially from the published Muʿtazilī literature) may undermine the relevance of moral ontology to this legal theory debate. If Muʿtazilī scholars saw their debate over moral ontology relevant to the before revelation question, one would expect to see more obvious references to it in their discussions of the before revelation controversy.

As mentioned above, Reinhart suggests three reasons explaining why Baṣrian-Muʿtazilīs take on permission whereas Baghdādīs choose proscription. I have just mentioned the first two. The third is a rigorous pious attitude towards doubtful acts common among scholars who adopt proscription, whether Baghdādī-Muʿtazilīs or others. Reinhart notes that proscription 'turned out to be the result of a pious scrupulousness (*warʿ* [sic]) that was entirely consonant with the ascetic skepticism of both the Baghdādī-Mu'tazilīs and the Ḥanbalīs such as Abū Yaʿlá'.[139] Commenting on the argument Abū

[138] For his short discussion of this debate, see Abū Rashīd al-Naysābūrī, *al-Masāʾil fī-l-khilāf*, 354–7.

[139] Reinhart, *Before Revelation*, 180. Also see p. 33. Wael Hallaq holds a similar opinion, he remarks that 'proscribers' saw it safer to proscribe, as

al-Ḥusayn attributes to his proscriber interlocutor – whom Reinhart believes to be the Baghdādī-Muʿtazilī Abū al-Qāsim al-Balkhī – he says

> the core of Abū l-Qāsim's argument is a fear that an act of unknown value *might* be an occasion of sin. The *ʿaql* knows only enough to recognize the possibility of transgression, and so, out of prudence, the *presumptive* assessment for all acts is Proscribed. Abū l-Qāsim is the technical and theological expression of the pietist impulse seen among Sufis and jurisprudential conservatives such as Aḥmad ibn Ḥanbal. In pietist literature this suspicion of the uncertain action, deliberately cultivated as a religious virtue, is called *scrupulousness* (*warʿ* [sic]); in practice scrupulousness manifests itself as an aversion to the uncertainly licit.... scrupulousness consists precisely in avoiding the dubious even though such avoidance is not, strictly speaking, Obligatory. Abū l-Qāsim's view of useful acts as Proscribed is then plausible against a background of praxic rigor and suspicion. Hence he says: When the act's value is unknown, consider it Proscribed, because it could possibly be corrupt.[140]

Reinhart's analysis resonates with Abū Yaʿlā's argument in support of proscription and the argument Abū al-Ḥusayn and Kalwadhānī attribute to their proscriber interlocutors. All three proscribers seem to hold that proscription is safer than permission. Abū Yaʿlā notes that choosing permission is a reckless option.[141] By proscription, humans free themselves from the risk of sinning. Proscription, rather than permission, seems more akin to jurists with an ascetic and a rigorist mentality.

Ascetic thought is not foreign to Muʿtazilīs, especially in their earlier periods. There are multiple theories explaining the earliest beginnings of Muʿtazilīs. Among those is the view that they started as a group of ascetic scholars. For example, Ignaz Goldziher writes that the term 'Muʿtazila' was initially a reference to those 'who

---

this would preclude the risk of performing prohibited acts. See Hallaq, *Islamic Legal Theories*, 115.

[140] Reinhart, *Before Revelation*, 32.

[141] Abū Yaʿlā, *al-ʿUdda fī uṣūl al-fiqh*, 1244.

withdrew' from the world and lived ascetic lives.[142] Furthermore, in his book *al-Intiṣār*, ʿAbd al-Raḥīm al-Khayyāṭ (d. ca. 300/913), a Baghdādī-Muʿtazilī, refers to his Baghdādī colleagues as *nussāk Baghdād* (the ascetics of Baghdad) and quotes Ibn al-Rāwandī (d. middle or end of fourth/tenth century)[143] using the same term in reference to Muʿtazilīs.[144]

Reinhart notes that the rigorist outlook of the early Muʿtazilīs was preserved more by the Baghdādī sub-school than the Baṣrian.[145] Proscription is also common among traditionist scholars, whom are known for their pietistic and ascetic tendencies.[146] This ascetic mentality and what Reinhart translates as scrupulousness piety might influence the shape of a jurist's hermeneutics. It might motivate him to adopt a more cautious and conservative hermeneutic, one that minimizes the place of doubt in law-making and consider it as enough grounds for proscription. Proscription, then, seems to be the answer that better suits an ascetic legal mind.

Reinhart mentions three possible reasons behind the Muʿtazilī split over the before revelation question. I have already challenged the first two, but the third seems a more probable reason for this

---

[142] Ignaz Goldziher, *Introduction to Islamic Theology and Law*, trans. Andreas and Ruth Hamori with introduction and additional notes by Bernard Lewis (New Jersey: Princeton University Press, 1981), 86.

[143] *EI*², s.v. 'Ibn al-Rāwandī or al-Rēwendī', (by P. Kraus and G. Vajda). Both authors favour the middle of fourth/tenth century as Ibn al-Rāwandī's most probable death date.

[144] Al-Khayyāṭ, *Kitāb al-Intiṣār*, 72–3. Reinhart also refers to Sarah Stroumsa's article titled 'The Beginnings of the Muʿtazilah Reconsidered' in which she depicts 'the founders of the Mu'tazilah as ascetics who withdrew from worldly pleasures and politics into devotion and missionary activity', see his *Before Revelation*, 182. See also Sarah Stroumsa, 'The Beginnings of the Muʿtazilah, Reconsidered', *Jerusalem Studies in Arabic and Islam* 6 (1985): 229–41.

[145] Reinhart, *Before Revelation*, 182.

[146] Reinhart, *Before Revelation*, 22–3. For a study of the ascetic and pietistic tendencies among traditionist scholars, Christopher Melchert, 'The Piety of the Hadith Folk', *International Journal of Middle East Studies* 34.3 (2002): 425–39.

split. The scrupulousness piety of the Baghdādī-Muʿtazilīs may have encouraged the formation of a rigorist and conservative hermeneutic that: interprets doubt in favour of proscription rather than permission, does not accept the absence of evidence as evidence of absence, and proscribes actions easier than it permits them. Such a rigorist hermeneutic would, most likely, prefer proscription to permission. The available literature does not indicate that there are, strictly, theological and metaphysical grounds for the Baghdādī-Baṣrian disagreement over the before revelation question. The Baghdādī-Muʿtazilī ascetic mentality creates epistemological and hermeneutical disagreements between them and the Baṣrians. These disagreements, rather than any theological and metaphysical variations, are probably the reason behind their different positions on the before revelation debate. Each Muʿtazilī sub-school answers the before revelation question in a manner suitable to its respective hermeneutics.

The Theoretical Foundations

In this section we will analyse arguments, both for and against, proscription. This should allow a better understanding of the theological and theoretical foundations not only of proscription, but of permission and suspension as well. The available information on proscription gives the impression that the major point of contention between jurists who uphold suspension and those who adopt proscription appears to be their disagreement over moral epistemology. This might be implied from the literature authored by jurists who promote suspension. For example, as explained before, Shīrāzī's rejection of proscription is based on his rejection of rational moral knowledge.[147] Samʿānī notes that his choice of suspension is a product of his belief that unaided reason cannot discern deontic assessments.[148] The late Shāfiʿī jurist Sayf al-Dīn al-Āmidī writes that embracing a revelational moral theory contradicts proscription.[149]

---

[147] See Shīrāzī, *Sharḥ al-Lumaʿ*, 977–9; Shīrāzī, *Tabṣira*, 533–4.

[148] Samʿānī, *Qawāṭiʿ al-adilla*, 3:419–20.

[149] Āmidī, *al-Iḥkām fī uṣūl al-aḥkām*, 1:127.

This might make some sense, for a jurist to consider an act or a thing proscribed before revelation, he must accept the ability of unaided reason to discern deontic knowledge. However, moral theory does not seem to have a consistent impact on a jurist's position on the before revelation debate. Scholars sharing a common moral theory will not necessarily share a common position on this debate. For example, the Ḥanbalī Abū Yaʿlā, despite choosing proscription, insists on his revelational moral theory. Baghdādī-Muʿtazilīs, on the other hand, described by medieval literature as proscribers, adopt a rational moral theory and a moral ontology that keeps the moral quality of an act an essential part of its ontological being.[150] This shows that jurists with very different moral theories uphold proscription. On the other hand, Baghdādī and Baṣrian Muʿtazilīs, both of whom believe in a rational moral theory, have two contradicting positions from proscription. Therefore, jurists disagree on the legal theory consequences of their moral theory. One cannot then assume that one particular moral theory will consistently lead to embracing a particular answer to the before revelation question.

Rather than a common moral theory, it appears that jurists who favour proscription share two common hermeneutical features. First, their rejection of the probative value of the absence of evidence. Jurists who uphold permission, including those discussed here, accept the absence of evidence as evidence of absence. ʿAbd al-Jabbār, Abū al-Ḥusayn, Ṣaymārī, Jaṣṣāṣ and Kalwadhānī all hold that if there is no evidence that a particular act is evil or harmful, this act must be good and permitted. For proscribers, the absence of evidence uncovering evil aspects in an act is not sufficient to preclude the possibility that this act might be evil. Therefore, all actions must be considered evil, thus proscribed, until there is evi-

---

[150] Commenting on finding Ḥanbalī jurists and Baghdādī-Muʿtazilīs sharing one legal theory position (i.e. proscription) Reinhart, rightly, observes '[t]he discovery that a number of prominent Ḥanbalīs shared a doctrine with the Baghdādī Muʿtazilīs -not just scandalous figures such as Ibn ʿAqīl but establishment figures such as Ibn Ḥāmid and Abū Yaʿlá- ought to cause us to rethink the notion of a dichotomous Islamic intellectual history'. See Reinhart, *Before Revelation*, 34.

dence proving that they are good and permitted. The second hermeneutical feature that seems common among proscribers is interpreting doubt in favour of proscription rather than permission. It appears that proscribers see doubt in itself as an aspect of evilness. It is enough to doubt that a particular act might be evil to consider it evil and, thus, proscribed. On the other hand, arguments advocating permission, ones utilised by permitters discussed above, show that jurists who choose permission do not consider doubt as an aspect of evilness. The possibility that an act is evil, for them, is not enough evidence to consider this act evil and thus proscribed.

The question now becomes: what makes jurists who adopt proscription see doubt as an aspect of evilness and refuse to accept the absence of evidence as evidence of absence? The examined literature suggests that asceticism and rigorous piety to be the most common factors among proscribers. I have also explained above that asceticism seems to have been common among Baghdādī-Muʿtazilīs. This is true about many traditionist and traditionalist jurists as well. Asceticism and scrupulousness piety might explain why proscribers see doubt as an aspect of evilness and refuse to accept the absence of evidence as evidence of absence. For an ascetic conservative legal mind, it is better to erroneously consider a permitted action as proscribed than to mistakenly permit an action that is actually proscribed. This ascetic approach to the law leads to the creation of a conservative extra-cautious hermeneutic. Such a hermeneutic will consider doubt an evidence for proscription rather than permission and refuse to consider the absence of evidence as evidence of absence. Common theological doctrines cannot explain why Abū Yaʿlā, other Ḥanbalīs and Baghdādī-Muʿtazilīs prefer proscription. What motivates them to assume proscription is their ascetic approach to the law and their scrupulous piety. Both encourage jurists from different theological backgrounds to embrace a strict conservative hermeneutic that, in turn, leads to embracing proscription rather than permission.

CONCLUSION

The before revelation question, like many legal theory questions, cannot be isolated from theological controversies. The theological debate that appears to have the greatest impact on this legal theory controversy is the debate around moral epistemology. This is obvious in the arguments the four Shāfiʿīs, who are examined here, utilize to support their position on this debate. ʿAbd al-Jabbār justifies upholding permission primarily by demonstrating that unaided reason is capable of acquiring moral and deontic knowledge. On the other hand, Shīrāzī, Juwaynī and Samʿānī vindicate suspension mainly by arguing that reason, without the assistance of revelation, is incapable of discerning such knowledge.

Another theological controversy relevant to the before revelation question is the Muʿtazilī-Ashʿarī/traditionalist debate around the definitions of divine justice and wisdom. The Muʿtazilīs define divine wisdom and justice as a group of constraints that God chose for Himself. These constraints come in the form of theological doctrines that are considered logical consequences of divine wisdom and justice. The ones that concern us most here are benevolence (*luṭf*), optimism (*al-ṣalāḥ wa-l-aṣlaḥ*) and the purposefulness of divine actions (*taʿlīl afʿāl Allāh*). ʿAbd al-Jabbār, as a Muʿtazilī, accepts these doctrines. For him, these fundamental Muʿtazilī tenets entail that God will always permit useful harmless actions and proscribe harmful ones. ʿAbd al-Jabbār's theology allows humans to predict divine laws even before they receive any divine guidance. Therefore, humans must not await the advent of revelation to ascertain the deontic qualification of useful actions. The fact that these Muʿtazilī doctrines play an important role in his justification of permission entails that they encouraged him to espouse permission.

Shīrāzī, Juwaynī and Samʿānī, as Ashʿarī and traditionalist scholars, have a very different perception of divine wisdom and justice. They vehemently refuse the Muʿtazilī concepts of benevolence, optimism and the purposefulness of divine actions. They rather hold that divine sovereignty and omnipotence require removing any constraints placed on divine actions and laws. For them, God is free to perform any action and impose any law, even if they may seem unreasonable to the human mind. This theology makes divine laws a group of capricious, unfathomable decisions. It makes it difficult for humans to predict divine laws and appreciate the rationale behind them. Therefore, in the absence of revelation, humans cannot predict divine laws. They cannot ascertain which actions will be permitted and which will be proscribed. All three jurists frequently use their understanding of divine omnipotence and sovereignty to argue for suspension and refute permission and proscription. This implies that their adoption of suspension is informed by their perception of divine wisdom and justice. It is quite clear that theology plays an essential role informing the position each jurist choses on the before revelation debate. Theology also shapes and determines the arguments used to justify a jurist's choice.

Having said this, one must note that the impact of theology on this aspect of legal theory does not seem consistent and uniform. As explained in the previous chapter, jurists often disagree on the legal implications of their theological doctrines. This is again noticeable in the before revelation debate. All three answers to the before revelation question can be found in all theological and legal schools. It is common to find followers of the same theological school embracing different answers to the before revelation question. It is also common to find jurists from different theological backgrounds sharing the same position on the before revelation debate.

For example, Muʿtazilīs, to a great extent, share a common perception of divine wisdom, divine justice and moral epistemology. Nonetheless, they are split; Baghdādī-Muʿtazilīs accept permission whereas Baṣrian-Muʿtazilīs adopt suspension. At the same time, Reinhart notes that proscription seems to be common among traditionalist jurists and is upheld by prominent Ḥanbalīs such as Abū Yaʿlā, Ibn Ḥāmid al-Warrāq (d. 403/1012), possibly Aḥmad b. Ḥanbal (d. 241/855) himself,[151] and others. Here we have two sub-Muʿtazilī schools with contradicting positions from the before revelation question. We also have traditionalists, including some Ḥanbalīs, sharing the same position with Baghdādī-Muʿtazilīs, despite both having almost contradicting theologies. Moreover, Māturīdī-Ḥanafī jurists, share a Māturīdī moral theory and, largely, a common definition of divine wisdom and justice. Nonetheless, a group of Māturīdīs prefer permission, such as Abū Zayd al-Dabūsī

---

[151] Reinhart, *Before Revelation*, 22–3. There is not conclusive information on Ibn Ḥanbali's position. A number of Ḥanbalī authors note that he might have adopted permission or proscription, see for example Kalwadhānī, *al-Tamhīd fī uṣūl al-fiqh*, 4:269–72; Ibn ʿAqīl, *al-Wāḍiḥ fī uṣūl al-fiqh*, 2:317; Abū Yaʿlā, *al-ʿUdda fī uṣūl al-fiqh*, 1238–41.

(d. ca. 430/1039) and Fakhr al-Islām al-Bazdawī (d. 482/1089),[152] whereas others opt for suspension, such as ʿAlāʾ al-Dīn al-Samarqandī (d. 539/1144?) and Abū al-Thanāʾ al-Lāmishī (fl. late fifth/eleventh century).[153] Ashʿarīs mainly embrace suspension but many of them, especially before the sixth/twelfth century, favour permission.

Each of these jurists believes that his position on the before revelation debate is in harmony with his theology. Scholars are often keen to present theological evidence and arguments justifying the answer they offer to the before revelation question. These theological arguments are probably aimed at members of the same

---

[152] Dabūsī, *Taqwīm al-adilla*, 458–61. Unfortunately, Fakhr al-Islām al-Bazdawī does not explicitly mention his position on the before revelation debate. However, Haytham Khazna deduces his acceptance of permission from the following legal theory opinion: in the case of two reports (*khabarān* sg. *khabar*) conflicting; one of them informs us of the permission of an act and another informs us of the proscription of the same act, Bazdawī says that the report proscribing the act should preponder (*yurajjaḥ*). Khanza notes that Bazdawī's justification of this opinion is based on his assumption that the by default status of acts is permission rather than proscription. Bazdawī justifies his choice saying that this would reduce the number of abrogations (*naskh*). He notes that if we accept the report that permits that act this would entail that there was a report that *first* proscribed this act and then another report came to abrogate this report and declare the act permitted. If this is the case then we would have two cases of abrogation, the first declaring an act proscribed and another declaring an act permitted. If we accept the proscribing report then we would only have one case of abrogation. The proscribing report would be abrogating an act known to be permitted. This argument, for good reasons, makes Khazna concludes that Bazdawī adopts permission. See Khazna, 'al-Ikhtilāfāt al-uṣūliyya', 189. For Bazdawī's statement, see Fakhr al-Islam Abū al-Ḥasan ʿAlī b. Muḥammad b. al-Ḥusayn b. ʿAbd al-Karīm al-Bazdawī (d. 482/1089), *Uṣūl al-Bazdawī* in ʿAlāʾ al-Dīn b. ʿAbd al-ʿAzīz b. Aḥmad al-Bukhārī (d. 730/1330), *Kashf al-asrār ʿan uṣūl Fakhr al-Islām al-Bazdawī*, 4vols ed. ʿAbd Allāh Maḥmūd Muḥammad ʿUmar (Beirut: Dār al-Kutub al-ʿIlmiyya, 1418/1997), 3:144–7. ʿAbd al-Aʿzīz al-Bukhārī's book is a commentary on al-Bazdawī's legal theory text.

[153] Samarqandī, *Mīzān al-uṣūl*, 283–4; Lāmishī, *Uṣūl al-fiqh*, 105–6.

theological school who hold a different position. Among the jurist's motives from these theological arguments is to show that their position on the before revelation debate is the logical outcome of their theology and not that of their opponent's. Theological doctrines certainly have a great impact on determining a jurist's position on the before revelation controversy. However, the influence of theology is not consistent on group and school level. Jurists who share a common theology disagree whether their theology entails permission, proscription, or suspension. Therefore, theology does not function as a 'standardizing factor' in legal theory. The acceptance of a common theology does not guarantee favouring similar answers to the before revelation debate.

This chapter has been chiefly an analysis of arguments for and against all three possible stands on the before revelation debate. This analysis uncovers some of the theoretical issues being implicitly discussed when a jurist ponders this debate. Among those issues is the predictability of divine legislations. Can humans predict divine laws on issues about which revelation does not comment? Is there a consistent rationale behind divine laws? Can humans use this rationale to create new legislation? The before revelation question is also a discussion on the interpretation of doubt. When in doubt about the legality of a particular action or thing, how should a jurist behave? Should he consider this act permitted, proscribed, or refrain from offering an answer all together? It is also a debate around the legal significance of the silence of revelation. In other words, can the silence of revelation (or the absence of evidence from revelation) function as a proof for any deontic qualification?

Rather than theology, it appears that a position on these hermeneutical questions consistently leads to preferring particular stands on the before revelation debate. Regardless of their theological orientation, jurists who refuse to consider the silence of revelation (or the absence of evidence) as evidence entailing any particular deontic qualification, often incline towards suspension. Scholars who regard the absence of evidence as sufficient legal evidence prefer either permission or proscription. Jurists who deem doubt an aspect of evilness opt for proscription, whereas those who refuse do not regard doubt as an evil aspect choose permission. Jurists who have an ascetic attitude tend to prefer proscription rather than permission or suspension. Jurists who espouse proscription come from various theological backgrounds, yet they often share this ascetic legal attitude. Scholars who uphold permission, despite their various theological orientations, share an optimistic attitude that refuse to consider doubt as evidence for proscription. They also interpret the absence of evidence as evidence for permission rather than proscription. Scholars who opt for suspension usually refuse to consider doubt and the absence of evidence as signs either for permission or proscription. Therefore, they abstain from any deontological assessment until the advent of the divine message.

The impact of these hermeneutical positions appears more consistent than that of theology. Jurists who adopt permission, proscription, or suspension share a common position on these hermeneutical debates, regardless of their theological discrepancies. As explained earlier, the impact of theology is obvious on the choices of individual jurists. However, since jurists disagree on the legal implications of their common theology, this impact is not consistent on a theological school level. Therefore, we often find different answers to the before revelation question within the same school of theology. On the other hand, jurists' positions on the above hermeneutical questions have a relatively more uniform impact on their answers to the before revelation question. Scholars who share a common perception of the legal significance of doubt and the absence of evidence often share a common position on the before revelation controversy.

CHAPTER FIVE: COUNT THE TRUTH(S)

INTRODUCTION

Pre-modern legal theory literature usually includes at least one chapter addressing the following questions: Are all jurists correct in their legal findings (*hal kull mujtahid muṣīb*)? Is truth single and universal (*hal al-ḥaqq wāḥid*), or there are equally valid multiple truths (*al-ḥaqq mutaʿaddid*)? The main concern of this controversy is to find out whether jurists with contradicting opinions are all correct or only one is correct while the rest are wrong. In other words, can contradicting deontic qualifications (sg. *ḥukm sharʿī*) be equally correct, or do plurality and contradiction necessitate the existence of error (*khaṭaʾ*)? These questions are part of a larger debate between scholars who insist on the singularity of the truth (a position that Muslim scholars call *takhṭiʾa*) and others who are ready to accept the plurality of truths (a position called *taṣwīb*).

As a point of departure for studying this debate, I will compare the positions of the our Shāfiʿī jurists, who constitute the centre of this study. This comparison is chiefly an analysis of the arguments they present in support of their views. The main aim of this analysis, and the chapter as a whole, is to explore and evaluate the impact of a jurist's theology on his stance regarding the above legal theory questions. To determine, or defend, his stance on the *taṣwīb-takhṭiʾa* debate, a jurist is compelled to raise further legal questions. Therefore, chapters on this debate examine other legal theory queries, such as the nature of divine law, whether it is determined (*muʿayyan* or *mutaʿayyin*) or indetermined (*ghayr muʿayyan* or *ghayr mutaʿayyin*). Answering this question requires (or determines) first to define the *ashbah*; a term we will encounter later. A definition of this term raises even more questions: What is the goal of *ijtihād* (*maṭlūb al-ijtihād*)? This inquiry requires identifying the role of the jurist in law-making and the obligation he is trying to accomplish during his *ijtihād*. Deciding on the latter issues necessitates a discussion of the role of probability (*ẓann*) in Islamic law. A jurist's answer to these questions will influence his toleration of legal and theological disagreements. As will become clearer through the chapter, these sub-questions are inseparable from the larger debate on the singularity or plurality of religious truth(s).

The study of this debate and the questions raised therein are indispensable for any solid understanding of Islam and its legal history. They are vital for understanding the different roles of God, revelation and jurists in the process of law-making. These questions are crucial for realizing the decentralized nature of Sunnī Islam and the role of religious scholarship, institutions and schools of law within the largest branch of Islam. Understanding these debates are important gateways for comprehending the epistemological and philosophical foundations of Islamic law and the literature produced by Muslim jurists. Without understanding these controversies, realizing the nature of Islamic law and its legal theory is impossible. The questions mentioned above, are, therefore, far from being marginal debates; they are major questions that help us dissect and understand important aspects of the Muslim legal culture, especially in its Sunnī version.

This chapter has seven main sections. The first is the current introduction; it introduces the main research question, defines important terms and surveys a sample of the most relevant secondary literature. The second section surveys the four Shāfiʿī jurists' positions on the toleration of disagreement in speculative theology and law (*fiqh*). The third examines the debate around the determination of divine law and the goal of *ijtihād*. The second and third sections provide important background information necessary for understanding the theoretical considerations that shape a jurist's position on the *taṣwīb-takhṭiʾa* debate.

As previously noted, this chapter mainly focuses on four Shāfiʿī jurists; three of them adopt *takhṭiʾa*. The fourth section investigates their versions of *takhṭiʾa* and analyses the arguments they put forward in support of their positions. Among the four Shāfiʿīs, ʿAbd al-Jabbār stands alone in promoting *taṣwīb*. The fifth section focuses on his stance and scrutinizes his supporting arguments. The analysis of the arguments for *taṣwīb* and *takhṭiʾa* aims at revealing the overriding assumptions and the theoretical and theological foundations of each position. The sixth section examines the impact of two theological doctrines considered relevant to this legal debate, namely optimism (*al-ṣalāḥ wa-l-aṣlaḥ*) and the possibility of God imposing an impossible obligation (*taklīf mā lā yuṭāq*). The final section is the conclusion in which I argue that epistemology is the aspect of theology with the most consistent and fundamental impact on a jurist's position on this legal theory debate; to a great extent, it determines which position he adopts. Creedal and doctrinal aspects of theology inform the position of individual jurists and shape their supporting arguments. However, their impact on group and theological school level appears less than consistent.

Terms and Definitions

In the introduction to this monograph, I have already mentioned a definition for speculative theology (*ʿilm al-kalām*). I also noted that the most common definition for it is a functional definition. I explained that speculative theology is an overarching discipline under which many sub-disciplines and topics are discussed, such as creation, divine attributes, eschatology, ethics, political authority and epistemology (*al-ʿulūm* or *al-maʿārif*), to mention only a few. The aspects of speculative theology that receive the greatest attention and prove to be the most controversial are the doctrinal and creedal aspects; ones that are usually associated with *ʿilm al-tawḥīd* or *ʿaqīda*. By doctrinal and creedal aspects, I am referring to doctrines primarily concerning divine attributes and divine actions. Discussions of divine attributes focus on the nature of God and the attributes that should be ascribed to Him (positive attributes, e.g. omniscience) and those that should be denied (negative attributes, e.g. impotence). Discussions of divine actions would include, for instance, debates around creation, prophecy, divine justice, freewill and predestination. The doctrinal aspects of speculative theology represent the core beliefs Muslims are expected to accept. Positions on these aspects often, though not exclusively, serve as the most important shibboleths for the different theological schools. They also occupy the largest parts of most theological works and are always debated with the greatest vigour.

Among the most relevant aspects of speculative theology to the legal theory issues raised in this chapter is epistemology. Epistemology, or the theory of knowledge, 'is the branch of philosophy concerned with enquiry into the nature, sources and validity of knowledge'.[1] This modern definition of epistemology will be valid if used to describe the topics often raised in the introductory chapters to most manuals of speculative theology. These chapters usually discuss, for instance, the following issues: definition of knowledge (*ḥadd al-ʿilm*), types of knowledge (*aqsām* or *anwāʿ al-ʿilm*), methods to acquire knowledge (*ṭuruq al-ʿilm*), definition of reason (*ḥadd al-ʿaql*), definition and regulations of speculative reasoning (*ḥadd wa-aḥkām al-naẓar*),[2] types of speculative reasoning (*anwāʿ al-naẓar*) and the conditions of valid speculative reasoning (*shurūṭ al-naẓar al-ṣaḥīḥ*).[3] The fact that these, and other, epistemological questions frequently appear at the beginning of theological works indicate that pre-modern Muslim theologians consider them to be an integral part, if not the foundation, of their discipline.

Epistemology is of primary importance to legal theory as well. Although less often and with fewer details than theological literature, it is not uncommon to find sections dedicated to the above

---

[1] A. C. Grayling, 'Epistemology', in *The Blackwell Companion to Philosophy*, ed. Nicholas Bunnin and E. P. Tsui-James (Oxford: Blackwell, 1996), 38. For more details on the definition of epistemology, see *The Encyclopedia of Philosophy*, s.v. 'Epistemology' (Richard Brandt); *The Encyclopedia of Philosophy*, 'Epistemology, History of' (D. W. Hamlyn); *Routledge Encyclopedia of Philosophy*, s.v. 'Epistemology' (Peter D. Klein).

[2] Translating *naẓar* as speculative reasoning is borrowed from Frank, 'The Science of Kalām', 12.

[3] For a sample of the introductory chapters in speculative theology literature that raises some of these questions, see Abū Bakr Muḥammad b. al-Ṭayyib b. al-Bāqillānī (d. 403/1013), *Kitāb al-Tamhīd*, ed. Richard McCarthy (Beirut: al-Maktaba al-Sharqiyya, 1957), 6–16; Abū Manṣūr ʿAbd al-Qāhir b. Ṭahir al-Tamīmī al-Baghdādī (d. 429/1037), *Kitāb Uṣūl al-dīn* (Istanbul: Dār al-Funūn al-Turkiyya, 1346/1928), 4–31; Abū al-Muʿīn [Maymūn b. Muḥammad b. Muḥammad] al-Nasafī (d. 508/1114), *Kitāb al-Tamhīd li-qawāʿid al-tawḥīd*, ed. Ḥabīb Allāh Ḥasan Aḥmad (Cairo: Dār al-Ṭibāʿa al-Muḥammadiyya, 1406/1986), 118–23; Bazdawī, *Uṣūl al-dīn*, 17–24 ; Juwaynī, *al-Shāmil fī uṣūl al-dīn*, 97–122; Abū Yaʿla, *al-Muʿtamad fī uṣūl al-dīn*, 19–29.

epistemological questions appearing at the beginning of legal theory manuals.[4] Moreover, epistemological questions are often raised during discussions of many legal theory topics such as: reports (*akhbār*) and their types, particularization (*takhṣīṣ*), abrogation (*naskh*), preponderance (*tarjīḥ*), jurisdiction of reason and revelation, types of evidence (*adilla*), deducing the *ratio legis* (*istinbāṭ al-ʿilla*), gradation of evidence (*tartīb al-adilla*), origin of languages (*mabdaʾ al-lughāt*) and most importantly *taṣwīb* and *takhṭiʾa*. Therefore, epistemology is not only a sub-discipline of speculative theology, it is an integral part of legal theory as well. It is relevant and indispensable for specialists of both disciplines.

The term *ijtihād* has already occurred several times. Zysow notes that it is not easy to find a satisfactory definition for this term.[5] This is certainly correct especially given that a jurist's definition of the term depends on his position on various legal theory debates. Therefore, phrasing a single definition of *ijtihād* that is applicable to all jurists is a tricky task. However, briefly and without going into the complications of this term, it may be defined as the total expenditure of effort (*istifrāgh al-wusʿ*)[6] to reach the deontic qualification of a particular action or case. In other words, it is the jurist's effort examining the available evidence (mainly Qurʾān and Sunna) trying to figure out the deontic qualification of a particular incident, whether covered or not by textual evidence (*naṣṣ*). This process includes utilizing legal methods and principles believed to be condoned by revelation, such as consensus, *qiyās*, public benefit, social custom (*ʿurf*) and the presumption of continuity (*istiṣḥāb*). This is in addition to the use of the numerous hermeneutical and

---

[4] See for example, Abū Bakr Muḥammad b. al-Ṭayyib al-Bāqillānī, *al-Taqrīb wa-l-irshād al-ṣaghīr*, 3 vols ed. ʿAbd al-Ḥamīd ʿAlī Abū Zunayd (Beirut: Muʾassasat al-Risāla, 1418/1998), 1:171–231; Ibn Ḥazm, *al-Iḥkām fī uṣūl al-aḥkām*, 1:13–29, 36–42, 65–75; Ghazālī, *Muṣtaṣfā*, 1:71–8, 88–92; Juwaynī, *Burhān*, 111–58; Shīrāzī, *Sharḥ al-Lumaʿ*, 145–56; Kalwadhānī, *Tamhīd*, 1:36–63; Abū Yaʿlā, *ʿUdda*, 76–100; Samʿānī, *Qawāṭiʿ*, 1:15–8, 26–30, 41–3.

[5] Zysow, *Economy of Certainty*, 259–60.

[6] This translation of *istifrāgh al-wusʿ* is borrowed from Weiss, *Spirit of Islamic Law*, 118.

linguistic tools of textual interpretation.[7] The process of *ijtihād* is a complicated process; not all jurists are considered competent for this process. A jurist qualified for this process is called a *mujtahid*.[8]

One final point on the definition of *ijtihād*. It is common for pre-modern scholars to associate *ijtihād* with *qiyās*. The eponym of the Shāfiʿī School, Muḥammad b. Idrīs al-Shāfiʿī, even considers both terms as synonyms.[9] However, the development of Muslim legal theory, in later centuries, created a difference between both terms. *Ijtihād* became, for many jurists, a more inclusive term. It became a reference to almost all methods used to deduce laws. In other words, *qiyās* became just one of many forms of *ijtihād*.[10] Still,

---

[7] For examples of pre-modern definitions of *ijtihād*, see Abū al-Walīd Sulaymān b. Khalaf al-Bājī (d. 463/1071), *Kitāb al-Ḥudūd fi-l-uṣūl*, ed. Nazīh Ḥammād (Beirut: Muʾassasat al-Zaʿbī, 1392/1973), 64; al-Khaṭīb al-Baghdādī, *al-Faqīh wa-l-mutafaqqih*, 1:447; Samʿānī, *Qawāṭiʿ*, 5:1; Shīrāzī, *Lumaʿ*, 258. For modern definitions, see for instance *EI*[2], s.v. 'Idjtihād' (J. Schacht and D. B. McDonald). Nādiya al-ʿUmarī presents a survey of the different, modern and pre-modern, definitions of the term, see her *al-Ijtihād fi-l-Islām*, 3rd ed. (Beirut: Muʾassasat al-Risāla, 1405/1985) 19–33.

[8] Therefore, although all *mujtahid*s are jurists, not all jurists are *mujtahid*s. Nevertheless, *in this chapter*, I use the term jurist and *mujtahid* interchangeably as synonyms. My usage of the term jurist is always a reference to jurists who are actually qualified for the practice of *ijtihād*. For information on the necessary qualifications for the practice of *ijtihād*, see for instance Weiss, *Search for God's Law*, 34, 679–82, 713–4; Zuḥaylī, *Uṣūl al-fiqh*, 1043–51.

[9] Muḥammad b. Idrīs al-Shāfiʿī (d. 204/820), *al-Risāla*, ed. Aḥmad Muḥammad Shākir (Beirut: Dār al-Kutub al-ʿIlmiyya, 199?), 477. It was Zysow who drew my attention to Shāfiʿī's comment, see his *Economy of Certainty*, 260. To the best of my knowledge, only few scholars remain committed to Shāfiʿī's equation of *ijtihād* with *qiyās*, see for instance Abū al-Ḥusayn ʿAlī b. ʿUmar al-Baghdādī known as Ibn al-Qaṣṣār (d. 397/1007), *Muqaddima fī uṣūl al-fiqh*, ed. Muṣṭafā Makhdūm (Riyadh: Dār al-Maʿlama, 1420/1998), 118–9; al-Ḥusayn b. Masʿūd al-Baghawī (d. 516/1122), *Sharḥ al-Sunna*, 16 vols ed. Shuʿayb al-Arnāʾūṭ (Beirut: al-Maktab al-Islāmī, 1403/1403), 10:116–7.

[10] Wael Hallaq suggests that this shift in the definition of *qiyās* started to happen soon after Shāfiʿī or even during his life time, see his *Origins*

pre-modern scholars often explain *ijtihād* and define the technical terms relevant to it by referring to methods used in *qiyās*; this will become clearer later in this chapter.

Taṣwīb and *takhṭiʾa* are terms central to the current chapter and some comments on them are necessary before going into the details of this study. *Taṣwīb* is a derivative of the three letter root *ṣ-w-b*. Among the meanings conveyed by this root are: truth, reaching the truth, aiming at a target, hitting a target and an opposite for the word 'error' (*khaṭaʾ*).[11] The word *takhṭiʾa* is a derivative of the root *kh-ṭ-ʾa*. This root is often used to denote the following connotations: to miss a target, to be wrong, to fail, to sin, intentional and unintentional error and sin, sinful and an opposite of the word 'correct' (*ṣawāb*).[12] Those are all lexical definitions (sg. *taʿrīf lughawī*). None of the examined pre-modern works on legal theory mentions the technical or the disciplinary definition (*taʿrīf iṣṭilāḥī*) of *taṣwīb* and *takhṭiʾa*.[13] Therefore, their connotation in legal theory literature

---

and Evolution, 114–5. The exact timing of this shift is not important for this study. What concerns us more here is that by the fifth/eleventh century the new more inclusive definition of *ijtihād* was predominant.

[11] Abū al-Qāsim Maḥmūd b. ʿUmar al-Zamakhsharī (d. 538/1144), *Asās al-balāgha* (n.p.: Dār al-Fikr, 1399/1979), 363–4 in CD-ROM *al-Jāmiʿ al-kabīr*; Abū al-Faḍl Muḥammad b. Mukarram b. Manẓūr (d. 711/1311–2), *Lisān al-ʿArab* (Beirut: Dār Ṣādir, 1980), 1:534–7 in CD-ROM *al-Jāmiʿ al-kabīr*. In some occasions, the editions used by *al-Jāmiʿ al-kabīr* database are different from the hard copy editions I consult. If I refer to an edition used by this database, the full and the concise note will be followed by the phrase 'in CD-ROM *al-Jāmiʿ al-kabīr*', otherwise all references are to the editions appearing for the first time as a full note.

[12] Manẓūr, *Lisān al-ʿArab*, 1:65–8 in CD-ROM *al-Jamiʿ al-kabīr*; Zamakhsharī, *Asās al-balāgha*, 1:167 in CD-ROM *al-Jāmiʿ al-kabīr*.

[13] For modern definitions and explanations of both terms and concepts, see Hamid Algar, 'Q. 21:78–9: A Qurʾanic Basis for *Ijtihād*?' *Journal of Qurʾanic Studies* 4.2 (2002), 4; Anver Emon, 'To Most Likely Know the Law: Objectivity, Authority, and Interpretation in Islamic Law', *Hebraic Political Studies* 4.4 (2009), 432; Hallaq, *Islamic Legal Theories*, 119–21; Weiss, *Spirit of Islamic Law*, 118; Zuḥaylī, *Uṣūl al-fiqh*, 1096; Namla, *Muhadhdhab*, 2349, 2356.

can only be inferred after monitoring their usage in these works. It appears from the examined literature that *taṣwīb*, for Muslim legal theoreticians, is the belief that different and contradicting deontic qualifications are all correct; as long as they are all based on, at least, inconclusive evidence (sg. *amāra* or *dalīl ẓannī*) and pronounced by *mujtahid*s who exhaust all efforts examining the accessible sources (jurists holding this position are called *muṣawwiba*). Whereas *takhṭiʾa* assumes the presence of one universally correct deontic qualification for each possible incident. Therefore, should jurists reach contradicting deontic qualifications, only one of their opinions can be correct; this is the one identical with the universally correct deontic qualification. The rest are nothing but error (jurists with this perception of the law are called *mukhaṭṭiʾa*).

As far as I can discern, authors writing in English, studying this debate, rarely use a one-word translation for *taṣwīb* or *takhṭiʾa*. A phrase of three or four words is often utilized, for example 'all *mujtahid*s are correct' for *taṣwīb* and 'only one *mujtahid* is correct' for *takhṭiʾa*.[14] Aron Zysow translates *taṣwīb* as infallibilism and *takhṭiʾa* as fallibilism.[15] Bernard Weiss, in his *Spirit of Islamic* Law, accepts this translation.[16] Abbas Poya is critical of Zysow's translations, and he translates neither *taṣwīb* nor *takhṭiʾa*. He uses the original Arabic words.[17] The term 'fallibilism' is certainly a misleading translation

---

[14] See for example Hallaq, *Islamic Legal Theories*, 119–21; Algar, 'A Qurʾānic Basis for *Ijtihād*'.

[15] Zysow, *Economy of Certainty*, esp. 259–78.

[16] Weiss, *Spirit of Islamic Law*, 117. However, in his earlier book *Search for God's Law*, he avoids using both translations. In reference to *taṣwīb*, Weiss often uses the phrase 'jurists are above error'; in reference to *takhṭiʾa* he uses the phrase 'jurists are involved in error'. For Weiss' section on the *taṣwīb-takhṭiʾa* debate, see *Search for God's Law*, 689–97. Weiss uses the term infallibilism in other contexts, mainly as a translation for the term *ʿiṣma* (i.e. immunity from error), especially that of the Prophet or the whole Muslim *umma*. See for instance his *Search for God's Law*, 198, 201, 207–9, 698.

[17] See Abbas Poya, *Anerkennung des Iǧtihād-Legitimation der Toleranz* (Berlin: Klaus Schwarz, 2003), 124 fn. 616. Gregor Schwarb agrees with Poya's criticisms of Zysow's translation of both terms, see his 'Capturing

for *takhṭiʾa*. Fallibilism is a concept usually associated with the writings of modern philosophers such as Charles Peirce (d. 1914) and Karl Popper (d. 1994). It holds that scientific knowledge should neither claim finality nor certainty. It is always tentative and probable. In fact, humans are incapable of reaching any definitive truth. This is due to the 'finite life span' of any scientific theory; the passage of time and the appearance of new theories do not only modify but might completely change and disprove current theories. This process of replacement and modification is a continuous process; what we consider today as correct might be disproved in the future, and future theories will continue to face a similar fate.[18]

This completely contradicts the basics of *takhṭiʾa* within Muslim legal theory. The *mukhaṭṭiʾa*, like modern fallibilist philosophers, make no claims of certainty and monopoly of the truth. However, the *mukhaṭṭiʾa* hold that there exists a single universal truth; there is a universally correct deontic qualification for each human action. Humans are, in many cases, capable of reaching this definitive truth. Jurists who uncover it are correct, whereas those who fail are in error. This universal truth is a divinely created truth; it is unchangeable, the passage of time and the appearance of new knowledge can neither modify nor upset it. Our perception of this truth might change, but the truth itself is constant. Therefore, translating *takhṭiʾa* as fallibilism is not only misleading but wrong. I have failed to find a satisfying alternative English translation. Therefore, to avoid misunderstandings, and having defined the term, I will not translate the term *takhṭiʾa* but continue to use the original Arabic.

The translation of *taṣwīb* as 'infallibilism' is not the best choice either. The *Oxford English Dictionary* define infallibility as the 'quality or fact of being… exempt from liability to error'. It describes infallible persons and their judgments as '[n]ot liable to be deceived or

---

the Meanings of God's Speech', 145 f.n. 133. In his brief encounter with the *taṣwīb-takhṭiʾa* debate, Schwarb does not attempt, as well, to translate both terms; he uses the original Arabic.

[18] This brief account of fallibilism is based on the *Routledge Encyclopedia of Philosophy*, s.v. 'fallibilism' (Nicholas Rescher); *The Oxford Companion to Philosophy*, s.v. 'fallibilism' (Nicholas Rescher).

mistaken; incapable of erring' and infallible things as '[n]ot liable to prove false, erroneous, or mistaken'.[19] These definitions are not completely foreign to *taṣwīb*. However, they are not an accurate definition for the Arabic term *taṣwīb* in its legal context. *Taṣwīb*, in Muslim legal theory, includes no claims to immunity from error.[20] It is rather a claim that all religious knowledge produced, under particular circumstances, is correct. A jurist who adopts *taṣwīb* does not consider himself immune from error. He remains correct as long as the knowledge he produces follows specific criteria. Jurists who fail to abide by these criteria are destined to fall in error. Furthermore, the English word 'infallibilism' might entail the existence of a universal (pontifical) truth according to which right and wrong can be decided. *Taṣwīb* is a doctrine that refuses the existence of a single universal truth; all knowledge (including contradicting information) is truthful; none of it can be wrong. Therefore, again, I am quite hesitant to translate *taṣwīb* as 'infallibilism' and *muṣawwiba* as 'infallibilists'. Due to the absence of an alternative adequate English translation, I will continue referring to both terms in their Arabic originals.[21]

Literature Review

Among the earliest works, in a European language, to focus on the plurality of truth debate, are the articles by Éric Chaumont and Marie Bernand. Their studies, however, pay more attention to the legal aspect of the debate without a detailed examination of its the-

---

[19] None of the consulted Encyclopedias and dictionaries of philosophy provide a definition for infallibilism, therefore I had to resort to language dictionaries.

[20] The Arabic term for immunity from error is *ʿiṣma* rather than *taṣwīb*. For information on the former term see *EI*², s.v. "ʿIṣma' (W. Madelung).

[21] In addition to Abbas Poya and Gregor Schwarb, other authors also refrain from translating both terms and use the original Arabic terms, see for example Birgit Krawietz, *Hierarchie der Rechtsquellen im tradierten sunnitischen Islam* (Berlin: Duncker and Humblot, 2002), 327–53; Rumee, *Narratives of Islamic Legal Theory*, 137–45; Emon, 'To Most Likely Know the Law'.

ological and epistemological dimensions.[22] Hamid Algar wrote an article on the use of the Qur'ānic verse 21:78–9 in support of both *taṣwīb* and *takhṭi'a*; again the theological dimension of the controversy is almost absent from his discussion.[23] Anver Emon's 'To Most Likely Know the Law' describes the epistemological and, to some extent, the theological points of contention between the *muṣawwiba* and the *mukhaṭṭi'a.* He notes that the debate dividing both groups is their disagreement whether 'God has a specific rule of law (*ḥukm muʿayyan*) in mind',[24] a question that I deal with extensively in this chapter. Despite their legal and theological differences, Emon emphasises the common grounds between the *muṣawwiba* and the *mukhaṭṭi'a.* He explains that both recognize the inevitability of interpretive agency and indeterminacy in the law. For both groups, the law is the human interpretation and representation of the divine Word; therefore, none of them equate the religious knowledge a jurist produces with the divine will. The two groups are equally aware of the uncertainty of Muslim law; yet, they equally accept the authority and validity of this uncertain law. However, they disagree on how to justify and affirm the authority of this law.[25]

Chapter five of Aron Zysow's 1984 doctoral dissertation, published as a book in 2013, studies the epistemological and theological aspects of primarily *taṣwīb.*[26] Zysow, rightly, notes that the disagreement over the goal of *ijtihād* is an important factor leading to the creation of this controversy. For the *muṣawwiba*, the goal of *ijti-*

---

[22] Éric Chaumont, "Tout chercheur qualifié dit-il juste?' (*hal kull muǧtahid muṣīb*) La question controversée du fondement de la légitimité de la controverse en Islam', in *La controverse religieuse et ses forms*, ed. Alain le Boulluec (Paris: Éditions du Cerf, 1995): 11–27; Marie Bernand, 'La problem de 'l'ašbah' ou les implications ontologiques de la règle juridico-religieuse', *Arabica* 37.2 (1990): 151–72. My understanding of both articles is not based on a professional translation of the French original, therefore it is neither complete nor thorough.

[23] Algar, 'A Qur'anic Basis for *Ijtihād*'.

[24] Emon, 'To Most Likely Know the Law', 432.

[25] Emon, 'To Most Likely Know the Law', 436–7, 439–40.

[26] Zysow, *Economy of Certainty,* 259–78.

hād is reaching inconclusive knowledge (*ẓann*); for *mukhaṭṭiʾa* probability and inconclusive knowledge are just one step towards another goal, i.e. the certain truth (*qaṭʿ* or *yaqīn*).[27] Zysow suggests two more conclusions that are particularly important for the current chapter.

First, he examines the epistemology of Abū Bakr al-Bāqillānī (d. 403/1013) that motivates him to favour *taṣwīb*. He concludes that Bāqillānī sees no fixed [or deterministic] relationship between inconclusive evidence (sg. *dalīl ẓannī* or *amāra*) and the inconclusive knowledge that may be deduced from it. This perception, notes Zysow, motivates Bāqillānī to favour *taṣwīb* rather than *takhṭiʾa*.[28] The current chapter argues that disagreements over the epistemo-

---

[27] Zysow, *Economy of Certainty*, 259–61.

[28] Zysow, *Economy of Certainty*, 261–2, 269–70. Inconclusive evidence is a reference to any textual or non-textual evidence that yields probable knowledge (*ẓann*, *ghālib al-ẓann*, or *ʿilm ẓannī*). Jurists sometimes disagree on which type of evidence yields this type of knowledge. However, the majority would consider solitary Prophetic traditions (sg. *khabar al-wāḥid*), *qiyās* and any equivocal normative text (i.e. a Qurʾānic verse or Prophetic tradition) as inconclusive. On the other hand, conclusive evidence (*dalīl qaṭʿī* or simply *dalīl*) is the evidence capable of yielding certain knowledge (*ʿilm* or *ʿilm qaṭʿī*). Again, scholars disagree on the type of evidence capable of producing this type of knowledge. The majority include all conclusively authentic (*qaṭʿī al-sanad*) textual evidence that is also unequivocal in its wording (*qaṭʿī al-dalāla*). This can be a consensus, a concurrent (*mutawātir*) Prophetic tradition, or a Qurʾānic verse. In addition, theologians often accept rational arguments as a source of certain knowledge. Certain knowledge is considered to be beyond doubt true, whereas inconclusive knowledge is often described as most probably correct. The majority of the available evidence covering law (*fiqh*) is inconclusive, therefore, for many jurists, our knowledge of jurisprudential (*fiqhī*) regulations can only, in most cases, be probable. Certainty occurs only in rare occasions in law. Whereas in speculative theology, Muslim scholars believe that there is conclusive evidence available revealing the truth for humans. Therefore, our knowledge of the 'correct creed' can be certain and beyond doubt. For more details on the issue of certainty and probability in Islamic law, see Sāmī al-Ṣalāḥāt, '*Khaṣāʾiṣ al-naṣṣ al-qaṭʿī ʿinda al-uṣūliyyīn*', *Islāmiyyat al-mʿarifa* 23 (1421/2000): 43–80; Weiss, *Spirit of Islamic Law*, 47–65, 88–122.

logical value of inconclusive evidence are a major point of contention between the *mukhaṭṭi'a* and the *muṣawwiba*; a conclusion that is in tune with Zysow's suggestion. However, Zysow's treatment of this legal theory debate pays close attention to *taṣwīb* without giving enough attention to *takhṭiʿa*. The nature and the foundations of one position will never be sufficiently understood without a thorough examination of the opposite stance. This chapter, therefore, examines both positions.

Zysow's second important conclusion is that the Muʿtazilī version of *taṣwīb* is 'built around' their theological doctrine of optimism (*al-ṣalāḥ wa-l-aṣlaḥ*), whereas the Ashʿarī version of the same legal position 'rests' on their rejection of the possibility of God imposing an impossible obligation (*taklīf mā lā yuṭāq*).[29] Optimism, notes Zysow, is the theological doctrine that motivates Muʿtazilīs to adopt *taṣwīb*.[30] Zysow's comments may be correct. As mentioned in previous chapters, jurists from different theological schools support the same legal theory position using different theological doctrines. However, I have also argued earlier that jurists belonging to the same school of theology interpret the legal consequences of their shared theology differently. This chapter contends that there is no one particular theological doctrine (optimism or otherwise) that can be consistently considered the precursor for *taṣwīb* or *takhṭi'a*, even within the same school of theology. Doctrinal and creedal aspects of speculative theology often shape a jurist's argument justifying his position on this debate, but rarely do they consistently require the adoption of particular positions in legal theory.

Almost two decades after Zysow submitted his doctoral dissertation, he published another article in which he discusses the

---

[29] Zysow, *Economy of Certainty*, 269. Excluding the possibility of God imposing an impossible obligation is another derivative of divine justice. For the Muʿtazilīs, requiring humans to perform an obligation that is unachievable, then holding them responsible for failing to fulfil this obligation is an evil and an unjust act. Therefore, they, in general, exclude the possibility of God imposing such an obligation. They argue that accepting the possibility of God requiring impossible obligations would render Him evil, unjust and undermine the authority of His revelation.

[30] Zysow, *Economy of Certainty*, 264–8.

connections between four legal theory debates and speculative theology within the Central Asian tradition of the Ḥanafī School. One section of this article focuses on the plurality of truth debate.[31] He describes this debate as the most theologically sensitive.[32] He qualifies his comment noting that the 'theological dispute is, however, precisely over the epistemic value of *ijtihād*'.[33] Again, Zysow here is, rightly, highlighting epistemological disagreements as an important aspect of this legal theory debate.

Most importantly, in the same article, Zysow discovers a change among Central Asian Ḥanafīs regarding the theological implications of the *taṣwīb-takhṭiʾa*. He observes that from the fifth/eleventh until the early eighth/fourteenth century, Central Asian Ḥanafīs saw the debate as having serious theological ramifications. They consider the acceptance of *taṣwīb* to be a result of embracing the Muʿtazilī doctrine of optimism. For Central Asian Ḥanafīs, argues Zysow, *taṣwīb* became synonyms with heresy and the adoption of deviant Muʿtazilī doctrines. Starting from the eighth/fourteenth century, the connection between *taṣwīb* and Muʿtazilī theology was being reviewed. On this change, Zysow quotes ʿAbd al-ʿAzīz al-Bukhārī (d. 730/1329) who dissociates *taṣwīb* from optimism and Muʾtazilī theology in general. After Bukhārī, most Central Asian Ḥanafīs do not consider *taṣwīb* a product of any theological 'deviancy'. The debate, in Zysow's words, is now de-theologized.

Zysow argues that this change was motived by a shift in the boundaries of 'orthodoxy'. Central Asian Ḥanafīs are aware that many Ashʿarīs adopt *taṣwīb*. In the eighth/fourteenth century, Ḥanafīs became more willing to accept Ashʿarīs as members in Sunnī 'orthodoxy'. Therefore, they had to find a way to accept the legal theory doctrines associated with Ashʿarīs, including *taṣwīb*. Ḥanafīs then decoupled *taṣwīb* from optimism. The latter became a legitimate legal theory position while the former remained a theological deviancy. Zysow's study shows that jurists in different periods of time disagree on the theological implications of the same

[31] Zysow, 'Muʿtazilism and Māturīdism', 239–47.

[32] Zysow, 'Muʿtazilism and Māturīdism', 239.

[33] Zysow, 'Muʿtazilism and Māturīdism', 239 footnote 18.

legal theory position. In this study, I show that even contemporaneous jurists debated the theological consequences of legal theory positions and the legal implications of their common theological doctrines.

Another study that examines the theological aspects of the *taṣwīb-takhṭiʾa* debate is chapters fifty three to fifty seven of Muḥammad al-ʿArūsī ʿAbd al-Qādir's *al-Masāʾil al-mushtaraka bayna uṣūl al-fiqh wa-uṣūl al-dīn* (published in 2009).[34] In a manner that is even more visible than Zysow, ʿAbd al-Qādir shows the impact of epistemological disagreements on the controversy under study. He offers two main conclusions that are relevant to this chapter. First, as mentioned below in more detail, there is a debate over the culpability (*taʾthīm*) of those Muslims who hold 'erroneous' theological beliefs, whether they will be held accountable for their wrong beliefs in the hereafter or whether they will be forgiven. He believes that this debate is caused by a disagreement over ranking the epistemological value of the knowledge produced by different types of evidence. A group of scholars (mainly traditionalists) hold that all types of evidence yield the same type of knowledge. In other words, all knowledge enjoys the same epistemic value and reliability. Another group of scholars (mainly speculative theologians and some legal theoreticians) distinguish between the knowledge produced by inconclusive and conclusive evidence (sg. *dalīl qaṭʿī*). The latter produces knowledge that is of a higher epistemic value than the former. ʿAbd al-Qādir explains that scholars who equate all types of evidence and the knowledge they produce hold that Muslims with erroneous theological beliefs are exonerated (sg. *maʿdhūr*) and will be forgiven in the hereafter.[35] Scholars who distinguish between the epistemic value of knowledge produced by conclusive and inconclusive evidence hold the opposite view. For them, Muslims with wrong theological beliefs are sinful (sg. *āthim*) and will be held accountable for their erroneous beliefs in the hereafter.[36] What is important to note here is that a jurist's epistemological positions

---

[34] ʿAbd al-Qādir, *al-Masāʾil al-mushtaraka*, 295–323.

[35] Translation borrowed from Weiss, *Search for God's Law*, 688.

[36] ʿAbd al-Qādir, *al-Masāʾil al-mushtaraka*, 304–7.

seem to be shaping some of his stances relevant to the *taṣwīb-takhṭi'a* debate.

ʿAbd al-Qādir's second conclusion is that *taṣwīb* is founded upon two assumptions. First, human knowledge of law is mainly inconclusive (*ẓannī*). This assumption is a consequence of distinguishing between the epistemological value of conclusive and inconclusive evidence. Second, *muṣawwiba* see the goal of *ijtihād* as the creation of probable knowledge rather than discovering a particular deontic qualification. This latter assumption requires adopting the 'undetermination of divine law', i.e. God does not determine a deontic qualification for every human action. All these assumptions are discussed in more detail in this chapter. It is enough, for the time being, to note that ʿAbd al-Qādir and Zysow, probably more than other modern authors, demonstrate the relevance of epistemological disagreements to the debate around the plurality of truth in Muslim legal theory. The different typologies of evidence and knowledge and the place of probability in Muslim legal thought are all epistemological controversies that significantly influence a jurist's position on the debate examined in this chapter. This influence is examined in more detail here.

Finally, it is common among modern studies of the *taṣwīb-takhṭi'a* debate to associate *taṣwīb* with Muʿtazilī legal thought. For example, ʿAbd al-Qādir, Zysow and Chaumont write that *taṣwīb* is a Muʿtazilī invention.[37] Moreover, Chaumont accepts Abū Isḥāq al-Shīrāzī's remark that Abū al-Ḥasan al-Ashʿarī's acceptance of *taṣwīb* is a remnant of his Muʿtazilī past.[38] Ulrich Rebstock notes that the Muʿtazilī-Ḥanafī jurist Abū al-Ḥusayn al-Baṣrī (d. 436/1044) is the first legal theoretician to fully develop the concept of *taṣwīb*.[39] This tendency has some resonance in pre-modern literature where a

---

[37] Chaumont, 'Tout chercheur qualifié dit-il juste?' 22. ʿAbd al-Qādir and Zysow identify Bāsrian-Muʿtazilīs as the ones who introduced this 'innovation', see ʿAbd al-Qādir, *al-Masā'il al-mushtaraka*, 314; Zysow, 'Muʿtazilism and Māturīdism', 243–4.

[38] Chaumont, 'Tout chercheur qualifié dit-il juste?' 22–3. For Shīrāzī's remark, see his *Sharḥ al-Lumaʿ*, 1048.

[39] Ulrich Rebstock. 'A Qāḍī's Errors', *Islamic Law and Society* 6.1 (1999), 7.

number of authors write that *taṣwīb* is a Muʿtazilī innovation.[40] This study challenges such perceptions. It contends that *taṣwīb* is not only a feature of Muʿtazilī legal theory. This position can be found among jurists from other theological backgrounds as well. Moreover, I am reluctant to connect *taṣwīb* or *takhṭiʾa* with any one particular theological school or doctrine.

This section was an attempt to review only a sample of the most relevant modern examinations of the debate around the multiplicity of the truth.[41] The next section examines the relationship between epistemology and the toleration of disagreement in speculative theology and law.

CULPABILITY FOR ERROR

Culpability (*taʾthīm*) is the concept of God holding humans responsible for error (*khaṭaʾ*) and sin (*ithm*) in this life and the next. The opposite is exoneration (*ʿudhr*); God pardoning a human for an error or a sin committed. This section asks the following question: Is a jurist vulnerable to divine blame and punishment for adopting a wrong jurisprudential (*fiqhī*) opinion or an erroneous theological belief? Answering this question depends first on deciding whether or not there is one universal truth in speculative theology and law. One must note here that since an acceptance of culpability entails that a jurist will be held accountable for his erroneous jurisprudential opinions, therefore culpability must also entail an equation of error with sin. Errors are just like sins; both invoke divine blame and punishment. As a result, an acceptance of culpability in law and speculative theology implies an intolerance of disagreement and variety. A jurist who adopts an incorrect jurisprudential or theolog-

[40] See for example, Zarkashī, *al-Baḥr al-muḥīṭ*, 6:243; Mardāwī, *al-Taḥbīr Sharḥ al-Taḥrīr*, 3941; Abū Yaʿlā, *al-ʿUdda fī uṣūl al-fiqh*, 1549.

[41] For more modern examinations of the *taṣwīb-takhṭiʾa* debate, see for example Asifa Quraishi, 'On Fallibility and Finality: Why Thinking like a Qadi Helps Me Understand American Constitutional Law', *Michigan State Law Review* 2 (2009): 339–60; Ahmed, *Narratives of Islamic Legal Theory*, 137–45; Krawietz, *Hierarchie der Rechtsquellen*, 327–53; Shtīwī, *ʿAlāqat ʿilm al-kalām bi-uṣūl al-fiqh*, 673–84; Weiss, *Spirit of Islamic Law*, 116–21; Weiss, *Search for God's Law*, 690–7.

ical opinion has committed both an error and a sin. Whereas exoneration, on the other hand, entails a distinction between error and sin. Jurists who unintentionally espouse the wrong positions are mistaken but are not sinful. This perception is more tolerant of disagreement and legal plurality. The next section examines culpability and *takhṭiʾa* in theology; the following one discusses them in the context of law.

Speculative Theology

ʿAbd al-Jabbār, Shīrāzī, Samʿānī and Juwaynī all adopt *takhṭiʾa* in theology.[42] In other words, in terms of dogma, only one doctrine is correct whereas all different ones are error. Naturally, each of them believes that his own creed is the only correct one. This unanimous position should not be surprising; excluding rare exceptions, the overwhelming majority of Muslim scholars adopt *takhṭiʾa* in theology.[43] However, all four are not unanimous on accepting culpability in theology; they disagree on the fate of those Muslims who deviate from the only true Muslim creed. Put differently, they are not unanimous on the fate of the followers of the different Muslim theological groups (e.g. Sunnī, Muʿtazilī, Ashʿarī, Shīʿī, Khārijī etc…) in the hereafter. Disagreements among those Muslims groups will certainly not concern the existence of God or the veracity of the Qurʾān, but will focus on theological controversies such as ones around political authority, divine attributes, freewill and predestination.

ʿAbd al-Jabbār is quite explicit: those who adopt a creed other than the correct one (i.e. his own Muʿtazilī creed) are infidels (*kuffār*) and will be punished in the afterlife for their error. Samʿānī is not as determined: he notes that the fate of those who follow an

42 Shīrāzī, *Tabṣira*, 496–7; Shīrāzī, *Lumaʿ*, 258; Shīrāzī, *Sharḥ al-Lumaʿ*, 1,43–4; ʿAbd al-Jabbār, *Mughnī*, 17:284, 355–7, 362; Juwaynī, *Burhān*, 1317–9; Samʿānī, *Qawāṭiʿ*, 5:11, 47, 62.

43 Abū Ḥāmid Muḥammad b. Muḥammad al-Ghazālī, *al-Mankhūl min taʿlīqāt al-uṣūl*, ed. Muḥammad Ḥasan Hītū (Damascus: Dār al-Fikr, 1970), 451; Rāzī, *al-Maḥṣūl fī ʿilm uṣūl al-fiqh*, 6:29; Abū Yaʿlā, *al-ʿUdda fī uṣūl al-fiqh*, 1540–1; Juwaynī, *Burhān*, 1316. See also Zuḥaylī, *Uṣūl al-fiqh*, 1091; ʿAbd al-Qādir, *al-Masāʾil al-mushtaraka*, 298.

erroneous creed is unknown. They might be forgiven, declared as profligates (*fussāq*),[44] or infidels.[45] Unfortunately, he does not mention the criteria according to which this will be decided.[46] Shīrāzī holds that [Muslims] adopting an erroneous creed will not be exonerated.[47] Juwaynī is the most lenient; Muslims who exhaust all efforts searching for the truth, yet their minds guide them to adopt an erroneous dogma are to be forgiven. The fact that they fail to reach the truth, despite all their efforts, entails that their minds do not bear (*lam taḥtamil*) the truth. Their minds cannot but embrace their chosen 'erroneous' dogma. Therefore, they must be exonerated. Yet, Juwaynī emphasizes that forgiving them does not legitimize their false creeds.[48]

Juwaynī does not offer an argument supporting his position. Samʿānī and Shīrāzī note that there is conclusive evidence (sg. *dalīl qaṭʿī*) establishing beyond doubt the only correct doctrine (by the correct creed they are, of course, referring to their own creed). Accordingly, all different doctrines are conclusively known to be wrong. Moreover, Shīrāzī adds that the presence of conclusive evidence rules out the possibility of exoneration.[49] On a similar tone, ʿAbd al-Jabbār argues that there is conclusive evidence revealing the correct Muʿtazilī creed. Consequently, all different ones are

---

[44] Translation borrowed from Weiss, *Search for God's Law*, 690.

[45] Samʿānī, *Qawāṭiʿ*, 5:47.

[46] In his short treatise *al-Intiṣār li-aṣḥāb al-ḥadīth*, Samʿānī is very critical of all theological groups; he often accuses them of misguidance (*ḍalāl*) and following their own whims (*ittibāʿ al-hawā*). However, he neither describes them as infidels nor mention whether their 'false' theological *ijtihād*s will lead to their punishment in the hereafter or their 'errors' will be exonerated, see Abū al-Muẓaffar Manṣūr b. Muḥammad Samʿānī, *Fuṣūl min Kitāb al-Intiṣār li-aṣḥāb al-ḥadīth*, ed. Muḥammad b. Ḥusayn al-Jīzānī (Riyadh: Maktabat Dār al-Minhāj 1428/[2007]).

[47] Shīrāzī, *Sharḥ al-Lumaʿ*, 1043–4.

[48] Juwaynī, *Burhān*, 1317–8. None of the four Shāfiʿīs under study distinguish between learned scholars (*ʿulamāʾ*) and average people (*ʿāmma*); their comments apply to both groups.

[49] Samʿānī, *Qawāṭiʿ*, 5:11–3; Shīrāzī, *Sharḥ al-Lumaʿ*, 1044; Shīrāzī, *Tabṣira*, 497.

conclusively known to be false. He adds that the presence of conclusive knowledge renders plurality and variety unacceptable.[50]

Neither the curt nature of the above arguments nor Juwaynī's disregard for justifying his position should be surprising. The vast majority of Muslim scholars accept *takhṭiʾa* in theology. There is no reason, then, to argue for a position that is widely accepted.[51] What is important to note here is that all three jurists justify their position on the same epistemological grounds: the presence of conclusive evidence and knowledge makes conclusive knowledge of the correct creed possible. This availability of this type of evidence and knowledge rules out *taṣwīb* and the acceptance of plurality. The irony is that almost all theologians accept the idea that conclusive evidence produces knowledge that is beyond doubt. However, they disagree on what constitutes conclusive evidence and on the dogmas deduced from this evidence.

Law (*fiqh*)

For the purpose of the whole study and before going into the details of this short section, one must highlight the difference between culpability (*taʾthīm*) and *takhṭiʾa*, especially in reference to law. As I have just mentioned above, the adoption of *takhṭiʾa* does not necessarily entail culpability or intolerance of legal plurality. The *mukhaṭṭiʾa* often acknowledge that, in many cases, the evidence available is not sufficient to conclusively reveal the only correct deontic qualification. Therefore, most of them hold that jurists who reach an erroneous deontic qualification are exonerated from their errors. Moreover, the *mukhaṭṭiʾa* neither claim conclusive knowledge of the truth nor conclusively render their opponents wrong. A jurist adopting *takhṭiʾa* believes that his own position is *most probably* correct and others with a different opinion are *most probably* wrong. Although the *mukhaṭṭiʾa* are certain that a single universal truth exists, this truth cannot always be conclusively iden-

---

[50] ʿAbd al-Jabbār, *Mughnī*, 17:358.

[51] ʿAbd al-Jabbār's argument for establishing *takhṭiʾa* in theology is longer than that of Samʿānī and Juwaynī. However, I mention here the part relevant to this study only. For his full argument, see ʿAbd al-Jabbār, *Mughnī*, 17:355–9.

tified.[52] This indetermination of the truth (*ikhfāʾ al-ḥaqq*) makes the toleration of legal variation an inescapable reality. It requires even the *mukhaṭṭiʾa* to acknowledge the legitimacy of different legal opinions and refuse culpability.[53] Nonetheless, this toleration does not apply to all aspects of law. This sub-section identifies the aspects in law in which disagreement is tolerated and those in which it is not.

Most Sunnī jurists hold that disagreement is neither allowed nor tolerated in deontic qualifications known via conclusive evidence (*dalīl qaṭʿī*). Examples of those qualifications include the obligatory nature of fasting Ramaḍān, paying *zakāt*, performing the *ḥajj* and the prohibition of murder, theft and extramarital sex.[54] The Shāfiʿī scholars, who are the focus of this study, do not adopt a unique position.[55] Shīrāzī describes jurists who adopt a deontic qualification that contradicts conclusive evidence as infidels (*kuffār*) or at best profligates (*fussāq*).[56] Samʿānī writes that disagreement is

---

[52] See for example, Ibn ʿAqīl, *al-Wāḍiḥ fī uṣūl al-fiqh*, 5:389–91; Abū Yaʿlā, *al-ʿUdda fī uṣūl al-fiqh*, 1568; Kalwadhānī, *al-Tamhīd fī uṣūl al-fiqh*, 4:336, 311, 325.

[53] It seems that only a minority of jurists, if any at all, accept culpability in law. Scholars who are usually mentioned as endorsing this position are Bishr al-Marīsī (d. 218/833), Abū Bakr b. al-Aṣamm (d. 200–1/816–7) and Ibn ʿUlayya (d. 218/833). For sources that attribute this position to all three scholars see, for instance Abū al-Fatḥ Aḥmad b. ʿAlī b. Barhān (d. 518/1124), *al-Wuṣūl ilā al-ūṣūl*, 2 vols ed. ʿAbd al-Ḥamīd ʿAlī Abū Zunayd (Riyadh: Maktabat al-Maʿārif, 1404/1984), 342–3; Shīrāzī, *Lumaʿ*, 260; Samʿānī, *Qawāṭiʿ*, 5:16–17. However, other sources, note that those three scholars adopt *takhṭiʾa* and do not mention that they adopt culpability. See for example, Ṣaymarī, *Masāʾil al-khilāf*, 303; Abū al-Ḥusayn, *Muʿtamad*, 949; ʿAbd al-Jabbār, *Mughnī*, 17:369; Abū Yaʿlā, *al-ʿUdda fī uṣūl al-fiqh*, 1548. Most pre-modern legal literature does not attribute culpability in law to any jurist at all, which might entail that this position was not accepted by any scholar in the first place.

[54] Khuḍarī, *Uṣūl al-Fiqh*, 374; Zuḥaylī, *Uṣūl al-fiqh*, 1095.

[55] In his *Burhān*, Juwaynī does not explicitly mention his position on the toleration of disagreement in *fiqh*.

[56] Shīrāzī, *Lumaʿ*, 259; Shīrāzī, *Sharḥ al-Lumaʿ*, 1045–6. Shīrāzī mentions two categories, first, deontic qualifications known by necessity (*bi-l-*

intolerable in deontic qualifications known via conclusive evidence; it is only acceptable in those qualifications know by inconclusive ones.[57] Even ʿAbd al-Jabbār, who accepts *taṣwīb*, adopts a similar position: *taṣwīb* is acceptable only in jurisprudential issues covered by inconclusive evidence; on the other hand, there is no place for legal variety in those area of law covered by conclusive evidence.[58]

An Epistemological Division

Our four Shāfiʿī jurists, like most other Sunnīs, accept *takhṭiʾa* in all topics (in speculative theology and law) covered by conclusive evidence.[59] Furthermore, excluding Juwaynī, the other three Shāfiʿīs accept culpability (*taʾthīm*) in all aspects of religion known via con-

---

ḍarūra) to have been practiced by the Prophet. He describes jurists refusing these qualifications as infidels. Examples of such practices include the ones just mentioned. The second category is the actions and obligations known not by necessity but rather via the consensus of the Companions or the scholars. He mentions no examples of such obligations. He describes jurists who defy such deontic qualifications as profligates and not infidels. It seems here that Shīrāzī is differentiating between deontic qualifications known via the Qurʾān and the concurrent Prophetic Sunna, on one hand, and those known via consensus, on the other. Defying the former category leads to infidelity but not the latter.

[57] Samʿānī, *Qawāṭiʿ*, 5:62.

[58] ʿAbd al-Jabbār, *Mughnī*, 17:362–3.

[59] Although none of the four jurists under study explicitly mention their position on the plurality of truth in the discipline of legal theory, however it is generally accepted that a similar typology applies to it. Legal theory is often perceived as a discipline whose knowledge is known via conclusive evidence; therefore, disagreement and *taṣwīb* are usually unacceptable in it, see Zuḥaylī, *Uṣūl al-fiqh*, 1091–2; Zysow, *Economy of Certainty*, 276. However, there is a debate whether all aspects of legal theory are known by conclusive evidence. For a brief discussion of this debate see Namla, *al-Khilāf al-lafẓī*, 1:38–9. Ironically, Ghazālī and the disputed author of *al-Talkhīṣ fī uṣūl al-fiqh* argue that they present conclusive evidence proving *taṣwīb*. Therefore, they know beyond any doubt that it is the *only* correct position rather than *takhṭiʾa*, see Ghazālī, *Mustaṣfā*, 4:32; Juwaynī [pseudo], *Talkhīṣ*, 3:353–4, 358.

clusive evidence, whereas all four jurists rule out culpability in aspects of religion deduced from inconclusive evidence (*dalīl ẓannī*).[60] The presence of conclusive evidence, in law as well as in speculative theology, rules out divine exoneration of error, tolerance of disagreement and makes identifying the only truth possible. This shows that for all four Shāfiʿīs, the border line between *taṣwīb* and *takhṭiʾa*, between tolerance and the intolerance of disagreement, is epistemological and not thematic. ʿAbd al-Jabbār is explicit: the method of knowledge determines whether the plurality of truths (*taʿaddud al-ḥaqq*) applies to the known information. For him, plurality is tolerable when this information is known via inconclusive evidence, but it is not tolerable when the information is known via conclusive evidence.[61] Said differently, the presence of conclusive knowledge (*ʿilm* or *yaqīn*), generated via conclusive evidence, rules out doubt and the plurality of the truth.

This common position is possible only because all four jurists share a common perception of the epistemological value of conclusive evidence. All four Shāfiʿīs hold that this type of evidence is capable of conclusively and unequivocally revealing the only correct position. In such cases, there is no need to accept plurality and forgive those who fail to reach the truth. The *taṣwib-takhṭiʾa* debate, then, only concerns issues covered and known by inconclusive evidence. This legal controversy, as will be noted below, is created by a disagreement over the epistemological value of inconclusive evidence. The four jurists' agreement over the epistemological value of conclusive evidence prevents this debate from including theological or jurisprudential issues known via conclusive evidence.

---

[60] It is interesting to note that although Juwaynī and Samʿānī show some leniency towards Muslims who adopt a different dogma, they show no similar leniency towards jurists who adopt jurisprudential positions that contradict what they consider to be conclusive evidence.

[61] ʿAbd al-Jabbār, *Mughnī*, 17:362. For other similar statements, see 17:357, 358.

THE DETERMINATION OF DIVINE LAW

The remaining of this chapter focuses, therefore, on the *taṣwīb-takhṭi'a* debate in relation to jurisprudential (*fiqhī*) matters covered by inconclusive evidence. This section provides important background information vital for analysing the theoretical motives that shape a jurist's position on the *taṣwīb-takhṭi'a* debate. A number of modern and pre-modern scholars have already noted that the debate around the determination (*taʿyīn*) of divine law lies at the core of the *taṣwīb-takhṭi'a* controversy.[62] This section examines the former debate and shows its relevance to any discussion of *taṣwīb* and *takhṭi'a*.

The debate around the determination of divine law asks whether divine law pre-exists a jurist's process of *ijtihād* or comes into being only after the end of this process. Said differently, does the jurist discover of create the law? Eventually, there are two main positions on this debate. The first position holds that divine law is determined (*mutaʿayyan* or *muʿayyan*); God determines a particular deontic qualification for every human action. Since eternity, God has already decided which actions are obligatory (*wājiba*), permitted (*mubāḥa*), proscribed (*maḥẓūra*), recommended (*mandūba*), or reprehensible (*makrūha*). Some of these predetermined deontic qualifications are to be found in the Qur'ān and the Sunna. However most of them are not. Jurists who accept the determination of divine law are often *mukhaṭṭi'a*.[63] For them, the only correct deontic qualifica-

[62] Among the modern scholars are Emon, 'To Most Likely Know the Law', 432; Chaumont, 'Tout chercheur qualifié dit-il juste?' 22; Zuḥaylī, *Uṣūl al-fiqh*, 1097. For pre-modern ones, see Shihāb al-Dīn Abī al-ʿAbbās Aḥmad b. Idrīs al-Ṣanhājī known as al-Qarāfī (d. 684/1285), *Nafā'is al-uṣūl fī sharḥ al-maḥṣūl*, ed. ʿĀdil ʿAbd al-Mawjūd and ʿAlī Muḥammad Muʿawwaḍ (Mecca: Maktabat Nizār Muṣṭafā al-Bāz, 1416/1995), 3889–90; Najm al-Dīn Sulaymān b. ʿAbd al-Qawī b. ʿAbd al-Karīm al-Ṭūfī (d. 716/1316), *Sharḥ Mukhtaṣar al-Rawḍa*, 3 vols ed. ʿAbd Allāh b. ʿAbd al-Muḥsin al-Turkī (Beirut: Mu'assasat al-Risāla, 1419/1998), 3:612; Asnawī, *Nihāyat al-sūl*, 4:558–9.

[63] Ghazālī, *Mustaṣfā*, 4:83; Shīrāzī, *Sharḥ al-Lumaʿ*, 1050; Samʿānī, *Qawāṭiʿ*, 5:56, Juwaynī [pseudo], *Talkhīṣ*, 3:384–5; Abū Yaʿlā, *al-ʿUdda fī uṣūl al-fiqh*, 1564, 1575. Those *muṣawwiba* who accept the determination of

tion is the one identical with pre-existing law; all the rest are wrong. The goal of *ijtihād* and the obligation of the *mujtahid*, in this case, is to discover God's predetermined laws, especially the ones not mentioned in the normative texts of Islam.

The second position of this debate sees divine law as an indetermined law. God does not predetermine a particular deontic qualification for every human action (excluding ones already mentioned in the Qur'ān and Sunna); the law is rather created by the *mujtahid*. In other words, divine law does not exist before the jurist's *ijtihād*; law is the product of this process.[64] Since divine law does not pre-exist the jurists' *ijtihād*, there can be no model laws according to which right and wrong can be decided. Jurists who exhaust all efforts investigating the available evidence will always produce a correct deontic qualification; none of them can be wrong. Thus, most scholars accepting this perception of divine law are *muṣawwiba*. For those who accept the indetermination of divine law, the goal of *ijtihād*, and the obligation of the jurist, cannot be the discovery of a pre-existing deontic qualification, simply because, for them, such qualifications do not exist. For such jurists, the goal of *ijtihād* and the task of the *mujtahid*, is to exhaust all efforts investigating the available evidence relevant to the jurisprudential case in question. This investigation should produce inconclusive knowledge about the deontic qualification that the jurist believes to be most probably correct. This inconclusive knowledge is the goal of *ijtihād*; it is also what the *mujtahid* is searching for.[65]

---

divine law often hold that jurists are not obliged to uncover the determined law. They are only required to search for it and act upon whatever probable knowledge their *ijtihād* produces, see for example Jaṣṣāṣ, *Fuṣūl*, 4:298, 319–24, 355, 365–71; Ṣaymarī, *Masā'il al-khilāf*, 297–303.

[64] See Weiss, *Spirit of Islamic Law*, 116, 118.

[65] For more details on both positions on the determination of divine law, see for instance Ṭūfī, *Sharḥ Mukhtaṣar al-Rawḍa*, 3:612–4.

Nature of the Verisimilitude (*ashbah*)[66]

The term verisimilitude (*ashbah*) often appears in debates around *taṣwīb* and *takhṭi'a* and is certainly relevant to any discussion of the determination of divine law. The Arabic word *ashbah* comes from the three letter root *sh-b-h*. Most derivatives of this root are used to describe any type of similarity between, for instance, the physical appearance of two persons, two objects, or even two ideas.[67] The main problem with the technical definition of this term is that different jurists define it differently, sometimes in reference to *ijtihād* and at others in reference to *qiyās*. Their definitions are usually influenced by their stance regarding the *taṣwīb-takhṭi'a* debate and the one around the determination of divine law. Despite the presence of many definitions, only two are relevant to our discussion here.

The first definition of the verisimilitude is that it is the deontic qualification (a jurist reaches through his *ijtihād*) that is identical with the qualification God has assigned, since eternity, for a particular human action. I call this perception of the *ashbah* the hard-verisimilitude theory. Only jurists who accept the determination of divine law can accept this definition. For most of them, the goal of *ijtihād* is the discovery of the determined deontic qualification (*ḥukm ashbah*). Therefore, the only correct qualification is this eternally assigned qualification; all the rest are wrong.[68] According to this understanding of the verisimilitude, God has already created the law before human existence. In this case, the verisimilar deontic qualification is nothing but the exact deontic qualification God created or determined for a particular human action.

The second definition of the verisimilitude is the one usually adopted by the jurists who accept the indetermination of divine law. I call their perception of this term the soft-verisimilitude. For

---

[66] Here, I am using Zysow's translation of the term *ashbah*, see his *Economy of Certainty*, esp. 262–76.

[67] For more information on the lexical definition of the three letter root *sh-b-h*, see Ibn Manẓūr, *Lisān al-ʿArab*, 13:503–6 in *al-Jāmiʿ al-kabīr*.

[68] For jurists who adopt this perception of the verisimilitude, see for example Ibn ʿAqīl, *al-Wāḍiḥ fī uṣūl al-fiqh*, 5:371; Ibn Barhān, *al-Wuṣūl ilā al-uṣūl*, 2:348.

them, the verisimilitude is probable knowledge (*ʿilm ẓannī* or *ghalabat al-ẓann*) about the deontic qualification they believe to be the most suitable to a case in question. In this case, the goal of *ijtihād* is to reach probable knowledge about the deontic qualification the jurist considers to be the most suitable for a particular case rather than finding a deontic qualification that God has determined for a case since eternity. For them, the requirement of the *mujtahid* is to exhaust all efforts investigating the accessible evidence until he reaches a deontic qualification *he* believes to be probably correct. This probable knowledge, in itself, is the 'verisimilar' deontic qualification. Given this perception of the verisimilitude, any deontic qualification a jurist reaches, after total expenditure of effort, must be correct.[69] It is important to note here that, according to this perception of the verisimilitude, the jurist is not trying to approximate divinely assigned law. This is because jurists adopting this perception believe that God did not assign particular laws for each human action. The jurist then is not trying to uncover a hitherto hidden law; he is rather creating the law. This point is discussed below in more detail.

The Muʿtazilī-Ḥanafī jurist Abū al-Ḥusayn al-Baṣrī rightly notes that before examining the *taṣwīb-takhṭiʾa* debate, one must first answer the question what the jurist is obliged to reach through his process of *ijtihād*.[70] An examination of the debate around the determination of divine law and a jurist's definition of the verisimilitude are necessary for answering this question. Part of the *taṣwīb-*

---

[69] For jurists who adopt the soft definition of the verisimilitude, see Ghazālī, *Mustaṣfā*, 4:43, 58, 83–92; ʿAbd al-Jabbār, *Mughnī*, 17:376–9. For more details on both and other definitions of the verisimilitude, see Shīrāzī, *Sharḥ al-Lumaʿ*, 1050–1; Abū al-Ḥusayn, *Muʿtamad*, 953–4. Zysow provides a brief discussion of the different definitions of the verisimilitude, see his *Economy of Certainty*, 267–9. There are other terms used to refer to the *ashbah*, such as the *aṣwab*, see Samarqandī, *Mīzān al-uṣūl*, 1136. Jaṣṣāṣ uses the term *naẓīr* in addition to *ashbah*, see his *Fuṣūl*, 4:330, 339. One gets the impression that *aṣwab* and *naẓīr* are archaic terms. Both do not disappear, but they become less common in legal theory literature after the fourth/tenth century.

[70] Abū al-Ḥusayn, *Muʿtamad*, 952. See also Zuḥaylī, *Uṣūl al-fiqh*, 1097.

takhṭiʾa controversy is a debate around the nature of the verisimilitude, its definition and the existence of a determined law that pre-exists the efforts of the jurist. The remaining of this section examines and compares the positions of the four Shāfiʿīs on these questions. This examination is important for understanding the difference between *taṣwīb* and *takhṭiʾa* and for clarifying the theoretical and theological points of contentions between both positions.[71]

A Single Determined Law

Shīrāzī and Samʿānī both adopt *takhṭiʾa* in law: only one deontic qualification is correct; the rest are wrong. They argue that God assigns evidence assisting humans to discover the correct deontic qualification. For them, the goal of *ijtihād* and the obligation of the jurist is to search for this evidence and uncover the correct deontic qualification.[72] Shīrāzī does not explicitly define the verisimilitude. However, he notes that the aim of dialectic disputations (sg.

---

[71] Having mentioned the different definitions of the *ashbah*, one must comment on the attempts to translate it. As mentioned before, Zysow translates the *ashbah* as the verisimilitude. Rebstock translates it as 'more similar', see his 'A Qāḍī's Errors', 11. Marie Bernand translates it as 'le plus ressemblant' or 'le plus proche par la resemblance', see her 'La problème de 'l'ašbah'. All these translations give the impression that the *ashbah* is the opinion or the theory that is the best approximation of the truth. These translations reflect only one of the definitions of the *ashbah*. However, none of these terms are accurate reflections of the hard or the soft theories of the *ashbah*. The hard-*ashbah* theory assumes that there is only one truth. The *ashbah* is the deontic qualification (*ḥukm sharʿī*) identical with this truth, not an approximation of it. The soft-*ashbah* refuses the existence of an ultimate truth against which one can decide whether a deontic qualification is a close approximation of it or not. The presence of multiple definitions of the term *ashbah* complicates translating it. However, due to the lack of a better alternative, I use Zysow's translation. Nonetheless, one should keep in mind the difference between the connotations of the term 'verisimilitude' in the English language and the connotations of the term *ashbah* in the discipline of Muslim legal theory.

[72] Shīrāzī, *Tabṣira*, 498; Shīrāzī, *Sharḥ al-Lumaʿ*, 1046, 1051; Samʿānī, *Qawāṭiʿ*, 5:19, 45–8, 51, 54, 56.

munāẓara) is to uncover God's predetermined deontic qualification (*al-ḥukm al-ashbah ʿinda Allāh taʿālā*).[73] This statement placed besides his adoption of *takhṭiʾa* reveals that he accepts the determination of divine law. For Shīrāzī, the aim of disputations, and thus *ijtihād*, is to uncover these determined deontic qualifications. Jurists who are successful have reached the correct qualification, all others are wrong. Nevertheless, mistaken jurists are not culpable. In fact, as a reward for intending to reach the truth, they receive half the reward reserved for the jurists who have managed to discover God's predetermined law.[74]

Samʿānī's chapter on *ijtihād* includes a perplexing statement. Although he is beyond doubt among the *mukhaṭṭiʾa*, he notes that he rejects the verisimilitude.[75] Yet, a closer look at his writings reveals that, just like Shīrāzī, he accepts the determination of divine law. He notes that there is only one correct deontic qualification for every human action. The aim of *ijtihād*, and the obligation of the jurist, is to uncover this deontic qualification.[76] To further clarify his position, Samʿānī mentions the archetypical case of *ijtihād*,

[73] Shīrāzī, *Tabṣira*, 502. Dialectic disputations (sg. *munāẓara*) are mainly theological and juridical disputes (often literary as well) in which two scholars promote opposing views, sometimes in front of an audience. This practice often occurs in the form of a question and answer. Dialectic disputations seem to have had a great impact on the literary style of legal and theological literature. Quite often authors adopt the *fanqala* style (*fā-in qāla qulnā*) where the author writes in the form of a question and an answer. The writer imagines the presence of an interlocutor always adopting the opposite position and trying to rebut his opinions. The author presents arguments against his imaginary interlocutor and in defence of his own views. For more details on dialectic disputations, see *EI*², s.v. 'Munāẓara' (E. Wagner); *EI*², s.v. '*Ikhtilāf*' (J. Schacht); *EI*², s.v. 'Masāʾil Wa-Adjwiba' (H. Daiber).

[74] Shīrāzī, *Sharḥ al-Lumaʿ*, 1046, 1051, 1064.

[75] Samʿānī, *Qawāṭiʿ*, 5:34.

[76] Samʿānī, *Qawāṭiʿ*, 5:19, 47–8, 52, 56.

that of searching for the direction of the *qibla*.[77] He writes that jurists or individuals searching for the *qibla* aim at finding its exact direction. He concludes saying that this should also be the aim of all processes of *ijtihād*. The goal of any *ijtihād* should be discovering the exact deontic qualification God has predetermined for each action (*maṭlūb al-mujtahidīn fi-l-ḥawādith ḥukm muʿayyān ʿinda Allāh taʿālā*).[78] This statement indicates that Samʿānī accepts the determination of divine law. Divine law is determined (just like the direction of the *qibla* is already determined); the verisimilitude is the deontic qualification identical with these determined laws. Jurists are required to uncover the verisimilitude. Successful jurists are correct; all the rest are wrong. However, jurists who exhaust all efforts searching for the truth, and yet reach a wrong deontic qualification, are exonerated and not held accountable for their failure.[79]

Juwaynī's goal of *ijtihād* is slightly different. Just like Shīrāzī and Samʿānī, he believes that divine law is determined. The only correct deontic qualification is the one identical with God's determined law.[80] The intended goal of any jurist is to discover these

---

[77] The *qibla* is the direction of the Kaʿba in Mecca which Muslims must face during ritual prayers (sg. *ṣalāt*). For more details, see *EI*², s.v. 'Ḳibla' (A. J. Wensinck and D. A. King).

[78] Samʿānī, *Qawāṭiʿ*, 5:48. For similar statements, see 5:45–8, 51. Given these statements, why then does Samʿānī, elsewhere, deny the existence of a verisimilitude? As mentioned above, the term *ashbah* is used by premodern jurists in reference to both the hard and the soft perceptions of the verisimilitude. A scholar, like Samʿānī, who adopts the hard-verisimilitude, would note that he rejects the verisimilitude. However, he is actually only rejecting the soft-verisimilitude. Interestingly, ʿAbd al-Jabbār, as mentioned below, argues against the existence of a verisimilitude. Yet, he remarks that the only accepted understanding of the verisimilitude is that it is the probable knowledge produced after *ijtihād* (i.e. the soft-verisimilitude), see his *Mughnī*, 17:377. Therefore, a scholar's statement rejecting the verisimilitude should not be taken at face value but placed within the larger context of his writings.

[79] Samʿānī, *Qawāṭiʿ*, 5:19, 56.

[80] Juwaynī, *Burhān*, 1324–6.

determined laws.[81] However, Juwaynī differs from them in that he notes that no jurist is required to reach anything beyond probable knowledge (*ẓann*).[82] Hence, for Juwaynī, the jurist's aim is not exactly to uncover God's determined deontic qualification, but, as he explicitly states, to only reach probable knowledge of it.[83] This difference is reflected in their descriptions of *ijtihād*. Shīrāzī describes *ijtihād* as the jurist's effort to uncover a deontic qualification.[84] Samʿānī notes that it is a search for the truth (*ṣawāb*) and an effort to deduce deontic qualifications from evidence.[85] Juwaynī, on the other hand, describes *ijtihād* as nothing but a search for probability (*ẓann*); once a jurist has reached probability he has completed his task. He insists that requiring a jurist to reach anything beyond probability would be an obligation impossible to fulfil.[86] In other words, for Juwaynī, the goal of *ijtihād* is not to uncover God's determined law; it is rather to only reach probable knowledge of it.[87]

Shīrāzī and Samʿānī do not state that the aim of *ijtihād* is to reach conclusive knowledge (*ʿilm*, *ʿilm qaṭʿī*, or *yaqīn*) about the correct deontic qualification. Neither do they say that inconclusive knowledge of these qualifications is a sufficient aim for *ijtihād*. Leaving this undecided might indicate that for both jurists a perfect process of *ijtihād* is expected to produce more than just inconclusive knowledge. Especially as both make it very clear that the obligation of the jurist is not to simply act upon the inconclusive knowledge resulting from his *ijtihād*. His obligation is, rather, to

---

[81] Juwaynī, *Burhān*, 1324–5.

[82] Juwaynī, *Burhān*, 1323–4.

[83] Juwaynī, *Burhān*, 1326.

[84] Shīrāzī, *Lumaʿ*, 258; Shīrāzī, *Sharḥ al-Lumaʿ*, 1043.

[85] Samʿānī, *Qawāṭiʿ*, 5:1.

[86] Juwaynī, *Burhān*, 1323.

[87] Juwaynī's opinion appears very similar to that of the Ḥanafī jurist, who followed Māturīdī theology, Abū Zayd al-Dabūsī. See Rumme Ahmed's explanation of Dabūsī's position in his *Narratives of Islamic Legal Theory*, 138–42. For Dabūsī's discussion of the topic see his, *Taqwīm al-adilla*, 407–17.

uncover and follow the truth.[88] This does not entail that inconclusive knowledge is invalid; if conclusive knowledge is not possible, then the jurist will have to settle with inconclusive knowledge. But the jurist starts his *ijtihād* with an attempt to uncover God's determined law and not only reach inconclusive knowledge of it.[89]

An Indetermined Law

The only jurist among the four under study to adopt *taṣwīb* is ʿAbd al-Jabbār. His writings I consulted do not include an explicit statement revealing his position on the determination of divine law. Nonetheless, his discussion of *taṣwīb* includes a number of references entailing that divine law is indetermined. He vehemently argues against the idea that the verisimilitude is God's determined deontic qualification.[90] He even notes that the verisimilitude should not be associated with God at all.[91] An examination of ʿAbd al-Jabbār's reference to the classical case of *ijtihād* might further clarify his position. He argues that none of the jurists searching for the *qibla* is actually required to find its direction.

> They are [rather] only required to investigate the signs (*al-fikr fi-l-amārāt*), reach probable knowledge, and act upon this knowledge. This applies to all cases of *ijtihād*. However, finding the *qibla* requires the presence of a *ʿayn* [a thing, i.e. the physical existence of the Kaʿba] to serve as a sign [for the jurist]. If this sign could exist without the existence of this *ʿayn*, searching for the *qibla* would not be impossible. This is just like original cases [*uṣūl*, sg. *aṣl*] in *ijtihād* [or *qiyās*]; they are necessary only because they serve as signs. If the verisimilitude is an original

---

[88] Shīrāzī, *Tabṣira*, 507–8; Shīrāzī, *Sharḥ al-Lumaʿ*, 1067; Samʿānī, *Qawāṭiʿ*, 5:57–8.

[89] On this point, see Weiss, *Spirit of Islamic Law*, 119.

[90] For his complete argument, see ʿAbd al-Jabbār, *Mughnī*, 17:376–9.

[91] ʿAbd al-Jabbār, *Mughnī*, 17:378.

> case [i.e. a sign for the jurist], then it is acceptable; any other understanding of the verisimilitude is not.[92]

The above passage includes important references. For our purpose here, it is crucial to note that ʿAbd al-Jabbār undermines the importance of the physical existence of the Kaʿba for a jurist searching for the *qibla*.[93] As mentioned before, searching for the *qibla* is the archetypical case of *ijtihād*. The Kaʿba resembles the object jurists are searching for during their *ijtihād*. For the *mukhaṭṭiʾa*, the Kaʿba represents God's determined law; the law all jurists are striving to find. ʿAbd al-Jabbār notes that the Kaʿba is necessary, when searching for the *qibla*, only because it serves as a sign that jurists can use during their *ijtihād*. If this sign could exist without the physical existence of the Kaʿba, the absence of the Kaʿba would have no influence on the jurist's search for the *qibla*. This is because, for ʿAbd al-Jabbār, jurists are not required to find the correct direction of the Kaʿba. They are simply required to investigate the signs indicating its direction, reach probable knowledge about its direction, and act upon this knowledge by facing whatever direction *they* believe to be probably that of the Kaʿba.

For ʿAbd al-Jabbār, the Kaʿba is not the ideal law jurists are expected to uncover. In fact, for him, this ideal law does not exist at all. The Kaʿba is nothing more than a sign that helps jurists reach probable knowledge of the *qibla*. Just as other evidence is a sign, not for God's determined law, but for reaching probability about the deontic qualification a *jurist* believes to be probably correct. Elsewhere, ʿAbd al-Jabbār notes that obligation (*taklīf*) is contingent upon the jurist's *ijtihād*, rather than upon a determined 'matter' (*al-taklīf mawqūf ʿalā ijtihādih dūna amr muʿayyan*).[94] In other words, obligation is not contingent upon determined laws; the jurist is not

---

[92] ʿAbd al-Jabbār, *Mughnī*, 17:379. Zysow's explanation of this argument was helpful in understanding ʿAbd al-Jabbār's difficult style of expression, see Zysow, *Economy of Certainty*, 266–7.

[93] Zysow writes that, for ʿAbd al-Jabbār, the physical existence of the Kaʿba is only an 'incidental feature of the obligation of directing oneself towards the *qibla*', see his *Economy of Certainty*, 267.

[94] ʿAbd al-Jabbār, *Mughnī*, 20/2:263.

searching for a particular deontic qualification to apply. Obligation is rather contingent upon whatever deontic qualification the jurist will reach via his *ijtihād.* At one point in his argument, ʿAbd al-Jabbār's interlocutor suggests that jurists are searching for the one deontic qualification that God would have chosen if He had assigned a particular law for the act in question.[95] ʿAbd al-Jabbār refuses this suggestion noting that it is very possible that God's deontic qualification would be whatever qualification the jurist would reach.[96] It is important to realize that for ʿAbd al-Jabbār divine law is neither homogeneous, monolithic nor determined. In ʿAbd al-Jabbār's legal framework, divine law is the result of the process of *ijtihād* conducted by each jurist; each jurist creates his own version of the divine law.

If divine law is indetermined, what then is the goal of *ijtihād*? What is the jurist searching for during his process of *ijithād*? As mentioned above, ʿAbd al-Jabbār plainly states that none of the jurists searching for the *qibla* are actually obliged to uncover its true direction. They are only required to investigate the signs for the direction of the *qibla*, and face whatever direction they believe to be, most probably, that of the *qibla.* From this example, it appears that the jurist has two main obligations, those can be also considered the goals of *ijtihād.* The first is total expenditure of effort investigating the available evidence relevant to the case in question. Second, the jurist is required to reach probable knowledge about the deontic qualification that *he* believes to be, probably, the most suitable for the case in question. Finally, a jurist is required to sincerely act upon his probable knowledge. God does not determine any laws; therefore, uncovering any of these laws (or finding the exact direction of the *qibla*) or even reaching probable knowledge about determined laws cannot be a target for *ijtihād.* For ʿAbd al-

[95] This is actually one of the many definitions of the verisimilitude, see Emon, 'To Most Likely Know the Law', 438.

[96] ʿAbd al-Jabbār, *Mughnī*, 17:378.

Jabbār, the performance of *ijtihād* becomes a goal in itself,[97] and the creation of probable knowledge is the second goal.[98]

Before ending this sub-section, we should comment on ʿAbd al-Jabbār's definition of the verisimilitude. As previously mentioned, ʿAbd al-Jabbār rejects defining it as God's determined deontic qualification. In another context, ʿAbd al-Jabbār notes that the verisimilitude is the original cases' deontic qualifications (*aḥkām al-uṣūl*).[99] In other words, it is the deontic qualification mentioned in textual evidence (Qurʾān or Sunna) used, during *qiyās*, to find the qualification of a case not covered by revelation (i.e. the novel case). Elsewhere, ʿAbd al-Jabbār quotes the famous Muʿtazilī authority Abū Hāshim al-Jubbāʾī (d. 321/933) saying that a jurist, examining a jurisprudential question, is only obliged to examine the available evidence. This obligation is fulfilled when the jurist reaches probable knowledge allowing him to identify the original case that reveals the deontic qualification of the novel case [during a process of *qiyās*]. Commenting on this statement, ʿAbd al-Jabbār notes that if the verisimilitude is the inconclusive knowledge resulting from the investigation of evidence, then it is acceptable; other understandings of it are not.[100]

Here we notice that ʿAbd al-Jabbār mentions two different descriptions of the verisimilitude. First, it is the deontic qualification of the original case. Second, it is the inconclusive knowledge produced after a process of *qiyās* or *ijtihād*. We have two options here; we can either conclude that ʿAbd al-Jabbār is inconsistent in his perception of the verisimilitude or we can attempt to harmonize both definitions. I prefer the latter option. Let's remember that previously ʿAbd al-Jabbār notes that original cases are necessary only because they serve as signs that jurists investigate to reach probable knowledge. Thus, one might suggest that for ʿAbd al-Jabbār the verisimilitude is the probable knowledge resulting from

---

97 See Zysow, *Economy of Certainty*, 271; ʿAbd al-Qādir, *al-Masāʾil al-mushtaraka*, 308.

98 On probability as a goal for *ijtihād*, see Zysow, *Economy of Certainty*, 266–7.

99 ʿAbd al-Jabbār, *Mughnī*, 17:379.

100 ʿAbd al-Jabbār, *Mughnī*, 17:377.

investigating the available signs, not only in *qiyās* but in other forms of *ijtihād* as well. It is important to note that nowhere does ʿAbd al-Jabbār suggests that the verisimilitude, or the goal of *ijtihād*, is probable knowledge of the correct or determined deontic qualification. This would contradict his rejection of the determination of divine law; for him determined and universally correct laws do not exist. For ʿAbd al-Jabbār, searching for probable knowledge about determined laws would be just like chasing a mirage or searching for an object that does not exist.

The difference between ʿAbd al-Jabbār's aim of *ijtihād* and that of Shīrāzī and Samʿānī is clear. The latter two refuse to consider probability as a purpose for *ijtihād*. For them the aim is to uncover God's determined deontic qualification and not only reach probable knowledge of it. The difference between ʿAbd al-Jabbār and Juwaynī might not be absolutely clear. In Juwaynī's view, the aim of the jurist's efforts is to reach probable knowledge about God's determined law. For ʿAbd al-Jabbār, the jurist is required to reach probable knowledge, not about a pre-assigned deontic qualification, but about the deontic qualification the jurist himself believes to be the most suitable for the case in question.

It is clear, I hope, that the above debates are dominated by epistemological discussions. The main points of contention between the four jurists revolve around the determination of divine law and the acceptance of probability as a goal for *ijtihād*. The latter is a debate around the requirements and standards of human knowledge. Are humans required to reach the 'truth' (*ḥaqq*)? Is probable and approximate knowledge of this 'truth' sufficient, or one must always aspire to certainty? Is certainty of the truth possible? The determination of divine law is largely a debate about the existence of this truth. It is a debate around the existence of a universal reality that should serve as the ideal that jurists aspire to. In the language of the pre-modern jurist, this reality is like a treasure – a *mujtahid* is digging the ground searching for it. For ʿAbd al-Jabbār, this reality (and this treasure) does not exist. In fact, the existence of any law (excluding ones already mentioned in the Qurʾān and Sunna) does not precede the jurist's *ijtihād*. Accordingly, for him and other *muṣawwiba*, *ijtihād* is a process that creates (*yunshiʾ*) a law that did not exist before the jurist's efforts. For the *mukhaṭṭiʾa*, on the other hand, *ijtihād* is a process that merely discovers (*yakshif*) a pre-existing body of laws. Having these discussions in mind, we now turn to a closer examination of the versions of *takhṭiʾa* and *taṣwīb* adopted by the four Shāfiʿīs jurists who are the main interest of this study. This discussion will further show that this debate is dominated by epistemological more than doctrinal and creedal questions.

THE SINGLE TRUTH

Takhṭiʾa is a position that assumes the existence of single absolute truth; there is only one correct answer to any jurisprudential question. Truth is far from being plural. Although Shīrāzī, Samʿānī and Juwaynī adopt this perception of the truth, they disagree, as mentioned above, on the goal of the process of *ijtihād*. This disagreement is not without consequences; it creates two versions of *takhṭiʾa*, one adopted by Juwaynī and another adopted by Shīrāzī and Samʿānī. This section explains each version and surveys the evidence that the jurists put forward in support of *takhṭiʾa*. The following section explains ʿAbd al-Jabbār's adoption of *taṣwīb* and analyses his supporting arguments. It then compares ʿAbd al-Jabbār's arguments to those of his three fellow Shāfiʿīs promoting *takhṭiʾa*. This comparison should, hopefully, shed more light on the theoretical points of contention between *taṣwīb* and *takhṭiʾa*, this should allow a better evaluation of the influence of theological disagreements on this legal debate.

Two Versions of *takhṭiʾa*

Shīrāzī's and Samʿānī's version of *takhṭiʾa* is quite simple. Both note that there is only one correct deontic qualification for each action. God has assigned enough evidence pointing towards the correct qualification. He made humans capable of noticing and understanding this evidence. Therefore, jurists are not only required to search for the correct qualification, but to find it and act upon it. Nevertheless, jurists who fail to uncover the truth are exonerated.[101] Both jurists imagine the presence of an interlocutor from the *muṣawwiba* who objects, saying that there is a consensus that jurists

---

[101] Shīrāzī, *Sharḥ al-Lumaʿ*, 1064, Shīrāzī, *Tabṣira*, 498; Samʿānī, *Qawāṭiʿ*, 5:47–8, 51–2, 54, 56.

are required to act upon whatever probable knowledge their *ijtihād* produces. Therefore, one cannot describe any jurist as mistaken. Shīrāzī and Samʿānī refuse this rationale saying that a jurist is not required to follow his probable knowledge; he is rather required to follow the truth. If he is successful in uncovering the only truth, then he is correct. A jurist who fails to reach the truth is simply in error; acting upon a wrong deontic qualification, even if based on the jurist's probable knowledge, can never be considered a correct action.[102]

Juwaynī seems to be adopting a position similar to that of this imaginary interlocutor. Unlike Shīrāzī and Samʿānī, he distinguishes between the goal of *ijtihād* (*maṭlūb al-ijtihād*) and the action required after this process. The latter might – or might not – be identical with God's determined deontic qualification. Like many other Sunnī scholars, Juwaynī holds that God requires jurists to act upon the probable knowledge resulting from their processes of *ijtihād*. Each process of *ijtihād* produces probable knowledge about the 'correct' deontic qualification for the action in question. Different jurists with distinct processes of *ijtihād* reach various deontic qualifications for the same action. Although Juwaynī insists that only one deontic qualification is correct, he contends that God does not require jurists to follow the correct deontic qualification. God rather obliges each individual jurist to act upon the probable knowledge produced via his own process of *ijtihād*.[103] Therefore, a jurist who acts upon his own inconclusive knowledge, even if not identical with the God's determined law, has fulfilled his obligation.

To further explain his position, Juwaynī mentions the example of searching for the *qibla*. We know that there is only one correct direction for the *qibla*. A jurist who searches for it and finds its exact direction has found the correct deontic qualification and has performed the correct action. A *mujtahid* who fails to find its exact direction has adopted the wrong deontic qualification. Yet, his action facing the direction he believes to be, most probably, that of the *qibla* is correct. Although his deontic qualification is wrong, his

[102] Shīrāzī, *Sharḥ al-Lumaʿ*, 1067; Shīrāzī, *Tabṣira*, 507–8; Samʿānī, *Qawāṭiʿ*, 5:58.

[103] Juwaynī, *Burhān*, 1323–6, 1328–9.

action remains correct.[104] Therefore, notes Juwaynī, a jurist who reaches a deontic qualification different from God's determined qualification is certainly mistaken (*mukhṭiʾ*). Nevertheless, his action is correct; he is correct (*muṣīb*) when he acts upon whatever probable knowledge he has reached via his *ijtihād.* Since God has obliged jurists to act upon their probable knowledge, one cannot describe the *action* (not the opinion) of those who fulfil this obligation as incorrect.[105] In other words, the opinions of jurists maybe right or wrong. However, all actions based on probable knowledge are correct.

This perception allows Juwaynī to distinguish between the goal of *ijtihād* and the action required after it. It allows him to distinguish between the correctness of the deontic qualification and the correctness of the action performed after *ijtihād.* There is only one correct deontic qualification; jurists who miss it are wrong. Yet, since jurists are only required to act upon their probable knowledge, their actions are always correct. Shīrāzī and Samʿānī make no such distinctions. For them, a jurist is required to uncover the truth and act upon it, rather than act upon his probable knowledge. Therefore, a jurist who reaches a wrong deontic qualification is both wrong in his *ijtihād* and wrong in his action. The correctness of the product of *ijtihād* and the action following it are indistinguishable. Although Juwaynī notes that he adopts a position between *takhṭiʾa* and *taṣwīb*,[106] nonetheless his insistence that there is only one correct deontic qualification for every human action places him among the ranks of the *mukhaṭṭiʾa.* Yet, Juwaynī's willingness to accept probability as a goal for *ijtihād* and the correctness of the actions of all jurists makes his version of *takhṭiʾa* less strict than that of Shīrāzī and Samʿānī.[107]

---

[104] Juwaynī, *Burhān*, 1325–6.

[105] Juwaynī, *Burhān*, 1325.

[106] Juwaynī, *Burhān*, 1323.

[107] Abbas Poya notes that Juwaynī adopts *taṣwīb*, see his, *Anerkennung des Iǧtihād*, 130. To support his understanding of Juwaynī's position Poya cites, Imām al-Ḥaramayn [Abū al-Maʿālī ʿAbd al-Malik b. ʿAbd Allāh] al-Juwaynī, *Kitāb al-Ijtihād min Kitāb al-Talkhīṣ*, ed. ʿAbd al-Ḥamīd Abū Zayd [sic] (Damascus; Beirut, [Dār al-Qalam; Dār al-ʿUlūm al-Thaqāfiyya]

Supporting Arguments

It is surprising that none of the three *mukhaṭṭiʾa* examined here mention arguments in support of their particular version of *takhṭiʾa*. Their supporting arguments are ones establishing *takhṭiʾa* in general and not a particular variant of it. Juwaynī's argument in support of *takhṭiʾa* is surprisingly short. I will outline his argument first then move to Shīrāzī's and Samʿānī's. To prove that there is only one correct answer for any jurisprudential question, Juwaynī put forward only two curt arguments. First, he notes that the same action or thing cannot be both permissible and prohibited at the same time. This is a reference to a common argument stating that *taṣwīb* leads to adopting contradicting deontic qualifications.[108] Second, he argues that any searcher (*ṭālib*, i.e. any jurist) needs a target to search for (*maṭlūb*). Therefore, it makes no sense that a jurist would be a searcher without a target. The target that he is searching for is the verisimilitude (i.e. the predetermined law).[109] Juwaynī stops here, however, the logical conclusion would be any jurist whose *ijtihād* uncovers anything but this verisimilitude would be in error.

1987), 27–70, which is republished in Juwaynī [pseudo], *Talkhīṣ*, 3:344–91. The author of *Talkhīṣ* clearly adopts *taṣwīb*. As mentioned in a previous chapter, there is a debate around the authorship of *Talkhīṣ*, whether it is Juwaynī's original work, his abridgment of Bāqillānī's *al-Taqrīb wa-l-irshād*, or Bāqillānī's abridgment of his own work (which seems unlikely). Even if we accept Juwaynī 's authorship of *Talkhīṣ* (which is possible), Juwaynī wrote it at an early stage of his career, see Donmez, 'Makānat Imām al-Ḥaramayn', 512. Whereas Juwaynī wrote his legal theory *magnum opus Burhān* at a later stage in his career. In this later book, Juwaynī adopts, in many cases, different legal theory positions than the ones expressed in *Talkhīṣ*. Therefore, *Burhān* should be considered Juwaynī's revised and modified (sometimes more sophisticated and refined) opinions on legal theory matters after years of learning and experience. His *Burhān*, thus, should certainly be studied beside *Talkhīṣ*. Unfortunately, Poya does not discuss Juwaynī's stance on *taṣwīb* as expressed in *Burhān*. The book does not appear in Poya's bibliography.

108 Juwaynī, *Burhān*, 1320.

109 Juwaynī, *Burhān*, 1324–5.

Samʿānī and Shīrāzī have more elaborate and longer arguments. However, I will only mention the ones relevant to the purpose of this study. First, both argue that *takhṭiʾa* is supported by the Companion's consensus. They assert that the Companions' practices and sayings imply that different deontic qualifications cannot all be correct. Shīrāzī and Samʿānī mention a number of reports attributed to prominent Companions, such as Abū Bakr, ʿUmar and ʿAlī, admitting that they might have expressed a wrong opinion, describing an opponent as mistaken, or blaming an opponent for holding an erroneous deontic qualification. Shīrāzī and Samʿānī argue that if these Companions believe that all deontic qualifications are correct, there would be no need to describe the opinion of another person or even one's self as error.[110] Both jurists take these reports as an indication for the occurrence of a consensus among the Prophet's Companions in support of *takhṭiʾa*. Samʿānī adds that the Companions' consensus is the strongest evidence establishing *takhṭiʾa*.[111]

Shīrāzī and Samʿānī mention two rational arguments that have no textual basis; only one is enough as an example. Both jurists note that two contradictory deontic qualifications are either correct, wrong, or one is correct while the other is wrong. They continue saying that two contradictory opinions cannot be correct; or else the same action would be proscribed and permitted at the same time, and this is impossible. Two contradictory qualifications cannot be wrong; otherwise this would entail that all the positions the Muslim *umma* embraces are all wrong. In this case they would have reached a consensus on an error. This would contradict a well-established doctrine that the *umma* can never unanimously agree on a false position. They conclude that the only acceptable answer is the last one; only one of the two contradictory opinions is correct

---

[110] For example, both jurists quote a report attributed to the first Caliph Abū Bakr, when asked about an inheritance case he prefaced his answer saying 'I can only state my opinion; if correct it is from God, if wrong it is from me and I ask for forgiveness'. For this and other similar reports, see Shīrāzī, *Sharḥ al-Lumaʿ*, 1052–54; Shīrāzī, *Tabṣira*, 500–1; Samʿānī, *Qawāṭiʿ*, 5:29–33.

[111] Samʿānī, *Qawāṭiʿ*, 5:28, 44.

and the other is wrong. If we accept their argument, then we must conclude that different deontic qualifications cannot all be correct.[112]

High Appreciation of Inconclusive Evidence

Now we move to the most important part of Shīrāzī's and Samʿānī's argument for *takhṭiʾa*. Their arguments, discussed here, are similar but not identical. Their imaginary interlocutors, who embrace *taṣwīb*, argue that there is no available evidence allowing humans to identify the only truth. Shīrāzī and Samʿānī refuse this claim; both note that the Qurʾān and the Sunna are evidence assigned by God allowing humans to identify the universally correct deontic qualification.[113] Their interlocutors also argue that the evidence effecting and producing a deontic qualification (*al-dalīl al-mūjib li-l-ḥukm*) is the jurist's probable knowledge (*ẓann al-mujtahid*) rather than the Qurʾān and the Sunna themselves.[114] They then conclude that since all probable knowledge (*ẓann*) has the same

---

[112] Shīrāzī, *Sharḥ al-Lumaʿ*, 1056; Shīrāzī, *Tabṣira*, 502; Samʿānī, *Qawāṭiʿ*, 5:36, 47. For their other rational arguments, see Shīrāzī, *Sharḥ al-Lumaʿ*, 1055; Shīrāzī, *Tabṣira*, 501; Samʿānī, *Qawāṭiʿ*, 5:42–3.

[113] Shīrāzī, *Sharḥ al-Lumaʿ*, 1064; Shīrāzī, *Tabṣira*, 498, 506; Samʿānī, *Qawāṭiʿ*, 5:46.

[114] *Al-mūjib li-l-ḥukm* is an expression often used in reference to the *ratio legis* during the process of *qiyās*. It is a phrase utilized to describe the factor that brings about or produces a particular deontic qualification. For example, in the archetypical case of *qiyās*, the *ratio legis* behind the prohibition of grape wine (*khamr*) is its inebriating quality. This quality, without going into unnecessary complications, is the effective factor that produces the Qurʾānic prohibition of consuming grape wine (*al-maʿnā al-mūjib li-l-ḥukm*). Here the four jurists under examination are employing this term in reference to the factors that brings about a deontic qualification. The debate here is whether the evidence that produces a deontic qualification are the texts (i.e. Qurʾān and Sunna) or this evidence is the probable knowledge the jurist produces after examining these texts. In other words, what makes a jurist adopt a particular deontic qualification? Is it the texts he examines, or the probable knowledge he reaches after the examination of these texts? Shīrāzī is adopting the former option.

epistemic value, all deontic qualifications based on this type of knowledge must be equally correct.[115]

Shīrāzī and Samʿānī refute this argument in two different ways that reveal a discrepancy in their epistemology. Both refuse the assumption that all probable knowledge is equal in its epistemic value. They note that preponderance (*tarjīḥ*) between various inconclusive knowledge (i.e. inconclusive deontic qualifications) is possible.[116] This means that the probable knowledge of one jurist might have more epistemic value than that of another. Furthermore, Shīrāzī, unlike Samʿānī, insists that the factor effecting and bringing about any deontic qualification is the evidence themselves (e.g. Qurānic verses and Prophetic traditions); deontic qualifications are produced by this evidence (*al-aḥkām tābiʿa li-l-adilla*), rather than the jurist's probable knowledge. He quotes Q 4:59 '[i]f you are in dispute over any matter, refer it to God and the Messenger'. Jurists, then, are required to refer to the Qurʾān and the Sunna to uncover the truth. Shīrāzī insists that the Qurʾān and the Sunna are the evidence disclosing the truth; probability, in itself, is not an evidence for the correct deontic qualification.[117]

Shīrāzī's interlocutor mentions another objection: if evidence were the factor producing deontic qualifications, then all jurists would reach the same conclusion after examining the same evidence, which is not always the case. He continues saying that a Shāfiʿī jurist reaches a deontic qualification different than the one a Ḥanafī reaches, despite both examining the same piece of evidence. Therefore, it must be the jurist's probable knowledge that is yielding the deontic qualifications rather than the evidence itself.[118] Furthermore, the same interlocutor, elsewhere, notes that different deontic qualifications are applicable to different people. For example, it is acceptable for individuals facing the threat of starvation to consume animal cadavers without proper slaughter rituals (*mayta*), but unacceptable to those in normal circumstances. Travelers per-

---

115 Shīrāzī, *Sharḥ al-Lumaʿ*, 1060.

116 Shīrāzī, *Sharḥ al-Lumaʿ*, 1061–2, 1069, 1071–2; Samʿānī, *Qawāṭiʿ*, 5:37–42, 59–60.

117 Shīrāzī, *Sharḥ al-Lumaʿ*, 1054–5, 1060–1; Shīrāzī, *Tabṣira*, 503.

118 Shīrāzī, *Sharḥ al-Lumaʿ*, 1062.

form half the required prostrations for the compulsory prayers while non-travellers (sg. *muqīm*) perform all required prostrations.[119] This proves that there is no one correct deontic qualification that applies to all humans.[120]

Shīrāzī rejects the above arguments. He contends that each inconclusive and conclusive evidence (*dalīl*)[121] has a uniform signification (*madlūl ʿāmm*); it conveys the same signification to all addressees. In other words, a Qurʾānic verse or a Prophetic tradition has only one intended meaning; they bear no multiple connotations. Each evidence is capable of revealing its intended signification to their addressees. Each Qurʾānic verse or Prophetic tradition communicates only one message to its audience. Consequently, concludes Shīrāzī, jurists who look into the same evidence should come up with the same interpretation and the same deontic qualification.[122] If jurists should reach different interpretations for the same evidence, only those who uncover the intended meaning are correct; all the rest are wrong. Individuals under duress (sg. *muḍṭarr*), but not others, are allowed to consume cadavers only because this is mentioned in revelation (Q 5:3, 6:119, 2:173). Travelers perform fewer prostrations in prayer only because this is clarified in the Prophetic Sunna. Different individuals have different deontic qualifications only when this is stipulated in a normative text (*naṣṣ*). Otherwise, any piece of evidence carries only one correct meaning applicable to all addressees. If evidence produces multiple significations, notes Shīrāzī, this would entail that revelation imposes contradicting deontic qualifications, permitting and proscribing the same action, and this is impossible.[123]

Now we turn to Samʿānī's rebuttal. His interlocutor also argues that evidence is not the factor effecting a deontic qualification.

---

[119] This unanimously agreed upon rule applies only to what is called *al-ṣalāwāt al-rubāʿiyya*, i.e. those prayers that include at least four prostrations, namely *ẓuhr*, *ʿaṣr* and *ʿishāʾ*.

[120] Shīrāzī, *Sharḥ al-Lumaʿ*, 1056–7.

[121] For Shīrāzī the term *dalīl* applies both to conclusive and inconclusive evidence, see his *Sharḥ al-Lumaʿ*, 155–6.

[122] Shīrāzī, *Sharḥ al-Lumaʿ*, 1059–62; Shīrāzī, *Tabṣira*, 503.

[123] Shīrāzī, *Sharḥ al-Lumaʿ*, 1062; Shīrāzī, *Tabṣira*, 504.

Rather, a jurist's inconclusive knowledge produced after examining this evidence is the factor yielding deontic qualifications. Like Shīrāzī, Samʿānī insists that evidence itself is the factor that produces a deontic qualification rather than the jurist's inconclusive knowledge.[124] However, unlike Shīrāzī, Samʿānī admits that inconclusive evidence has no one uniform signification; they are incapable of communicating the same message to all addressees. Therefore, different jurists investigating the same inconclusive evidence will deduce different interpretations and thus reach different deontic qualifications.[125] Now, Samʿānī faces a question that Shīrāzī does not. If inconclusive evidence has no uniform signification, how then can jurists uncover the only correct deontic qualification? What makes a deontic qualification correct and another false? In fact, why adopt *takhṭiʾa* rather than *taṣwīb*?

Despite being aware of this shortcoming, Samʿānī does not put forward an explicit argument to fortify his position. However, at some point, he notes that if there are different deontic qualifications, each supported by different inconclusive evidence (*amārāt*),[126]

---

[124] Samʿānī, *Qawāṭiʿ*, 5:49–50.

[125] Samʿānī, *Qawāṭiʿ*, 5:47.

[126] Samʿānī defines *dalīl* (pl. *adilla*) as the guide to a pursued object (*wa-ammā al-dalīl fa-huwa al-murshid ilā al-maṭlūb*). He notes that most traditionalist jurists (*fuqahāʾ*) make no distinction between conclusive and inconclusive evidence, they refer to both as *adilla*. Whereas speculative theologians (*mutakallimūn*) reserve the term *dalīl* only to those evidence capable of yielding conclusive knowledge whereas they utilize the term *amāra* in reference to evidence yielding nothing more than inconclusive knowledge. See Samʿānī, *Qawāṭiʿ*, 1:42–3. Samʿānī's definition does not exclude inconclusive evidence from being *adilla*. However, still, it is not clear to me whether he adopts the terminology common among the traditionalist jurists or the one common among the speculative theologians. In his *Qawāṭiʿ*, in most cases, he gives the impression that he reserves the term *dalīl* for conclusive evidence and *amāra* for inconclusive evidence (see for instance Abū al-Muẓaffar Manṣūr b. Muḥammad b. ʿAbd al-Jabbār al-Samʿnāī, *Qawāṭiʿ al-adilla fī uṣūl al-fiqh*, 2 vols ed. Muḥammad Ḥasan al-Shāfiʿī (Beirut: Dār al-Kutub al-ʿIlmiyya, 1418/1997), 1:475, 477, 2:73, 79, 83, 187, 2:323 in *al-Jāmiʿ al-kabīr*). At other times, he uses the term *dalīl* in

then the jurist is required to adopt the deontic qualification supported by the single strongest inconclusive evidence. A jurist who forsakes the strongest evidence to adopt a weaker one would simply be in error.[127] Most importantly, elsewhere, Samʿānī notes that

> God has assigned conclusive evidence (*dalāla*) informing us of the deontic qualifications we are required to follow. This is because He requires us to act upon the strongest and most deserving *rationes legis* (*aqwā al-ʿilal wa-awlāhā*). God assigned methods through which we can *certainly* know which of the *inconclusive* evidence conveys the correct deontic qualification. The conclusive evidence is the evidence establishing the probative value of *qiyās*. Know that if we deduce the rationale (*maʿnā*, i.e. *ratio legis*) from an original case, once we find this rationale in a novel case, we must *certainly* know that the deontic qualification of the novel case is that of the original case… Although our knowledge of the deduced rationale is *probable*, nonetheless our knowledge of the deontic qualification of the novel case is *certain*.[128]

This statement includes an unjustified epistemological leap; the inconclusive knowledge produced by *qiyās* suddenly, and without proper explanation, turns into conclusive knowledge.[129] Samʿānī

---

reference to both conclusive and inconclusive evidence (see for example his *Qawāṭiʿ*, 1:85, 2:193 in *al-Jāmiʿ al-kabīr*). Nonetheless, I did not come across a case in which he uses the term *amāra* in reference to anything but inconclusive evidence. Therefore, I interpret his use of the term *dalīl* as a reference to both inconclusive and conclusive evidence unless there are obvious signs that he is only referring only to conclusive ones. On the other hand, I interpret his use of the term *amāra* as a reference only to inconclusive evidence.

[127] Samʿānī, *Qawāṭiʿ*, 5:37.

[128] Samʿānī, *Qawāṭiʿ*, 5:45.

[129] Commenting on Abū al-Ḥusayn al-Baṣrī's and ʿAbd al-Jabbār's acceptance of an identical epistemic leap, El-Tobgui notes that '[i]t is not altogether clear exactly how or why this shift from a judgment of prevalent probability (*ghalabat al-ẓann*) to conclusive knowledge (*'ilm*) should occur…', see Carl Sharif El-Tobgui, 'The Epistemology of *Qiyas* and *Ta'lil*

admits that our knowledge of the *ratio legis* (or rationale) is probable. Nonetheless, he explicitly states that our knowledge of the deontic qualification of the novel case, deduced via this *ratio legis*, is certain.

One wonders, why does Samʿānī mention *qiyās* and *rationes legis* in the middle of an argument establishing *takhṭiʾa*? The above quote is Samʿānī's reply to his interlocutor, who adopts *taṣwīb*. His interlocutor objects saying that if there were only one single truth, God would have assigned conclusive evidence revealing this truth. Samʿānī's words must be read as a rebuttal of this objection. It seems here that Samʿānī is noting that the epistemic leap that occurs in *qiyās*, which is the archetypical method of *ijtihād*, occurs also in all forms of *ijtihād*. In the above quote, Samʿānī explicitly states that God has assigned evidence allowing us to *certainly* identify the strongest available *inconclusive* evidence that reveal the correct deontic qualification. Once we know which of the inconclusive evidences is the strongest, we *certainly* know that the deontic qualification supported by this particular *inconclusive* evidence is the correct one. In this case, the knowledge produced by the strongest inconclusive evidence becomes conclusive. Therefore, although Samʿānī admits that most of the available evidence is inconclusive, there are still ways to reach conclusive knowledge via this inconclusive evidence.

Samʿānī, here, seems to be referring to what is usually known as the belief of preponderance (*iʿtiqād al-rujḥān*).[130] This concept assumes the presence of conclusive evidence identifying one particular inconclusive evidence as the strongest among other evidence of the same type. In this case, the jurist certainly knows that this particular inconclusive evidence is more deserving (*awlā*) of being followed than all others. Therefore, the jurist's adoption of the deontic qualification supported by this *inconclusive* evidence is *conclusively* known to be the correct choice, although the epistemological

---

between The Mu'tazilite Abu 'L-Husayn al-Basri and Ibn Hazm al-Zahiri', *UCLA Journal of Islamic and Near Eastern Law* 2.2 (2002–3), 296. Zysow describes this epistemic leap as a 'displacement of certainty', see his *Economy of Certainty*, 27, 266.

130 Translation borrowed from Zysow, *Economy of Certainty*, 261.

value of the evidence itself remains inconclusive.[131] This concept allows Samʿānī to claim that certain knowledge of the only truth, despite the absence of conclusive knowledge, is possible. Therefore, for him, the claim that there is no sufficient evidence to certainly uncover the truth is unfounded. The inconclusive evidence available is sufficient to allow a jurist to reach conclusive knowledge of the only one correct deontic qualification.

Samʿānī's version of *takhṭiʾa* appears less strict than Shīrāzī's. This might be inferred from his acknowledgment that inconclusive evidence cannot yield a single signification to all addressees. However, it is important to note here that both Shīrāzī's and Samʿānī's arguments in support of *takhṭiʾa* are based on the idea that the available inconclusive evidence is sufficient for revealing the only correct deontic qualification. For Shīrāzī, this is possible because all textual evidence (conclusive and inconclusive) yields only one signification for all addressees. Jurists who exhaust all efforts examining the same piece of evidence should reach the same conclusion. For Samʿānī, this is possible because God has assigned evidence for humans allowing them to certainly identify the strongest inconclusive evidence that reveals the only correct deontic qualification. To appreciate the significance of Shīrāzī's and Samʿānī's arguments we will have to compare them to ʿAbd al-Jabbār's version of *taṣwīb* and his supporting evidence.[132]

MULTIPLE TRUTHS

ʿAbd al-Jabbār adopts the exact opposite position of Shīrāzī and Samʿānī. As previously mentioned, he holds that divine law is indetermined; God does not determine a deontic qualification for each human action. Therefore, for him, the jurist cannot be obliged to

---

[131] For more details on the belief of preponderance, see for example, Saʿd al-Dīn Masʿūd b. ʿUmar al-Taftāzānī (d. 793/1390), *Sharḥ al-Talwīḥ ʿalā al-Tawḍīḥ li-matn al-Tanqīḥ fī uṣūl al-fiqh*, 2 vols ed. Zakariyyā ʿUmayrāt (Beirut: Dār al-Kutub al-ʿIlmiyya, 1416/1996), 2:216–7 in *al-Jāmiʿ al-kabīr*; Zarkashī, *Baḥr*, 1:74.

[132] Shīrāzī and Samʿānī present their arguments in support of *takhṭiʾa* in a different order than the one followed here. I reorganized their argument to allow a briefer and clearer presentation of them.

uncover a determined deontic qualification, simply because such qualifications do not exist. Rather, the jurist is required to investigate evidence and reach probability about the deontic qualification he believes to be the most suitable.[133] Since what all jurists are required to reach is probable knowledge, all the probable knowledge produced via their *ijtihād*s is correct.

This does not imply that any deontic qualification produced by any jurist is valid. ʿAbd al-Jabbār mentions four conditions for accepting the plurality of truths (*taʿaddud al-ḥaqq*). First, it is accepted only in law, whereas in theology there is only one truth. Second, the multiplicity of truths is acceptable only in the absence of conclusive knowledge. The latter is sufficient to uncover the only truth. Once the truth is apparent, all humans are required to follow it. Third, for an opinion to be correct it must be based on [at least] probable knowledge (*ghālib al-ẓann*),[134] i.e. it must be based, as a minimum, on inconclusive evidence. ʿAbd al-Jabbār describes an opinion that is not based on any evidence as doubt (*shakk* or *ẓann sawdāwī*), and this is invalid. Finally, elsewhere, ʿAbd al-Jabbār adds that only a deontic qualification expressed by a jurist who exhausts all efforts during his *ijtihād* can be correct. Jurists who fall short of exhausting their efforts cannot be correct.[135] All deontic qualifications that fulfil these four criteria, for ʿAbd al-Jabbār, are correct.[136]

Supporting Arguments

ʿAbd al-Jabbār has a chapter dedicated to vindicating *taṣwīb*.[137] In this chapter, he puts forward two main arguments. The first is the practice and the consensus of the Prophet's Companions. ʿAbd al-

---

133 ʿAbd al-Jabbār, *Mughnī*, 17:379.

134 ʿAbd al-Jabbār, *Mughnī*, 17:357.

135 ʿAbd al-Jabbār, *Mughnī*, 17:369. He makes this comment in reference to those jurists searching for the *qibla*. However, since searching for the *qibla* is the archetypical case of *ijtihād*, it must be taken as a comment applicable to all cases of *ijtihād*.

136 It is not clear to me whether ʿAbd al-Jabbār would consider any deontic qualification that does not fulfil these criteria as automatically incorrect or not meeting these criteria allows the possibility of error.

137 ʿAbd al-Jabbār, *Mughnī*, 17:364–75.

Jabbār notes that the Companions have disagreed over many jurisprudential questions. Nonetheless, they all unanimously refrain from blaming each other for holding a [wrong] jurisprudential position. He argues that this unanimous position entails a consensus on the part of the Companions establishing *taṣwīb.* He adds that this consensus is impossible without the presence of conclusive evidence motivating them all to adopt the same opinion. Therefore, concludes ʿAbd al-Jabbār, Companions must have been aware of a Prophetic tradition proving *taṣwīb.* The fact that we today are not aware of this tradition is not important, because the Companions' consensus is sufficient evidence that this tradition existed among them.[138]

Furthermore, ʿAbd al-Jabbār writes that we have confirmed reports showing Companions accepting the practice of issuing independent jurisprudential opinions (sg. *raʾy*).[139] It is also common to find them changing their jurisprudential opinions. Both practices, argues ʿAbd al-Jabbār, are impossible without accepting *taṣwīb.*[140] He adds that Companions [who held leading political positions] appointed individuals, whom they disagreed with, as judges and allowed them to pass judgments according to their own *ijtihād.*[141] This shows, for ʿAbd al-Jabbār, that the Companions tolerated jurisprudential disagreements. He takes such reports as a sign that the Companions unanimously tolerated legal plurality. For him, this unanimous tolerance functions as a consensus (*ijmāʿ*) in favour of *taṣwīb.*

ʿAbd al-Jabbār's second argument for *taṣwīb* depends on the Muʿtazilī understanding of divine justice, especially on its derivative doctrine that precludes the possibility of God imposing unattaina-

---

[138] ʿAbd al-Jabbār, *Mughnī,* 17:364.

[139] *Raʾy* is often used to describe the conclusion a jurist reaches after a process of *ijtihād* that is not entirely based on textual evidence (sg. *naṣṣ*) but more on speculative and rational tools such as *qiyās* and juristic preference (*istiḥsān*). For more on *raʾy*, see *EI*[2], s.v. 'Raʾy' (Jeanette Wakin and A. Zysow); *EI*[3], s.v. 'Ahl al-raʾy' (Peter C. Hennigan).

[140] ʿAbd al-Jabbār, *Mughnī,* 17:365.

[141] ʿAbd al-Jabbār, *Mughnī,* 17;366. See an additional argument based on the practice of the Companions in the same page.

ble obligations. He argues that if truth were single (*law kān al-ḥaqq wāḥid*, i.e. if there were only one correct deontic qualification for every human action), there would have been conclusive evidence (sg. *dalīl*) identifying this truth. God will not oblige humans to reach a single truth without first providing sufficient evidence to guide humans to this particular truth. Such a requirement, in the absence of adequate evidence, would constitute an obligation impossible to fulfil.[142] For Muʿtazilīs, the theological repercussions of requiring impossible obligations are well known. As previously mentioned, if God were to impose such obligations, this would entail that He is unjust, not worthy of worship and His revelations are not a reliable source of knowledge. Implications that would repel not only Muʿtazilīs, but all Muslims.

ʿAbd al-Jabbār's argument is premised on the assumption that there exists no conclusive evidence revealing a single truth. Given that God is just and that He never imposes impossible obligations, the absence of conclusive evidence revealing a single truth must therefore indicate that this single truth does not exist in the first place. ʿAbd al-Jabbār assumes that if a single truth exists, God would have provided humans with suitable evidence guiding them to this universal truth. He then concludes that if a single truth does not exist, then no jurist can be described as erroneous. The nonexistence of a universal truth entails the nonexistence of a yardstick deciding which is correct and which is not. Put differently, the absence of truth also entails the absence of error.

One should note that this is not a question of tolerating disagreement and plurality; this is simply a belief that in the absence of a single truth, all knowledge produced, according to the previously mentioned four conditions, must be correct. If a single truth should exist, then disagreement will not be tolerated. ʿAbd al-Jabbār explicitly refuses the opinion of those *mukhaṭṭiʾa* who say that despite the presence of evidence, mistaken jurists are exonerated.[143] He insists that the presence of evidence excludes the possibility of pardoning mistaken jurists. He notes that jurists who fall in error are culpable (sg. *āthim*), will face divine punishment, and if

---

142 ʿAbd al-Jabbār, *Mughnī*, 17:366–8.

143 ʿAbd al-Jabbār, *Mughnī*, 17:371–2. See also 17:374–5.

their error is serious they might be considered profligates or even infidels.[144] This position entails that, for ʿAbd al-Jabbār, error is equivalent to sin; error definitely leads to punishment. Therefore, God always provides conclusive evidence revealing the single truth, if this truth existed. In the absence of such evidence, in the absence of a single truth, no jurist deserves blame and punishment and no jurist should be described as erroneous.

Low Appreciation of Inconclusive Evidence

The previous section surveyed ʿAbd al-Jabbār's argument in support of *taṣwīb* as it appears in a chapter dedicated to this purpose. However, there are few other statements that occur in another chapter that are not only crucial for understanding his above argument but also crucial for recognizing his motives for adopting *taṣwīb*. ʿAbd al-Jabbār begins a chapter titled 'Identifying issues in law in which the truth is single and issues in which all jurists are correct',[145] noting that

> the determining factor here is the method [of knowledge]; truth is single in [issues] known via certain knowledge (*ʿilm*) and supported by conclusive evidence (*dalīl*). All other issues would be known only via prevalent probability (*ghālib al-ẓann*); in such issues all jurists are correct… The same applies to the rational disciplines (*ʿaqliyyāt*). This is because obligation (*taklīf*) does not differ in issues supported by conclusive evidence and known via certain knowledge, whereas obligation differs in what is known via probable knowledge [i.e. supported by inconclusive evidence], in such issues all opinions are correct. This also applies to law (*sharʿiyyāt*).[146]

ʿAbd al-Jabbār's concluding remark is a key statement here. Unfortunately, he does not plainly inform his readers why probable knowledge and inconclusive evidence, in law and theology, produces different obligations (i.e. deontic qualifications) whereas conclusive evidence produces the same obligation. Understanding this last

---

144 ʿAbd al-Jabbār, *Mughnī*, 17:368–9, 374.

145 ʿAbd al-Jabbār, *Mughnī*, 17:362–3.

146 ʿAbd al-Jabbār, *Mughnī*, 17:362.

statement is the gateway for understanding ʿAbd al-Jabbār's epistemology. To better understand and appreciate this last comment, one must turn to similar statements in the literature of other authors who adopt *taṣwīb*.

I found some help in a statement by Abū Ḥāmid al-Ghazālī in his *Mustaṣfā*. Ghazālī, who accepts *taṣwīb*,[147] notes that describing inconclusive evidence (*al-adilla al-ẓanniyya*) as evidence (*adilla*, sg. *dalīl*) is only an allegorical description. Actually, he notes, they are not evidence at all. This is caused by the fact that they are not true or essential evidence (*adillā fī-anfusihā*); they are rather contingent evidence (*adilla iḍāfiyya*). They do not essentially (*fī-nafsihā*) signify any particular signification. Their signification is rather contingent upon the state of the jurist examining them. Different jurists investigating the same inconclusive evidence might, quite possibly, reach different conclusions. Ghazālī continues saying that each jurist interprets this type of evidence influenced by his own temperament, background, experience and profession. In other words, inconclusive evidence yields different significations for different jurists; each according to his own disposition. He even notes that the same jurist who examines the same inconclusive evidence, but in two different situations, might reach two different conclusions. In sum, inconclusive evidence in itself includes no one particular signification; it is incapable of uniformly conveying a single message to all humans.[148]

---

[147] Ghazālī, *Mustaṣfā*, 4:53–8.

[148] Ghazālī, *Mustaṣfā*, 4:53–6. Part of Ghazālī's passage is translated in Schwarb, 'Capturing the Meanings of God's Speech', 146. Also see Zysow's discussion of Bāqillānī's version of *taṣwīb* in his *Economy of Certainty*, 269– 71. Zysow's discussion and Schwarb's translation of this statement were helpful in finding the appropriate English terms for expressing Ghazālī's and ʿAbd al-Jabbār's ideas in English. For other similar statements in works by authors adopting *taṣwīb*, see Shihāb al-Dīn Abū al-ʿAbbās Aḥmad b. Idrīs al-Qarāfī, *Sharḥ Tanqīḥ al-Fuṣūl fī ikhtiṣār al-Maḥṣūl fī uṣūl al-fiqh*, ed. Maktab al-Buḥūth wa-l-Dirāsāt fī Dār al-Fikr (Beirut: Dār al-Fikr, 1424/2004), 345; Qarāfī, *Nafā'is al-uṣūl*, 3886; Ṭufī, *Sharḥ Mukhtaṣar al-Rawḍa*, 614–5. These pre-modern sources were also helpful in deciphering ʿAbd al-Jabbār's unclear statement.

Ghazālī here is arguing that there is no fixed relationship between inconclusive evidence and the knowledge produced after examining it. The knowledge a jurist deduces from this type of evidence is a product of his own disposition and context rather than a product of an inherent meaning within this particular type of evidence. Nothing guarantees that inconclusive evidence will produce the same connotation each time it is examined. Therefore, in the absence of conclusive evidence, requiring humans to uncover a single truth is an obligation impossible to fulfil.[149] Ghazālī's key claims here are: first, inconclusive evidence cannot contain any one specific and determined signification, thus it is not fit for conveying a universal truth and a standard message to all addressees. Second, a jurist imposes his own interpretation on this type of evidence; therefore, inconclusive evidence cannot enforce a particular interpretation or meaning on any addressee.

Now, we can go back to ʿAbd al-Jabbār's statement. As mentioned above, he notes that conclusive evidence and certain knowledge produce one obligation, i.e. one deontic qualification. This is because conclusive evidence is capable of conveying the same connotation to all jurists. This connotation is the only correct interpretation; all jurists are required to adopt it. Ghazālī's statement explains why ʿAbd al-Jabbār notes that probable knowledge and inconclusive evidence yield multiple obligations. Inconclusive evidence is incapable of conveying the same signification to all humans. Therefore, different jurists deduce different deontic qualifications and obligations from the same piece of inconclusive evidence. If there were one universal truth, God would not have used inconclusive evidence to communicate this truth to humans.

It is very important to note that for ʿAbd al-Jabbār God's choice to communicate most of His laws through inconclusive evidence is not an accident. Commenting on God's use of equivocal speech to communicate with humans, ʿAbd al-Jabbār notes that as long as God does not make available to humans the evidence informing them of the only correct interpretation of His equivocal speech, this means that He intends all the possible interpretations of this speech. God deliberately chooses to express Himself in pol-

---

[149] Ghazālī, *Mustaṣfā*, 4:53.

yvalent words; ones that are capable of communicating the multiple meanings He intends. If His intention were to communicate a single meaning, He would either use unequivocal speech or provide evidence showing the only correct connotation of His equivocal speech. The absence of this evidence entails that all equivocal parts of revelation must be seen as purposely designed to yield multiple significations. All these multiple significations are intended by God; thus, all of them are correct. The same applies to Prophetic traditions.[150] The key point here is that in all issues covered by inconclusive evidence, God does not have a single truth to communicate. For ʿAbd al-Jabbār, there are numerous truths. Those truths are as many as all the possible interpretations God's multifaceted speech can convey.[151]

---

[150] ʿAbd al-Jabbār, *Mughnī*, 17:83–5. ʿAbd al-Jabbār notes that one does not have to pronounce two different statements to communicate two different messages. Sometimes only one statement is sufficient, see his *Mughnī*, 17:84.

[151] Of course, not all interpretations are valid. Muʿtazilīs often argue that Qurʾānic verses and Prophetic traditions should always be interpreted in harmony with 'reason'. By reason they are mainly referring to the Muʿtazilī principles of divine unity and justice (*al-tawḥīd wa-l-ʿadl*). They believe that both doctrines are established by rational arguments rather than ones based on revelation. For Muʿtazilīs, any correct process of rational speculation will always guide humans to accept both principles. Moreover, Muʿtazilīs consider both tenets to be indispensable for preserving the justice, wisdom and divinity of God. If any of these tenets are undermined, God's divinity will be undermined as well. He will not deserve to be worshiped and His revelation will lose credibility. Therefore, they assume that any interpretation of revelation that contradicts their understanding of divine unity and justice to be wrong. For example, any understanding of a Qurʾānic verse or Prophetic tradition that would result in imposing an impossible obligation must be excluded. For more details, see for example ʿAbd al-Jabbār, *Mughnī*, 12:166, 16:395, 17:93, 315; Abū al-Ḥusayn, *Muʿtamad*, 179–81, 371, 405, 886–8, 908, 931.

An Epistemological Debate

Shīrāzī's and Samʿānī's argument in support of *takhṭiʾa* mainly depends upon their high appreciation of inconclusive evidence. ʿAbd al-Jabbār's argument in support of *taṣwīb* primarily rests upon his low appreciation of the same type of evidence. What both arguments have in common is an obvious concern with epistemology more than doctrinal and creedal aspects of speculative theology. Each jurist is trying to prove his legal theory doctrine by referring, above all, to his epistemology. For Shīrāzī inconclusive evidence is true evidence; it is capable of conveying a uniform signification to all humans. For Samʿānī, extra evidence assists inconclusive evidence to reveal a standard signification to all addressees. Both agree that conclusive evidence is not the only path to discern God's legislative intent; inconclusive ones are adequate for realizing this task. Jurists who successfully interpret this evidence and uncover God's predetermined law are correct; those who fail are in error. There is only one truth; inconclusive evidence is sufficient to disclose this truth to the jurist who does the effort examining and searching for it.

ʿAbd al-Jabbār adopts a totally different epistemology; inconclusive evidence cannot convey a single signification to all addressees. It is contingent evidence; its connotation is contingent upon the interpretation of each single jurist. Furthermore, God does not have a single legislative intent; He accepts multiple deontic qualifications for the same action. This is exactly why He deliberately chose to communicate His message through inconclusive evidence, being the type of evidence that is capable of yielding multiple meanings. When He wills to communicate a single truth, He uses conclusive evidence. Therefore, the absence of such evidence should always be a sign for the absence of a single and a universal legal truth that God intends.[152]

---

[152] David Vishanoff argues that ʿAbd al-Jabbār sees revelation as a perfect tool capable of clearly disclosing the divine message, see his *Islamic Hermeneutics*, 122–51. My conclusions here should not necessarily be in contradiction with Vishanoff's remarks. Vishanoff is aware that for ʿAbd al-Jabbār equivocal speech has multiple meanings and all of these meanings are indeed intended by God, see for instance pp. 119, 125, 138. I

Other than their references to epistemology, Shīrāzī's and Samʿānī's arguments for *takhṭiʾa* include almost no other references to speculative theology. None of them depends on particular doctrinal tenets to justify his adoption of *takhṭiʾa.* The absence of such theological references might entail that their adoption of *takhṭiʾa* is not greatly informed by their creed and dogma. Their continuous references to epistemology indicate that their epistemology is the single most important aspect of theology that shaped their stance on the *taṣwīb-takhṭiʾa* debate. ʿAbd al-Jabbār's argument for *taṣwīb* is different. Epistemology is certainly his major concern and it clearly influenced his position on the debate under study. However, he also depends on doctrinal tenets such as divine justice (and especially on its derivative doctrine that excludes the possibility of God requiring an impossible obligation) to justify his adoption of *taṣwīb.* This might entail that his Muʿtazilī background, especially his understanding of divine justice, encouraged him to adopt *taṣwīb.* The remaining part of this chapter examines the influence of two theological doctrines on the *taṣwīb-takhṭiʾa* debate, trying to understand how far, if at all, they influence a jurist's position on this legal theory controversy.

THEOLOGY AND THE MULTIPLICITY OF TRUTH

As noted previously, Zysow contends that optimism is the foundation of the Muʿtazilī version of *taṣwīb* whereas excluding the possibility of God requiring unachievable obligations is the basis of the Ashʿarī variant of the same doctrine. Moreover, David Vishanoff argues that ʿAbd al-Jabbār's Muʿtazilī theology heavily influenced

---

have mentioned that, for ʿAbd al-Jabbār, in many cases, God wills to communicate multiple meanings by the same text. Therefore, He deliberately chooses an equivocal mode of speech. This equivocal speech is the best vehicle capable of signifying a multifaceted message. Since God's choice of using equivocal speech is deliberate, and since He actually intends delivering multiple messages by the same text, therefore the equivocal nature of revelation should not be seen as an aspect of ambiguity. It is rather the clearest and most suitable method capable of successfully delivering the polyvalent message intended by God.

his hermeneutics.[153] Vishanoff identifies divine justice,[154] optimism,[155] incorporeity,[156] and the uncreated nature of the Qurʾān[157] to be among the Muʿtazilī doctrines that shaped ʿAbd al-Jabbār's hermeneutics and epistemology. An examination of the impact of all these theological controversies on the *taṣwīb-takhṭiʾa* debate would require huge space and cause frequent repetitions. Therefore, I have chosen to focus on the two theological doctrines that appear, more often than others, in the pre-modern treatments of the *taṣwīb-takhṭiʾa* discussion, namely the possibility of God requiring an impossible obligation and optimism. The first sub-section focuses on the former, the second on the latter. The primary aim here is to explore in what way, if at all, these doctrines inform a jurist's position on the *taṣwīb-takhṭiʾa* debate. To realize this aim, we will take a step backward and examine the literature not only of the four Shāfiʿīs, who are the focus of the current study, but also examine the writings of other major jurists on the subject. This should allow a better appreciation of the impact of both doctrines on the *taṣwīb-takhṭiʾa* controversy and situate the writings of the four Shāfiʿīs in a wider context.

Impossible Obligations

Among the controversial issues that might bring speculative theology and legal theory close is the debate around the possibility of God imposing an impossible obligation. There are two major categories for such obligations, first, the essentially impossible (*al-muḥāl li-dhātih*). This includes actions that are in themselves impossible to perform, such as simultaneously performing two contradictory actions or creating an already existing being. The second category is the impossible due to an external condition (*al-muḥāl li-ghayrih*). This includes actions that are not impossible in themselves but ones that God knows will never occur or ones that God has informed humans will not occur. The most oft-cited example of this type of

---

153 See for instance, Vishanoff, *Islamic Hermeneutics*, 120, 150.

154 Vishanoff, *Islamic Hermeneutics*, 139.

155 Vishanoff, *Islamic Hermeneutics*, 123.

156 Vishanoff, *Islamic Hermeneutics*, 142.

157 Vishanoff, *Islamic Hermeneutics*, 145–50.

impossible obligation is the case of the Prophet's uncle Abū Lahab who rejects Islam and violently opposes the message of his nephew. Accepting the message of Islam is not an unrealisable obligation in itself. However, Q 111:1–3 informs Muslims that Abū Lahab will suffer punishment in hellfire. For Muslims, this represents a divine prediction of the future; Abū Lahab will not repent and will die as a non-believer. Although Abū Lahab is, in theory, still required to accept Islam and will be punished if he does not, Muslims believe that God has informed them that Abū Lahab will never accept the Muslim message. Therefore, for many Muslims this is a case in which a human, namely Abū Lahab, is obliged to meet an obligation that he is destined not to fulfil. It is not an inherently impossible obligation, but one that became impossible after the Qur'ānic verses foretold the future of Abū Lahab.[158]

The debate over whether God does (or could) require (or has required) unfeasible obligations is entangled with other theological controversies, most importantly free will and predestination, but going into the details of these debates is beyond the scope of this study. It is enough to know here that most Muʿtazilīs hold that God will not (or cannot) impose an impossible obligation.[159] Most Ashʿarīs and traditionalists, on the other hand, do not exclude this possibility. A few Ashʿarīs, like the jurist Ibn al-ʿArabī (d. 543/1148), Āmidī (d. 631/1233) and Ibn Rashīq (d. 632/1234) reject the possibility of God imposing an essentially impossible obligation.[160] A notable Ashʿarī exception is Ghazālī, who rules out the

---

[158] For more information on both types of impossible obligations, see Juwaynī, *Irshād*, 226–8; Āmidī, *Iḥkām*, 179–85.

[159] Some pre-modern authors note that Baghdādī-Muʿtazilīs exclude the possibility of God imposing an obligation that is essentially impossible, but they accept the possibility of God imposing an obligation that is impossible due to external conditions. See for instance Āmidī, *Iḥkām*, 1:180.

[160] Al-Ḥusayn b. Rashīq (d. 632/1243), *Lubāb al-maḥṣūl fī ʿilm al-uṣūl*, 2 vols ed. Muḥammad Ghazālī ʿUmar Jābī (Dubai: Dār al-Buḥūth li-l-Dirāsāt al-Islāmiyya wa-Iḥyāʾ al-Turāth, 1422/2001), 250–2; Abū Bakr [Muḥammad b. ʿAbd Allāh] b. al-ʿArabī (d. 543/1148), *al-Maḥṣūl fī uṣūl al-*

possibility of God imposing an unattainable obligation of any kind.[161]

The impossibility of God requiring unachievable obligations often appears in arguments in support of *taṣwīb*. As mentioned above, it is an important part of ʿAbd al-Jabbār's justification of *taṣwīb*. Although less patently, other Muʿtazilīs also utilize the same doctrine in support of *taṣwīb*. Abū al-Ḥusayn al-Baṣrī, Jaṣṣāṣ and Imām Abū Yaḥyā al-Nāṭiq bi-l-Ḥaqq all note that the absence of conclusive evidence covering particular aspects of law indicates that God did not predetermine one correct deontic qualification for these aspects. If humans were required to follow one particular deontic qualification, God would have provided them with conclusive evidence revealing this qualification.[162] In his vindication of *taṣwīb*, the Ashʿarī-Shāfiʿī Ghazālī mentions an identical argument.[163] Interestingly, although the famous Ḥanbalī Najm al-Dīn al-Ṭūfī (d. 716/1316) does not exclude the possibility of God imposing an impossible obligation,[164] he mentions an argument identical to that of ʿAbd al-Jabbār in support of his adoption of *taṣwīb*.[165] The frequent appearances of this doctrine in arguments promoting *taṣwīb*, in the literature of jurists from different theologi-

---

fiqh, ed. Ḥusayn ʿAlī al-Yadarī and Saʿīd ʿAbd al-Laṭīf Fūda (Amman: Dār al-Bayāriq, 1420/1999), 25; Āmidī, *Iḥkām*, 1:180–2.

161 Ghazālī, *Mustaṣfā*, 1:290–9. This is only a brief description of the Ashʿarī and traditionalist stance that certainly lacks nuance. For a concise survey of this debate, see ʿAbd al-Qādir, *al-Masāʾil al-mushtaraka*, 137–46. For pre-modern discussions of this controversy, see for instance Juwaynī, *Irshād*, 226–8; Bāqillānī, *Tamhīd*, 293–5; Abū Yaʿlā, *al-ʿUdda fī uṣūl al-fiqh*, 392. A similar position is to be found among many Māturīdīs, see for instance Bazdawī, *Uṣūl al-dīn*, 128; Nasafī, *Tamhīd*, 263–7.

162 Abū al-Ḥusayn, *Muʿtamad*, 972–3; Abū al-Ḥusayn [pseudo], *Sharḥ al-ʿUmad*, 2:266–9; Jaṣṣāṣ, *Fuṣūl*, 4:302–3, 312.

163 Ghazālī, *Mustaṣfā*, 4:43–4, 53, 56, 111.

164 Sulaymān b. ʿAbd al-Qawī al-Ṭūfī, *al-Bulbul fī uṣūl al-fiqh* (Riyadh: Maktabat al-Imām al-Shāfiʿī, 1410/[1990]), 15–6; Ṭūfī, *Sharḥ Mukhtaṣar al-Rawḍa*, 1:224–41.

165 Ṭūfī, *Sharḥ Mukhtaṣar al-Rawḍa*, 615.

cal backgrounds, might imply that it encourages scholars to side with this legal theory position.

However, jurists who adopt *takhṭiʾa* do not favour this legal theory position despite the constitution of an impossible obligation. They often attempt to rebut their opponents' claim that *takhṭiʾa* leads to the imposition of an unattainable obligation. The Ẓāhirī Ibn Ḥazm (d. 456/1064), for example, argues that uncovering the correct deontic qualification is not an unfeasible task; many have managed to discern the truth, and there is no reason to believe that more people will not continue to do so in the future.[166] The Ashʿarī-Mālikī Ibn Rashīq, the Shāfiʿī Samʿānī and the traditionalist-Ḥanbalīs Ibn Qudāma (d. 620/1223) and Ibn al-Najjār (d. 972/1565) all write that since mistaken jurists are exonerated for reaching the wrong deontic qualification, there is no place for the *muṣawwiba*'s claim that *takhṭiʾa* entails requiring an impossible obligation.[167] The *mukhaṭṭiʾa*, therefore, do not adopt *takhṭiʾa* because they accept the possibility of God requiring an impossible obligation. They rather present arguments showing that their position does not bring about an unachievable duty.

Furthermore, the Ḥanbalī jurist Abū al-Khaṭṭāb al-Kalwadhānī (d. 510/1116) adopts *takhṭiʾa* and does not exclude the possibility of God imposing an impossible obligation.[168] Nonetheless, he argues that we know that there is only one truth, consequently it is impossible that God would require humans to reach this single truth without first assigning evidence revealing it. Therefore, we must assume that there exists evidence allowing humans to

---

[166] Ibn Ḥazm, *Iḥkām*, 5:79.

[167] Muḥammad b. Aḥmad b. ʿAbd al-ʿAzīz al-Fatūḥī known as Ibn al-Najjār (d. 972/1565), *Sharḥ al-Kawkab al-munīr*, 4 vols ed. Muḥammad al-Zuḥaylī and Nazīh Ḥammād (Riyadh: Maktabat al-ʿUbaykān, 1413/1993), 4:490, 492; ʿAbd Allāh b. Aḥmad b. Qudāma (d. 620/1223), *Rawḍat al-nāẓir wa-jannat al-munāẓir*, ed. Maḥmūd Muḥammad ʿUthmān (Riyadh: Dār al-Zāḥim, 1425/2005), 394; Samʿānī, *Qawāṭiʿ*, 5:47; Ibn Rashīq, *Lubāb al-maḥṣūl*, 716.

[168] Kalwadhānī, *Tamhīd*, 1:263–9. Here he only excludes the possibility of God imposing an essentially impossible obligation but not an obligation that is impossible due to an external condition.

discern the only truth.[169] Kalwadhānī turns ʿAbd al-Jabbār's argument around and uses it to support *takhṭiʾa*. He starts first by assuming that there is a single truth. He then argues that since God does not require impossible obligations, therefore we know that there must be evidence revealing this truth for humans. What is surprising here is that although Kalwadhānī does not exclude the possibility of God imposing unachievable obligations, he does not refrain from using this doctrine to justify his adoption of *takhṭiʾa*.

It is also important to note that among the ranks of the *muṣawwiba* there are jurists who accept and others who preclude the possibility of God obligating a duty that is unattainable. Among those who rule out this possibility are many of the Baṣrian-Muʿtazilīs in addition to the Ashʿarī scholar Ghazālī.[170] Whereas the Ashʿarīs Bāqillānī, Shihāb al-Dīn al-Qarāfī (d. 684/1285), Ibn al-ʿArabī in addition to the Ḥanbalī Najm al-Dīn al-Ṭūfī adopt *taṣwīb* and hold that God can impose impossible obligations.[171] Numerous other Ashʿarī and traditionalist scholars espouse *takhṭiʾa* while also sharing the same theological position.[172] Ghazālī's posi-

---

[169] Kalwadhānī, *Tamhīd*, 4:338.

[170] The position of Ghazālī's teacher, Juwaynī, is not entirely consistent. In his *Irshād* he accepts the possibility of God imposing an impossible obligation (see his *Irshād*, 226–8). In his *Burhān* he excludes this possibility, see *Burhān*, 104–5. Yet we know that in *Burhān* he adopts *takhṭiʾa*.

[171] For their acceptance of this theological doctrine, see Bāqillānī, *Tamhīd*, 293–5; Ibn al-ʿArabī, *Maḥṣūl*, 25; Qarāfī, *Sharḥ Tanqīḥ al-Fuṣūl*, 115–6. For their adoption of *taṣwīb*, see Qarāfī, *Nafāʾis al-uṣūl*, 3876–908 (especially 3876, 3883), Ibn al-ʿArabī, *Maḥṣūl*, 152–3. Bāqillānī's extant legal theory book (*Taqrīb*) does not include a section on this debate. However, pre-modern sources are unanimous that he adopts *taṣwīb*, see for example Bājī, *Iḥkām al-fuṣūl*, 714; Juwaynī [pseudo], *Talkhīṣ*, 3:340–1; Juwaynī, *Burhān*, 1319; Ghazālī, *Mustaṣfā*, 4:48–9; Abū Yaʿlā, *ʿUdda*, 1550.

[172] See for instance, Rāzī, *Maḥṣūl*, 6:29–64; al-Khaṭīb al-Baghdādī, *Kitāb al-Faqīh*, 2:114–27; Āmidī, *Iḥkām*, 4:215–42; Ibn Qudāma, *Rawḍat al-nāẓir*, 381; Bāji, *Iḥkām al-fuṣūl*, 713–27; Ibn al-Qaṣṣār, *Muqaddima fī uṣūl al-fiqh*, 268–72; Abū Yaʿlā, *ʿUdda*, 1540–78; Ibn ʿAqīl, *Wāḍiḥ*, 5:351–91; Kalwadhānī, *Tamhīd*, 4:317–66. In addition of course to Shīrāzī, Juwaynī and Samʿānī.

tion is particularly interesting. In his earlier book *Mankhūl*, he excludes the possibility of God requiring an unfeasible obligation. At the same time, he accepts a version of *takhṭiʾa* that is identical to that of his teacher Juwaynī. Later in his career, Ghazālī wrote his legal theory *magnum opus Mustaṣfā*. In this work, he still insists that imposing impossible obligations are unacceptable. Yet, he changes his legal theory position and adopts a version of *taṣwīb* identical to that of ʿAbd al-Jabbār. The fact that he changed his legal theory position without altering his theological stance shows that for him a position on this theological question has no direct impact on his decision to adopt *taṣwīb* or *takhṭiʾa*.[173]

What we notice here is that there are *muṣawwiba* and *mukhaṭṭiʾa* on both sides of this theological debate. Accepting and rejecting the possibility of God imposing an impossible obligation is used both to support *takhṭiʾa* and *taṣwīb*. Therefore, there is not enough evidence that one position on this theological controversy consistently encourages jurists to adopt either *taṣwīb* or *takhṭiʾa*. This is because jurists disagree on the legal theory consequences of this theological debate. Some jurists consider excluding the possibility of God imposing impossible obligations as a precursor for *taṣwīb*. Others see it as a precursor to *takhṭiʾa*. While other jurists, probably like Ghazālī, see no connection between this theological debate and the legal controversy over the multiplicity of the truth. Therefore, we see him changing his position on the *taṣwīb-takhṭiʾa* debate without changing his position that precludes the idea of God imposing unattainable duties. Excluding impossible obligations does not appear, then, as the doctrine that unites the *muṣawwiba*. It does not appear to be part of the common conceptual framework that allows jurists from different theological backgrounds to adopt *taṣwīb*. However, each individual jurist probably believes that his position on the multiplicity of the truth to be in harmony with (or a product of) his position on impossible obligations. Yet, since jurists disagree on the legal ramifications of the impossible obligations debate,

---

[173] For Ghazālī's rejection of the possibility of God imposing an impossible obligation, see his *Mankhūl*, 22–8; *Mustaṣfā*, 1:288–99. For his acceptance of *takhṭiʾa* and rejection of *taṣwīb*, see *Mankhūl*, 451–61. For his acceptance of *taṣwīb* and rejection of *takhṭiʾa*, see his *Mustaṣfā*, 4:30–111.

a position on this debate has no uniform impact on group and school level. Sharing the same position on this debate does not guarantee sharing the same position on the *taṣwīb-takhṭiʾa* question.

Optimism

As previously explained, optimism is a Muʿtazilī doctrine. It promotes that God will (or must) always guarantee human optimal benefit in this life and the one to come. Ashʿarīs and traditionalists consider this Muʿtazilī tenet a restriction on the absolute omnipotence of God. For them God's actions cannot be regulated or determined by any factor other than His own will. Therefore, they often refuse to accept any doctrine that requires God to act in a predetermined manner. For them, nothing can guarantee that divine actions will consistently aim at realizing optimal human benefit.

Optimism often appears in Muʿtazilī arguments in support of *taṣwīb*. For example, Ṣaymarī, Jaṣṣāṣ, Abū al-Ḥusayn al-Baṣrī and Imām Abū Yaḥyā al-Nāṭiq bi-l-Ḥaqq all argue that revelation aims at realizing the optimal benefit of humans. Different humans have diverse interests in different times and different contexts. Therefore, it is only natural to have diverse, but equally correct, deontic qualifications each designed to realize the optimal benefit of each individual in a particular context. An action beneficial for ʿAmr is permitted, but in a different context the same action might be harmful for Zayd, thus it must be proscribed.[174] ʿAbd al-Jabbār's argument for *taṣwīb* appears also to be influenced by the Muʿtazilī doctrines of optimism and benevolence (*luṭf*). The latter requires God to always facilitate salvation to humans; this obviously demands the clarification of revelation. Moreover, an ambiguous revelation can hardly be more beneficial to humans than a clear one. Therefore, the absence of conclusive evidence should not be seen as a sign of ambiguity, but rather a deliberate choice on the part of God. He purposely abandons conclusive evidence to use inconclu-

---

[174] Jaṣṣāṣ, *Fuṣūl*, 4:358; Abū al-Ḥusayn, *Muʿtamad*, 961, 962–3, 968–9; Abū al-Ḥusayn [pseudo], *Sharḥ al-ʿUmad*, 2:241–3; Ṣaymarī, *Masāʾil al-khilāf*, 309.

sive ones that are more capable of delivering the multiple meanings that He wants to communicate to humans. ʿAbd al-Jabbār makes no explicit reference to benevolence or optimism. However, the impact of both doctrines can be noticed between the lines of his argument.

On the other hand, there are *mukhaṭṭiʾa* who, despite their rejection of this doctrine, are keen to show that an adoption of optimism should lead to *takhṭiʾa* rather than *taṣwīb*. The Ashʿarī scholar Fakhr al-Dīn al-Rāzī (d. 606/1209) argues that optimism should require God to explicitly reveal the correct deontic qualification that would realize human optimal benefit, rather than leave humans unguided.[175] Abū al-Khaṭṭāb al-Kalwadhānī writes that *taṣwīb* entails that all deontic qualifications are correct, including harmful ones and others that fall short of realizing optimal benefit. The only correct deontic qualification must be the one which realizes optimal human benefit; all the rest are wrong.[176] Finally, Shihāb al-Dīn al-Qarāfī quotes Shaykh ʿIzz al-Dīn saying that *taṣwīb* contradicts optimism.[177] We find here jurists using optimism this time to establish *takhṭiʾa* and disprove *taṣwīb*. Pre-modern jurists, therefore, are not unanimous on the legal theory consequences of optimism; some hold that it leads to an adoption of *taṣwīb* whereas others maintain that it leads to the adoption of *takhṭiʾa*.

What might confirm this conclusion is that the *muṣawwiba* themselves are split over optimism. Baṣrian-Muʿtazilīs who accept *taṣwīb*, as mentioned above, adopt optimism. Ashʿarīs on the other hand reject optimism, yet some of them adopt *taṣwīb*, such as Ghazālī, Bāqillānī, Ibn al-ʿArabī and Qarāfī. The Ḥanbalī jurist Ṭūfī adopts *taṣwīb* while sharing the same Ashʿarī contempt for optimism.[178] Those scholars must have considered their rejection of optimism not a logical impediment for adopting *taṣwīb*, whereas

---

[175] Rāzī, *Maḥṣūl*, 6:59.

[176] Kalwadhānī, *Tamhīd*, 4:344.

[177] Qarāfī, *Nafāʾis al-uṣūl*, 3901. Qarāfī here is probably referring to his famous Shāfiʿī teacher ʿIzz al-Dīn b. ʿAbd al-Salām (d. 660/1262), nicknamed Sulṭān al-ʿUlamāʾ.

[178] For Ṭūfī's rejection of optimism, see his *Sharḥ Mukhtaṣar al-Rawḍa*, 1:409–10.

Muʿtazilīs probably consider *taṣwīb* a logical product for their belief in optimism. Again jurists are in disagreement over the legal theory implications of accepting or rejecting optimism. Optimism is utilized as an argument for and against *taṣwīb*. The adoption of *taṣwīb* is neither monopolized by those who refuse nor by those who accept optimism. Knowing a jurist's position on this theological doctrine does not help predicting his position on the *taṣwīb-takhṭiʾa* debate.

The Māturīdī-Ḥanafī Fakhr al-Islām al-Bazdawī (d. 484/1089) notes that Muʿtazilīs adopt the multiplicity of truths as a result of their belief in the doctrine of optimism.[179] Commenting on this statement, ʿAlāʾ al-Dīn al-Bukhārī (d. 730/1330) notes that since, for Muʿtazilīs, guaranteeing human optimal benefit is a duty on God, therefore all jurists must be correct. It is conclusively better for a jurist to be correct and receive full reward than risk committing an error. Bukhārī then concludes that *taṣwīb* must be a product of the Muʿtazilī espousal of optimism. Nonetheless, he notes that *taṣwīb* does not necessarily entail an adoption of optimism; many Sunnīs (*ahl al-sunna*) embrace *taṣwīb* without accepting optimism. Therefore, he adds that those Muʿtazilīs who take on *taṣwīb* base their decision on optimism, whereas those Sunnīs who favour *taṣwīb* base their decision on precluding the possibility of God requiring an unachievable duty.[180] As explained before, Zysow argues that early Central Asian Ḥanafīs saw that *taṣwīb* is premised on accepting the 'deviant' Muʿtazilī doctrine of optimism. Based on Bukhārī's above statement, Zysow argues that later Central Asian Ḥanafīs decoupled optimism and *taṣwīb*. The later was 'de-Muʿtazilized'; it was dissociated from the Muʿtazilī doctrine of optimism and thus became a legitimate legal theory position.[181] This further shows that the theological implications of legal theory debates change through time. I have argued above that even contem-

---

[179] Bazdawī, *Uṣūl al-Bazdawī*, 4:43.

[180] ʿAlāʾ al-Dīn b. ʿAbd al-ʿAzīz b. Aḥmad al-Bukhārī (d. 730/1330), *Kashf al-asrār ʿan uṣūl Fakhr al-Islām al-Bazdawī*, 4 vols ed. ʿAbd Allāh Maḥmūd Muḥammad ʿUmar (Beirut: Dār al-Kutub al-ʿIlmiyya, 1418/1997), 4:43–4.

[181] Zysow, 'Muʿtazilism and Māturīdism', 239–47.

poraneous jurists disagree on the theological implications of *taṣwīb* and its relationship to theological doctrines such as optimism and the validity of impossible obligations; such disagreement makes it difficult for theology to have a consistent impact on the legal theory of scholars belonging to the same theological trend.

Based on Bukhārī's opinion, mentioned in the above paragraph, Zysow argues elsewhere that

> [t]he fundamental theological difference between the Muʿtazilite and the Ashʿarite versions is that Muʿtazilite infallibilism [i.e. *taṣwīb*] is built around the doctrine of optimism, while for Ashʿarism infallibilism rests on the theological principle that God will not impose what is impossible.[182]

Like many other modern scholars of Islam, Zysow often argues that theology is a major catalyst shaping a jurist's position on different questions of legal theory. It is a major argument for the current and previous chapters that different jurists from different theological backgrounds often utilize different – sometimes even contradicting – theological arguments to justify the same legal theory opinion. On the other hand, it is common to see different jurists using the same theological doctrine to justify contradicting positions in legal theory. This might imply that a jurist's theological background determines which theological doctrines he uses to support a particular position in legal theory; more than his theological background deciding which legal theory position he should favour.

The two doctrines that most often appear in pre-modern treatments of this debate are optimism and the possibility of God requiring an impossible obligation. Both doctrines are used to prove and disprove both positions from the debate. We even find that scholars who refuse these doctrines utilize them in support of the legal theory position of their choice (e.g. Kalwadhānī and Ṭūfī). This information may lead to one of two, or maybe both, conclusions. First, as mentioned before, jurists are not unanimous on the legal theory implications of the same theological doctrine. Therefore, we often find the same theological doctrine used to justify and

[182] Zysow, *Economy of Certainty*, 269.

refute the same legal theory position. Second, this information may also imply that some jurists do not strictly shape their legal theory in response to their theological background; they do not contemplate about the legal consequences of their dogma, then form a legal theory that is a reflection of it. Some jurists adopt the legal theory common among their legal school and then seek theological justifications for their theories. In such cases, the impact of theology on the arguments a jurist uses to justify his legal theory is more profound than its impact on his decision which legal theory position to adopt.

CONCLUSION

The *taṣwīb-takhṭiʾa* debate and the questions raised during any discussion of it, provide indispensable foundational knowledge for any profound understanding of Muslim legal history and culture(s). This chapter focuses on one aspect of this debate, namely the impact of a jurist's theological background on determining his stance regarding *taṣwīb* and *takhṭiʾa*. The point of departure for studying the impact of theology on this legal theory controversy is the literature of four Shāfiʿī jurists who belong to three different theological schools. The Muʿtazilī ʿAbd al-Jabbār's version of *taṣwīb* is almost identical to that of the Ashʿarīs Bāqillānī and Ghazālī. Shīrāzī espouses a rigid, but not the most rigid, form of *takhṭiʾa*. Juwaynī rightly describes himself as adopting a middle position between *takhṭiʾa* and *taṣwīb*. Samʿānī's version of *takhṭiʾa* occupies a place between Shīrāzī's rigid version and Juwaynī's more lenient one.

At the beginning of this chapter, I have explained that speculative theology is a huge discipline that addresses many different sub-topics. Among the major concerns of speculative theology is what I describe as the doctrinal aspect of theology. This aspect is mainly concerned with divine attributes and actions; topics that are often associated with *ʿilm al-tawḥid* or *ʿaqīda*. Another important sub-topic within speculative theology is epistemology (*al-ʿulūm wa-l-maʿārif*). This aspect of speculative theology is mainly concerned with the theory of knowledge; a concern that is certainly relevant to legal theory. This chapter tries to evaluate the impact of speculative theology on the *taṣwīb-takhṭiʾa* debate and identify which aspects of theology influence this important legal theory controversy and in what way.

It appears that jurists disagree on the aspects of speculative theology that are relevant to this legal theory debate. For example, Shīrāzī's, Samʿānī's and Juwaynī's arguments supporting *takhṭiʾa* are almost free from doctrinal and creedal references. They do not explicitly depend on any particular theological doctrine as a justification for their acceptance of *takhṭiʾa.* This might indicate that they see no direct connection between their doctrinal aspects of speculative theology and their choice to adopt *takhṭiʾa.* On the other hand, ʿAbd al-Jabbār's argument for *taṣwīb* depends on his Muʿtazilī understanding of divine justice, especially on a derivative doctrine that excludes the possibility of God requiring an impossible obligation. This might indicate that both theological doctrines are among ʿAbd al-Jabbār's motives for adopting *taṣwīb.*

The inclusion of doctrinal discussions in this aspect of legal theory is not an exclusive Muʿtazilī phenomenon. The two theological debates that often appear in discussions of *taṣwīb* and *takhṭiʾa* are the ones around optimism and the possibility of God requiring an impossible obligation. Among the non-Muʿtazilī jurists who raise both theological doctrines in their treatment of this legal theory question are: Ibn Ḥazm, Bazdawī, Kalwadhānī, Ibn Rashīq, Razī and Qarāfī, to mention only a few. We also find Muʿtazilīs who raised both theological topics in their discussion of *taṣwīb* and *takhṭiʾa,* such as Ṣaymarī, Abū al-Ḥusayn al-Baṣrī, in addition to ʿAbd al-Jabbār. For these jurists both theological doctrines must be among the most relevant doctrines to their position on *taṣwīb* and *takhṭiʾa.* They consider both doctrines as factors that shape or determine their position on this debate. These jurists utilize both doctrines to justify their legal theory choices and prove that they are in harmony with their creed.

However, it is important to note that jurists occasionally disagree on the legal theory implications of the same theological doctrine. Therefore, theology does not always have a consistent impact on the legal theory of jurists sharing the same theological beliefs. This can be noticed in the debate around the multiplicity of the truth. We often find the same theological doctrine used, by different jurists, to justify both *taṣwīb* and *takhṭiʾa.* We also find jurists from different theological trends justifying their adoption of *taṣwīb* using contradicting theological doctrines. This also applies to *takhṭiʾa.* As explained before, optimism and the impossibility of God requiring an unachievable obligation are used to argue for and against *taṣwīb* and *takhṭiʾa*. For some jurists, optimism leads to favouring *taṣwīb*, whereas for others it leads to embracing *takhṭiʾa*. Each jurist believes that his own legal position is the natural outcome of his theology. The decision of each individual jurist to adopt either *taṣwīb* or *takhṭiʾa* is, in many cases, informed by his theological doctrines. However, disagreements over the legal theory implications of the same theological doctrine limit the ability of theology to have a consistent impact on the legal theory of jurists belonging to the same theological trend. Since jurists disagree on the legal entailments of their common theology, theology often does not have a standardizing effect on their legal theory. Therefore, jurists from the same theological background do not necessary share the same position on the *taṣwīb-takhṭiʾa* debate, despite the impact of theology on the position of individual jurists. The influence of theological doctrines at a group level appears inconsistent and seems less obvious than its influence on individual scholars.

The use of contradicting theological arguments to support the same legal theory opinion may also imply that such arguments are formed in retrospect. As explained before, we often find jurists with a common position on optimism and the possibility of God requiring unattainable obligations using the same doctrine to argue, at times, for *taṣwīb* and, at others, for *takhṭiʾa*. This is also true about *takhṭiʾa*. This may give the impression that they are arguments formed retrospectively to an already made legal choice more than theoretical motives motivating a jurist to adopt one or the other legal stance. Jurists decide on their legal theory positions and then seek theological justifications for their choices. An Ashʿarī who adopts *taṣwīb* would utilize his dogma to justify his choice. A Muʿtazilī who adopts the same legal theory position will probably use the exact opposite theological doctrines to justify the same legal theory position. In this case, theological doctrines would be factors that shape a jurist's arguments supporting his legal theory positions more than factors determining those positions. It is also crucial to know that a jurist's legal orientation may shape or influence his understanding of the legal consequences of his theology. For example, a Shāfiʿī jurist may interpret the legal implications of his theology in manner that would confirm his Shāfiʿī legal theory. Each jurist may tend to favour the interpretation that would suit the legal theory positions common among his legal school.

Rather than the doctrinal aspects of speculative theology, it appears that epistemology is the single aspect of speculative theology with the most profound and most consistent impact on a jurist's stance on the *taṣwīb-takhṭiʾa* debate, both on individual and group level. A jurist's position on the goal of *ijtihād*, role of probability in legislation and epistemological value of inconclusive evidence consistently determine whether he adopts *takhṭiʾa* or *taṣwīb*. Jurists who adopt *takhṭiʾa* tend to elevate the epistemological value of inconclusive evidence. This type of evidence, for many *mukhaṭṭiʾa*, can reveal a standard signification to all addressees. The *muṣawwiba*, on the other hand, tend to undermine the epistemological significance of inconclusive evidence. They often hold that such evidence is incapable of conveying a single universal message; it always yields multiple significations. *Muṣawwiba*, moreover, usually allow probability a greater role in legislation; probability in itself can be a goal for *ijtihād*. The *mukhaṭṭiʾa* tend to limit the role of probability as a goal for *ijtihād*. Probability, for many, is seen as unfit for being the jurist's goal. A jurist's aim is to uncover the divinely determined deontic qualification for the action in question. Yet, if certain knowledge of this deontic qualification is unachievable, a jurist must settle with probable knowledge of it. Knowledge of jurist's position on these epistemological questions can usually help predict his position on the *taṣwīb-takhṭiʾa* debate, whereas knowledge of a jurist's theological background does not usually reveal much about his position on this legal controversy.

The main difference, therefore, between the *mukhaṭṭiʾa* and the *muṣawwiba* is a set of epistemological rather than doctrinal differences. The Ashʿarī theologian and Shāfiʿī jurist Ghazālī writes that

> the origin of this error [i.e. *takhṭiʾa*] is that the *fuqahāʾ* [a reference to traditionalist jurists] give more weight to inconclusive evidence; they believe they are true evidence rather than contingent ones, and this is sheer error.[183]

On the other hand, the traditionalist Shāfiʿī jurist Samʿānī, who is certainly among the *fuqahāʾ* Ghazālī is criticizing, remarks that

---

183 Ghazālī, *Mustaṣfā*, 4:56.

> I have pondered and found that most who embrace *taṣwīb* are the speculative theologians (*mutakallimūn*). Those [are scholars] who have no enough knowledge in law (*fiqh*) and the laws of *sharīʿa*. They fail to acquire the honour of this discipline and fail to understand the methods of the Qur'ān and the Sunna.

Few lines later he concludes that

> they [i.e. speculative theologians] approach law with feeble and confused minds... They say that a *mujtahid* is only obliged to reach probable knowledge, one that he reaches via inconclusive evidence. [For them] a *mujtahid* can never be obliged anything beyond that [i.e. probability]. They believe that there exists no single truth that can be searched for. They also say that a *mujtahid* is only obliged to act upon the probable knowledge produced via inconclusive evidence rather than conclusive ones. They [even] note that in law there exists no conclusive evidence in the first place.[184]

The above quotations reveal two important aspects in the *taṣwīb-takhṭi'a* debate. First, Ghazālī's criticism of *takhṭi'a* is addressed to the *fuqahā'*; a term that can be a reference to any jurist. However, quite often, it is used as a reference to traditionalist jurists, ones who stay aloof from speculative theology and are critical of its speculative methods. On the other hand, Samʿānī notes that most who adopt *taṣwīb* are speculative theologians. Other pre-modern scholars make similar comments. Such comments become more important when they are made by, relatively, late scholars who had a wonderful birds-eye view of earlier legal theory literature. For example, Jamāl al-Din al-Asnawī (d. 772/1370) notes that most Ashʿarīs and Muʿtazilīs adopt *taṣwīb*. Qarāfī and Shawkānī (d. 1255/1839) say that most theologians are *muṣawwiba*.[185] A number

---

184 Samʿānī, *Qawāṭiʿ*, 5:53–4.

185 Asnawī, *Nihāyat al-sūl*, 4:560; Qarāfī, *Sharḥ Tanqīḥ al-Fuṣūl*, 344; Shawkānī, *Irshād*, 1074. On the other hand, the famous Ḥanbalī jurist Taqī al-Dīn b. Taymiyya notes that most Ashʿarīs adopt *takhṭi'a*, see Taqī al-Dīn Abū al-ʿAbbās Aḥmad b. ʿAbd al-Ḥalīm b. Taymiyya (d. 728/1328) and others, *al-Muswwada fī uṣūl al-fiqh*, collected by Aḥmad b. Muḥammad

of modern scholars seem convinced by these comments. Zuḥaylī notes that Ashʿarīs and Muʿtazilīs accept *taṣwīb*.[186] Zysow and Schwarb note that most speculative theologians adopt one or the other version of *taṣwīb*.[187]

Zysow is not surprised by the popularity of *taṣwīb* among theologians. He notes that this may be explained by the fact that *taṣwīb* denigrates law and elevates speculative theology, Sufism, and legal theory. For the *muṣawwiba*, truth is single only in theology, whereas in law the rule is the multiplicity of truths. *Takhṭiʾa*, on the other hand, makes no distinction between speculative theology and law; there is only one truth in both disciplines. Therefore, theologians incline towards the position that enhances the prestige of their major discipline.[188] Zysow's explanation is based on self-interest; theologians prefer *taṣwīb* because it elevates the status of their discipline. However, this justification does not provide a conceptual or a philosophical explanation for the popularity of *taṣwīb* among theologians and *takhṭiʾa* among the *fuqahāʾ*. It does not explain what exactly it is in the intellectual formation of speculative theologians and traditionalist jurists that motivates them to favour a particular position on the multiplicity of truth.

I could not, admittedly, find an explanation better than Zysow's. However, there is one suggestion that I might – quite hesitantly – put forward. Muslim theologians do not share a common epistemology; neither do traditionalist jurists. However, traditionalist jurists are usually reputed with an epistemology that elevates the value of inconclusive evidence. They, in many cases, refuse to draw a sharp and clear distinction between inconclusive and

---

b. Aḥmad b. ʿAbd al-Ghanī al-Harrānī (d. 745/1344), ed. Muḥammad Muḥyī al-Dīn ʿAbd al-Ḥamīd (Cairo: Maṭbaʿat al-Madanī, n.d.), 497. However, Ibn Taymiyya's opinion is uncommon among the examined pre-modern sources.

[186] Zuḥaylī, *Uṣūl al-fiqh*, 1099.

[187] Schwarb, 'Capturing the Meanings of God's Speech', 149; Zysow, *Economy of Certainty*, 275–6. The latter writes that most theologians of the classical period adopt *taṣwīb*, which might indicate that this is not necessarily true in later periods.

[188] Zysow, *Economy of Certainty*, 275–6.

conclusive knowledge and evidence. Speculative theologians, on the other hand, undermine the epistemological value of inconclusive evidence. They award inconclusive evidence a (relatively) narrow role in establishing knowledge when compared to traditionalists. Theologians often draw clearer distinctions between inconclusive and conclusive knowledge and evidence. They usually adopt a clear hierarchy of evidence where conclusive evidence is obviously placed above inconclusive ones.[189] The epistemology of the theologians is often more refined and sophisticated than the epistemology common among many –though certainly not all – traditionalist jurists. Theologians' frequent involvement in debates with non-Muslims and Muslims from other theological schools encourages them to create an epistemology better designed to withstand philosophical criticisms from non-Muslim as well as Muslim scholars of all disciplines.

The reason behind the popularity of *taṣwīb* among theologians cannot be common theological doctrines; in fact, they were vehemently arguing about the correct dogma. What brings theologians together then is a similar epistemology that makes them, more than traditionalists, receptive of *taṣwīb.* Given their low appreciation of inconclusive evidence, and given that most jurisprudential (*fiqhī*) issues are covered by this type of evidence, uncovering a single truth seems to be a difficult task. The same might be attributed to traditionalist jurists. The reason for the popularity of *takhṭiʾa* among their ranks is their epistemology. Their high appreciation of inconclusive evidence makes the absence of conclusive evidence an unconcerning fact. For them, inconclusive evidence is capable of disclosing the universal truth for those jurists who sincerely exhaust all efforts investigating this type of evidence. The *taṣwīb-takhṭiʾa*

---

[189] For a brief comparison between the epistemology common among the speculative theologians and that of the traditionalist jurists, see ʿAbd al-Karīm, *al-Tajdīd wa-l-mujaddidūn*, 135–8; ʿAbd al-Qādir, *al-Masāʾil al-mushtaraka*, 23–35. Both authors are modern traditionalist jurists who present the opinions of the theologians to refute them and establish those of the traditionalists. However, their accounts are sufficient as a brief introduction to the debate.

debate, therefore, is primarily a debate concerned more with different epistemological outlooks than different theological ones.

The second important feature of the *taṣwīb-takhṭiʾa* debate that Ghazālī's and Samʿānī's quotes reveal might confirm my above explanation. Both quotations imply that the major points of contention between the *mukhaṭṭiʾa* and the *muṣawwiba* are epistemological differences rather than anything else. Ghazālī singles out the disagreement over the epistemological value of inconclusive evidence as the major cause of this disagreement. The origin of *takhṭiʾa* is the traditionalist jurists' insistence that inconclusive evidence is true and essential evidence. In other words, the foundation of their position is their belief that inconclusive evidence is capable of yielding a uniform signification to all addressees. Samʿānī, on the other hand, notes that theologians adopt *taṣwīb* because they hold that jurists are not required to reach anything beyond probable knowledge, jurists are required to act upon whatever inconclusive knowledge they reach and most importantly because they deny the existence of conclusive evidence covering most aspects of law. Both Ghazālī and Samʿānī cite epistemological disagreements as causes for the disagreement between the *mukhaṭṭiʾa* and the *muṣawwiba*. Both describe epistemological beliefs as the basis of both positions. None of them mention doctrinal controversies as among the foundations of this legal theory controversy.

This debate, therefore, is mainly an epistemological debate between two groups of scholars with different epistemological outlooks. It is common to find scholars from different theological backgrounds sharing the same position on the *taṣwīb-takhṭiʾa* debate. Common theological doctrines can never be the theoretical framework that brings the *muṣawwiba* or the *mukhaṭṭiʾa* together. What seems capable of bringing both groups together, despite their considerable theological disagreements, is their similar (certainly not identical) epistemology. Epistemological aspects of theology, more than doctrinal ones, have a consistent impact on a jurists' position on the multiplicity of the truth. The common factor among the majority of the scholars who adopt *taṣwīb* is a similar epistemology, one that undermines the epistemological value of inconclusive evidence. Whereas the common factor among jurists who adopt *takhṭiʾa* is a similar (again certainly not identical) epistemological outlook, one that elevates the epistemological value of inconclusive evidence.

It is therefore not surprising to find sections on *taṣwīb* and *takhṭi'a*, in pre-modern legal theory literature, mainly dominated by epistemological discussions without giving doctrinal concerns equal attention. All this shows that the single aspect of speculative theology with the most fundamental and consistent impact on the *taṣwīb-takhṭi'a* debate is epistemology. Creedal and doctrinal aspects of theology inform the legal theory choices of individual jurists and shape their supporting arguments. Disagreements over the legal theory implications of doctrines prevent theological doctrines from having a consistent impact on the *taṣwīb-takhṭi'a* debate at a group level. Epistemology, on the other hand, manages to have a more uniform impact both at an individual and at a group level. Jurists often interpret the legal theory implications of their common epistemology in a similar fashion. Therefore, jurists with a similar epistemological outlook often share the same position on the multiplicity of the truth. A jurist's answer to the question how many truth(s) exist, is largely determined by his epistemology more than his doctrinal theology.

CONCLUSION

This study has focused on four Shāfiʿī jurists who follow three different theological traditions. It is primarily a comparison of their positions on three aspects of legal theory, namely the use of *rationes legis* and *qiyās* in law-making, the deontic qualification of human actions before the advent of revelation and the plurality of truth. We have been mainly concerned with examining the nature of the relationship between their theology and their legal theory and exploring the impact of their theological doctrines on the formation of their views in legal theory. This study is also, most importantly, an analysis of the arguments the four jurists use to support their legal theory positions and refute that of their opponents. The arguments a jurist offers to support his legal theory choices have many functions, including their role as explanations for why he adopts particular legal theory stands and not others. Analysing those arguments, therefore, is important for recognizing to what extent a jurist's theology informs and shapes his choices in legal theory. Should a jurist's argument refer to theological doctrines as a justification for embracing a particular legal theory position, this indicates that the doctrines he mentions are among the motives for favouring this particular legal theory stand. Furthermore, theological justifications mentioned in legal theory literature are often arguments directed towards jurists who share the author's theological background but adopt different stances in legal theory. Jurists use these theological justifications to prove that their own legal theory choices are the logical outcome of their theology and demonstrate the harmony between their dogma and their legal theory.

The four Shāfiʿī jurists' *uṣūl al-fiqh* writings examined for this study show that they often utilize theological arguments to support their legal theory views. The theological debates that are most often used for this purpose are those around the definition of divine wisdom and justice, moral theory, divine omnipotence, optimism and the purposefulness of divine actions. Throughout this study, I have highlighted cases where a jurist's position on these theological doctrines informs, if not determines, his legal theory choices. I have also mentioned cases in which disagreements on these doctrines, among the four Shāfiʿīs who are studied here, lead to discrepancies in their legal theory.

For example, in the chapter on *qiyās*, I explained that the Muʿtazilī jurist ʿAbd al-Jabbār allows benefit (*maṣlaḥa*) and human reason an almost unlimited role in discovering the *rationes legis* behind deontic qualifications mentioned in the Qurʾān or Prophetic Sunna. To justify his position, he refers to the Muʿtazilī principles of optimism and rational ethics. He argues that God only imposes laws that guarantee human optimal benefit; therefore, the benefit that a divine law brings must also be its *rationes legis*. He adds that human reason is capable of distinguishing between harmless (thus good) and harmful (therefore evil) acts. He concludes that humans can rely on this knowledge to uncover the *ratio legis* of the laws mentioned in the normative texts of Islam and the benefits they bestow on humans. Juwaynī and Samʿānī refuse the Muʿtazilī concept of optimism; for them, God is not obliged to guarantee optimal human benefit. Furthermore, their theology undermines the ability of unaided human reason to ascertain moral knowledge. They use these theological doctrines to prove that only benefits mentioned in revelation, and not ones known via unaided reason, can function as indicators for the correct *rationes legis*. Each jurist supports his legal theory stand by reference to his theological doctrines. This shows that their legal theory choice in this context is motivated, at least partially, by their theology. Furthermore, citing contradicting theological doctrines to support contradicting positions in legal theory may entail that this legal theory disagreement is a product of theological divergences between those jurists.

Another similar situation is their position on the before revelation debate. For ʿAbd al-Jabbār, all harmless actions are permitted even before the advent (or in the absence) of divine revelation. He supports his position by noting that human reason has an innate capacity to discern moral and deontic knowledge without any external assistance. Furthermore, his understanding of divine justice and wisdom entails that God always permits harmless actions and prohibits harmful ones. This allows humans to predict divine laws, even before receiving any divine message. On the other hand,

Shīrāzī, Juwaynī and Samʿānī hold that humans should suspend all deontic qualifications, until they receive revelation. They offer their moral theory as evidence for this legal theory position. All three argue that human reason cannot attain moral and deontic knowledge, without guidance from revelation. Therefore, before revelation humans have no access to this type of knowledge. Furthermore, their understanding of divine omnipotence renders divine laws unpredictable prior to revelation. Unlike Muʿtazilīs, they insist that nothing obliges God to permit harmless actions and prohibit harmful ones. Only revelation ensures humans that God abides by these principles. Therefore, prior to revelation, humans are, mostly, not in a position to recognize which actions God permits and which ones He prohibits.

Discussions of the debate around the plurality of truth also include references to speculative theology. ʿAbd al-Jabbār, for example, uses his Muʿtazilī theology to defend the plurality of truth in law. One of his supporting arguments depends on the Muʿtazilī concept of divine justice, especially a derivative doctrine that excludes the possibility of God imposing impossible obligations. Most Muslim jurists agree that conclusive evidence (*adilla qaṭʿiyya*) is rare in the area of law. ʿAbd al-Jabbār argues that if truth were single, God would have assigned enough conclusive evidence capable of unequivocally revealing the single truth to humans; anything otherwise would render discovering this single truth an obligation impossible to fulfil. Since, for Muʿtazilīs, God does not require unachievable obligations, the absence of conclusive evidence in law rules out the singularity of truth. In law, multiple and even contradicting opinions for the same case may all be equally correct.

These are some of the examples we have discussed for cases in which a jurist uses his theological doctrines as evidence supporting his legal theory choices. The appearance of such arguments indicates that in these and similar cases a jurist's theology informs and helps to shape his legal theory stances. Jurists make choices in legal theory that are sensitive to their theology. They adopt the legal theory stands they believe to be in harmony with their creed; or at least avoid ones that appear, to them, in contradiction with their theological beliefs. Jurists who use theological justifications for legal theory positions see theology as requiring the adoption of particular stands in legal theory. For such jurists, theology is among the factors that shape and inform legal theory. However, it is important to note that the impact of speculative theology on legal theory is far from uniform and consistent. This is mainly due to the fact that jurists, even those who are members of the same theological tradition, often disagree on the legal theory entailments of their theological doctrines. Therefore, jurists sharing the same theological outlook do not necessarily favour similar positions in legal theory.

For example, ʿAbd al-Jabbār uses optimism and rational moral theory to argue that benefit and human reason should be widely used to deduce *rationes legis* in processes of *qiyās*. His Muʿtazilī student Abū al-Ḥusayn al-Baṣrī (in addition to the earlier Ḥanafī authority Jaṣṣāṣ), refers to the same Muʿtazilī doctrines to argue for restricting the use of benefit and human reason in deducing *rationes legis*. Both ʿAbd al-Jabbār and Abū al-Ḥusayn are contemporary Muʿtazilīs; they accept optimism and share a similar moral theory. However, they have contradicting interpretations for the legal theory consequences of their common theological doctrines.

A similar phenomenon is evident in the before revelation debate. ʿAbd al-Jabbār uses his rational moral theory and his Muʿtazilī perception of divine wisdom and justice to justify his adoption of permission. The Ashʿarīs Juwaynī and Shīrāzī and the traditionalist Samʿānī support their adoption of suspension by showing the inability of the human mind to ascertain moral and deontic knowledge without the aid of revelation. If we only focus on this sample of scholars, we may gain the impression that positions in this debate are divided along theological lines. Jurists who embrace an Ashʿarī or a traditionalist theology and undermine the ability of human reason to ascertain moral knowledge favour suspension. Whereas Muʿtazilī jurists who embrace a rationalist moral theory adopt permission. However, if we take a step backward and look at a larger sample of jurists and more schools of theology, as explained in chapter four, we see that theological schools are often split over this aspect of legal theory. Baghdādī-Muʿtazilīs use their rational moral theory and their understanding of divine justice and wisdom to establish proscription; Baṣrian-Muʿtazilīs, like ʿAbd al-Jabbār, use the same doctrines to argue for permission. The Ashʿarī School is similarly diverse. The same doctrines used by Juwaynī and Shīrāzī to argue for suspension are used by other Ashʿarīs to vindicate permission or proscription. As noted by Kevin Reinhart, all three answers to the before revelation question can be found in all theological and legal schools. It is common to find followers of the same theological tradition embracing different answers to the before revelation question. It is also common to find jurists from diverse theological backgrounds sharing the same position on the before revelation question.

The same applies to the debate around the plurality of truth. ʿAbd al-Jabbār's argument for the plurality of the truth draws heavily on his Muʿtazilī theology. He refers mainly to the Muʿtazilī concept of divine justice, especially to two derivative doctrines, namely optimism and the impossibility of God requiring unattainable obligations. His argument entails that the adoption of both theological doctrines must lead to embracing the plurality of truth. Yet, we also find that other Muʿtazilī scholars use the same theological doctrines to argue for the singularity of truth in law. This shows that Muʿtazilīs disagree on the legal theory requirements of their common doctrines. Each group favours the legal theory positions it believes to be the logical reflection of its theology. The situation among Ashʿarīs is not very different. Ashʿarī scholars reject the Muʿtazilī understanding of divine justice. For many of them, reason does not exclude the possibility of God imposing an impossible obligation nor does it guarantee that God's laws maintain human optimal benefit. A group of Ashʿarī scholars holds that their theology entails the adoption of the singularity of truth whereas others argue that the same theology requires favouring the plurality of truth. What we notice here is that jurists who share the same theology do not agree on the legal theory implications of their common dogmas. We occasionally find jurists from the same theological school adopting contradicting positions on the legal theory entailments of their shared theology.

It is also worth noting that embracing contradicting theological doctrines do not necessarily trigger disagreements in legal theory. For example, the Ẓāhirī School is known for its rejection of the Sunnī concept of *qiyās*. As explained previously, Aron Zysow notes that Ẓāhirīs are split over the valid ethical theory. A group favours a rational ethical theory; another group restricts the capacity of human reason to discern ethical knowledge and depends mainly on revelation as a source for this type of assessments. Zysow explains that Ẓāhirīs who favour a rational ethical theory use this theory as evidence against the authority of *qiyās*; Ẓāhirīs who embrace a less rational moral theory use their theory to argue for the same stand on *qiyās*. Here we find jurists followers of the same legal trend using two contradicting theological positions to justify the same Ẓāhirī legal stand.[1] Each group of jurists probably holds that their own theology is the more reliable foundation for their stand in legal theory. Another similar example from Shīʿī Islam, Twelver legal theory is often characterized by rejecting the authority of *qiyās*. The Akhbārī legal school, a Twelver Shīʿī sub-school, is divided over the validity of Ṣūfī and mystical knowledge. However, Akhbārīs, like many Shīʿīs, refuse *qiyās*. Robert Gleave shows that anti-Ṣūfī Akhbārī jurists only use traditions attributed to the Shīʿī Imāms to argue against the authority of *qiyās*. Those Akhbārīs, who accept Ṣūfism, use philosophical and mystical arguments never used by anti-Ṣūfī Akhbārīs, to reject *qiyās*.[2] Each group of jurists refutes legal theory in a manner that is in harmony with its theology. This reveals a number of points. First, this further shows that theological disagreements do not always lead to discrepancies in legal theory. Second, jurists within the same legal trend occasionally have different theological foundations for their common positions in legal theory. Finally, a jurist's theology has a strong impact on determining the argument he uses to justify his legal theory.

Pre-modern jurists often use theological doctrines and arguments as justifications and explanations for their choices in legal theory. They use them as evidence establishing the validity of their legal theory positions. This reveals that theology is among the factors informing the legal theory choices of such jurists. A jurist's theology may prompt him to favour certain positions in legal theory and avoid others. However, as explained earlier, jurists who belong to the same theological tradition, often use the same theological doctrine to argue for two contradicting positions in legal theory. This proves that they disagree on the legal theory implications of their common theology. For one jurist a doctrine leads to adopting a particular legal theory position; for another jurist the same doc-

---

[1] Zysow, *Economy of Certainty*, 182.

[2] Robert Gleave, 'Scriptural Sufism and Scriptural Anti-Sufism: Theology and Mysticism amongst the Shīʿī Akhbāriyya', in *Sufism and Theology*, ed. Ayman Shihadeh (Edinburgh: Edinburgh University Press, 2007), 170–2.

trine may produce a contradicting outcome in legal theory. These disagreements hinder theology from having a consistent and uniform impact on group and theological school level. Jurists who share the same theological doctrines may adopt opposing positions in legal theory. Each jurist believes that his legal theory is the logical outcome of his creed. Therefore, theology does not have a standardizing effect in legal theory; sharing a common theology does not necessarily lead to adopting a common legal theory. At the same time, theological disagreements do not always cause discrepancies in legal theory nor do they regularly prevent jurists from membership in the same school of law.

There might be an additional explanation for the inconsistent impact of speculative theology on legal theory. The use of contradicting theological doctrines to justify the same legal theory position may also imply that some jurists do not strictly shape their legal theory in response to their theological beliefs; they do not contemplate about the legal consequences of their dogma, and then form a legal theory that is a reflection of it. Some jurists adopt the legal theory common within their legal school and then, retrospectively, seek theological justifications for their theories. For example, an Ashʿarī who adopts the plurality of truth would utilize his dogma to justify his choice. A Muʿtazilī may use the exact opposite theological doctrines to defend the same position in legal theory. In such cases, theology would be informing and shaping arguments for already determined legal theory positions, rather than informing a jurist's decision which legal theory stand to adopt. These efforts do not have to be seen as disingenuous attempts to theologically justify whatever legal theory position dominant within a jurist's school of law. They may also indicate that a jurist's legal orientation influences and shapes his understanding of the legal theory entailments of his own theology. A Shāfiʿī jurist, due to his Shāfiʿī education and upbringing, may be tempted, consciously or unconsciously, to interpret the legal implications of his theology in a manner that is compatible with (or would confirm) his Shāfiʿī legal theory.

In all cases, and regardless of the reasons, pre-modern Muslim jurists disagree on the legal theory implications of their theology. Furthermore, jurists who are members of the same school of law have different theological justifications for the same position in legal theory. These disagreements entail that there are no agreed upon theological foundations for Sunnī legal theories. Shāfiʿī legal theory, for instance, is supported and founded upon various theological doctrines. Ashʿarī-Shāfiʿī jurists ground their legal theory on their Ashʿarī theology, traditionalists base their Shāfiʿī legal theory on their doctrines, whereas Shāfiʿī-Mūʿtazilī scholars justify and support the validity of their Shāfiʿī legal theory using their distinct theology. The same can be noticed in the Ḥanafī and Mālikī schools of law; jurists use their different theological dogmas to support the legal theory of their choice. Therefore, we occasionally find contradicting theological doctrines used to support the same view in legal theory. This does not mean that Muslim jurists do not share any common theological foundations for their legal theory. The unanimously accepted theological foundations for Muslim (and not only Sunnī) legal theory are the basic Muslim doctrines accepted by most (if not all) Muslims. Those include, for instance, divine unity (*tawḥīd*), the veracity of revelation, the Prophethood of the Prophet Muḥammad, resurrection, reward and punishment in the afterlife, etc. These doctrines do not require the adoption of specific views in legal theory. However, they are the theological foundations required to establish the authority and the need for a Muslim legal theory in the first place.

Disagreements around the theological foundations of legal theory mean that none of the major legal theory stands that distinguish Sunnī legal theory (or individual schools of law) became associated with only one theological doctrine or a particular school of theology. For example, accepting the authority of *qiyās* and consensus are shibboleth of Sunnī legal theory. Members of Sunnī schools of law, regardless of their theological backgrounds accept these legal theory tools. Ashʿarī, Māturīdī and traditionalist jurists each use their own theology to vindicate the authority of both methods. It is not uncommon to find contradicting theological doctrines used to establish the authority of *qiyās* and consensus. Thus, accepting legal theory, consensus, or any other major legal theory method is not strictly associated with only one theological doctrine or trend. This entails that the adoption of Sunnī legal theory does not require adopting the teachings of any theological school. This is also true of individual Sunnī legal schools. Membership in the Shāfiʿī, Ḥanafī, or Mālikī School does not require membership in any particular theological trend. Nothing in the legal theory of these schools necessitates embracing specific theological doctrines, other than accepting the Muslim message, the authority of the

Qur'ān and the Prophetic Sunna. Therefore, doctrinal disagreements, within Islam, do not prevent jurists from joining the same school of law.

The four Shāfiʿī jurists studied here (and probably many others) seem keen to limit the legal theory discrepancies caused by their theological debates. However, it is not obvious to me whether this eagerness is a cause or an effect. It is not clear to me whether the presence of jurists from diverse theological backgrounds in the same legal school created the need to limit discrepancies in legal theory caused by theological disagreements, or whether the fact that theological disagreements do not produce discrepancies in legal theory allowed jurists from different theological trends to exist within the same school of law. This limitation is crucial to maintaining (or creating) a degree of conformity within Sunnī schools. Excluding the Ḥanbalī, the three other Sunnī legal schools contain jurists from various theological backgrounds. The Shāfiʿī School, for instance, includes Muʿtazilī, Ashʿarī and traditionalist jurists. Therefore, it is common to find significant theological disagreements among jurists who are members of the same legal school. The concept of a legal school assumes, and requires, some level of conformity among its members. Without some degree of uniformity, schools of law would split, disintegrate and there would be no need to have schools of law in the first place. If theological disagreements are going to cause significant discrepancies in legal theory, this may ruin the common theoretical foundations of every school of law. Therefore, either from the beginning of the formation of legal schools or in retrospect, there had to be a bridle limiting the impact of theology on legal theory. This bridle makes it possible for jurists from different theological backgrounds, within the same legal school, to hold similar legal methodology doctrines, regardless of theological disagreements.

Even beyond the legal school level, jurists who are members of Sunnī schools of law accept the legitimacy of each other's law and legal theory. Unlike in theology, disagreements in law and legal theory are highly tolerated. A traditionalist-Shāfiʿī jurist accepts the validity of the legal conclusions of a Muʿtazilī-Ḥanafī jurist, although they reject each other's theology. As explained in chapter two, Wael Hallaq argues that following the *miḥna* initiated by the Abbasid Caliph Ma'mūn (d. 218/833) and starting from the fourth/tenth century, a synthesis between rationalist and traditionalist trends in Islam was created. Rationalist jurists accept elements common among traditionalist jurists and traditionalist jurists accept elements from rationalist legal theory. This synthesis, argues Hallaq, created Sunnī legal theory as we know it in the fourth/tenth century and afterwards. This does not mean that Sunnī legal theory became monolithic; there still existed various trends within it, some of them are more rational or traditional than others. However, jurists following the Sunnī schools of law all accept the authority of the Qurʾān and the Sunna as normative sources and accept a group of non-textual and rational methods in law-making, such as *qiyās*. Legal theory became the discipline in which jurists from different theological and philosophical perspectives could co-exist and interact. This rationalist-traditionalist synthesis allows traditionalist jurists and speculative theologians, of all types, to accept the legitimacy of each other's legal teachings, regardless of their theological disagreements. It allows legal theory (and law) to be the discipline in which jurists from various theological and philosophical perspectives can co-exist and interact.

It is important to note that the compromise between speculative theologians and traditionalists was mainly limited to the field of legal theory and law. Speculative theologians maintained their highly speculative theology and traditionalists remained committed to their relatively scripturalist methods in theology. Despite their highly tolerant attitude in the legal disciplines, Muslim scholars remained, to a large extent, exclusivist in theology. The creation of a middle ground in legal theory, but not in theology, could not have been possible without limiting the legal theory disagreements produced by theological differences. This limitation allowed traditionalists and speculative theologians to accept each other's legal theory and adopt similar legal theory positions without presenting similar compromises in the field of theology. Common membership in a legal school and sharing common position in legal theory do not require sharing a common theology. Therefore, in legal theory, traditionalist jurists and speculative theologians manage to reach a middle position whereas in theology both remain at odds. Reaching a compromise in legal theory does not require also reaching a compromise in speculative theology.

The disciplines of speculative theology and legal theory are strongly intertwined. Pre-modern legal theory writings often include theological discussions. Jurists are also frequently keen to harmonize their positions in legal theory with their theological doctrines. They usually present theological justifications for their legal theory positions and adopt the legal theory stands they believe to be in harmony with their theology. Therefore, a jurist's theology informs and helps to shape his legal theory. However, as explained earlier, jurists disagree on the legal theory ramifications of their theological doctrines. These disagreements entail that theology influences the legal theory of individual jurists; however, on group level this influence is not consistent. Two jurists sharing the same theological beliefs may interpret the legal theory consequences of their common creed differently. Therefore, theology does not have a standardizing effect on legal theory; the adoption of a common theology will not necessarily lead to sharing a common legal theory. The absence of this standardizing effect prevents the creation of legal schools or legal theories that are attached to particular theological schools. No school of theology created its own legal theory that is founded upon its theology. Individual jurists made legal theory choices based on their own understanding of the legal theory entailments of their theology. However, disagreements around these entailments prevent members of the same theological school from creating a common legal theory based on a shared understanding of the legal theory requirements of their theology.

Now, I hope it is clear why it is possible – and common – to find jurists from varied theological backgrounds within the same school of law. Muʿtazilīs, traditionalists, Ṣūfīs, jurists with an interest in philosophy and those who refuse philosophy all can adopt one of the different forms of Sunnī legal theory and become members in one of the Sunnī schools of law. They share the same teachers, read the same legal literature and comfortably accept the legitimacy of each other's legal theory and law. Their vehement theological and philosophical debates do not prevent them from co-existing within the same legal school or from accepting the validity of their opponents' legal positions. The presence of various theological traditions within the same school does not mean that jurists were not interested in harmonizing their legal theory with their theology. Each jurist had his own theological justifications for adopting the legal theory of his choice. The legal theory of individual scholars is in harmony with their own understanding of the legal implications of their theology. However, disagreements over the legal theory entailments of theology make it unnecessary, or impossible, to harmonize the legal theory of a specific school of law with the doctrines of a specific theological trend.

My study has attempted to nuance our perception of the function of speculative theology in legal theory and better understand the relationship between both disciplines. For many jurists, legal theory has theological foundations. Pre-modern jurists in Islam are often keen to clarify the theological underpinnings of their legal theory and present theological justifications for their stands in legal theory. However, the same jurists disagree on the proper theological foundations of individual legal theory stands; they disagree on the legal theory entailments of their theology. Therefore, sharing a common theology does not necessarily lead to sharing similar positions in legal theory; sharing a common legal theory does not require sharing a common theology. It is not common to find a legal theory position that requires embracing a particular theological tradition; we rarely find a theological doctrine that consistently leads to the adoption of a specific position in legal theory. Although theology has an impact on the legal theory of individual jurists, on group level this impact is not consistent. Theology prompts different results in legal theory, even for jurists who are members of the same theological trend. Yes, theology often informs the legal theory of individual jurists, but no one particular theology shapes the legal theory of a school of law.

والله أعلم

SOURCES IN ARABIC

The authors and works by the same authors are listed in alphabetical order. This order does not take into consideration al-, Abū, and Ibn.

Al-ʿAdnī, Abū Muḥammad Ṣalāḥ b. Fattīnī Kantūsh. *Akhṭāʾ al-uṣūliyyīn fi-l-ʿaqīda*. Sanaa: Dār al-Āthār, 1427/2006.

Āl ʿAbd al-Laṭīf, Aḥmad b. ʿAbd al-Laṭīf b. ʿAbd Allāh. *Manhaj Imām al-Ḥaramayn fī dirāsat al-ʿaqīda*. Riyadh: Markaz al-Malik Fayṣal li-l-Buḥūth wa-l-Dirāsāt al-Islāmiyya, 1414/1993.

ʿAbd Allāh, Khālid ʿAbd al-Laṭīf Muḥammad Nūr. *Masāʾil uṣūl al-dīn al-mabḥūtha fī-uṣūl al-fiqh*. Medina: Islamic University, 1426/[2005].

Al-Āmidī, ʿAlī b. Muḥammad (d. 631/1233). *Al-Iḥkām fī uṣūl al-aḥkām*, 4 vols. Edited by ʿAbd al-Razzāq ʿAfīfī. Riyadh: Dār al-Ṣaymaʿī, 1424/2003.

Ibn ʿAqīl, Abū al-Wafāʾ ʿAlī (d. 513/1119). *Kitāb al-Funūn*. Edited by George Makdisi and Iḥsān ʿAbbās. Damascus: Majmaʿ al-Lugha al-ʿArabiyya, 1392/[1972].

———. *Al-Wāḍiḥ fī uṣūl al-fiqh*, 5 vols. Edited by ʿAbd Allāh b. ʿAbd al-Muḥsin al-Turkī. Beirut: Muʾassasat al-Risāla, 1420/1998.

Ibn al-ʿArabī, Abū Bakr [Muḥammad b. ʿAbd Allāh] (d. 543/1148). *Al-Maḥṣūl fī uṣūl al-fiqh*. Edited by Ḥusayn ʿAlī al-Yadarī and Saʿīd ʿAbd al-Laṭīf Fūda. Amman: Dār al-Bayāriq, 1420/1999.

Ibn ʿĀshūr, Muḥammad al-Ṭāhir. *Tafsīr al-taḥrīr wa-l-tanwīr*, 2 vols. Tunis: al-Dār al-Tūnisiyya li-l-Nashr, n.d.

Al-Asnawī, Jamāl al-Dīn ʿAbd al-Raḥīm b. al-Ḥasan (d. 772/1370). *Nihāyat al-sūl fī Sharḥ Minhāj al-uṣūl*, 4 vols. Beirut (?):ʿĀlam al-Kutub, 1982(?).

Ibn al-Athīr, ʿIzz al-Dīn Abū al-Ḥasan ʿAlī b. Abī al-Karam known as. *Al-Kāmil fi-l-tārīkh*, 13 vols. Edited by Carolus J. Tornberg. Beirut: Dār Ṣādir, 1966.

ʿAṭiyya, Jamāl al-Dīn. *Al-Tanẓīr al-fiqhī*. N.p: N.p., 1987.

Al-Badawī, Yūsuf Aḥmad. 'Al-Khaṣā'iṣ al-uṣūliyya li-madrasat al-mutakallimīn'. *Al-Majalla al-Urduniyya fi-l-dirāsāt al-Islāmiyya* 5.4 (2009): no page numbers.

Al-Baghawī, al-Ḥusayn b. Masʿūd (d. 516/1122). *Sharḥ al-Sunna*, 16 vols. Edited by Shuʿayb al-Arnāʾūṭ. Beirut: al-Maktab al-Islāmī, 1403/1403.

Al-Baghdādī, Abū Manṣūr ʿAbd al-Qāhir b. Ṭahir al-Tamīmī (d. 429/1037). *Kitāb Uṣūl al-dīn*. Istanbul: Dār al-Funūn al-Turkiyya, 1346/1928.

Al-Bājī, Abū al-Walīd Sulaymān b. Khalaf (d. 474/1081). *Iḥkām al-fuṣūl fī aḥkām al-uṣūl*. Edited by ʿAbd al-Majīd Turkī. Beirut: Dār al-Gharb al-Islāmī, 1995.

———. *al-Ishāra fī uṣūl al-fiqh*. 2nd ed. Edited by ʿĀdil ʿAbd al-Mawjūd and ʿAlī ʿAwaḍ. Riyadh: Maktabat Nizār Muṣṭafā al-Bāz, 1418/1997.

———. *Kitāb al-Ḥudūd fi-l-uṣūl*. Edited by Nazīh Ḥammād. Beirut: Muʾassasat al-Zaʿbī, 1392/1973.

Al-Bākistānī, Zakariyyā b. Ghulām Qādir. *Tawḍīḥ uṣūl al-fiqh ʿalā manhaj ahl al-ḥadīth*. Dammam: Dār Ibn al-Jawzī, 1428[/2007].

Balkā, Ilyās. *Al-Wujūd bayna al-sababiyya wa-l-niẓām*. Herndon, Virginia: al-Maʿhad al-ʿĀlamī li-l-Fikr al-Islāmī, 2009.

Al-Balkhī, Abū al-Qāsim ʿAbd Allāh al-Kaʿbī (d. 319/931). *Qabūl al-akhbār wa-maʿrifat al-rijāl*, 2 vols. Edited by Abū ʿAmr al-Ḥusaynī ʿAmr b. ʿAbd al-Raḥīm. Beirut: Dār al-Kutub al-ʿIlmiyya, 2000.

Baqā, Muḥammad Maẓhar. *Muʿjam al-uṣūliyyīn*. Mecca: Jāmiʿat Umm al-Qurā, 1414/[1993].

Al-Bāqillānī, Abū Bakr Muḥammad b. al-Ṭayyib (d. 403/1013). *Kitāb al-Tamhīd*. Edited by Richard McCarthy. Beirut: al-Maktaba al-Sharqiyya, 1957.

———. *al-Taqrīb wa-l-irshād al-ṣaghīr*, 3 vols. Edited by ʿAbd al-Ḥamīd ʿAlī Abū Zunayd. Beirut: Muʾassasat al-Risāla, 1418/1998.

Al-Bardīsī, Muḥammad Zakariyyā. *Uṣūl al-fiqh*. Cairo: Dār al-Thaqāfa li-l-Nashr wa-l-Tawzīʿ, n.d.

Ibn Barhān, Abū al-Fatḥ Aḥmad b. ʿAlī (d. 518/1124). *Al-Wuṣūl ilā al-ūṣūl*, 2 vols. Edited by ʿAbd al-Ḥamīd ʿAlī Abū Zunayd. Riyadh: Maktabat al-Maʿārif, 1403/1983.

Al-Bayḍāwī, ʿAbd Allāh b. ʿUmar (d. 685/1286?). *Minhāj al-wuṣūl ilā ʿilm al-uṣūl*. Edited by Muṣṭafā Shaykh Muṣṭafā. Damascus: Muʾassasat al-Risāla, 2006.

Al-Bazdawī, Abū al-Yusr Muḥammad (d. 493/1099). *Uṣūl al-dīn*. Edited Hans Peter Linss. Cairo: al-Maktaba al-Azhariyya li-l-Turāth, 1424/2003. (This is probably a reprint of the Cairo: Dār Iḥyāʾ al-Kutub al-ʿArabiyya, 1963 edition)

Al-Bazdawī, Fakhr al-Islam Abū al-Ḥasan ʿAlī b. Muḥammad b. al-Ḥusayn b. ʿAbd al-Karīm (d. 482/1089). *Uṣūl al-Bazdawī*. In ʿAlāʾ al-Dīn b. ʿAbd al-ʿAzīz b. Aḥmad al-Bukhārī (d. 730/1330). *Kashf al-asrār ʿan uṣūl Fakhr al-Islām al-Bazdawī*, 4vols. Edited by ʿAbd Allāh Maḥmūd Muḥammad ʿUmar. Beirut: Dār al-Kutub al-ʿIlmiyya, 1418/1997.

Al-Bukhārī, ʿAlāʾ al-Dīn b. ʿAbd al-ʿAzīz b. Aḥmad (d. 730/1330). *Kashf al-asrār ʿan uṣūl Fakhr al-Islām al-Bazdawī*, 4vols. Edited by ʿAbd Allāh Maḥmūd Muḥammad ʿUmar. Beirut: Dār al-Kutub al-ʿIlmiyya, 1418/1997.

Al-Burāk, ʿAbd al-Nāṣir b. Nāṣir and Yāsir b. Saʿd Badr al-ʿAskar. *Sharḥ al-qaṣīda al-dāliyya*. Riyadh: Dār Ibn al-Jawzī, 1430/2009.

Al-Dabūsī, Abū Zayd ʿUbayd Allāh b. ʿUmar ʿIsā (d. 430/1038–9). *Taqwīm al-adilla fī uṣūl al-fiqh*. Edited by Khalīl al-Mīs. Beirut: Dar al-Kutub al-ʿIlmiyya, 2007.

Al-Dawālībī, Muḥammad Maʿrūf. *Al-Madkhal ilā ʿilm uṣūl al-fiqh*. 5th ed. Beirut: Dār al-ʿIlm li-l-Malāyīn, 1385/1965.

Al-Dhahabī, Muḥammad b. Aḥmad b. ʿUthmān (d. 748/1348 or 753/1352–3). *Al-ʿIbar fī khabar man ghabar*, 5 vols. 2nd ed. Edited by Ṣalāḥ al-Dīn al-Munjid. Kuwait: Maṭbaʿat Ḥukumat al-Kuwayt, 1984.

———. *Siyar aʿlām al-nubalāʾ*, 23 vols. Edited by Shuʿayb al-Arnāʾūṭ and Muḥammad al-ʿIrqisūsī. Beirut: Muʾassasat al-Risala, 1413[/1992].

———. *Tarīkh al-Islām wa-wafayāt al-mashāhīr wa-l-aʿlām*, 52 vols. Edited by ʿUmar ʿAbd al-Salām Tadmurī. Beirut: Dār al-Kitāb al-ʿArabī, 1987/1407.

Al-Dīb, ʿAbd al-ʿAẓīm. *Fiqh Imām al-Ḥaramayn.* N.p,: N.p., 1405/1985.

Donmez, Ibrāhīm Kāfī. 'Makānat Imām al-Ḥaramayn fī uṣūl al-fiqh'. In *al-Dhikrā al-alfiyya li-Imām al-Ḥaramayn.* Edited by ʿAbd al-Aẓīm al-Dīb and Muḥammad Ṣāliḥ al-Shīb, 506–42. Doha: University of Qatar, 2000.

Dughaym, Samīḥ. *Falsafat al-qudur fī fikr al-Muʿtazila.* 2nd ed. Beirut: Dār al-Fikr al-Lubnānī, 1992.

———. *Mawsūʿat muṣṭalaḥāt al-Ashʿarī wa-l-Qāḍī ʿAbd al-Jabbār.* Beirut: Maktabat Lubnan, 2002.

Al-Ḍuwayḥī, ʿAlī b. Saʿd b. Ṣāliḥ. *Ārāʾ al-muʿtazila al-uṣūliyya.* Riyadh: Maktabat al-Rashīd, 1415/1995.

Al-Farābī, Abū Naṣr Muḥammad (d. 339/950). *Iḥṣāʾ al-ʿulūm.* 2nd ed. Edited by ʿUthmān Amīn. Egypt: Maṭbaʿat al-Iʿtimād, 1949.

Farghalī, Muḥammad Maḥmūd. *Buḥūth fi-l-qiyās* Alexandria: Dār al-Kitāb al-Jāmiʿī, 1981.

———. *Mujarrad maqalāt al-shaykh Abī al-Ḥasan al-Ashaʿrī.* Edited by Aḥmad ʿAbd al-Raḥīm al-Sāyaiḥ. Cairo: Maktabat al-Thaqāfa al-Dīniyya, 1425/2005.

Al-Ghazālī, Abū Ḥāmid Muḥammad b. Muḥammad (d. 505/1111). *Al-Mankhūl min taʿliqāt al-uṣūl.* Edited by Muḥammad Ḥasan Hītū. Beirut: Dār al-Fikr, 1970.

———. *Al-Munqidh min al-ḍalāl.* Edited by Saʿd Karīm al-Fiqī. Alexandria: Dār Ibn Khaldūn, n.d.

———. *Al-Mustaṣfā min ʿilm al-uṣūl.* Edited by Ḥamza b. Zuhayr Ḥāfiẓ. Medina (?): Sharikat al-Madīna al-Munawwara li-l-Ṭibāʿa (?), 1413/1992 (?).

———. *Shifāʾ al-ghalīl fī bayān al-shabah wa-l-mukhīl wa-masālik al-taʿlīl.* Edited by Ḥamad al-Kabīsī (?). Baghdad: Maṭbaʿat al-Irshād, 1390/1971.

Haniyya, Māzin. 'Takhṣīṣ al-ʿilla'. *Majallat al-Jāmiʿa al-Islāmiyya* [Gaza] 12.2 (2004): 343–66.

Ḥarfūsh, Ashraf. *Falsafat al-kalām ʿinda Imām al-Ḥaramayn al-Juwaynī.* Damascus: Al-Ḥikma, 1415/1994.

Ibn Ḥazm, Abū Muḥammad ʿAlī b. Aḥmad b. Saʿīd (d. 456/1064). *Al-Iḥkām fī uṣūl al-aḥkām*, 8 vols. Edited by Aḥmad Muḥammad Shākir. Cairo: Maktabat al-Khanjī, 1345–7/1926–9.

Hītū, Muḥammad Ḥasan. *Al-Imām al-Shīrāzī.* Beirut: Dār al-Fikr, 1980.

Abū al-Ḥusayn Muḥammad b. ʿAlī b. al-Ṭayyib al-Baṣrī (d. 436/1044). *Kitāb al-Muʿtamad fī uṣūl al-fiqh.* Edited by Muḥammad Ḥamīdullāh and others. Damascus: al-Maʿhad al-ʿIlmī al-Faransī li-l-Dirāsāt al-ʿArabiyya, 1965.

———. [pseudo] *Sharḥ al-ʿUmad*, 2 vols. Edited by ʿAbd al-Ḥamīd b. ʿAlī Abū Zunayd. Medina: Maktabat al-ʿUlūm wa-l-Ḥikam, 1410/[1990].

Al-Ījī, ʿAḍud Allāh wa-l-Dīn ʿAbd al-Raḥmān b. Aḥmad (d. 756/1355). *Al-Mawāqif fī ʿilm al-kalām.* Beirut: ʿĀlam al-Kutub, n.d.

Ilāhī, Muḥammad Manẓūr. *Al-Qiyās fi-l-ʿibādāt: ḥukmuh wa-atharuh.* Riyadh: Maktabat al-Rushd, 1424/2004.

Imām, Zakariyyā Bashīr ʿAlī. 'Qiyās al-ghāʾib ʿalā al-shāhid'. *Majallat al-Sharīʿa wa-l-qānūn, jāmiʿat al-Imārāt al-ʿArabiyya al-Muttaḥida* 8 (1415/1994): 143–202.

Ismāʿīl, Shaʿbān Muḥammad. *Dirāsāt ḥawl al-ijmāʿ wa-l-qiyās.* Alexandria: Maktabat al-Nahḍa al-Miṣriyya, 1989.

ʿAbd al-Jabbār b. Aḥmad al-Hamadhānī (d. 415/1024). [pseudo] *al-Majmūʿ fi-l-muḥīṭ bi-l-taklīf.* Collected by Abū Muḥammad al-Ḥasan b. Aḥmad b. Mattawayh (fl. fifth/eleventh century). Edited by J. Peters. Beirut: Dār al-Mashriq, 1999.

———. *al-Mughnī fī abwāb al-tawḥīd wa-l-ʿadl*, 20 vols. Edited by Ṭāhā Ḥusayn and others. Cairo: Wizārat al-Thaqāfa wa-l-Irshād al-Qawmī, 1960–9.

———. *al-Mukhtaṣar fī uṣūl al-dīn.* In *Rasāʾil al-ʿadl wa-l-tawḥīd.* Edited by Muḥammad ʿImāra, 317–89. Cairo: Dār al-Shurūq, 1988.

——— [pseudo], *Sharḥ al-uṣūl al-khamsa.* Edited by ʿAbd al-Karīm ʿUthmān. Cairo: Maktabat Wahba, 1416/1996.

Al-Jalaynad, Muḥammad al-Sayyid. *Qaḍiyyat al-khayr wa-l-sharr fi-l-fikr al-Islāmī.* 2nd ed. Cairo: Maṭbaʿat al-Ḥalabī, 1981.

Al-Jāmiʿ al-kabīr li-kutub al-turāth al-Islāmī wa-l-ʿArabī (CD-ROM). 5th ed. Amman: Markaz al-Turāth li-l-Barmajiyyāt, 2012.

Al-Jaṣṣāṣ, Aḥmad b. ʿAlī al-Rāzī (d. 370/981). *Uṣūl al-fiqh al-musammā al-fuṣūl fi-l-uṣūl*, 4 vols. 2nd ed. Edited by ʿUjayl Jāsim al-Nashmī. Kuwait: Wizārat al-Awqāf wa-l-Shuʾūn al-Islāmiyya, 1414/1994.

Ibn al-Jawzī, Abū al-Faraj ʿAbd al-Raḥmān (d. 597/1200). *Al-Muntaẓam fī tārīkh al-mulūk wa-l-umam*, 18 vols. Edited by Muḥammad ʿAbd al-Qādir ʿAṭā and others. Beirut: Dār al-Kutub al-ʿIlmiyya, 1412/1992.

Al-Jīzānī, Muḥammad b. Ḥusayn b. Ḥasan. *Maʿālim uṣūl al-fiqh.* Dammam: Dār Ibn al-Jawzī, 1416/1996.

Al-Jushamī, Abū Saʿd al-Muḥsin b. Muḥammad Karāma al-Ḥākim (d. 484/1101). *Sharḥ al-ʿUyūn.* In *Faḍl al-iʿtizāl wa-ṭabaqāt al-Muʿtazila.* Edited by Fuʾād Sayyid, 362–93. Tunis: al-Dār al-Tūnisiyya lil-Nashr, 1974.

Al-Juwaynī, Abū al-Maʿālī ʿAbd al-Malik b. ʿAbd Allah b. Yūsuf (d. 478/1085). *Al-ʿAqīda al-niẓāmiyya fī al-arkān al-Islāmiyya.* Edited by Muḥammad Zāhid al-Kawtharī. Cairo al-Maktaba al-Azhariyya, 1992.

———. *Al-Burhān fī uṣūl al-fiqh.* Edited by ʿAbd al-ʿAzīm al-Dīb. Doha: Maṭābiʿ al-Dawḥa al-Ḥadītha, 1399/[1979].

———. *al-Ghiyāthī: Ghiyāth al-umam fi-l-tiyāth al-ẓulam.* 2nd ed. Edited by ʿAbd Al-ʿAẓīm al-Dīb. N.p: N.p., 1401/1981.

———. *Al-Kāfiya fi-l-jadal.* Edited by Fawqiyya Ḥusayn Maḥmūd. Cairo: Maṭbaʿat ʿĪsā al-Bābī al-Ḥalabī, 1979.

———. *Kitāb al-Irshād ilā qawāṭiʿ al-adilla fī uṣūl al-iʿtiqād.* Edited by Muḥammad Yūsuf Mūsā and ʿAlī ʿAbd al-Munʿim ʿAbd al-Ḥamīd. Cairo: Maktabat al-Khānjī, 1369/1950.

———. (?) *Kitāb al-Talkhīṣ fī uṣūl al-fiqh*, 3 vols. Edited by ʿAbd Allāh Jawlam al-Nibālī and Bashīr Aḥmad al-ʿUmarī. Beirut: Dār al-Bashāʾir al-Islāmiyya, 1428[/2007].

———. *Lumaʿ al-adilla fī qawāʿid ahl al-Sunna wa-l-jamāʿa.* Edited by Fawqiyya Ḥusayn Maḥmūd. Cairo: al-Muʾassasa al-Miṣriyya al-ʿĀmma li-l-Taʾlīf wa-l-Anbāʾ wa-l-Nashr, 1385/1965.

———. *Matn al-Waraqāt wa-yalīh naẓm al-waraqāt li-l-Shaykh Sharaf al-Dīn al-ʿAmrīṭī.* Riyadh: Dār al-Ṣaymaʿī, 1416/1996.

———. *Al-Shāmil fī uṣūl al-dīn.* Edited by ʿAlī Sāmī al-Nashshār. Alexandria: Muʾassasat al-Maʿārif, 1969.

Al-Kalwadhānī, Maḥfūẓ b. Aḥmad b. al-Ḥasan Abū al-Khaṭṭāb (d. 510/1117). *Al-Tamhīd fī uṣūl al-fiqh*, 4 vols. Edited by Mufīd Muḥammad Abū ʿAmsha. Mecca: Umm al-Qurā University, 1406/1985.

ʿAbd al-Karīm, Abū al-Faḍl ʿAbd al-Salām b. Muḥammad Ibn. *al-Tajdīd wa-l-mujaddidūn fī uṣūl al-fiqh.* 3rd ed.1424/2003. Reprint, Cairo: al-Maktaba al-Islāmiyya, 1427/2007.

Ibn Kathīr, Abū al-Fidāʾ Ismāʿīl b. ʿUmar (d. 774/1373). *Al-Bidāya wa-l-nihāya*, 14 vols. Beirut: Maktabat al-Maʿārif, 1966. In CD-ROM *al-Jāmiʿ al-kābīr.*

Ibn Khaldūn, ʿAbd al-Raḥmān (d. 808/1406). *Al-Muqaddima*, 5 vols. Edited by ʿAbd al-Salām al-Shaddādī. Casablanca: Khizānat Ibn Khaldūn Bayt al-Funūn wa-l-ʿUlūm wa-l-Ādāb, 2005.

Khallāf, ʿAbd al-Wahhāb. *ʿIlm uṣūl al-fiqh.* 8th ed. N.p.: Maktabat al-Daʿwa al-Islāmiyya, 2002.

Ibn Khallikān, Shams al-Dīn Aḥmad (d. 681/1282). *Wafayāt al-aʿyān wa-anbāʾ abnāʾ al-zamān*, 7 vols. Edited by Iḥsān ʿAbbās. Lebanon: Dar al-Thaqāfa, n.d.

Al-Khaṭīb al-Baghdādī, Abū Bakr Aḥmad b. ʿAlī b. Thābith (d. 463/1071). *Kitāb al-Faqīh wa-l-mutafaqqih*, 2 vols. Edited by ʿĀdil b. Yūsuf al-ʿAzāzī. Riyadh: Dār Ibn al-Jawzī, 1417/1996.

Al-Khaṭṭāf, Ḥasan. 'Qiyās al-ghāʾib ʿalā al-shāhid wa-dawruh fī takwīn al-ʿaql al-iʿtizālī'. *Islāmiyyat al-maʿrifa* 44 (2006): 91–128.

Al-Khayyāṭ, Abū al-Ḥusayn ʿAbd al-Raḥīm b. Muḥammad b. ʿUthmān (d. ca. 300/913). *Kitāb al-Intiṣār wa-l-radd ʿalā Ibn al-Rāwandī al-mulḥid.* 2nd ed. Edited by H. Y. Nyberg. 1344/1925. Reprint, Beirut: Awrāq Sharqiyya, 1423/1993.

Khazna, Haytham ʿAbd al-Ḥamīd ʿAlī. 'Al-Ikhtilāfāt al-uṣūliyya bayna madrasaty al-ʿIrāq wa-Samarqand wa-atharuhā fī uṣūl al-fiqh al-Ḥanafī'. PhD., Jordanian University, 2004.

Al-Khuḍarī, Muḥammad. *Uṣūl al-fiqh.* 6th ed. Cairo: al-Maktaba al-Tijāriyya, al-Kubrā, 1389/1969.

Al-Khunn, Muṣṭafā Saʿīd. *Abḥāth ḥawl uṣūl al-fiqh*. Beirut: Dār al-Kalim al-Ṭayyib, 2000/1420.

———. *Dirāsa tārīkhiyya li-l-fiqh wa-uṣūlih*. Damascus: al-Sharika al-ʿArabiyya al-Muttaḥida li-l-Tawzīʿ, 1984/1404.

Al-Lāmishī, Abū al-Thanāʾ Maḥmūd b. Zayd (fl. late fifth/eleventh and early sixth/tenth century). *Kitāb fī Uṣūl al-fiqh*. Edited by ʿAbd al-Majīd Turkī. Beirut: Dār al-Gharb al-Islāmī, 1995.

Maḥmūd, Fawqiyya Ḥusayn. Introduction to Imām al-Ḥaramayn Abū al-Maʿālī ʿAbd al-Malik al-Juwaynī. *Lumaʿ al-adilla fī-qawāʿid ʿaqāʾid ahl al-Sunna wa-l-Jamāʿa*. Edited Fawqiyya Ḥusayn Maḥmūd, 3–72. Cairo: al-Dār al-Miṣriyya li-l-Taʾlīf wa-l-Tarjama, 1385/1965.

———. *Al-Juwaynī Imām al-Ḥaramayn*. Cairo: al-Muʾassasa al-Miṣriyya al-ʿĀmma li-l-Taʾlīf wa-l-Anbāʾ wa-l-Nashr, 1970.

Ibn Manẓūr, Abū al-Faḍl Muḥammad b. Mukarram (d. 711/1311–2). *Lisān al-ʿArab*. Beirut: Dār Ṣādir, 1980. In CD-ROM *al-Jāmiʿ al-kabīr*.

Al-Mardāwī, Abū al-Ḥasan ʿAlāʾ al-Dīn ʿAlī b. Sulaymān (d. 885/1480). *Al-Taḥbīr sharḥ al-Taḥrīr fī uṣūl al-fiqh*. Edited by ʿAbd al-Raḥmān b. ʿAbd Allāh al-Jibrīn and others. Riyadh: Maktabat al-Rushd, 1421/2000.

Ibn Mufliḥ, Burhān al-Dīn Ibrāhīm b. Muḥammad b. ʿAbd Allāh b. Muḥammad (d. 884/1479). *Al-Maqṣad al-arshad fī dhikr aṣḥāb al-Imām Aḥmad*, 3 vols. Edited ʿAbd al-Raḥmān b. Sulaymān al-ʿUthaymīn. Riyadh: Maktabat al-Rushd, 1410/1990. In CD-ROM *al-Jāmiʿ al-kabīr*.

Abū al-Muʿīn [Maymūn b. Muḥammad b. Muḥammad] al-Nasafī (d. 508/1114). *Kitāb al-Tamhīd li-qawāʿid al-tawḥīd*. Edited Ḥabīb Allāh Ḥasan Aḥmad. Cairo: Dār al-Ṭibāʿa al-Muḥammadiyya, 1406/1986.

Ibn al-Murtaḍā, Aḥmad b. Yaḥyā (d. 840/1437). *Kitāb Ṭabaqāt al-Muʿtazila*. Edited by Susanna Diwald-Wilzer. Beirut: al-Maktaba al-Kāthūlīkiyya, 1407/1987.

Nādir, Albīr Naṣrī. *Falsafat al-Muʿtazila*, 2 vols. Alexandria: Maṭbaʿat Dār Nashr al-Thaqāfa, 1950.

Ibn al-Najjār, Muḥammad b. Aḥmad b. ʿAbd al-ʿAzīz al-Fatūḥī known as (d. 972/1565). *Sharḥ al-Kawkab al-munīr*, 4 vols. Edited by Muḥammad al-Zuḥaylī and Nazīh Ḥammād. Riyadh: Maktabat al-ʿUbaykān, 1413/1993.

Al-Namla, ʿAbd al-Karīm b. ʿAlī b. Muḥammad. *Al-Jāmiʿ li-masāʾil uṣūl al-fiqh al-Islāmī*. Riyadh: Maktabat al-Rushd, 2000/1420.

———. *Al-Khilāf al-lafẓī ʿinda al-uṣūliyyīn*, 2 vols. 1417/1996. Reprint, Riyadh: Maktabat al-Rushd, 1420/1999.

———. *Al-Muhaẓẓab fī ʿilm uṣūl al-fiqh al-muqāran*. Riyadh: Maktabat al-Rushd, 1999.

Abū al-Naṣr, Muḥammad ʿAbd al-ʿAẓīm. *al-Salājiqa: Tārīkhahum al-siyāsī wa-l-ʿaskarī*. Giza, Egypt: ʿEin [sic] for Human and Social Studies, 2001.

Al-Naysābūrī, Saʿīd b. Muḥammad b. Saʿīd Abū Rashīd (d. after 415/1024). *Al-Masāʾil fī-l-khilāf bayna al-Baṣriyyīn wa-l-Baghdādiyyīn*. Edited by Maʿn Ziyāda and Riḍwān al-Sayyid. Tripoli, Libya: Maʿhad al-Inmāʾ al-ʿArabī, 1979.

Ibn Qāḍī Shuhba, Abū Bakr b. Aḥmad b. Muḥammad b. ʿUmar (d. 851/1448). *Ṭabaqāt al-Shāfiʿiyya*, 4 vols. Edited by al-Ḥāfiẓ ʿAbd al-ʿAlīm Khān. Beirut: ʿĀlam al-Kutub, 1407/[1987].

ʿAbd al-Qādir, Muḥammad al-ʿArūsī. *al-Masāʾil al-mushtaraka bayna uṣūl al-fiqh wa-uṣūl al-dīn*. 2nd ed. Riyadh: Maktabat al-Rushd, 1430/2009.

Al-Qaḥṭānī, Muḥammad Aḥmad. *Manāhij al-uṣūliyyīn fī-l-taʾlīf*. N.p. Dār al-Wafāʾ li-l-Ṭibāʿa wa-l-Nashr, n.d.

Al-Qaraḍāwī, Yūsuf. 'Tarjamat al-Imām al-Juwaynī bayna al-muʾarrikhīn: al-Dhahabī wa-l-Subkī'. In *al-Dhikrā al-alfiyya li-Imām al-Ḥaramayn al-Juwaynī*. Edited by ʿAbd al-ʿAẓīm al-Dīb and Muḥammad Ṣāliḥ al-Shīb, 85–123. Doha: University of Qatar, 2000.

Al-Qarāfī , Shihāb al-Dīn Abī al-ʿAbbās Aḥmad b. Idrīs al-Ṣanhājī known as (d. 684/1285). *Nafāʾis al-uṣūl fī sharḥ al-Maḥṣūl*. Edited by ʿĀdil ʿAbd al-Mawjūd and ʿAlī Muḥammad Muʿawwaḍ. Mecca: Maktabat Nizār Muṣṭafā al-Bāz, 1416/1995.

———. *Sharḥ Tanqīḥ al-fuṣūl fī ikhtiṣār al-Maḥṣūl fī uṣūl al-fiqh*. Edited by Maktab al-Buḥūth wa-l-Dirāsāt fī Dār al-Fikr. Beirut: Dār al-Fikr, 1424/2004.

Ibn al-Qaṣṣār, Abū al-Ḥusayn ʿAlī b. ʿUmar al-Baghdādī known as (d. 397/1007). *Muqaddima fī uṣūl al-fiqh*. Edited by Muṣṭafā Makhdūm. Riyadh: Dār al-Maʿlama, 1420/1998.

Al-Qazwīnī, ʿAbd al-Karīm b. Muḥammad al-Rāfiʿī (d. 623/1226). *Al-Tadwīn fī akhbār Qazwīn*, 4 vols. Edited by ʿAzīz Allāh al-ʿAṭṭārī. Beirut: Dār al-Kutub al-ʿIlmiyya, 1987.

Ibn Qudāma, ʿAbd Allāh b. Aḥmad (d. 620/1223). *Rawḍat al-nāẓir wa-jannat al-munāẓir*. Edited by Maḥmūd Muḥammad ʿUthmān. Riyadh: Dār al-Zāḥim, 1425/2005.

Al-Qūṣī, Muḥammad ʿAbd al-Faḍīl. 'Malāmiḥ al-madhhab al-kalāmī ʿinda al-Juwaynī'. In *al-Dhikrā al-alfiyya li-Imām al-Ḥaramayn al-Juwaynī*. Edited by ʿAbd al-ʿAẓīm al-Dīb and Muḥammad Ṣāliḥ al-Shīb, 355–78. Doha: University of Qatar, 2000.

Ibn Rashīq, al-Ḥusayn (d. 632/1243). *Lubāb al-maḥṣūl fī ʿilm al-uṣūl*, 2 vols. Edited by Muḥammad Ghazālī ʿUmar Jābī. Dubai: Dār al-Buḥūth li-l-Dirāsāt al-Islāmiyya wa-Iḥyāʾ al-Turāth, 1422/2001.

Al-Rāzī, Fakhr al-Dīn Muḥammad b. ʿUmar b. al-Ḥusayn (d. 606/1209). *Al-Maḥṣūl fī ʿilm uṣūl al-fiqh*, 6 vols. 2nd ed. Edited by Ṭāhā Jābir Fayyāḍ al-ʿUlwānī. Beirut: Muʾassasat al-Risāla, 1412/1992.

Abū Saʿda, Muhrā Ḥasan. *Al-Ittijāh al-ʿaqlī fī mushkilat al-maʿrifa ʿinda al-Muʿtazila*. Cairo: Dār al-Fikr al-ʿArabī, 1993.

Al-Saʿdī, ʿAbd al-Ḥakīm ʿAbd al-Raḥmān Asʿd. *Mabāḥith al-ʿilla ʿinda al-uṣūliyyīn*. 2nd ed. Beirut: Dār al-Bashāʾir al-Islāmiyya, 1421/2000.

Ṣadr al-Sharīʿa ʿUbayd Allāh b. Masʿūd al-Maḥbūbī (d. 747/1346). *Al-Tawḍīḥ li-matn al-tanqīḥ fī uṣūl al-fiqh*. Published in Saʿd al-Dīn Masʿūd b. ʿUmar al-Taftāzānī (d. 792/1390). *Sharḥ al-Talwīḥ ʿalā al-Tawḍīḥ li-matn al-Tanqīḥ fī uṣūl al-fiqh*, 2 vols. Edited by Zakariyyā ʿUmayrāt. Beirut: Dār al-Kutub al-ʿIlmiyya, 1996.

Ibn al- Ṣalāḥ, Abū ʿAmr ʿUthmān b. ʿAbd al-Raḥmān (d. 643/1245). *Ṭabaqāt al-fuqahāʾ al-Shāfiʿiyya*, 2 vols. Edited by Muḥyī al-Dīn ʿAlī Najīb. Beirut: Dār al-Bashāʾir al-Islāmiyya, 1992.

Al-Ṣalāḥāt, Sāmī. '*Khaṣā'iṣ al-naṣṣ al-qaṭ'ī 'inda al-uṣūliyyīn*'. *Islāmiyyat al-m'arifa* 23 (1421/2000): 43–80.

Salhab, Rāmī b. Muḥammad. *Al-Qiyās fi-l-'ibādāt wa-taṭbīqātuh fi-l-madhhab al-Shāfi'ī.* Beirut: Dār Ibn Ḥazm, 2010.

Al-Sam'ānī, Abū al-Muẓaffar Manṣūr b. Muḥammad b. 'Abd al-Jabbār (d. 489/1096). *Fuṣūl min Kitāb al-Intiṣār li-aṣḥāb al-ḥadīth.* Edited Muḥammad b. Ḥusayn al-Jīzānī. Riyadh: Maktabat Dār al-Minhāj 1428/[2007].

———. *Qawāṭi' al-adilla fī uṣūl al-fiqh*, 5 vols. Edited by Muḥammad Ḥasan Ismā'īl al-Shāfi'ī. Beirut: Dār Iḥyā' al-Kutub al-'Ilmiyya, 1997.

Al-Samarqandī, 'Alā' al-Dīn Abū Bakr Muḥammad b. Aḥmad. (d. 539/1144?). *Mīzān al-uṣūl fī natā'ij al-'uqūl.* In 'Abd al-Malik b. 'Abd al-Raḥmān As'd al-Sa'dī. '*Mīzān al-uṣūl fī natā'ij al-'uqūl*'. PhD., Umm al-Qurā University, 1404/1984.

Al-Ṣan'ānī [known as al-Amīr al-Ṣan'ānī], Muḥammad b. Ismā'īl (d. 1182/1769). *Subul al-salām sharḥ Bulūgh al-marām min adillat al-aḥkām.* 4th ed. Edited by Muḥammad b. 'Abd al-'Azīz al-Khūlī. Beirut: Dār Iḥyā' al-Turāth al-'Arabī, 1379[/1959]. In CD-ROM *al-Jāmi' al-kabīr.*

Sānū, Quṭb Muṣṭafā. *Adāwāt al-naẓar al-ijtihādī al-manshūd fī ḍaw' al-wāqi' al-mu'āṣir.* Beirut: Dār al-Fikr, 2000.

———. 'Al-Mutakallimūn wa-uṣūl al-fiqh: Qirā'a fī jadaliyyat al-'alāqa bayna 'ilmay al-uṣūl wa-l-kalām'. *Islāmiyyat al-ma'rifa* 9 (1997): 37–70.

———. *Qirā'a ma'rifiyya fi-l-fikr al-uṣūlī.* Kuwait: Wizārat al-Awqāf wa-l-Shu'ūn al-Islāmiyya, 1428/2007.

Al-Sarakhsī, Aḥmad b. Abī Sahl (d. 490/1097). *Uṣūl al-Sarakhsī*, 2 vols. Edited by Abū al-Wafa al-Afghānī. Beirut: Dar al-Kutub al-'Ilmiyya, 1414/[1993].

Al-Ṣarīfīnī, Ibrāhīm b. Muḥammad b. al-Azhar (d. 641/1243). *Al-Muntakhab min al-Siyāq l-tārīkh Naysābūr.* Edited by Muḥammd Aḥmad 'Abd al-'Azīz. Beirut: Dār al-Kutub al-'Ilmiyya, 1409/1989.

Al-Ṣaymarī, Ḥusayn b. 'Alī (d. 436/1045). *Kitāb Masā'il al-khilāf fī uṣūl al-fiqh.* In 'Les problems de divergences en méthodologie juridique: Presentation, analyse et edition critique'. By Abdelouahad Jahdani. PhD diss., Universite de Provence, 1991.

Al-Sayyid, Muḥammad Ṣāliḥ Muḥammad. *Aṣālat ʿilm al-kalām*. Cairo: Dār al-Tawfīq al-Namūdhajiyya, 1986.

Sazkīn, Fuʾād. *Tārīkh al-turāth al-ʿarabī*, 9 vols. Translated by Maḥmūd Fahmī Ḥijāzī, ʿArafa Muṣṭafā, and Saʿīd ʿAbd al-Raḥīm. Riyadh: Jāmiʿat al-Imām Muḥammad b. Saʿūd al-Islāmiyya, 1411/1991.

Al-Shāfiʿī, Ḥasan Maḥmūd. *al-Madkhal ilā dirāsat ʿilm al-kalām*. 2nd ed. Karachi: Idārat al-Qurʾān wa-l-ʿUlūm al-Islāmiyya, 1422/2001.

Al-Shāfiʿī, Muḥammad b. Idrīs (d. 204/820). *Al-Risāla*. 2nd ed. Edited by Aḥmad Shākir. Beirut: Dār al-Kutub al-ʿIlmiyya, 199?.

Al-Shahrānī, ʿĀyiḍ b. ʿAbd Allāh b. ʿAbd al-ʿAzīz. *Al-Taḥsīn wa-l-taqbīḥ al-ʿaqliyyān wa-atharuhumā fī masāʾil uṣūl al-fiqh*, 3 vols. Riyadh: Kunūz Ishbīliyya, 1429/2008.

Shalabī, Muḥammad Muṣṭafā. *Taʿlīl al-aḥkām*. 2nd ed. Beirut: Dār al-Nahḍa al-ʿArabiyya, 1981.

Shams al-Dīn, Muḥammad Mahdī. *Al-Tajdīd fi-l-fikr al-Islāmī*. Beirut: Dār al-Manhal al-Lubnānī, 1417/1997.

Al-Shawkānī, Muḥammad b. ʿAlī (d. 1255/1839). *Irshād al-fuḥūl fī taḥqīq al-ḥaqq min ʿilm al-uṣūl*. Edited by Abū Ḥafṣ Sāmī b. al-ʿArabī al-Atharī. Riyadh: Dār al-Faḍīla, 1421/2000.

Al-Shīrāzī, Abū Isḥāq Ibrāhīm b. ʿAlī b. Yūsuf al-Fīrūzabādī (d. 476/1083). *Al-Ishāra ilā madhhab ahl al-ḥaqq*. Edited by Muḥammad al-Sayyid al-Jalaynad. Cairo: Wizārat al-Awqāf, 1420/1999.

———. *Al-Lumaʿ fī uṣūl al-fiqh*. Edited by Muḥyī al-Dīn Mistū and Yūsuf ʿAlī Bidīwī. Beirut: Dār al-Kalim al-Ṭayyib, 1416/1995.

———. *Sharḥ al-Lumaʿ*, 2 vols. Edited by ʿAbd al-Majīd Turkī. Beirut: Dār al-Gharb al-Islāmī, 1988.

———. *Al-Tabṣira fī uṣūl al-fiqh*. 2nd ed. Edited by Muḥammad Ḥasan Hītū. Damascus: Dār al-Fikr, 1403/1983.

———. *Al-Mulakhkhaṣ fi-l-jadal fī uṣūl al-fiqh*. In Muḥammad Yūsuf Ākhindijān Niyāzī. '*Al-Mulakhkhaṣ fi-l-jadal fī uṣūl al-fiqh*'. M.A. diss., University of Umm al-Qurā, 1987.

Al-Shithrī, Saʿd b. Nāṣir b. ʿAbd al-ʿAzīz. '*Qiyās al-ʿaks: Ḥaqīqatuh wa-ḥukmuh*'. *Majallat Umm al-Qurā li-ʿulūm al-Sharīʿa wa-l-lugha al-ʿArabiyya wa-ādābihā* 28 (1424[/2003]): 433–455.

Al-Shtīwī, Muḥammad b. ʿAlī al-Jīlānī. *ʿAlāqat ʿilm uṣūl al-fiqh bi-ʿilm al-kalām*. Beirut: Maktabat Ḥasan al-ʿAṣriyya,1431/2010.

Al-Shūwaykh, ʿĀdil. *Taʿlīl al-aḥkām fi-l-sharīʿa al-Islāmiyya*. Tanta, Egypt: Dār al-Bashāʾir li-l-Thaqāfa wa-l-ʿUlūm, 1420/2000.

Sirāj, Muḥammad Aḥmad . *Madkhal li-dirāsat tārīkh al-fiqh al-Islāmī*. Cairo: Saʿd Samak lil-Naskh wal-Ṭibāʿa, 1995.

Al-Subkī, Tāj al-Dīn b. ʿAlī b. ʿAbd al-Kāfī (d. 771/1370). *Ṭabaqāt al-Shāfiʿiyya al-kubrā*, 10 vols. 2nd ed. Edited by Maḥmūd Muḥammad al-Ṭanāḥī and ʿAbd al-Fattāḥ Muḥammad al-Ḥulw. N.p.: Hajr lil-Ṭibāʿa wa-l-Nashr, 1413/[1993].

Al-Suyūṭī, Abū al-Faḍl ʿAbd al-Raḥmān b. Jalāl al-Dīn (d. 911/1505). *Tarīkh al-khulafāʾ*. Cairo: al-Maṭbaʿa al-Munīriyya, 1351/1932.

Al-Taftazānī, Saʿd al-Dīn Masʿūd b. ʿUmar (d. 793/1390). *Sharḥ al-Maqāṣid min ʿilm al-kalām*, 2 vols. Pakistan: Dār al-Maʿārif al-Nuʿmāniyya, 1401/1981.

———. *Sharḥ al-Talwīḥ ʿalā al-Tawḍīḥ li-matn al-Tanqīḥ fī uṣūl al-fiqh*, 2 vols. Edited by Zakariyyā ʿUmayrāt. Beirut: Dār al-Kutub al-ʿIlmiyya, 1416/1996.

Ibn Taymiyya, Taqī al-Dīn Abū al-ʿAbbās Aḥmad b. ʿAbd al-Ḥalīm (d. 728/1328) and others. *Al-Muswwada fī uṣūl al-fiqh*. Collected by Aḥmad b. Muḥammad b. Aḥmad b. ʿAbd al-Ghanī al-Ḥarrānī (d. 745/1344). Edited by Muḥammad Muḥyī al-Dīn ʿAbd al-Ḥamīd. Cairo: Maṭbaʿat al-Madanī, n.d.

Al-Ṭūfī, Najm al-Dīn Sulaymān b. ʿAbd al-Qawī b. ʿAbd al-Karīm (d. 716/1316). *Al-Bulbul fī uṣūl al-fiqh*. Riyadh: Maktabat al-Imām al-Shāfiʿī, 1410/[1990].

———. *Sharḥ Mukhtaṣar al-Rawḍa*, 3 vols. Edited by ʿAbd Allāh b. ʿAbd al-Muḥsin al-Turkī. Beirut: Muʾassasat al-Risāla, 1419/1998.

Turkī, Ibrāhīm. *Al-Sababiyya ʿinda al-qāḍī ʿAbd al-Jabbār*. Alexandria: Dār al-Wafāʾ, 2004.

Turkī, ʿAbd al-Majīd. Introduction to *Sharḥ al-Lumaʿ fī uṣūl al-fiqh*, by Abū Isḥāq Ibrāhīm al-Shīrāzī, 2 vols, 1:5–116. Edited by

ʿAbd al-Majīd Turkī. Tunis: Dār al-Gharb al-Islāmī, 1429/2008.

Al-ʿUmarī, Nādiya Sharīf. *al-Ijtihād fi-l-Islām*, 3rd ed. Beirut: Muʾassasat al-Risāla, 1405/1985.

———. *Al-Qiyās fi-l-tashrīʿ al-Islāmī.* Giza, Egypt: Dār Hajr li-l-Ṭibāʿa wa-l-Nashr wa-l-Tawzīʿ, 1407/1987.

Al-Usmandī, Muḥammad b. ʿAbd al-Ḥamīd (d. 552/1158). *Badhl al-naẓar fī uṣūl al-fiqh.* Edited by Muḥammad Zakī ʿAbd al-Barr. Cairo: Maktabat al-Turāth, 1412/1992.

ʿUthmān, ʿAbd al-Karīm. *Qāḍī al-Quḍāt ʿAbd al-Jabbār b. Aḥmad al-Hamadhānī.* Beirut: Dār al-ʿArabiyya, 1968.

Al-Yāfiʿī, Abū Muḥammd ʿAbd Allāh b. Asʿad b. ʿAlī b. Sulaymān (d. 768/1367). *Mirʾāt al-janān wa-ʿibrat al-yuqẓān*, 4 vols. Cairo: Dār al-Kitāb al-Islāmī, 1413/1993. In CD-ROM *al-Jāmiʿ al-kabīr.*

Abū Yaʿlā Muḥammad b. al-Ḥusayn al-Farrāʾ (d. 458/1066). *Al-ʿUdda fī uṣūl al-fiqh.* 2nd ed. Edited by Aḥmad b. ʿAlī Sīr al-Mubārkī. 1400/1980. Reprint, Riyadh: Muʾassasat al-Risāla, 1410/1990.

———. *Kitāb al-Muʿtamad fī uṣūl al-dīn.* Edited by Wadīʿ Zaydān Ḥaddād. Beirut: Dār al-Mashriq, 1974.

Al-Zamakhsharī, Abū al-Qāsim Maḥmūd b. ʿUmar (d. 538/1144). *Asās al-balāgha.* N.p.: Dār al-Fikr, 1399/1979. In CD-ROM *al-Jāmiʿ al-kabīr.*

Al-Zarkashī, Badr al-Dīn Muḥammad b. Bahādur (d. 794/1392). *Al-Baḥr al-muḥīṭ fī uṣūl al-fiqh*, 6 vols. Edited by ʿAbd al-Qādir ʿAbd Allāh al-ʿĀnī. Kuwait: Wizārat al-Awqāf wa-l-Shuʾūn al-Islāmiyya, 1413/1992.

Zayna, Ḥusnī. *Al-ʿAql ʿinda al-Muʿtazila: Taṣawwur al-ʿaql ʿinda al-Qāḍī ʿAbd al-Jabbār.* Beirut: Dār al-Āfāq al-Jadīda, 1978.

Al-Zuḥaylī, Muḥammad. *Al-Imām al-Juwaynī.* 2nd ed. Damascus: Dar al-Qalam, 1992.

SOURCES IN ENGLISH AND EUROPEAN LANGUAGES

Authors and texts by the same author are listed in alphabetical order. The alphabetical order of the works listed does not take into consideration the word 'the' and the letter 'A' when they appear at the beginning of a title.

Abou El Fadl, Khaled. *The Great Theft: Wrestling Islam from the Extremists*. New York: Harper One, 2007.

Abrahamov, Binyamin. 'The *bi-lā kayfa* Doctrine and its Foundations in Islamic Theology'. *Arabica* 42 (1995): 365–79.

Ahmad, Ahmad Atif. Structural Interrelations of Theory and Practice in Islamic Law*: A Study of Six Works of Medieval Islamic Jurisprudence*. Leiden: Brill, 2006.

Ahmed, Rumee. *Narratives of Islamic Legal Theory*. Oxford: Oxford University Press, 2012.

Algar, Hamid. 'Q. 21:78–9: A Qur'anic Basis for *Ijtihād*?' *Journal of Qur'anic Studies* 4.2 (2002): 1–22.

Bausani, A. 'Religion in the Saljuq Period'. In *The Cambridge History of Iran*. Edited by John Andrew Boyle. Vol. 5, *The Saljuq and Mongol Periods*, 283–302. Cambridge: Cambridge University Press, 1968.

Bedir, Murteza. 'The Early Development of Hanafi Usul al-Fiqh'. PhD diss., University of Manchester, 1999.

Bernand, Marie. *L'accord unanime de la communauté comme fondement des statuts légaux de l'Islam d'après Abu l-Husayn al-Basri*. Paris: J. Vrin, 1970.

———. 'La problem de 'l'ašbah' ou les implications ontologiques de la règle juridico-religieuse'. *Arabica* 37.2 (1990): 151–72.

———. *La Profession de foi d'Abū Isḥāq al-Šīrāzī.* Cairo: Institut français d'archéologie orientale, 1987.

Bosworth, C. Edmund. 'The Political and Dynastic History of the Iranian World (A.D. 1000–1217)'. In *The Cambridge History of Iran.* Edited by John Boyle. Vol 5, *The Saljuq and Mongol Periods,* 1–202. Cambridge: Cambridge University Press, 1968.

Brockelmann, Carl. *Geschichte der arabischen Litteratur.* Leiden: Brill, 1943.

———. *Geschichte der arabischen Litteratur. Erster Supllementband.* Leiden: Brill, 1937.

Brunschvig, Robert. 'Logic and Law in Classical Islam'. In *Logic in Classical Islamic Culture.* Edited by G. E. von Grunebaum, 9–20. Wiesbaden: Otto Harrassowitz, 1970.

Bulliet, Richard. *The Patricians of Nishapur: A Study in Medieval Islamic Social History.* Cambridge: Harvard University Press, 1972.

———. 'The Political-Religious History of Nishapur in the Eleventh Century'. In *Islamic Civilization* 950–1150. Edited by D. S. Richards, 71–91. Oxford: Cassirer, 1973.

Busse, Heribert. *Chalif und Grosskönig: Die Buyiden im Iraq (945–1055).* Beirut: Orient-Institut der deutschen morgenländische Gesellschaft, 1969.

———. 'Iran under the Buyids'. In *The Cambridge History of Iran.* Edited by Richard Nelson Frye. Vol. 4, *From the Arab Invasion to the Saljuqs,* 250–304. Cambridge: Cambridge University Press, 1975.

———. 'The Revival of Persian Kingship under the Būyids'. In *Islamic Civilization 950–1150.* Edited by D. S. Richards, 47–70. London: B. Cassirer, 1973.

Chaumont, Éric. 'Encore au sujet de l'Ash'arisme d'Abû Isḥâq Ash-Shîrâzî'. *Studia Islamica* 74 (1991): 167–77.

———. "Tout chercheur qualifié dit-il juste?' (*hal kull muǧtahid muṣīb*) La question controversée du fondement de la légitimité de la controverse en Islam'. In *La controverse religieuse et ses forms.* Edited by Alain le Boulluec, 11–27. Paris: Éditions du Cerf, 1995.

Donohue, John J. *The Buwayhid Dynasty in Iraq 334H./945 to 403H./1012: Shaping Institutions for the Future*. Leiden: Brill, 2003.

Eissa, Mohamed Ahmed Abdelrahman. 'Abū al-Ḥusayn al-Baṣrī's Use of Reason in *ʿIlm al-Kalām and Uṣūl al-Fiqh*'. *Al-Shajarah Journal of the International Institute of Islamic Thought and Civilization* 16.1 (2011): 1–45.

———. "The Mutʿazili Criteria for Evaluating Prophetic Traditions with Special Reference to Usul al-Fiqh." M.A. diss., American University in Cairo, 2008.

El Shamsy, Ahmed. 'The Social Construction of Orthodoxy'. In *The Cambridge Companion to Classical Islamic Theology*. Edited by Tim Winter, 91–118. Cambridge: Cambridge University Press, 2008.

———. 'The Wisdom of God's Law: Two Theories'. In *Islamic Law in Theory*. Edited by A. Kevin Reinhart and Robert Gleave, 19–38. Leiden: Brill, 2014.

El-Tobgui, Carl Sharif. 'The Epistemology of *Qiyas* and *Ta'lil* between The Mu'tazilite Abu 'L-Husayn al-Basri and Ibn Hazm al-Zahiri'. *UCLA Journal of Islamic and Near Eastern Law* 2.2 (2002–3): 281–354.

Emon, Anver. *Islamic Natural Law Theories*. Oxford: Oxford University Press, 2010.

———. 'Natural Law and Natural Rights in Islamic Law'. *Journal of Law and Religion* 20.2 (2004 -2005): 351–395.

———. 'To Most Likely Know the Law: Objectivity, Authority, and Interpretation in Islamic Law'. *Hebraic Political Studies* 4.4 (2009): 415–40.

Encyclopaedia of Islam [online]. 2nd ed. Edited by P. Bearman, T. Bianquis, C. E. Bosworth, E. van Donzel and W. P. Heinrichs. Brill Online (http://referenceworks.brillonline.com/ browse/ encyclopaedia-of-islam-2).

Encyclopaedia of Islam [online]. 3rd ed. Edited by Kate Fleet, Gudrun Krämer, Denis Matringe, John Nawas, Everett Rowson. Brill Online (http://referenceworks.brillonline.com/browse/ encyclopaedia-of-islam-3).

Encylopædia Britanica [online] (www.britannica.com).

The Encyclopedia of Philosophy. 8 vols. Edited by Paul Edwards and others. London: Collier Macmillan, 1967.

Ephrat, Daphna. *A Learned Society in Transition: The Sunni ʿUlamāʾ of Eleventh-Century Baghdad*. Albany, New York: State University of New York Press, 2000.

Evkuran, Mehmet. 'The Problem of Causality in Islamic Thought'. *Journal of Islamic Research* 2.2 (2009): 115–27.

Fadel, Mohammad H. 'The True, the Good, and the Reasonable: The Theological and Ethical Roots of Public Reasoning in Islamic Law'. *The Canadian Journal of Law and Jurisprudence* 21.1 (2008): 1–65.

Fazlur Rahman. 'Functional Interdependence of Law and Theology'. In *Theology and Law in Islam*. Edited by G. E. von Grunebaum, 89–99. Wiesbaden: Otto Harrassowitz, 1971.

———. *Islam and Modernity*. Chicago: The University of Chicago Press, 1982.

———. *Islamic Methodology in History*. Karachi: Central Institute of Islamic Research, 1965.

———. 'Law and Ethics in Islam'. In *Ethics in Islam*. Edited by R. G. Hovannisian, 3–15. Malibu, California: Undena Publications, 1985.

———. *Major Themes of the Qur'an*. 2nd ed. Chicago: University of Chicago Press, 2009.

———. *Revival and Reform in Islam*. Oxford: One World, 2000.

Frank, Richard. *Beings and their Attributes the Teachings of the Basrian School of the Muʿtazila in the Classical Period*. Albany: State University of New York, 1978.

———. 'Knowledge and Taqlid: The Foundations of Religious Belief in Classical Ashʿarism'. *Journal of the American Oriental Society* 109 (1989): 37–62.

———. 'The Science of Kalām'. *Arabic Sciences and Philosophy* 2 (1992): 7–37.

———. 'The Structure of Created Causality According to al-Ašʿarî: An Analysis of the Kitâb al-Lumaʿ'. *Studia Islamica* 25 (1966): 82–164.

Gilliot, C. 'Deux professions de foi du juriste théologien aš'arite Abū Isḥāq aš-Šīrāzī'. *Studia Islamica* 68 (1988): 170–196.

Gimaret, D. 'Les Usul al-Hamsa du Qadi Abd al-Jabbar et leurs Commentaires'. *Annales Islamologiques* 15 (1979): 47–96.

Gleave, Robert. Forward to *The Economy of Certainty*. By Aron Zysow, xi-xix. Atlanta, Georgia: Lockwood Press, 2013.

———. *Inevitable Doubt: Two Theories of Shīʿī Jurisprudence*. Leiden: Brill, 2000.

———. 'Scriptural Sufism and Scriptural Anti-Sufism: Theology and Mysticism amongst the Shīʿī Akhbāriyya'. In *Sufism and Theology*. Edited by Ayman Shihadeh, 158–76. Edinburgh: Edinburgh University Press, 2007.

Goldziher, Ignaz. *Introduction to Islamic Theology and Law*. Translated by Andreas and Ruth Hamori with introduction and additional notes by Bernard Lewis. New Jersey: Princeton University Press, 1981.

———. *Muslim Studies*, 2 vols. Edited by M. Stern. Translated by C. R. Barber and M. Stern. Albany: State University of New York, 1971.

———. *The Ẓāhirīs: Their Doctrine and Their History*. Translated by Wolfgang Behn. Leiden: Brill, 1971.

Grayling, A. C. 'Epistemology'. In *The Blackwell Companion to Philosophy*. Edited by Nicholas Bunnin and E. P. Tsui-James, 37–61. Oxford: Blackwell, 1996.

Hallaq, Wael. *Authority, continuity and change in Islamic law*. Cambridge: Cambridge University Press, 2001.

———. 'Considerations on the Function and Character of Sunni Legal Theory'. *Journal of the American Oriental Society* 104 (1984): 679–689.

———. *A History of Islamic Legal Theories: An Introduction to Sunnī Uṣūl al-Fiqh*. Cambridge: Cambridge University Press, 1997.

———. *An Introduction to Islamic law*. Cambridge: Cambridge University Press, 2009.

———. 'Logic, Formal Arguments and Formalization of Arguments in Sunnī Jurisprudence'. *Arabica*, 37 (1990): 315–358.

———. 'The Logic of Legal Reasoning in Religious and non-Religious Cultures: The Case of Islamic Law and the Common Law'. *Cleveland State Law Review* 34 (1985): 79–96.

———. 'Non-Analogical Arguments in Sunni Juridical Qiyas'. *Arabica*, 36 (1989): 286–306.

———. 'On the Authoritativeness of Sunni Consensus'. *International Journal of Middle East Studies* 18 (1986): 427–54.

———. *The Origins and Evolution of Islamic law*. Cambridge: Cambridge University Press, 2005.

———. *Sharīʿa: Theory, Practice, Transformations*. Cambridge: Cambridge University Press, 2009.

———. 'A Tenth-Eleventh Century Treatise on Juridical Dialectic'. *Muslim World* 77 (1987): 197–228.

———. 'Was al-Shafiʿi the Master Architect of Islamic Jurisprudence?' *International Journal of Middle East Studies* 25.4 (1993): 587–605.

Hanne, Eric. *Putting the Caliph in his Place*. Madison, New Jersy: Fairleigh Dickinson University Press, 2007.

Hasan, Ahmad. 'The Legal Cause in Islamic Jurisprudence: An Analysis of ʿillat al-ḥukm'. *Islamic Studies* [Islamabad] 19.4 (1980): 247–70.

———. 'Rationality of Islamic Legal Injunctions: The Problem of Valuation (*taʿlīl*)'. *Islamic Studies* [Islamabad] 13 (1974): 95–109.

Heemskerk, Margaretha T. *Suffering in the Muʿtazilite Theology: ʿAbd al-Jabbar's Teaching on Pain and Divine Justice*. Leiden; Boston: Brill, 2000.

Hourani, George. *Islamic Rationalism: The Ethics of ʿAbd al-Jabbār*. Oxford: Clarendon Press, 1971.

———. 'The Rationalist Ethics of ʿAbd al-Jabbar'. In *Reason and Tradition in Islamic Ethics*. Edited by George Hourani, 98–108. Cambridge: Cambridge University Press, 1985.

———. *Reason and Tradition in Islamic Ethics*. Cambridge: Cambridge University Press, 1985.

Jackson, Sherman A. 'Function and Formalism: Toward a Functional Analysis of *Uṣūl al-fiqh*'. In *Studies in Islamic Legal Theory*. Edited by Bernard Weiss, 177–201. Leiden: Brill, 2002.

Johansen, Baber. *Contingency in a Sacred Law: Legal and Ethical Norms in Muslim Fiqh* Leiden: Brill, 1999.

Juynboll, G.H.A. *Muslim Tradition: Studies in Chronology, Provenance, and Authority of Early ḥadīth*. Cambridge: Cambridge University Press, 1983.

Kabir, Mafizullah. *The Buwayhid Dynasty of Baghdad.* Calcutta: Iran Society, 1964.

Kamali, Mohammad Hashim. *Principles of Islamic Jurisprudence.* 3rd ed. Cambridge: Islamic Texts Societies, 2003.

Kennedy, Hugh. *The Court of the Caliphs.* London: Weidenfeld and Nicolson, 2004.

Kraemer, Joel. *Humanism in the Renaissance of Islam: The Cultural Revival during the Būyid Age.* Leiden: Brill, 1986.

Krawietz, Birgit. *Hierarchie der Rechtsquellen im tradierten sunnitischen Islam.* Berlin: Duncker and Humblot, 2002.

Klopfer, Helmut. *Das Dogma des Imâm al-Ḥaramain al-Djuwainî.* Cairo: al-Arab Salaheddine Boustany, 1958.

Lange, Christian. *Justice, Punishment, and the Medieval Muslim Imagination.* Cambridge: Cambridge University Press, 2008.

———. 'Sins, Expiation and Non-Rationality in Ḥanafī and Shāfiʿī *Fiqh*'. In *Islamic Law in Theory.* Edited by A. Kevin Reinhart and Robert Gleave, 143–75. Leiden: Brill, 2014.

Laoust, Henri. *La Politique de Gazali.* Paris: P. Geuthner, 1970.

———. *Les Schismes dans l'Islam.* Paris: Payot, 1965.

Leaman, Oliver. *An Introduction to Classical Islamic Philosophy.* 2nd ed. Cambridge: Cambridge University Press, 2004.

———. Review of *Before Revelation: The Boundaries of Muslim Moral Thought*, by A. K. Reinhart. *British Journal of Middle Eastern Studies* 22.1/2 (1995): 140–1.

Madelung, Wilferd. *Der Imam al-Qasim b. Ibrahim.* Berlin: Walter de Gruyter, 1965.

———. *Religious Trends in Early Islamic Iran.* Albany, N.Y.: The Persian Heritage Foundation, 1988.

———. 'The Spread of Māturīdism and the Turks'. In *Actos do IV Congresso de Estudos Árabes e Islâmicos, Coimbra-Lisboa 1968*, 109–168. Ledien: Brill, 1971.

Makdisi, George. 'Ashʿari and the Ashʿarites in Islamic Religious History I'. *Studia Islamica* 17 (1962): 37–80.

———. *Ibn ʿAqil: Religion and Culture in Classical Islam.* Edinburgh: Edinburgh University Press, 1997.

———. 'The Juridical Theology of Shâfi'î: Origins and Significance of *Uṣûl al-Fiqh*'. *Studia Islamica* 59 (1984): 5–47.

———. *The Rise of Colleges: Institutions of Learning in Islam and the West.* Edinburgh: Edinburgh University Press, 1981.

———. *The Rise of Humanism in Classical Islam and the Christian West.* Edinburgh: Edinburgh University Press, 1990.

———. 'Significance of Sunni Schools of Law in Islamic Religious History'. *International Journal of Middle Eastern Studies* 10 (1979): 1–8.

———, 'The Sunni Revival'. In *Islamic Civilization, 950–1150.* Edited by D. S. Richards, 155–68. Oxford: Bruni Cassirer, 1973.

Melchert, Christopher. *The Formation of the Sunni Schools of Law.* Leiden: Brill, 1997.

———. 'The Piety of the Hadith Folk'. *International Journal of Middle East Studies* 34.3 (2002): 425–39.

———. 'Religious Policies of the Caliphs from al-Mutawakkil to al-Muqtadir A H 232–295/A D 847–908'. *Islamic Law and Society* (1996): 316–42.

———. Review of *Kitāb al-Lumaʿ fī uṣūl al-fiqh, Le Livre des Rais illuminant les fondements de la compréhension de la Loi*, by Abū Isḥāq Ibrāhīm al-Shīrāzī, translated by Éric Chaumont, *Islamic Law and Society* 9 (2002): 116–9.

———. 'Traditionist-Jurisprudents and the Framing of Islamic law'. *Islamic Law and Society* 8 (2001): 383–406.

Mez, Adam. *The Renaissance of Islam.* Translated by Khuda Bakhsh and D. S. Margoliouth. Patna: The Jubilee Printing and Publishing House, 1937.

Motzki, Harald. *The Origins of Islamic Jurisprudence: Meccan Fiqh before the Classical Schools.* Translated by Marion H. Katz. Leiden: Brill, 2002.

Nagel, Tilman. *The History of Islamic Theology.* Translated by Thomas Thornton. Princeton: Markus Wiener, 2000.

Opwis, Felicitas. *Maṣlaḥa and the Purpose of the Law: Islamic Discourse on Legal Change from the 4th/10th to the 8th/14th Century*. Leiden: Brill, 2010.

Ormsby, Eric. Review of Before Revelation: The Boundaries of Muslim Moral Thought, by A. Kevin Reinhart. *Islamic Law and Society* 5.1 (1998): 118–23.

The Oxford Companion to Philosophy. Edited by Ted Honderich. Oxford: Oxford University Press, 1995.

Peters, J. R. T. M. *God's Created Speech*. Leiden: E. J. Brill, 1976.

Quraishi, Asifa. 'On Fallibility and Finality: Why Thinking like a Qadi Helps Me Understand American Constitutional Law'. *Michigan State Law Review* 2 (2009): 339–60.

The Qur'ān. Translated by M. A. S. Abdel Haleem. 2004. Reprint, Oxford: Oxford University Press, 2005.

Ramadan, Tariq. *Radical Reform: Islamic Ethics and Liberation*. Oxford: Oxford University Press, 2009.

Rayan, Sobhi. 'Al-Ghazâlî's Use of the Terms darûrah and 'âdah in his Theory of Causality'. *Islamic Culture* 78.3 (2004): 77–98.

Rebstock, Ulrich. 'A Qāḍī's Errors'. *Islamic Law and Society* 6.1 (1999): 1–37.

Reinhart, Kevin A. *Before Revelation: The Boundaries of Muslim Moral Thought*. Albany: State University of New York Press, 1995.

———. 'Like the Difference between Heaven and Earth: Ḥanafī and Shāfiʿī Discussions of *Farḍ* and *Wājib* in Theology and Uṣūl'. In *Studies in Islamic Legal Theory*. Edited by Bernard G. Weiss, 205–34. Leiden: Brill, 2002.

———. Response to Eric Ormsby's review of *Before Revelation: The Boundaries of Muslim Moral Thought*, by A. K. Reinhart. *Islamic Law and Society* 6.3 (1999): 419–20.

Routledge Encyclopedia of Philosophy. 10 vols. Edited by Edward Craig and others. London: Routledge, 1998.

Sadeghi, Behnam. *The Logic of Law-making in Islam: Women and Prayer in the Legal Tradition*. Cambridge: Cambridge University Press, 2013.

Schacht, Joseph. *The Origins of Muhammadan Jurisprudence*. 3rd ed. 1950. Reprint, Oxford: Clarendon Press, 1967.

Schwarb, Gregor. 'Capturing the meanings of God's speech: the relevance of *uṣūl al-fiqh* to an understanding of *uṣūl al-tafsīr* in Jewish and Muslim *kalām*'. In *A Word Fitly Spoken: Studies in Medieval Exegesis of the Hebrew Bible and the Quran.* Edited by Meir M. Bar Asher, 111–56. Jerusalem: The Ben-Zui Institute for the History of Jewish Communities in the East, 2007.

Songur, Haluk. 'Two Approaches to the Particularization of Effective Cause (takhsis al-ʿillah) in Islamic Legal Theory'. *Süleyman Demirel Üniversitesi İlahiyat Fakültesi Dergisi* 17 (2006): 15–26.

Stewart, Devin. Review of *Kitāb al-Lumaʿ fī uṣūl al-fiqh* (*Le Livre des Rais illuminant les fondements de la compréhension de la Loi*), by Abū Isḥāq Ibrāhīm al-Shīrāzī, translated by Éric Chaumont. *Journal of the American Oriental Society* 123.1 (2003): 246–47.

Stroumsa, Sarah. 'The Beginnings of the Muʿtazilah Reconsidered'. *Jerusalem Studies in Arabic and Islam* 6 (1985): 229–41.

Van Renterghem, Vanessa. 'Controlling and Developing Baghdad: Caliphs, Sultans, and the Balance of Power in the Abbasid Capital'. In *The Seljuqs: Politics, Society, and Culture.* Edited by Christian Lange and Songül Mecit, 117–38. Edinburgh: Edinburgh University Press, 2011.

Vasalou, Sophia. *Moral Agents and their Deserts: The Character of Muʿtazilite Ethics.* Princeton: Princeton University Press, 2008.

Vikør, Knut S. *Between God and the Sultan.* Oxford: Oxford University Press, 2006.

Vishanoff, David R. *The Formation of Islamic Hermeneutics: How Sunni Legal Theorists Imagined a Revealed Law.* New Haven, Connecticut: American Oriental Society, 2011.

Watt, William Montgomery. *Islamic Theology and Philosophy.* 2nd ed. Edinburgh: Edinburgh University Press, 2003.

Weiss, Bernard G. *The Search for God's Law: Islamic Jurisprudence in the Writings of Sayf al-Dīn al-Āmidī.* Salt Lake City: University of Utah Press, 1992.

———. *The Spirit of Islamic Law.* 1998. Reprint, Athens, Georgia: University of Georgia Press, 2006.

Winter, Tim. Introduction to *The Cambridge Companion to Classical Islamic Theology.* Edited by Tim Winter, 1–18. Cambridge: Cambridge University Press, 2008.

Wisnovsky, Robert. *Avicenna's Metaphysics in Context.* London: Duckworth, 2003.

Wolfson, Harry A. *The Philosophy of the Kalām.* Cambridge: Harvard University Press, 1976.

Zysow, Aron. *The Economy of Certainty: An Introduction to the Typology of Islamic Legal Theory.* Atlanta, Georgia: Lockwood Press, 2013.

———. 'The Economy of Certainty: An Introduction to the Typology of Islamic Legal Theory'. PhD diss., Harvard University, 1984.

———. 'Muʿtazilism and Māturidism in Ḥanafī Legal Theory'. In *Studies in Islamic Legal Theory.* Edited by Bernard G. Weiss, 235–65. Leiden: Brill, 2002.

———. 'Two Theories of the Obligation to Obey God's Commands'. In *The Law Applied: Contextualizing the Islamic Sharīʿa.* Edited by Peri Bearman and others, 397–421. London: I. B. Tauris, 2008.

INDEX

The Index is arranged in alphabetical order; this order does not take into consideration al-, Abū and Ibn.

www.ingramcontent.com/pod-product-compliance
Lightning Source LLC
LaVergne TN
LVHW011529200926
848484LV00001B/203

* 9 7 8 1 4 6 3 2 0 6 1 8 5 *